The
Population
of Singapore
Second Edition

The **Institute of Southeast Asian Studies (ISEAS)** was established as an autonomous organization in 1968. It is a regional centre dedicated to the study of socio-political, security and economic trends and developments in Southeast Asia and its wider geostrategic and economic environment.

The Institute's research programmes are the Regional Economic Studies (RES, including ASEAN and APEC), Regional Strategic and Political Studies (RSPS), and Regional Social and Cultural Studies (RSCS).

ISEAS Publishing, an established academic press, has issued almost 2,000 books and journals. It is the largest scholarly publisher of research about Southeast Asia from within the region. ISEAS Publishing works with many other academic and trade publishers and distributors to disseminate important research and analyses from and about Southeast Asia to the rest of the world.

Saw Swee-Hock

The Population of Singapore

Second Edition

ISEAS Institute of Southeast Asian Studies
Singapore

First published in Singapore in 2007 by ISEAS Publishing
Institute of Southeast Asian Studies
30 Heng Mui Keng Terrace
Pasir Panjang
Singapore 119614

E-mail: publish@iseas.edu.sg
Website: <http://bookshop.iseas.edu.sg>

The responsibility for facts and opinions in this publication rests exclusively with the author and his interpretations do not necessarily reflect the views or the policy of the publisher or its supporters.

ISEAS Library Cataloguing-in-Publication Data

Saw Swee-Hock, 1931–
   The population of Singapore.
   1. Singapore—Population policy.
   2. Singapore—Population.
   3. Demography—Singapore.
   I. Title
HB3645 A3S271   2007

ISBN: 978-981-230-738-5 (hard cover)
ISBN: 978-981-230-739-2 (PDF)

Typeset by Superskill Graphics Pte Ltd
Printed in Singapore by Utopia Press Pte Ltd

Contents

List of Tables

List of Figures

Preface

The city-state of Singapore, with a small cosmopolitan population, is well known for its accomplishments in many areas of social and economic development brought about by a strong and stable government. Among the more significant characteristics are the clean and crime-free environment, the remarkable public housing programme, the air transport system centred on a first-rate airport and national airline, the world-class seaport, and the high standard of living. The per capita income was estimated to reach US$32,810 in 1997, higher than that recorded for Australia, Hong Kong, the United States, the United Kingdom, Germany, and many European countries. In the field of demography, the most prominent achievements are the effective population control programme and the rapid decline in fertility to replacement level in 1975. These two characteristics, together with other major features of the population, are discussed in considerable detail in this book.

It has always been my fervent desire to incorporate my research findings on the different aspects of Singapore's demographics into a single cohesive work. Not surprisingly, this ambitious project has taken a long time to realize. Pressure of work prior to my retirement from academia did not permit me to make any sustained effort to prepare the manuscript, and intensive writing could only be realized during my study leave spent in the Department of Statistics at the University of Hong Kong in 1991, and in Wolfson College, University of Cambridge, in the following year. Thereafter, progress on the manuscript was delayed further by the late release of the results of the 1990 Population Census. In giving the finishing touches to the manuscript in the late nineties, I took the opportunity to include whatever data that were pertinent and available for the years up to 1997 to supplement the census data. The final product incorporated in this book has been carefully designed to meet its overall objective of presenting a comprehensive and up-to-date account of population trends and patterns in Singapore.

In the preparation of this book I was fortunate to receive the assistance of many organizations and individuals. In particular, I would like to mention the excellent facilities offered at the National University of Singapore, the University of Hong Kong, and the University of Cambridge. I am greatly indebted to my wife, Cheng Siok Hwa, for her comments on the manuscript. My grateful thanks go to Professor Chia Siow Yue, Director of the Institute of Southeast Asian Studies, for her encouragement. Needless to say, any opinions and shortcomings in the book are entirely my own.

Saw Swee-Hock
June 1997

Preface to Second Edition

The original edition of this book on *The Population of Singapore* presents an analysis of population trends and patterns in Singapore in eleven chapters covering the period from its foundation in the early nineteenth century to around the year 1997. In designing the second edition, I have expanded the book by increasing the number of chapters to thirteen and by including data, particularly those from the 2000 Population Census and the 2005 General Household Survey, that have been made available up to 2005, or even 2006 in some instances. The old chapter on Population Control has been split into two, one entitled Family Planning, Abortion and Sterilisation and the other Fertility Policies and Programmes. A new chapter on the very current topic, Immigration Policies and Programmes, has been added. The last chapter on Future Population Trends incorporates the results of my latest projection of the resident population and, for the first time, the resident labour force. As for the other chapters, they have been updated by including materials that have been made available up to the year 2006 or so. Overall, the changes have resulted in a book that is clearly more current and comprehensive.

In preparing the second edition of the book, I have benefited from the valuable assistance of many organisations and individuals. My thanks go to the numerous government organisations for supplying me with the necessary materials and statistics. My research has been greatly facilitated by the assistance and conducive facilities offered at the London School of Economics Library, the National University Library, and the Institute of Southeast Asian Studies. I wish to thank Ambassador K Kesavapany, Director of ISEAS, for his generous hospitality and Mrs Triena Ong, Managing Editor of ISEAS Publications Unit, for bringing out this edition expeditiously. I wish to reiterate that any opinions and shortcomings are entirely my own.

Saw Swee-Hock
June 2007

1

Background

In this introductory chapter, we will present a concise account of the geography and history of Singapore before commencing on the study of the population of the country. Some knowledge of these two aspects of the country will provide the necessary background information for a better appreciation of the population trends and patterns that will be discussed in the various chapters. The evolution of the population has indeed been intertwined with the geographical setting as well as the historical development of the country. We will also provide a brief description of the demographic information upon which this study is based so as to facilitate the interpretation of the statistical data included in the book.

GEOGRAPHICAL SETTING

The Republic of Singapore comprises the main island of Singapore and some 54 small islets within its territorial waters and jurisdiction. The country has a total land area of only 699.4 square kilometres, 500 of which are taken up by the diamond-shaped main island, which is 41.8 kilometres in length and 22.5 kilometres in breath. Singapore is situated at longitude 103° 50' East and latitude 1° 17' North, and at the southern extremity of Peninsular Malaysia to which it is linked by the old rail-and-road causeway and a new bridge spanning the Straits of Johor. In its wider context, the Republic occupies a strategic position on the principal sea, air, telecommunications and trade routes between Europe and the Far East and Oceania.

The topography of Singapore is one lacking in contrast as the whole country is of very low elevation with a few small hills no higher

1

than 166 metres. There are many rivers, with the larger ones, such as the Kranji and Seletar rivers, used as catchment areas for reservoirs, and, of course, the Singapore River which flows through the very heart of the city area. The lowland forests that used to cover the island in the early days have retreated with the advance of roads, houses, office buildings, factories and cultivated vegetation. What remains are some small pockets of protected reserves, such as the Bukit Timah Nature Reserve and the Kranji Reserve, totalling some 2,797 hectares. The built-up area is dominated by tall office buildings in the city, public housing high-rise apartments in the new towns, and factories which are concentrated mainly in the industrial town of Jurong on the western side of the main island.

Singapore, being only 136.8 kilometres north of the Equator, has an equatorial climate with uniformly high temperatures throughout the year, high humidity and fairly abundant rainfall. The average temperature is about 28°C, humidity about 70 per cent, and rainfall about 2,400 millimetres per year. Owing to its proximity to the sea, the nights in most places are invariably breezy and somewhat cool. There is an absence of marked seasonal changes although December is often the wettest and coolest month.

HISTORICAL BACKGROUND

The origin of Tumasik or Old Singapore remains shrouded in antiquity and the date of the founding of the first settlement is not known. According to the *Sejarah Melayu* (Malay Annals), an Indian prince. Sang Nila Utama, who was a ruler of Palembang, sailed to Temasek. On landing. Sang Nila Utama and his party saw a strange beast which they took to be a lion. This was considered a good omen and the new settlement was given the name "Singapura", or Lion City. No date is given in the *Sejarah Melayu*, but there is some evidence to suggest that the founding of Singapore dates back to the seventh century.

The early history of Tumasik that has survived is little more than a recital of piracy, invasion and siege. As part of the Sri Vijaya Empire, it was attacked by invaders like the Chola King, Rajindrachola I, who devastated the settlement in 1025. In the fourteenth century, it became part of the Majapahit Empire and was subjected to frequent attacks and periods of control by Siam which was struggling with Majapahit for domination over the Malay Peninsula. In 1402, a Siamese force was sent against Parameswara, a Palembang prince who had killed the pro-Siamese ruler of Tumasik and taken his place. Parameswara fled north and subsequently founded Malacca, which rose rapidly as a trading centre because of its strategic position in the Straits of Malacca.

When Malacca was captured by the Portugese in 1511, it was already a flourishing port and capital of the Malacca Sultanate, while Singapore remained largely a mangrove swamp inhabited by some fishermen and pirates. But by 1641 the Portugese had surrendered Malacca to the Dutch, who became the main rival to the British for commercial and political ascendancy in the East Indies and the Malay Peninsula.[1] The British position was strengthened somewhat by the founding of Penang in 1786, but this provided only control over the northern approach to the Straits of Malacca. However, effective Dutch control along the Straits could be exercised from Malacca and along the Sunda Straits from Batavia. The only other British port in the area, Bencoolen in Sumatra, was too far away to be of much use, and hence a base at the southern end of the Malacca Straits was essential to the British interest.

The British Governor of Bencoolen, Thomas Stamford Raffles, tried to secure control of the Sunda Straits by establishing a British post at Semangka Bay and later at Callambyan Bay, but these attempts proved to be unsuccessful. In late 1818 he tried to set up a settlement in Riau but failed again as it was seized by the Dutch in November 1818. Finally, he landed at Singapore on 29 January 1819, and the next day he concluded a treaty with Temenggong Abdul Rahman who was the ruler of the small Malay community. This was followed by a series of three treaties with the Temenggong and Sultan Hussein, the eldest son of Sultan Mahmud of Johor, which in return for certain monetary payments, allowed the British to finally alienate the whole island in August 1824.

Singapore started as a Residency controlled from Bencoolen, and in 1824 it was transferred to the jurisdiction of the British in Calcutta. In 1832, the three British settlements of Penang, Malacca and Singapore were put under the charge of a Governor stationed in Singapore, which eventually became the centre of government for the Straits Settlements encompassing these three colonies. With increasing British penetration into the Malay states in other parts of the Malay Peninsula, Singapore came to serve as a collecting and distributing centre not only for goods but also for people. Chinese and Indian migrants streamed through Singapore into the hinterland, while many also came to work and live on the island. The opening of the Suez Canal, the coming of the steamship, the setting up of international telegraph and the expansion of the tin and rubber industries all contributed to the growth of Singapore in the nineteenth and early twentieth centuries.

Until the outbreak of World War II, Singapore was governed like any other British colony, with a Governor appointed by the Colonial Office and assisted by an Executive Council with an official majority and a Legislative Council, which from 1924 had an equal number of official and unofficial members. The colonial government was swept away on 2 February 1942 when the British surrendered Singapore to the Japanese invasion forces. With the unconditional surrender of Japan following the dropping of the atomic bomb on Hiroshima and Nagasaki, Singapore was handed back to the British on 5 September 1945. Singapore was temporarily under the British military administration until 27 March 1946 when it became a separate Crown Colony, distinct from the Federation of Malaysia covering the whole of the peninsula.

The first constitutional reform was held in April 1955 with elections to fill the 25 seats in the new legislative body known as the Assembly, which had additionally a Speaker, 3 ex-officio members, and 4 nominated members.[2] The Chief Minister of this Assembly was David Marshall, but he resigned about a year later when he failed to reach an agreement with the British on further steps towards self-government. Lim Yew Hock became the next Chief Minister, and during his tenure of office an agreement was finally reached in March 1957 whereby Singapore would attain full internal self-government with a completely elected Legislative Assembly of 51 members. External affairs and defence remained under British control.

In the elections held on 30 May 1957, the People's Action Party (PAP) won 43 of the 51 seats and formed the new government, with Lee Kuan Yew as the Prime Minister of the new state. Towards the end of that year, Yusof bin Ishak was installed as the first Yang di-Pertuan Negara, or President. Some four years later, on 9 July 1963, Singapore joined Malaya, Sabah and Sarawak to form the Federation of Malaysia. This union did not run smoothly, and on 9 August 1965 Singapore separated from Malaysia and became an independent and sovereign state within the Commonwealth. With full powers to manage the affairs of the state, the PAP government, led by Lee Kuan Yew, proceeded to embark on a series of measures designed to expedite the social and economic development of the country. Since then, the PAP has remained in government, with Lee Kuan Yew as Prime Minister until November 1990 when Goh Chok Tong took over. In 2004, Lee Hsien Loong became the third Prime Minister of Singapore.

ECONOMY

During the whole colonial period, the economy of Singapore was dominated by entrepôt trade, facilitated by a good natural harbour, excellent port facilities, low-cost ancillary services such as shipping, banking and insurance, and a strategic geographical location. The trade consisted of an inflow of raw materials from Peninsular Malaysia and other neighbouring countries, and their re-export after being processed, and the import of manufactured goods from the West for distribution to these countries. The primary products of the region such as rubber, coffee, pepper, copra, coconut oil, rattan and timber are sorted, graded and re-exported to the West. Manufactured goods, foodstuffs, and machinery of all kinds were imported from Europe and America for distribution to the neighbouring countries. The pre-eminent position of entrepôt trade was reflected in the tertiary sector absorbing about 72 per cent of the labour force in 1957.

The entrepôt trade suffered a severe setback in 1964 when Indonesian confrontation of the formation of Malaysia broke out, sending the economy into a tailspin. When confrontation was eventually terminated in 1966, normal trading relations with the neighbouring countries were restored. Apart from this temporary setback, there was the emergence of economic nationalism in the region, resulting in an increasing tendency for goods to bypass Singapore. After attaining independence in 1965, the island state embarked on a diversification programme by focusing on industrialisation to offset the decline in entrepôt trade and to provide employment to the rapidly growing population. New and medium scale industries over a wide front were set up to produce plywood, cables, steelpipes, electrical appliances and textiles. This was soon accompanied by heavy industries such as steel mills, dry docks, heavy engineering works, and oil refineries. In more recent years, the economy was further strengthened with the promotion of tourism, financial services, petrochemicals and pharmaceuticals.

The economy of Singapore has undergone dramatic changes to emerge as a very advanced one nowadays viewed in terms of the economic structure and per capita income. Transport, communications, power and other basic facilities are well developed; standards of public administration are high and efficient; and social institutions and services are modern and efficient, the proportion of the workforce engaged in the main occupational groups amounted to about 29 per cent in professional and technical, 13 per cent in administrative and managerial, 18 per cent in manufacturing, 12 per cent in business services, and 5 per cent in financial services. The per capita income was estimated to reach the high of $44,666 in 2005, propelling Singapore into the small club of rich countries in the world.[3]

DEMOGRAPHIC DATA

In this section, we will describe very briefly the sources of demographic data upon which this study is based, while a full account is presented in the Appendix. The counting of the people of Singapore dates back to 1824, and thereafter seven similar head counts were made by 1836. The crude statistics of these counts were collected and published by T. J. Newbold.[4] Three further counts were conducted in 1840, 1849 and 1860, and the results, by sex and race, were reproduced by T. Braddell in his book.[5] The statistics produced from these counts are very narrow in scope and subject to serious errors in some cases.

More comprehensive and reliable statistics were made available through the series of regular population censuses conducted from 1871. These censuses were held once every ten years up to 1931; no census was taken in 1941 because of World War II. The first post-war census was completed in 1947, followed by another in 1957. The next census was conducted thirteen, instead of ten, years later in 1970 in order to coincide with the United Nations recommendation that countries should shift their census to that year. Since then, three decennial censuses were held in 1980, and 1990 and 2000.

The other major set of statistics required for our study was taken from the vital registration system, which was introduced in 1872. However, the birth and death statistics for the early years are not obtainable, as these figures were first made available only in 1886. For many years, only a few basic statistics were collected, and it was only after World War II that major improvements in the collection system were introduced so as to produce more detailed and useful figures.

The third source of data originated from the system of registering marriages and divorces. Muslim marriages are registered in the Registry of Muslim Marriages, while divorces are finalised and registered in the Shariah Court. The registration of Muslim marriages has always been compulsory, but the registration of non-Muslim marriages was only made compulsory with the enactment of the Women's Charter in September 1961. For this study, we were able to obtain statistics of all marriages solemnised in Singapore only from this date onwards. Whatever statistics that are made available are quite comprehensive and accurate.

In addition to the above three major sources of demographic statistics, the study has also utilised data from various publications. These publications are listed in the Bibliography.

Notes

1. D.G.E. Hall, *A History of South-East Asia* (London: Macmillion, 1958).
2. C.M. Turnbull, *A History of Singapore, 1819–1975* (Kuala Lumpur: Oxford University Press, 1977).
3. Singapore, *Singapore Yearbook of Statistics, 2006* (Singapore: Department of Statistics, 2006).
4. T. J. Newbold, *Political and Statistical Account of the British Settlements in the Straits of Malacca* (London: John Murray, 1839).
5. T. Braddell, *Statistics of the British Possessions in the Straits of Malacca* (Pinang: Pinang Gazette Printing Office, 1861).

2

Population Growth and Distribution

In studying the history of the population in Singapore, it is best to commence with the year 1819 when Stamford Raffles first landed on the practically uninhabited island. To trace back to the period before this date, which is shrouded in myths and legends and with no reliable records, would be difficult and treading on unsafe ground. Even for the early nineteenth century, the data compiled from the various head counts are not completely accurate. Prior to World War II, the growth of the population was essentially through immigration as the indigenous inhabitants were few in number and contributed little to this growth. After the war, immigration was subjected to increasingly tighter control, and natural increase became the principal factor of population growth.

EARLY SETTLEMENT

In 1811 a band of about one hundred Malays from Johor, led by the Temenggong who was an officer of the Sultan of Johor, migrated southwards and settled on the banks of the Singapore River.[1] At that time, however, the country was already populated by a small group of natives known as the *orang laut*, or sea gypsies, who were fishermen and pirates living exclusively in their boats along the small rivers.[2] According to T. J. Newbold, when Raffles landed on the island on 28 January 1819, the population numbered about 150, living in a few shabby huts under the rule of the Temenggong.[3] About 120 of them were said to be Malays and the rest Chinese. These figures are probably nothing more than an informed guess, but they cannot be far off the mark since the population then was extremely small. In any case, it is known for sure that during

8

the next few months the population increased very rapidly through a great influx of immigrants.

The first people to be attracted by the many opportunities for making profits in the new trading post of Singapore were inhabitants from the older Dutch settlement of Malacca on the west coast of Peninsular Malaysia. In spite of the severe measures adopted by the Dutch to prevent their subjects from sailing to Singapore and the petty pirates in the waters of the Straits of Malacca, hundreds managed to find their way to the new settlement.[4] Among these new arrivals, the majority were Malays and the rest were Chinese. By the middle of 1819, Raffles claimed that the population had risen to about 5,000, as stated in his letter to the Duchess of Somerset on 11 June 1819. His famous words were, "My new colony thrives most rapidly. We have not been established four months and it has received an ascension of population exceeding 5,000 principally Chinese, and this number is daily increasing".[5]

According to the same source, the population was said to have numbered between 10,000 and 12,000 by August 1820. However, a completely different account is presented by Thomas Braddell, who gives the figure of 5,874 as the total population in 1821.[6] In the absence of a perfect method of verifying this figure, it can perhaps be surmised that the enthusiasm of Raffles had led him to exaggerate somewhat, and it is more likely that Braddell, writing with the detachment of a decade later, is nearer the truth. Besides, Raffles had also erred in over-estimating the proportion of Chinese when he remarked that they formed the majority. Braddell estimated that the Chinese numbered 1,150 and the Malays 4,724 in 1821, and in fact it was not until the early 1830s that the former did outnumber the latter.

The news about the establishment of the free port of Singapore in the centre of an area rich in trade soon spread far and wide, and traders and settlers from places outside Peninsular Malaysia began to flock to the island. The news soon reached the southern parts of China and Chinese traders, who had previously travelled to such places as Malacca, Brunei and Manila, found it safer and more profitable to visit Singapore instead.[7] The first junk arrived from Amoy in February 1812 and ushered in a series of such voyages, normally ending at the close of the Northeast Monsoon in March or April, which brought the Chinese traders and settlers into the country.[8]

At about the same time, news of the British trading centre in Singapore reached the Indian sub-continent, and Indian traders soon came to the island in fairly large numbers. Apart from traders, there were indentured labourers and convicts among the steady stream of Indians coming into the country in the first few years. The early Indians were mainly Chuliahs and Tamils from South India, but subsequently there came also such northern Indians as the Sikhs (also known locally as Bengalis) and Pathans.

A third major group were the Indonesian immigrants who came from the neighbouring islands in the East Indies in the south. Among them were the Javanese, Bugis and Balinese who were shrewd traders and merchants. Being persons of the same racial stock, these newcomers intermingled with the Malays and became assimilated through marriage and other affiliations.

PRE-WAR POPULATION GROWTH

The large influence of immigrants led to a rapid increase in the population of the colony, which reached 10,683 by the time the first head count was taken in January 1824. This implies that in a matter of only three years after 1821 the population had more than doubled. The figures for the rest of the period up to 1947 are laid out in Table 2.1. The general feature conveyed by these figures is one of uninterrupted population growth

TABLE 2.1
Population Growth, 1824–1947

Year	Population ('000)	Increase ('000)	Annual Growth Rate
1824	10,683	—	—
1830	16,634	5,951	7.7
1840	35,389	18,755	7.8
1849	52,891	17,502	4.6
1860	81,734	28,843	4.0
1871	96,087	14,353	1.5
1881	137,722	41,635	3.7
1891	181,602	43,880	2.6
1901	226,842	45,240	2.3
1911	303,321	76,479	3.0
1921	418,358	115,037	3.3
1931	557,745	139,387	2.9
1947	938,144	380,399	3.2

during the whole period with, however, some variation in the actual growth rates attained at different times.

The figures reveal that the population continued to grow rapidly, and within a short span of twenty-five years it had been enlarged by about five times, to reach 52,891 in 1849. The annual growth rate amounted to 7.7 per cent during 1824–30, 7.8 per cent during 1830–40, and 4.6 per cent during 1840–49. The annual rate of increase experienced in these early years was the highest in the demographic history of the country, and has never been equalled since then.

In the second half of the nineteenth century, the population did not grow as fast and managed to expand by only four times to reach 226,842 in 1901. The slackening in population growth is reflected in the annual growth rate, which declined from 4.0 per cent during 1849–60 to the low of 2.3 per cent during 1891–1901. The exceptionally low rate of 1.5 per cent recorded during 1860–71 was not accurate, being affected by the unreliability of the 1860 census which appears to have overcounted the population by a large but unknown quantum.[9] What in fact occurred was that the population grew at an average rate of more than 1.5 per cent during 1860–71, and less than 4.0 per cent during the preceding period 1849–60.

In the twentieth century, the population increased fourfold from 226,842 in 1901 to 938,144 in 1947. After slackening in the late nineteenth century, the growth rate gathered momentum again and was raised to 3.0 per cent during 1901–11, and 3.3 per cent during 1911–21. The drop to 2.9 per cent during 1921–31 was due to the restriction of immigrants from China and India during the World Depression in the early thirties. In the final period, 1931–47, the growth rate recovered to 3.2 per cent. It should be recalled that the population census scheduled for 1941 was postponed on account of the imminence of war breaking out in Singapore, and hence there is no population figure for that year. The Japanese occupation of Singapore ended on 5 September 1945, and the census date was set for 23 September 1947. It should be noted that there must have been a large movement of people into Singapore during those two years, which boosted the 1947 census figure.

For a better understanding of how the population grew over the years, we will supplement the census figures with birth and death statistics to examine the components of population growth. Table 2.2 presents a summary of the components of population growth since 1881 when vital statistics for a complete intercensal period first became

TABLE 2.2
Components of Population Growth, 1881–1947

Intercensal Period	Population Increase	Natural Increase	Net Migrational Increase
1881–91	43,857	−30,932	74,798
1891–01	45,980	−42,542	88,522
1901–11	75,729	−59,978	135,707
1911–21	115,037	−35,594	150,631
1921–31	139,387	18,176	212,211
1931–47	380,399	178,296	202,103

available. The data indicate the relative importance of fertility, mortality, and migration as factors determining population growth.

In spite of the absence of data for the years prior to 1881, it is quite safe to say that the excess of deaths over births had existed right from 1819 until 1921, as revealed by the figure in Table 2.2. The resultant negative natural increase in those days was due to the low number of births and the high level of deaths. The number of births in any particular year was low on account of the absence of normal family life for most men, whose families were left behind in their own country, apart from the high proportion of bachelors among the immigrants. In contrast, the annual number of deaths was usually high because of the deadly tropical and infectious diseases like malaria, cholera, dysentry and tuberculosis, and the poor health conditions prevailing then. It was the large-scale immigration that arrested the reduction in population which would otherwise result from the negative natural increase, and turned the tide in favour of a fairly-high rate of population growth in those days up to 1921.

From the early 1920s, the number of births began to rise faster than the number of deaths, with the result that a positive natural increase began to emerge and grow bigger. But migration continued to play a more dominant role in population growth up to 1941. The period was characterised by a continuous decline in the crude death rate, from about 32 in 1921 to 21 per thousand population in 1941 as devastating tropical diseases such as malaria were brought under effective control, and by a slow but steady rise in the crude birth rate from 28 in 1921 to 44.7 in 1941, caused primarily by the normalising of the sex ratio.

Consequently, a widening of the demographic gap between the birth rate and the death rate ensued, and was reflected in a higher natural increase. It should be mentioned that during the Japanese Occupation from February 1942 to September 1945 there was no immigration from China and the Indian sub-continent.

The multiracial character of the population calls for an investigation of the interesting differences in the pattern of population growth experienced by the three main races in the country. Table 2.3 shows the annual rate of population increase of each race for the various periods from 1824 to 1947. Two general features are revealed by the figures. First, there are certainly variations in the annual rate of population increase recorded by each of the three main races. Secondly, the Indians were exposed to more violent fluctuations in their growth rates caused by frequent ups and downs in migration between the Indian sub-continent and Singapore. By comparison, the Malay rate was somewhat steadier, and the Chinese rate went through only minor oscillations.

From the peak level of 12.0 per cent per annum registered in 1824–30, the growth rate of the Chinese was reduced rapidly during the first two decades. Thereafter, it increased very slowly but steadily to about 3 per cent towards the close of the nineteenth century, and then remained at slightly above this level during the first half of the present century.

TABLE 2.3
Annual Rate of Population Growth for Three Main Races, 1824–1947

Period	Chinese	Malays	Indians
1824–30	12.0	2.9	16.7
1830–40	10.4	5.6	5.8
1840–49	5.0	2.9	7.2
1849–60	5.4	5.2	6.8
1860–71	0.4	4.4	−1.5
1871–81	4.8	2.4	0.2
1881–91	3.5	0.1	2.9
1891–01	3.0	0.0	0.6
1901–11	3.0	1.5	5.0
1911–21	3.7	2.5	1.5
1921–31	2.9	2.0	4.6
1931–47	3.5	3.6	1.9

During the intercensal period 1901–11, the Chinese population grew by about 55,500; the negative natural increase amounted to 53,300 and hence the net migrational increase was 108,800. The same pattern was repeated in the following period, 1911–21. During 1921–31, a positive natural increase emerged, but migration continued to persist as the dominant factor of population growth. The 1931–47 period witnessed a complete swing, with natural increase (175,500) becoming more important than net migration (134,300).

By comparison, the figures for the Indian growth rate reveal great fluctuations on account of the vagaries of migration between Singapore and the Indian sub-continent. It is obvious that the growth rate fluctuated from one intercensal period to another with no clear long-term trend. Another interesting feature is that the two greatest extremes in the growth rate were recorded by the Indians. The highest rate of increase by any race was the 16.7 per cent registered by the Indians during the period 1824–30, and the lowest was also experienced by the Indians during the period 1860–71 when they registered a negative growth rate

TABLE 2.4
Components of Population Growth for
Three Main Races, 1901–1947

Intercensal Period	Population Increase	Natural Increase	Net Migrational Increase
		Chinese	
1901–11	55,500	−53,300	108,800
1911–21	95,600	−36,600	132,200
1921–31	103,500	9,600	93,900
1931–47	310,800	176,500	134,300
		Malays	
1901–11	5,800	−1,800	7,600
1911–21	11,800	600	11,200
1921–31	11,400	5,700	5,700
1931–47	48,800	8,100	40,700
		Indians	
1901–11	10,700	−4,500	15,200
1911–21	4,500	−3,800	8,400
1921–31	18,500	−1,300	19,800
1931–47	18,200	900	17,300

of 1.5 per cent. As for the components of population growth, the negative natural increase persisted until the period 1921–31 when it amounted to 1,300 as against the net migrational samples of 19,800.

According to the figures in Table 2.3, the Malay population grew at a slower pace than the Chinese population during the major part of the pre-war days. The immigration of Malays into the country has always been at a much lower level than that of the Chinese or the Indians. This is also the reason for the Malay population not experiencing exceptionally high growth rates, which can only come about as a result of great waves of migration. The negative natural increase also existed among the Malays, but it lasted only until 1901–11. The earlier emergence of a positive natural increase was a manifestation of the more settled nature of the Malay community with normal family lives.

POST-WAR POPULATION GROWTH

A publication of the Economic Commission for Asia and the Pacific (ESCAP) issued in 1959 stated: "The rate of population growth in Asia and the Far East has accelerated in recent years because mortality has rapidly declined while fertility, on the contrary, has remained constant."[10] This was indeed an apt description of the position in Singapore during the early post-war years. In the second post-war census, held in 1957, the population numbered 1,445,929 compared to the figure of 938,144 enumerated in the preceding census of 1947 (see Table 2.5). This gives an increase of 507,785 or an annual growth rate of 4.5 per cent, which was the highest ever recorded in the present century. It would appear somewhat baffling that the high rate could have been attained in

TABLE 2.5
Population Growth, 1947–2006

Year	Population ('000)	Increase ('000)	Annual Growth Rate
1947	938,144	—	—
1957	1,445,929	507,785	4.5
1970	2,074,507	628,578	2.8
1980	2,413,945	339,438	1.5
1990	3,047,132	633,187	2.4
2000	4,017,733	970,601	2.8
2006	4,483,900	466,167	1.8

the absence of large-scale immigration such as had occurred in the pre-war days. There is, however, a perfectly logical explanation to this phenomenon.

Firstly, the immediate post-war years witnessed a rapid decline in the crude death rate from 13.3 in 1947 to 7.4 per thousand population in 1957 and a maintenance of the crude birth rate at a high level of about 45 per thousand population. Consequently, the intercensal period was characterised by a very high rate of natural increase, equivalent to about 3.5 per cent per annum. Secondly, within the migrational factor there was a marked shift from net migrational gain from overseas countries to net migrational gain from Peninsular Malaysia. The magnitude of this essentially urbanisation movement may be deduced from the following figures:

Period	Population Growth	Natural Increase	Net Migration
1947–57	507,800	395,600	112,200

The net migrational increase of 112,200 for 1947–57 represents the net total of migration (including that from Peninsular Malaysia). But it has been estimated that the population of Singapore was depleted by a net migrational loss of some 29,200 during this period to overseas countries, other than Peninsular Malaysia. Adding 29,200 to the figure 112,200 yields an estimated total net migrational gain from Peninsular Malaysia of some 141,400, which is equivalent to approximately 14,100 persons per year, or an annual rate of increase of about 1 per cent. This is the factor that was responsible for inflating an annual natural increase of about 3.5 per cent to the high annual population growth rate of 4.5 per cent.

For Singapore and Peninsular Malaysia as a whole, the population increase during the 1947–57 period amounted to 1,880,800, but the natural increase for the same period was 2,020,100, thus giving a net outward (or overseas) migration of 139,300. On the other hand, the estimated volume of outward migration based on land, sea and air arrival and departure statistics was 104,500 for Singapore and Peninsular Malaysia, broken down into 82,600 for the latter and 21,900 for the former. Applying this percentage distribution between the two territories to the actual migrational deficit of 139,300 will give us an estimate of

29,200 for Singapore, while the remaining 110,100 was for Peninsular Malaysia. At that time the two territories were still colonies under British rule and the movement of people between them was completely free.

The third post-war census conducted in 1970 yielded a population of 2,074,507, an increase of 628,578 or 2.8 per cent per annum compared with the population in 1947. The intercensal period witnessed certain important developments which were responsible for reducing the rate of population increase to a comparatively low level. While the decline in mortality was very rapid in the early post-war years, it naturally slackened somewhat as mortality approached the lowest possible level. The crude death rate was lowered from 7.4 in 1957 to 5.2 per thousand in 1970. The other more significant development was that fertility, having remained at its peak for many decades, finally commenced to fall in 1958, and very sharply too. From the high of 42.7, the crude birth rate was brought down to 22.1 per thousand population in 1970.

The third development was in respect of migration between Singapore and Peninsular Malaysia, which was not maintained at the previously high level. The growth of towns and increasing job opportunities in Peninsular Malaysia led to a slowdown in the migration of people southwards into Singapore. Additionally, the free movement of people between the two countries was put to an end with the imposition of immigration control after Singapore's separation from Malaysia in August 1965. The relatively slow volume of migration between the two countries may be observed from the following figures:

Period	Population Growth	Natural Increase	Net Migration
1957–70	628,600	438,249	164,185

The rigid control of immigration from Peninsular Malaysia since August 1965 and from other countries after the Japanese occupation resulted in a net migration surplus of only 33,000. Migration has become a negligible factor of population growth.

In the fourth post-war census held in 1980, the population of Singapore was enumerated to be 2,413,945 compared with 2,074,507 counted in the 1970 census. This gives an increase of 339,438 or 16.4 per cent for the ten-year intercensal period. The average annual rate of population growth implied in these figures was 1.5 per cent, the lowest ever recorded since the holding of a modem census more than one hundred years ago in 1871. One of the major consequences of the exceptionally low rate of population growth was the acute shortage of labour, and hence the importation of foreign workers in recent years.

The remarkable slackening in the rate of population growth was caused by the sharp decline in fertility brought about by, apart from social and economic factors, the successful population control programme introduced by the government. During the intercensal period, the crude birth rate was reduced from 22.1 in 1970 to 17.1 per thousand population in 1980. The crude death rate stayed stationary at about 5.2 per thousand population during the period, while net migrational surplus also remained at a very low level. This is illustrated by the following figures:

Period	Population Growth	Natural Increase	Net Migration
1970–80	339,400	315,400	24,000

The low figure of 24,000 for the net migrational surplus reflects the continuation of the tight control exercised over immigration from Peninsula Malaysia and other countries.

According to the census held in June 1990, the population of Singapore was enumerated as 3,047,132, an increase of 633,187, or 26.2 per cent, an improvement over the 1.5 per cent recorded during the previous intercensal period 1970–80. Of the total population increase during 1980–90, some 438,249, or 69.2 per cent were contributed by natural increase, and 194,938 or 30.8 per cent by net migration. The re-emergence of migration as an important factor of population growth was due partly to a conscious effort in admitting more foreigners to settle in Singapore to compensate for the slow population growth and to the recruitment of more foreign low-skilled workers to relieve the tight labour market.

Period	Population Growth	Natural Increase	Net Migration
1980–90	633,187	438,249	194,938

The latest census conducted in June 2000 yielded a population of 4,017,733, up by 970,601 or 24.2 per cent from the previous figure of

3,047,132 in 1990. The average rate of annual increase has continued to accelerate to 2.8 per cent during this latest intercensal period. Of the total population increase during 1990–2000, some 330,030 or 34.0 per cent were contributed by natural increase and 640,571 or 66 per cent by net migration. The diminishing role played by natural increase in the population growth of Singapore may be attributed to fertility continuing to remain well below the replacement level. The low level of natural increase, coupled with sustained economic growth, necessitated the greater inflow of foreigners.

Period	Population Growth	Natural Increase	Net Migration
1990–2000	970,601	330,030	640,571

In recent years, there was a further slackening in the rate of population growth, being lowered to 1.8 per cent during 2000–2006.

RECENT POPULATION GROWTH

The growth of population in the new millennium will be examined in greater detail in terms of the data for twelve-month periods as well as for the resident and non-resident population. In the census the resident population is defined to include Singapore citizens and Singapore permanent residents, and all other persons are included in the non-resident population. The latter group comprised of, among others, low-skilled foreigners holding work permits, skilled foreigners and their family members with employment pass, and foreign students studying in private commercial schools, government schools, polytechnics and universities. Another noteworthy point is that since the figures in the first column of Table 2.6 are for mid-year entrants, the figures in the other two columns would refer to the twelve-month period from mid-year to mid-year rather than for the calendar years.

The increase in the total population during the first twelve-month period 2000–01 amounted to 113,467 or 2.8 per cent, similar to the average annual growth rate recorded in the last intercensal period 1990–2000. In the next twelve-month period, the increase tumbled to 40,100 or 1.0 per cent, and continued downtrend to 13,900 or 0.3 per cent during the twelve-month period 2002–03. Thereafter, the recovery in the

TABLE 2.6
Growth of Resident and Non-Resident Population, 2000–2006

Mid-Year	Number	Increase	
		Number	Percentage
Total Population			
2000	4,017,733	—	—
2001	4,131,200	113,467	2.8
2002	4,171,300	40,100	1.0
2003	4,185,200	13,900	0.3
2004	4,240,300	55,100	1.3
2005	4,351,400	111,100	2.6
2006	4,483,900	132,500	3.0
Resident Population			
2000	3,263,209	—	—
2001	3,319,100	55,891	1.7
2002	3,378,300	59,200	1.8
2003	3,437,300	59,000	1.7
2004	3,486,900	49,600	1.4
2005	3,553,500	66,600	1.9
2006	3,608,500	55,000	1.5
Non-Resident Population			
2000	754,524	—	—
2001	812,100	57,576	7.6
2002	793,000	−19,100	−2.4
2003	747,900	−45,100	−5.7
2004	753,400	5,500	0.7
2005	797,900	44,500	5.9
2006	875,400	77,500	9.7

population growth was just as rapid, with the increase rising to 55,100 or 1.4 per cent during 2003–04, 111,100 or 2.6 per cent during 2004–05, and quickly 312,500 or 3.0 per cent during 2005–06.

A completely different pattern of population growth was displayed by the two components of the total population. The dominant group represented by the resident population experienced a fairly steady increase, due to natural increase being the principal factor of population growth. While the amount of increase ranged from about 50,000 to

67,000, the annual rate of increase was also quite stable, generally below 2 per cent. The small group of non-resident population, mostly foreigners on short-term stay, was subjected to violent changes, up by 57,576 or 7.6 per cent during the first twelve-month period 2000–01, and down the very next period to 19,000 or 2.4 per cent as the economy continued to contract. This downward tendency gathered momentum in the period 2002–03 when a decrease of 45,000 or 5.7 per cent was recorded. Thereafter, an upturn occurred, with a modest increase of 5,500 or 0.7 per cent during 2003–04. In the last two periods, the non-resident population resumed its high growth rate, 44,500 or 5.9 per cent during 2004–05 and 77,500 or 9.7 per cent during the latest period.

A greater insight into the dynamics of recent population growth is provided in Table 2.7 showing the components of population growth. Natural increase has in fact registered a steady but declining trend on account of a declining number of births and a rising number of deaths. It fell regularly from 29,828 in 2000–01 to the low of 21,158 in 2003–2004, and then recovered very slightly in the last two periods. Net migration, on the other hand, has recorded a down-up movement in recent years. Starting with a surplus of 83,639 in 2000–01, net migration dipped to 15,478 in the next twelve-month period and even to a deficit of 9,583 in 2002–03. For the next period, a surplus of 33,942 appeared, and continued to be enlarged to 89,633 and 130,500 in the last two periods.

A major difference in the two sets of figures is that the natural increase represents the addition of babies and net migration the addition of mainly foreign adults to the total population. It should be pointed out

TABLE 2.7

Components of Total Population Growth, 2000–2006

Mid-year to Mid-year	Population Growth	Natural Increase	Net Migration
2000–01	113,467	29,828	83,639
2001–02	40,000	24,622	15,478
2002–03	13,900	23,483	–9,583
2003–04	55,100	21,158	33,942
2004–05	111,100	21,467	89,633
2005–06	132,500	21,671	130,500

that the figures for net migration do not in any way represent the normal net inflow of foreigners seeking a permanent new home in Singapore. In the main, they refer to transient foreigners entering the country to work on short-term stints in the various sectors of the economy suffering from acute labour shortages. Changes in the size of these foreigners are determined by the state of the economy in the country. The downward movement in net migration, and hence the decline in the non-resident population noted earlier, was caused by the economic slump triggered by the Sars crisis, the electronics downturn, and companies restructuring and downsizing their work force in Singapore.

Information on the two components of the total population was first collected in the 1970 Census, with 2,074,500 or 27.1 per cent resident population and the other 60,900 or 2.9 per cent non-resident population. Ten years later in 1980 there were 2,282,100 or 94.5 per cent residents and 131,800 or 5.5 per cent non-residents. A dramatic change occurred in the last two censuses, with the non-residents lifted to 311,300 or 10.2 per cent in 1990 and to 754,500 or 18.8 per cent in 2000. The high population of transient non-residents, or foreigners, enumerated in 1990 and 2000 has resulted in a major departure in the presentation of the census results. Almost all the census tables were based on the resident population only in order to present a truer profile of the population in Singapore. This new method of tabulating the census data since 1990 will be reflected in certain parts of this study where data are available for the resident population only.

POPULATION DISTRIBUTION

The geographical distribution of the population of Singapore will be analysed in terms of Development Guide Plan (DGP) regions used by the Urban Redevelopment Authority. For our purpose, the DGP regions are grouped into six broad areas known as Central, East, Northeast, North, West, and Islands and Others. As can be seen in the map (Figure 2.1), the Central Water Catchment area and the Training Area reserved for military exercises are included in the Others category together with some sixty islets in the Islands category.[11] The population distribution according to these broad regions for 1980 and 1990 is presented in Table 2.8.

With the continuous drift of the population in the Central region to the government-built new towns and private housing estates in the outlying areas in the eighties, the population in the Central region

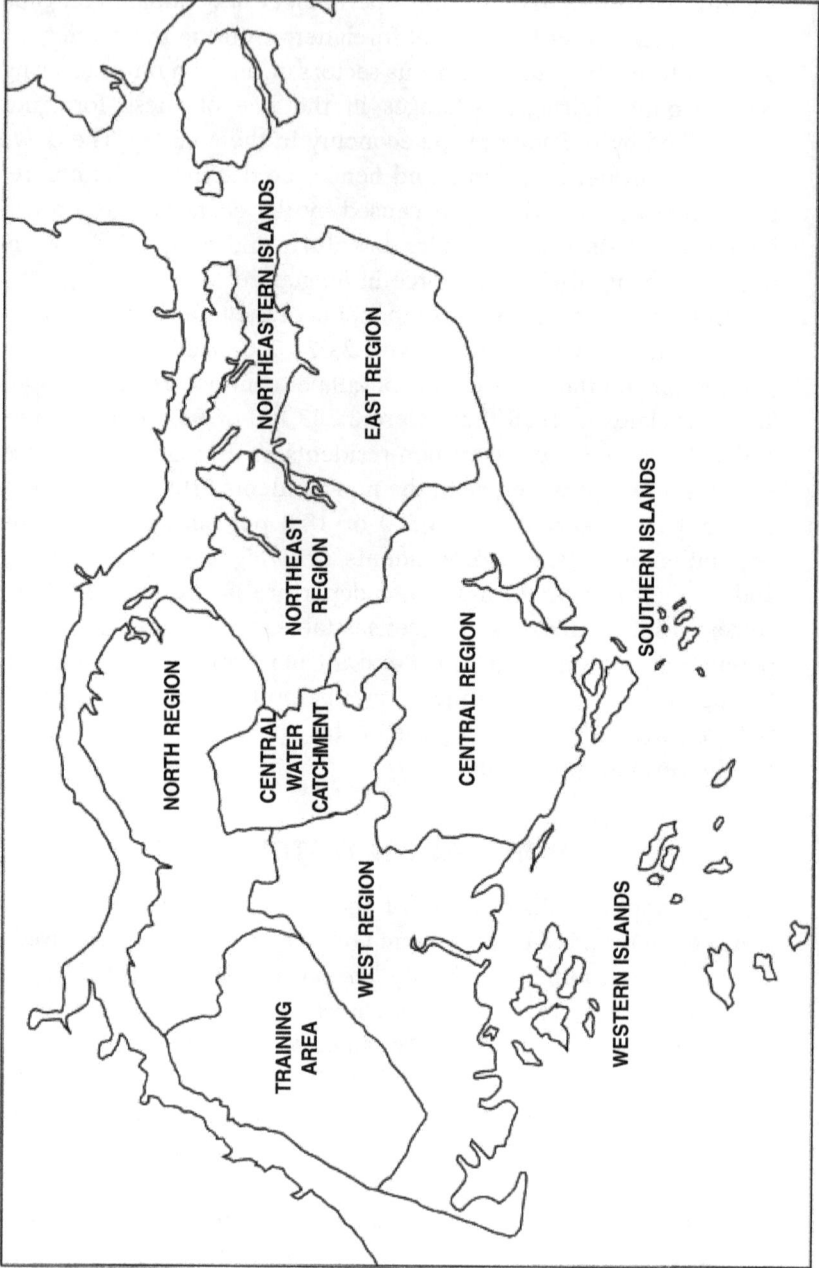

FIGURE 2.1
Development Guide Plan Regions

TABLE 2.8

Distribution of Total Population by Region, 1980 and 1990

Region	1980		1990		1980–1990 Increase	
	Number	%	Number	%	Number	%
Central	1,363,669	56.5	1,129,859	37.5	−233,810	−17.0
East	318,040	13.2	525,902	17.4	207,862	65.0
Northeast	326,611	13.5	505,934	16.8	179,323	55.0
North	107,254	4.5	259,068	8.6	151,814	142.0
West	268,654	11.1	582,678	19.3	314,024	117.0
Islands & Others	29,717	1.2	12,938	0.4	−16,779	−57.0
Total	2,413,945	100.0	3,016,379	100.0	602,434	25.0

declined from 1,364,000 in 1980 to 1,130,000 in 1990. An increase in population was recorded in the other regions, except in the Islands and Others region. The islanders from the various islets have also moved into subsidised apartments in the new towns, while negligible population changes would occur in the Central Water Catchment and Training areas. The greatest population expansion was recorded in the North region, with an increase of 142 per cent, followed closely by the West region with 117 per cent. Much slower expansion was recorded in the East region (65 per cent) and in the Northeast region (55 per cent).

As a result of the above population shifts, the people of Singapore are now more dispersed over the country. By 1990, only 30 per cent of the population stayed in the Central region, and fairly similar proportions were found in three other regions. Some 19 per cent of the population stayed in the West region, 17 per cent in the East region, and another 17 per cent in the Northeast region. A much lower 9 per cent inhabited the North region, and less than 1 per cent in the Islands and Others region. The population density in 1990 was 9,515 persons per square kilometre in the Central region, 8,323 in the Northeast region, 6,006 in the East region, 5,487 in the West region, 2,804 in the North region, and only 74 in the Islands and Others region. The overall population density of Singapore was 4,705 persons per square kilometre.

We have not included the figures for 2000 in Table 2.8 because the information concerning the distribution of the population by region was available for the resident population only and not for the total population supplied in the 2000 Census report.[12] Although the figures

TABLE 2.9

Distribution of Resident Population by Region, 2000

Region	Number	Percentage
Central	895,052	27.4
East	654,096	20.0
Northeast	566,589	17.4
North	394,912	12.1
West	741,921	22.7
Islands & Others	10,639	0.3
Total	**3,263,209**	**100.0**

presented in Table 2.9 are not strictly comparable to those shown in Table 2.8, some broad conclusions can be inferred from the two sets of data. The proportion of the resident population staying in the Central region stood at the lower figure of 27.4 per cent in 2000 as against the 37.5 per cent of the total population in 1990. All the other four regions have in fact recorded a larger share of the resident population in 2000 as compared with the share of the total population registered in 1990. There is therefore some evidence to suggest that the dispersion of the population from the crowded Central region to the outlying parts of the country have taken place during the latest intercensal period. For sure, this geographical dispersion of the population will continue in the years ahead.

Notes

1. T. J. Newbold, *Political and Statistical Account of the British Settlements in the Straits of Malacca* (London: John Murray, 1839), p. 2.
2. W.W. Skeat and H. H. Ridley, "The Orang Laut of Singapore", *Journal of the Straits Branch of the Royal Asiatic Society* 33 (January 1900): 247.
3. Newbold, op. cit, p. 2.
4. Song Ong Siang, *One Hundred Years' History of the Chinese in Singapore* (London: John Murray, 1923), p. 6.
5. Lady Sophia Raffles, *Memoir of the Life and Public Services of Sir Thomas Stamford Raffles, FRC etc. Particularly in the Government of India, 1811–16 and of Bencoolen and Its Dependencies, 1817–24; with Details of Commerce and Resources of the Eastern Archipelago, and Selection from His Correspondence* (London: John Murray, 1830), p. 383.

6. T. Braddell, *Statistics of the British Possessions in the Straits of Malacca* (Pinang: Pinang Gazette Printing Office, 1861).
7. Song, op. cit., p. 7.
8. Victor Purcell, *The Chinese in Malaya* (London: Oxford University Press, 1948), p. 70.
9. J.F.A. McNair, C.S. Walker and A. Knight, "Report of the Census Officers for the Straits Settlement of Singapore", *Blue Book of the Straits Settlements 1871* (Singapore: Statistical Office, 1872), p. 8.
10. United Nations, "Population Trends and Related Problems of Economic Development in ECAFE Region", *Economic Bulletin for Asia and the Far East* 1, no. 1 (June 1959): 2.
11. Cheng Lim Keak, *Geographic Analysis of the Singapore Population* (Singapore: Department of Statistics, 1995).
12. Leow Bee Geok, *2000 Census of Population, Geographic Distribution and Travel*, Statistical Release No. 4 (Singapore: Department of Statistics, 2001).

3

Changing Population Structure

In this chapter we will discuss the structure of the population in terms of ethnic groups, sex composition, age structure, religious composition and citizenship pattern. The structure of the population has evolved over many decades in accordance with not only demographic determinants like migration, mortality and fertility, but also social and economic forces. These variables have exerted their influence in different ways and in varying degrees on each aspect of the population structure. In Singapore, international migration, to be discussed in the next chapter, has left its pervasive and permanent imprint on many facets of the population structure.

ETHNIC AND DIALECT COMPOSITION

The multiracial society of Singapore has evolved from a long history of migration from the nearby countries of Malaysia, Indonesia, China and India since its establishment in 1819. With such a heterogeneous population exhibiting major differences in religion, language, culture and customs, the collection of data on the various ethnic and dialect groups is certainly necessary for the purpose of studying the race differentials in population growth and structure, nuptiality, fertility, and so on. This has always been recognised and the item on race has always been a mandatory one in the census questionnaire used since 1871.

In the population censuses, the concept of ethnic group has been used in the usual sense to connote groups or communities belonging to the same stock or ethnological origin having common bonds of culture, customs, and language. By tradition, the respondents have been classified according to four main ethnic groups in the country, with each group subdivided into specific community or dialect groups. In cases where the person has mixed parentage, the ethnic group of the father has been used. The term "Chinese" covers all persons of Chinese origin, and is subdivided into specific dialect groups such as Hokkien, Teochew, Cantonese, Hainanese, Hakka, and so forth. "Malays" includes all persons of Malay or Indonesian origin, and is subdivided into Malays, Javanese, Boyanese, Bugis, and so forth. The term "Indians" has not been uniformly defined in the past, but nowadays it is used to refer to all persons from the Indian sub-continent, such as Indians, Pakistanis, Bangladeshis, and Sri Lankans. It is subdivided into Tamils, Malayalis, Punjabis, Gujeratis, and so forth. Finally, the term "Others" is used to cover all the other ethnic groups, such as Eurasians, Arabs, Thais, Filipinos, Japanese, Americans, Europeans, and many other small groups.

The changes in ethnic composition according to the above fourfold classification are depicted in Table 3.1. Singapore has never had a sizeable native population since it was founded by Stamford Raffles in 1819; the Chinese and Indians are immigrant people and so are most of the Malays. Throughout the demographic history, these three races have made up the majority of the total population; their combined proportion has persisted at around 96 per cent. Although the predominant position of these three ethnic groups has always remained, their relative share of the total population underwent some major changes in the nineteenth century. In this connection, the early figures underline the less known fact that the Malays were the dominant race in Singapore during the first two decades or so after the founding of the colonial settlement. In 1824 there were 6,431, or 60.2 per cent, Malays compared with 3,317, or 31.0 per cent, Chinese. The proportion of Malays was reduced to 45.9 per cent in 1930, but was still higher than the Chinese at 39.4 per cent. By 1836 the Malays, with a total of 12,497 persons, were outnumbered by the Chinese, whose total was 13,749, and since then the population has remained predominantly Chinese in composition.

From the much reduced proportion of 41.7 per cent in 1836, the Malays continued to experience a diminution in their share of the total population as the inflow of Chinese immigrants into the colony gathered momentum. The proportion of Malays was reduced further to 32.2 per cent in 1849, 27.6 per cent in 1871, and 15.8 per cent in 1901. In the twentieth century, it decreased very slowly to reach the record low of 11.7 per cent in 1931, followed by a slow recovery to about 15.0 per cent in 1970. Thereafter, it remained around the 14 per cent level until

TABLE 3.1
Distribution of Population by Race, 1824–2006

Year	Chinese	Malays	Indians	Others	Total
			Number		
1824	3,317	6,431	756	179	10,683
1830	6,555	7,640	1,913	526	16,634
1836	13,749	12,538	2,932	765	29,984
1849	27,988	17,039	6,284	1,580	52,891
1871	54,572	26,141	10,313	3,790	94,816
1881	86,766	33,012	12,086	5,858	137,722
1891	121,906	35,956	16,009	7,727	181,602
1901	164,041	35,988	17,047	9,768	226,842
1911	219,577	41,806	27,755	14,183	303,321
1921	315,151	53,595	32,314	17,298	418,358
1931	418,640	65,014	50,811	23,280	557,745
1947	729,473	113,803	71,927	22,941	938,144
1957	1,090,596	197,059	129,510	28,764	1,445,929
1970	1,579,866	311,379	145,169	38,093	2,074,507
1980	1,856,237	351,508	154,632	51,568	2,413,945
1990	2,252,700	408,000	229,500	126,200	3,016,400
2000*	2,505,379	453,633	257,791	46,406	3,263,209
2006*	2,713,200	490,500	319,100	85,500	3,608,500
			Percentage		
1824	31.0	60.2	7.1	1.7	100.0
1830	39.4	45.9	11.5	3.2	100.0
1836	45.9	41.7	9.9	2.6	100.0
1849	52.9	32.2	11.9	3.0	100.0
1871	57.6	27.6	10.9	4.0	100.0
1881	63.0	24.0	8.8	4.3	100.0
1891	67.1	19.7	8.8	4.3	100.0
1901	72.1	15.8	7.8	4.3	100.0
1911	72.4	13.8	9.2	4.7	100.0
1921	75.3	12.8	7.7	4.2	100.0
1931	75.1	11.7	9.1	4.2	100.0
1947	77.8	12.1	7.7	2.4	100.0
1957	75.4	13.6	9.0	2.0	100.0
1970	76.2	15.0	7.0	1.8	100.0
1980	76.9	14.6	6.4	2.1	100.0
1990	74.7	13.5	7.6	4.2	100.0
2000*	76.7	13.9	7.9	1.4	100.0
2006*	75.2	13.6	8.8	2.4	100.0

*Resident population only.

2006. Moving in the opposite direction was the proportion of Chinese, rising from 31.0 per cent in 1824 to 52.9 per cent in 1849, 72.1 per cent in 1901, and 77.8 per cent in 1947. The Chinese proportion has remained somewhat stable at about 75 per cent. The figures given in Table 3.1 underline the contrary movements in the proportion of these two races occurring mainly in the nineteenth century rather than in the present century.

The Indians have, by comparison, maintained a much more stable proportion of the total population during the larger part of the whole period. It stood at 7.1 per cent in 1824 and rose to a peak of 11.9 per cent in 1849, after which it fell to 8.8 per cent in 1881. Since then, it has fluctuated around the neighbourhood of 8 per cent. As for the mixed group of minority races known as "Others", the proportion has never exceeded 5 per cent. In the colonial days, this group comprised mainly Eurasians and Europeans, but nowadays it is an extremely mixed group, with sizeable numbers of foreign professionals and their family members.

Of the total resident population of 3,263,209 enumerated in 2000, some 2,505,379, or 76.7 per cent, were Chinese, and hence the not unexpected widespread influence of this group in the social and economic activities of the country. Within the 2,505,379 Chinese resident population, there were the many dialect-speaking communities led by the Hokkiens, who numbered 1,028,485, or 41.1 per cent. This community was way ahead of the Teochews, who came in second with 526,197, or 21.0 per cent. The Cantonese occupied third position with 385,630, or 15.4 per cent. The fourth and fifth were extremely close, and they were the Hakkas with 198,435, or 7.9 per cent, and the Hainanese with 167,594, or 5.5 per cent. The much smaller groups, with numbers ranging from about 47,000 to 22,000, were the Foochows, the Henghuas, and the Shanghainese. Though unified by a common written character, the Chinese are differentiated by many dialect-speaking communities, with some minor specialisation by each group in certain economic activities. Apart from intermarriages among these communities, the government has been attempting to unify them by persuading them to adopt Mandarin as the common language in their workplace and at home.

By comparison the 453,633 Malay resident population in 2000 was far more homogeneous as an ethnic group, with the large number of 309,716, or 68.3 per cent, being Malays. The other much smaller communities were the Javanese with 80,062, or 17.6 per cent, and Boyanese with 51,849, or 11.4 per cent. Most of these minority communities, although originating from Indonesia, have lived in Singapore for many generations and for all practical purposes have been classified as Malays. What is perhaps more significant is that in Singapore they normally communicate in Bahasa Melayu even though their own written and spoken language may vary somewhat. We must also remember that they have a common religion in Islam and over the years have intermarried freely.

The Indian resident population as an ethnic group, numbering 257,791 in 2000, was rather heterogeneous, being differentiated by distinct language divisions as well as national boundaries, represented by India, Pakistan, Bangladesh, and Sri Lanka. The Tamils, regardless of which country they originated from, constituted the largest group, with 150,184 or 58.3 per cent. The much smaller language groups were the Malayalis with 21,736, or 8.4 per cent, the Sikhs with 13,188, or 8.8 per cent, and the Hindustanis with 5,064, or 3.4 per cent. Apart from different spoken languages, various components of the Indian population have their own written languages. In religion, the Indians are sharply divided between the Hindus, the Muslims, the Buddhists, and the Christians, to mention only the important ones.

The fourth ethnic group, denoted as "Others" in the census tables, must necessarily be extremely mixed, viewed in terms of nationality, language, and religion. Of the 46,406 resident population classified as "Others" in 2000, 15,045, or 32.4 per cent, were Eurasians, 7,517, or 16.2 per cent, Arabs, 11,067, or 25.8 per cent, Caucasians, and 3,219, or 3.3 per cent, Filipinos. Even the Caucasians, or Whites as they are known in other countries, were a rather mixed lot, considered in terms of nationality and language. There were the Dutch, French, Germans, Italians, and the English-speaking component represented by the English, Scottish, Americans, Canadians, Australians, and New Zealanders. Considered as a whole, the "Others" constitute a vital segment of the population of Singapore in view of their valuable contribution to the development process of the country.

SEX COMPOSITION

In a population closed completely to migration, the sex composition is determined by the slight excess of boys at birth. This is, however, counterbalanced by the boys being subject to higher mortality at almost all ages so that eventually the sex ratio of the general population becomes near normal, with fairly even numbers of each sex. In countries where immigration of predominantly males has been a major factor of population growth, one can expect the sex ratio to deviate from the normal pattern. This was true in the case of Singapore, considering the past immigration of predominantly men, discussed in the previous chapter. In the course of time, a gradual movement towards a more balanced sex ratio will occur as the proportion of female immigrants rises, the volume of natural increase becomes larger, and the flow of immigration diminishes to a low level.

The sex composition of the population is examined in Table 3.2 in terms of the number of males per thousand females. Three phases in the evolution of the sex ratio may be distinguished. First, from 1824 to 1849 the general movement of the sex ratio was towards greater disparity, rising from 1,987 males per thousand females to a peak of 3,905. This may be attributed to the declining proportion of the more settled Malay

TABLE 3.2
Sex Ratio by Race, 1824–2006

Year	Total	Chinese	Malays	Indians
1824	1,987	8,188	1,058	5,878
1830	2,763	11,275	1,141	10,387
1836	3,148	14,642	1,168	9,580
1849	3,905	11,500	1,421	6,499
1871	3,189	6,147	1,267	4,294
1881	3,088	5,112	1,281	3,943
1891	3,209	4,680	1,383	4,216
1901	2,938	3,871	1,279	4,129
1911	2,453	2,790	1,172	4,914
1921	2,044	2,123	1,230	5,021
1931	1,713	1,656	1,161	5,189
1947	1,217	1,132	1,208	2,903
1957	1,117	1,039	1,101	2,001
1970	1,047	1,017	1,036	1,518
1980	1,042	1,015	1,072	1,323
1990	1,023	1,012*	1,041*	1,181*
2000*	996	990	1,031	1,043
2006*	982	972	996	1,063

*Resident population only.

population with a relatively balanced sex ratio and to an increase in the proportion of Chinese and Indians through an influx of primarily male immigrants from China and the Indian sub-continent. The second phase covers the second half of the nineteenth century. During this period, the sex ratio was almost stationary at around 3,100 males per thousand females. The third phase covers the present century when a continuous movement of the sex ratio towards parity may be observed. The improvement from 2,938 in 1901 to 2,044 in 1921 was engendered solely by a rising proportion of women among new immigrants, mostly wives of immigrant settlers who had decided to live permanently on the island.

For the period 1921–47, the improvement may be attributed to a larger proportion of female immigrants as well as to the growing volume of natural increase. By far the most important impetus was the official policy in the late 1930s of making "every endeavor to improve the sex ratio among immigrants by means of the Indian Immigration Committee and the Aliens Ordinance of 1933 whereby women were admitted free of quota restrictions until 1938".[1] By 1947, the sex ratio had further improved to reach a more favourable level of 1,217. As natural increase assumed its role as the prime growth factor, the sex ratio moved towards 1,117 in 1957 and 1,049 in 1970. It showed very little improvement in the 1980 census when it stood at 1,042, but improved considerably to 1,023 in 1990 as more foreign female workers were admitted to alleviate the acute shortage of labour. The figures for the resident population only shows that the sex ratio dropped to 996 in 2000 and 982 in 2006, due to the exclusion of the non-resident population which has more males than females.

In examining the movement in the Chinese sex ratio, we should bear in mind that a main feature of Chinese immigration in the early nineteenth century was that for quite a long time the male immigrants did not bring their womenfolk with them. Being only temporary residents, the Chinese immigrants preferred to leave their wives and children in China; the majority of them could not afford to bring their families; the authorities in China, though lax in preventing the emigration of males, took precautions to discourage women from going overseas in order to maintain a strong hold on the overseas Chinese and to ensure remittances from them.[2] There is reason to believe that the women enumerated in the early censuses did not come directly from China but were mixed-blood Malacca Baba women. Referring to the year 1837, C.B. Buckley wrote, "Up to this time, no Chinese women had come to Singapore from China, and the newspaper said that, in fact, only two genuine Chinese women were, or at any time had been in the place, and they were two small-footed ladies who had been, some years before, exhibited in England."[3] It is not surprising that the Chinese sex ratio at that time was most abnormal, with about 15,000 males per thousand females.

As the ban on female immigrants from China was lifted and as the Chinese community in Singapore assumed a more settled nature, a larger number of women came. The result was a gradual normalising of the sex ratio, from 14,642 in 1836 to 1,656 in 1931. From the mid-1930s the movement of the Chinese ratio towards parity was accelerated by the bigger volume of natural increase and by the Colonial Government's policy of encouraging female immigration through the Aliens Ordinance 1933, by which women were admitted free of quota restrictions. The flow of immigration ceased after the outbreak of war in December 1941 and in the early post-war years, but the high rate of natural increase continued the process of normalising the Chinese sex ratio. By 1947 the ratio had improved to 1,132 and continued to improve in the post-war years to reach the almost even ratio of 1,015 in 1980. The sex ratio of the Chinese resident population stood at 1,012 in 1990, and even went down to 990 in 2000 and 972 in 2006, with more females than males for the first time.

The Indian sex ratio also commenced at a very uneven level at the beginning, with 5,878 males per thousand females in 1824. The ratio rose to 10,387 in 1830, and thereafter it fell to 3,943 in 1881. The unbalanced sex ratio may be ascribed to the immigrants being predominantly male workers, and to those married ones leaving their wives and children at home in India. Unlike the Chinese sex ratio which moved downwards continuously, the Indian sex ratio rose again after 1881 to reach 5,189 in 1931, and only after that did it follow a definite downtrend. Even so, the uneven nature of the Indian sex ratio, by comparison, persisted for a long time until the post-war years. This is because there has always been a lesser tendency among the Indians to settle permanently in Singapore. Even in 2006, the sex ratio of the Indian resident population still remained quite uneven at 1,063.

The sex ratio of the Malays differs from those of the Chinese and the Indians in two respects. In the first place, the Malays, though comprising some immigrant elements, have constituted a predominantly settled community and have exhibited a near balanced sex ratio right from the early days. Even in 1824, the Malay sex ratio was quite normal at 1,058 males per thousand females. The second special feature is that the Malay sex ratio did not follow any definite path, and went through an up-down movement as determined by the fluctuations in the relatively low volume of immigrants. The Malay sex ratio went up and down many times within the range of 1,030 and 1,420 over the years. But in more recent years, the sex ratio of the Malay resident population improved from 1,041 in 1990 to 1,031 in 2000, and to the more balance level of 996 in 2006.

Another important aspect of the study of the sex composition concerns the changes that have occurred among the five broad age groups, as shown in Table 3.3. The sex ratio in the youngest sex group, 0–4 years, has always been the most normal, and over the years the least changes were recorded. In this age group, the two principal factors that determine the sex ratio is the proportion of boys and girls at birth and the differential child mortality between the two sexes. There are always more male than female babies born, but this is subsequently counter-balanced by a heavier mortality among males than females. The net effect is still a slight excess of males over females in this age group, as can be observed in the table. However, we need to mention that this sex ratio may also be affected by the greater under-enumeration of girls than boys at the censuses. In the next age group, 5–14 years, the sex ratio was affected by migration to a very minor extent, and hence there was still a relatively small excess of boys over girls.

The sex ratio in the next two groups, within the working ages of 15 and 59, was abnormal at most times. This is a reflection of the large extent to which the migration of predominantly male workers has affected the structure of the population. In the 15–29 age group, there were slightly three times more males right up to 1947. After that, the

TABLE 3.3

Sex Ratio by Broad Age Group, 1881–2006

Age Group	1881	1901	1921	1947	1970	1990	2000*	2006*
0–4	1,105	1,038	1,029	1,132	1,058	1,074	1,072	1,051
5–14	1,136	1,202	1,069	1,208	1,056	1,078	1,067	1,061
15–29	3,227	3,291	2,427	2,998	1,033	1,004	996	989
30–59	4,855	3,900	2,770	1,243	1,093	1,020	998	984
60 and over	4,875	1,683	1,468	953	877	861	865	849

* Resident Population only.

normalisation of the sex ratio became pronounced. The older working age group, 30–59, recorded a more uneven ratio of slightly less than five times more males in 1881, but experienced a rapid normalisation of the ratio over the years. As the male workers grew older and stayed longer in Singapore, they would be more inclined to bring their families into the country to settle down for good. The marked normalisation in the 15–29 age group recorded in the 1980s was due to the greater inflow of female domestic maids.

Similar figures for 2000 and 2006 are available for the resident population and not for the total population. In both years, the sex ratio shows that there were less males than females since the non-resident population, with a high proportion of males in the working age groups, has been excluded. In 2006 the sex ratio stood at 989 in the 15–29 age group, and this drops progressively to 984 and 849 in the next two higher age groups. This may be attributed to the higher mortality among the males than the females in resident population, not so much affected by migration.

AGE STRUCTURE

The item on age has always been included in the population censuses conducted in Singapore because of its usefulness with regard to many aspects of demographic analysis and social and economic planning. Recognising the importance of the age item, many interrelated questions and special precautions were adopted to ensure reliable age reporting. The prime aim was to obtain the completed age, or the age at last birthday of a person, reckoned by the Western method in accordance with the Gregorian solar calendar. There are, in fact, other methods of reckoning ages and in accordance with other types of calenders. In Singapore, there is the special case of the Chinese reckoning ages by means of their own method according to the Chinese lunar calendar. To overcome this problem, a technique of collecting and converting the Chinese ages reckoned according to their traditional method into the required ages in the censuses was used.[4] The elaborate system of collecting ages in the censuses has resulted in exceptionally good quality statistics that are relatively free from the usual errors, such as digital preference and overstatement at old age.

In studying the population structure of a country, it is necessary to examine the age distribution in view of its significant influence on the amount of labour available, the supply of marriageable partners, the absolute number of births and deaths, and the extent and type of dependency burden. In a closed population unaffected by international migration, the age structure is determined mainly by the level of fertility and the mortality level over the age range. In such a population, the data when plotted on a graph will resemble a pyramid with the largest number at the base and becoming smaller upwards with the advance of age. The higher the level of fertility in the immediate past, the broader will be the base of the age pyramid. However, the usual pyramid shape may be distorted by certain factors, such as exceptionally heavy mortality among combat soldiers during war times, dramatic decline in the number of births, and heavy immigration or emigration at certain ages. The brief conceptual framework outlined here will facilitate our understanding of Table 3.4 and Figure 3.1.

A useful method of studying the age structure of Singapore is to analyse it in terms of five functional broad age groups, as presented in Table 3.4. The pre-school group, under 5 years of age, increased rapidly

TABLE 3.4
Distribution of Population by Broad Age Group, 1901–2006

Age Group	1901	1931	1947	1957	1970	1980	1990	2000*	2006*
	Number ('000)								
0–4	12.5	49.1	144.5	264.7	235.4	193.7	228.6	213.3	196.5
5–14	25.6	96.5	222.7	354.4	569.4	459.4	418.8	485.5	501.6
15–29	98.5	184.0	246.7	366.7	582.9	837.1	907.6	671.5	729.6
30–59	75.9	204.1	320.5	404.8	568.5	750.1	1,207.5	1,522.2	1,753.4
60 and over	3.7	24.0	33.7	55.3	118.3	173.6	258.9	348.7	427.3
Total	216.2	557.7	938.1	1,444.9	2,074.5	2,413.9	3,016.4	3,243.2	3,608.4
	Percentage								
0–4	5.8	8.8	12.2	18.3	11.4	8.0	7.6	6.6	5.5
5–14	11.8	17.3	23.7	24.5	27.4	19.0	13.9	15.0	13.9
15–29	45.6	33.0	26.3	25.4	28.1	34.7	30.1	20.7	20.2
30–59	35.1	36.6	34.2	28.0	27.4	31.1	40.1	46.9	48.6
60 and over	1.7	4.3	3.6	3.8	5.7	7.2	8.4	10.8	11.8
Total	100.0	100.0	100.0	100.0	100.0	100.0	100.0	100.0	100.0

* Resident Population only.

from 12,500, or 5.8 per cent, in 1901 to a peak of 264,700, or 18.3 per cent, in 1957, and thereafter declined steadily to 228,600, or 7.6 per cent, in 1990. This was engendered by the decreasing number of births resulting from the sharp fall in fertility to below the replacement level in 1975, and the continuation of this low level since then. The essentially school-going population aged 5–14 also recorded an increase from 25,600 in 1901 to a peak of 569,400 in 1970. In the next two decades the number declined to reach 418,800 in 1990 as the shrinking birth rate began to take effect. This has resulted in a fall in school enrolment and a shrinkage in the supply of new entrants into the labour force.

In the young working group aged 15–29, the number rose consistently right up to 1990 when it stood at 907,600, an increase of slightly more than nine times from 98,500 in 1981. The same continuous increase was also recorded by the older working-age group 30–59, rising from 75,900 in 1901 to 1,207,500 in 1990. This represents a more pronounced rise of slightly less than sixteen times during the same period. It should be pointed out that sizeable numbers in these two working-age groups in 1990 were foreign workers engaged in the various sectors of the economy on employment passes or work permits. As for the last age group of 60 years and over, the number was enlarged by about seventy times from 3,700 to 258,900 in the last nine decades. The present trend towards a sharp rise in old persons is indicative of the presence of the population ageing process in Singapore.

We can also look at the age data given in Table 3.4 in terms of dependency burden. If we define the young dependency burden as the proportion of the population below 15 years, it can be observed that the young dependency burden stood at 17.6 per cent in 1901 and became heavier over the years, to peak at 42.8 per cent in 1957. Since then, the young dependency burden has been lightened, slowly at first but gathering speed in recent years to reach the low of 21.5 per cent in 1990. On the other hand, the old dependency burden, defined as the proportion of those aged 60 and over, has been relatively light in Singapore, but has become heavier in the last three decades. In 1957, the old dependency burden amounted to only 3.8 per cent, but more than doubled by 1990 when it stood at 8.4 per cent.

Another way of looking at the problem is that approximately 53.4 per cent of the population supported the other 46.6 per cent of the young and old dependants in 1957, but by 1990 the dependency burden had lightened, with 70.2 per cent supporting 29.9 per cent. There was,

FIGURE 3.1
Age Pyramids, 1931–2005

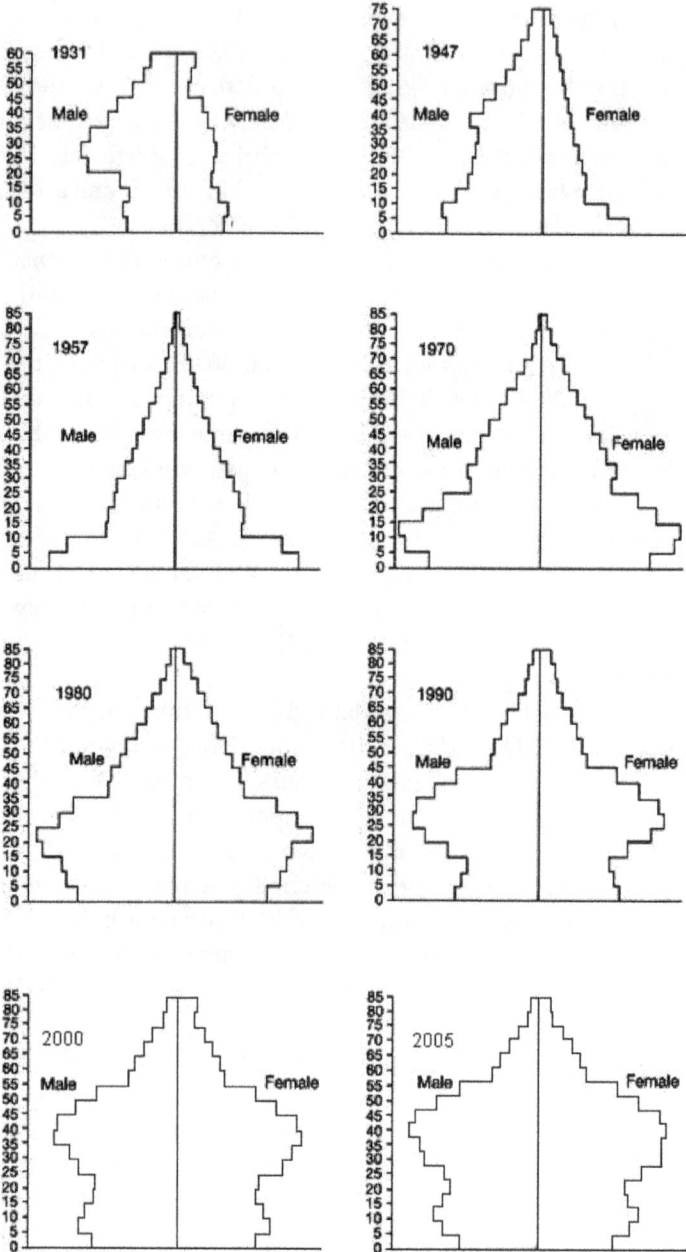

however, a decided shift from supporting young dependants to old dependants, a phenomenon that is expected to continue indefinitely in the future as fertility continues at below or near replacement level.

Another method of examining the age structure of the population is by means of the age pyramids depicted in Figure 3.1. The 1931 age pyramid represents the typical example of an abnormal age structure with a big bulge at the working ages on account of heavy immigration of working-age persons from mainly China and India. The relatively bigger bulge in the male section of the pyramid may be ascribed to the predominance of men among the immigrant workers. In due course, the reduction of immigrants during and immediately after the war led to the reduction of the bulge at the working ages in the 1947 pyramid. A decade later in 1957 the bulge had completely disappeared so that the

FIGURE 3.2

Age Pyramids of Resident Population by Race, 2005

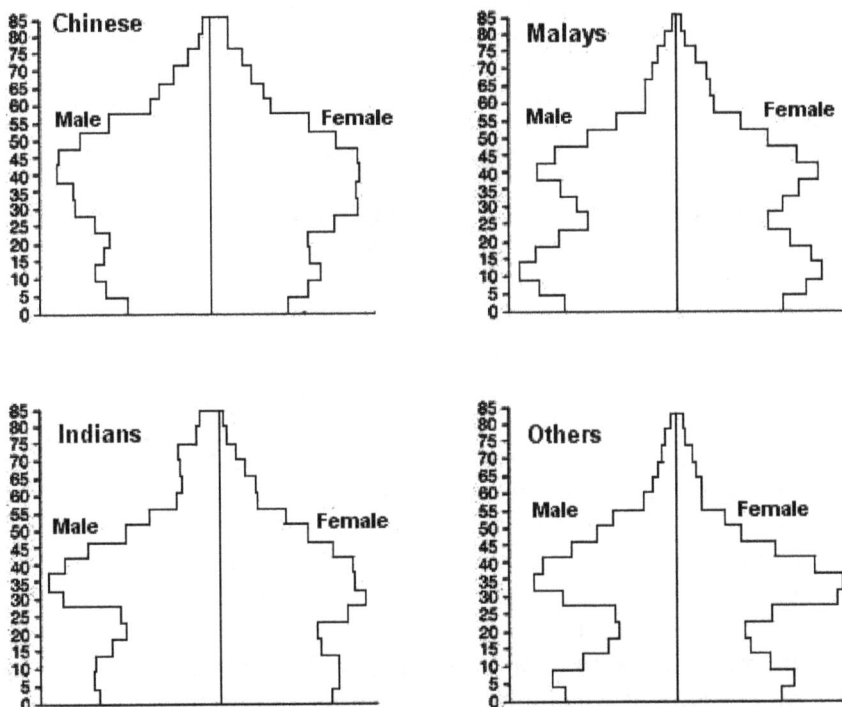

usual pyramid shape prevailed, with quite a broad base engendered by the rapid increase in the number of births after the war.

The next stage in the evolution of the age structure commenced with the continuous fall in the number of births first experienced in 1957. The interesting outcome was the appearance of the depression at the very base of the pyramid, as may be noticed in the 1970 age pyramid, which by that time had already witnessed the complete disappearance of the working-age bulge. The relentless decline in the number of births in the seventies led to an enlargement of the depression at the base of the 1980 age pyramid extending upwards to the teenage group and becoming progressively depressed downwards to the youngest group of 0–4 years.

The general shape of the age pyramid in 1990 has remained almost unaltered, except that the depression at the base has extended upwards slightly. Curiously enough, a new kind of bulge generated by a combination of rapidly increasing births and rapidly decreasing births subsequently has now emerged, and this time its presence is equally felt in both the male and female sections. Briefly, the age pyramid of Singapore has therefore evolved from an abnormal pyramid with a working-age bulge to a normal but broad-based pyramid, and then a unique pyramid with a shrinking base and a new teenage bulge. The age pyramids of the main racial groups are depicted in Figure 3.2.

RELIGIOUS COMPOSITION

Though not as important as race which affects almost every aspect of the demographics of Singapore, religion deserves some attention in view of its underlying influence on nuptiality, fertility, and the population control programme. Religious differences have a strong tendency to reinforce racial and cultural identities of the people and have thus presented serious obstacles to effective racial intermingling in the country. Furthermore, the resurgence of religious fervour in recent years has propelled religion into the forefront as the key factor that determines the racial and political harmony of the nation.[5] A study of the religious composition of the population is, however, handicapped by the inherent difficulties encountered in the collection of information on religion, which involves a wide range of personal beliefs and attitudes. The information, if collected, is generally less precise and accurate than other types of statistics compiled in a population census, which has to be taken into account when interpreting census data on religion.

Unlike the items on race, sex and age, information on religion has not always been collected in the population census. Whilst religion was included as an item in the questionnaire used in the 1911, 1921 and 1931 censuses, it was omitted in the first three post-war censuses held in 1947, 1957 and 1970, and re-introduced in the two later censuses. The information on religion was collected only from persons aged 10 and above, and the religion stated by the respondent was accepted by the enumerators. Those who reported that they were free-thinkers or atheists and those who did not give an answer to the question were all classified under "No Religion". Those who professed to follow the teachings of the Chinese sages, such as Confucius, Mencius and Lao Zi, and those who practised ancestor worship and other sects were collectively included under "Taoism". The other religions indicated in Table 3.5 for the resident population is self-explanatory.

The major religions in the country have been firmly established and the religious affiliations of the resident population have remained essentially unchanged over the years. This is manifested in the figures for 1980, 1990 and 2000, where the changes appear to be significant for only Buddhism and Taoism. The proportion of the resident population professing to practise Buddhism rose from 26.7 per cent in 1980 to 31.1 per cent in 1990 and 42.5 per cent in 2000, while that for Taoism fell from 30.0 per cent to 22.4 per cent and even to the low of 8.5 per cent

TABLE 3.5

Percentage Distribution of Resident Population Aged 10 and Over by Religion and Race, 1980–2000

Religion	Total			Race (2000)			
	1980	1990	2000	Chinese	Malays	Indian	Others
Buddhism	26.7	31.1	42.5	53.6	0.0	0.6	13.7
Taoism	30.0	22.4	8.5	10.8	0.0	0.0	0.2
Islam	16.2	15.4	14.9	0.3	99.6	25.6	22.3
Christianity	9.9	12.5	14.6	16.5	0.3	12.1	53.3
Hinduism	3.6	3.7	4.0	0.0	0.0	55.4	1.1
Other Religions	0.5	0.6	0.6	0.3	0.2	5.6	1.3
No Religion	13.1	14.3	14.8	18.3	0.0	0.5	8.1
Total	100.0	100.0	100.0	100.0	100.0	100.0	100.0

in 2000 during the same period. However, the difference between these two religions is not clear-cut among the Chinese, particularly the older and less educated.[6] If we combine the two figures, the changes occurring during the decade is less conspicuous, decreasing from 56.7 per cent to 53.5 per cent and 51.0 per cent in 2000. The population professing Islam fell slightly from 16.2 per cent in 1980 to 15.4 per cent in 1990 and 14.9 per cent in 2000, and that professing Hinduism rose marginally from 3.6 per cent to 3.7 per cent, and 4.0 per cent in 2000 during the same period. By far the greatest increase was registered by the Christians, with a rise of 3.5 percentage points from 9.9 per cent to 12.5 per cent, and finally even reached 14.6 per cent.

We will now look at the pattern of religious affiliations as reflected in the 2000 census. Buddhism was professed by the largest group of people, 1,060,662 persons, or 42.5 per cent, followed very closely by Islam with 371,660 persons, or 14.9 per cent. The third position was taken up by Christianity which was professed by 364,087 persons, or 14.6 per cent, and the fourth place by Taoism with 212,344 persons, or 8.5 per cent. Hinduism was a minor religion practised by 99,904 persons, or 4.0 per cent. This pattern of religious affiliations is of course determined to a large extent by the ethnic composition of the population discussed earlier.

The best example of a close distribution of religion along racial lines are the Malays with as high as 99.6 per cent of their members professing the Islamic faith. The vast majority of them are Sunni Muslims belonging to the Islam Shafei school of thought. In fact, Islam is one of the principal criteria used to determine whether a person is classified as Malay for some official or legal purposes. Unlike other religions, the influence of Islam on its followers is quite permanent as there is no provision in Islamic laws for the conversion of a Muslim to another religion or for the renunciation of Islam. Under such conditions, the Malays will always be identified with Islam, and the small number of non-Muslims among this community are those who originate from Indonesia.

By and large, the Chinese are adherents of one principal faith, Buddhism. Some 53.6 per cent of the Chinese professed to follow Buddhism. A sizeable proportion, 16.5 per cent, of the Chinese are Christians, this followed by Taoism with 10.8 per cent. By comparison, the Chinese had the largest proportion of free-thinkers and atheists, and also people with no religion (18.3 per cent).

In the case of the Indians, the main religion is Hinduism, which was followed by some 55.4 per cent of the group. Among the fair proportion of 25.6 per cent practising Islam were the Pakistanis and Bangladeshis. The third important religion reported by the Indians was Christianity, with 15.1 per cent. The figures for Others, encompassing mainly foreign workers and their families, show that Christianity was the dominant religion (53.3 per cent). Most of them were Caucasians, besides the Eurasian Singaporeans.

Another useful way of looking at the religious patterns is to examine the racial composition of the people belonging to a particular religion. The most obvious feature is that almost all those who follow Taoism are Chinese. To a large extent this is also true in the case of Buddhism, with a majority of Chinese (99.5 per cent), though there were some Indians and Thais professing this religion too. Those practising Islam were predominantly Malays (84.4 per cent), and the other group of some importance were the Indians (12.4 per cent). Only the Christian community appeared to escape this close identification of race with religion since it has appreciable numbers of Chinese, Indians, Eurasians, and Caucasians from many countries. As a matter of interest, the close overlap of race and religion was cited in the 1947 Census Report as the reason for not collecting information on religion,[7] and this was apparently the same reason for its exclusion in the 1957 and 1970 censuses.

LITERACY PATTERN

In the population censuses held in Singapore, literacy has always been defined as the ability of the respondent to read with understanding a newspaper in the language specified. For operational purposes during the field-work stage, the declaration of ability on the part of the respondent was accepted without further question or a test being actually administered by the enumerators. Moreover, it was a common practice to collect the information on literacy from only persons aged 10 and over. Another noteworthy point is that, being a multiracial society, the information was collected in terms of the different languages used in the country. This will allow us to examine the changes in the literacy pattern among the various languages, which is, of course, a result of the past educational system in respect of the language medium of instruction.

One convenient method of measuring the degree of literacy among a particular group of persons is by means of the general literacy rate, which may be defined as the number of literate persons per thousand population aged 10 and over. The general literacy rates, by ethnic group and sex, for the last four census years are given in Table 3.6. The 1990 and 2000 figures are for resident population only. As expected, there has been an improvement in the general literacy rate over the years, moving up sharply from 523 per thousand population aged 10 and over in 1957 to 722 in 1970, and then to 840 in 1980. During the same period, the greatest improvement of 364 points was recorded by the Chinese, compared with a lesser improvement of 146 points by the Indians. The Malays occupied an intermediate position with an improvement of 243 points. Notwithstanding these diverse movements, the Chinese literacy rate in 1980 was still the lowest (826) and the Indian literacy rate the highest (898), with the Malay rate (865) standing in between. The same relative position in the general literacy rates among these three ethnic

TABLE 3.6
General Literacy Rates by Race and Sex, 1957–2000

Race	1957	1970	1980	1990*	2000*
			Both Sexes		
All Races	523	722	840	901	925
Chinese	462	697	826	895	921
Malays Indians	622	770	865	917	936
Indians	752	839	898	930	951
Others	940	959	977	974	971
			Males		
All Races	686	838	915	955	966
Chinese	626	820	909	953	963
Malays Indians	821	892	932	967	976
Indians	816	886	928	953	975
Others	972	975	985	982	988
			Females		
All Races	336	601	762	847	886
Chinese	295	575	744	838	880
Malays	392	642	793	865	899
Indians	550	759	857	904	926
Others	905	942	967	966	957

* Resident population only.

groups was displayed by the 1990 and 2000 rates, which refer to the resident population only.

The figures for each of the two sexes, also shown in Table 3.6, reveal that the general literacy rate has improved faster among the females in the last three decades or so. The male general literacy rate increased from 686 in 1957 to 915 in 1980, whilst the female rate experienced a more pronounced improvement from 336 to 762 during the same period. The 1990 and 2000 figures for resident population suggest that a similar greater improvement was also experienced by females in the eighties. Another important feature of the table refers to all the three major races experiencing a greater improvement in the general literacy rate among the females. Singapore has certainly witnessed important changes leading to a more favourable attitude towards education and employment for women. The overall effect is that the gap between the male and female literacy rate has narrowed considerably over the years, but with the men still enjoying a high literacy rate.

In recent years, much attention has been focused on the progress and problems associated with bilingualism, particularly in schools and work situations. Recognising the importance of bilingualism, the census authorities have generated very useful information showing literacy of respondents in a particular language as well as in two or more languages. The detailed classification of literacy in more than one official language has been tabulated for only combinations of the other official languages and English owing to constraints of coding and tabulation which made it necessary to limit the number of sub-classifications. There is also good reason to believe that the number of persons literate in two or more languages other than English would be negligible. Incidentally, the other official languages besides English are Chinese, Malay and Tamil.

The distribution of literate persons aged 10 and over by language is presented in Table 3.7. Of the total 1,125,524 literate persons in 1970, 904,422 or 80.3 per cent were monolingual, being literate in only one of the four official languages. This position changed significantly to 62.0 per cent in 1980, and appeared to have declined further judging from the figure of 53.5 per cent for resident population in 1990, and 43.9 per cent for 2000. Conversely, the same period saw a major shift in the proportion of multilingual persons upwards from 19.1 per cent in 1970 to 37.5 per cent in 1980, 46.0 per cent in 1990 and 56.0 per cent in 2000 in respect of the resident population. Supplementary figures given in the census

TABLE 3.7

Literate Persons Aged 10 and Over by Language Literate In, 1970–2000

Languages Literate In	Number				Percentage			
	1970	1980	1990*	2000*	1970	1980	1990*	2000*
One Official Language	904,422	1,079,344	1,086,500	1,012,183	80.3	62.0	53.5	43.9
Two or More Official Languages	214,751	628,789	935,100	1,293,463	19.1	37.5	46.0	56.0
Non-Official Languages	6,351	8,275	9,800	3,119	0.6	0.5	0.5	0.1
Total	1,125,524	1,676,408	2,031,400	2,308,765	100.0	100.0	100.0	100.0
English	327,006	320,416	385,900	353,801	29.0	19.1	19.0	15.3
Chinese	455,735	604,374	606,000	580,369	40.5	36.0	29.8	25.1
Malay	96,525	93,269	75,900	62,721	8.6	5.6	3.7	2.7
Tamil	25,156	21,285	18,700	15,293	2.2	1.3	0.9	0.7
English & Chinese	99,781	377,614	635,600	877,510	8.9	22.5	31.3	38.0
English & Malay	80,975	188,504	235,200	283,342	7.2	11.3	11.6	12.6
English & Tamil	17,720	35,162	45,200	64,074	1.6	2.1	2.2	2.8
Other Two or More	16,275	27,509	22,700	68,536	1.4	1.6	1.1	3.0
Non-Official Languages	6,351	8,275	6,200	3,119	0.6	0.5	0.3	0.1
Total	1,125,524	1,676,408	2,031,400	2,308,765	100.0	100.0	100.0	100.0

*Resident population only.

reports indicate that this spread of multilingualism took place among all the main ethnic groups. Singapore's educational policy based on bilingualism was undoubtedly responsible for the remarkable inroads made into the spread of bilingualism in all sections of the population.

The emphasis on learning English and the mother tongue has naturally boosted the proportion literate in English and any one of the other three official languages. The proportion of literate persons in English and Chinese was raised from 8.9 per cent in 1970 to 22.5 per cent in 1980. In the case of English and Malay, the proportion rose from 7.2 per cent to 11.3 per cent, and the proportion for English and Tamil rose from 1.6 per cent to 2.1 per cent. What these changes mean is that the old monolingual type of persons, commonly known as English-educated, Chinese-educated, Malay-educated and Tamil-educated, would give way to multilingual persons. Among the resident population in 1990, 19.0 per cent of the literate persons could speak only English, compared with 45.1 per cent who could speak both English and one of the other three official languages. The position improved further in 2000 when 15.3 per cent could speak only English, and 53.4 per cent could speak English and one of the other three languages. It is probably true to say that not all Chinese children would opt for English and Chinese; some might select English and Malay, or a foreign language instead. On the other hand, a small minority of Malay and Indian children might opt for English and Chinese rather than Malay or Tamil. These were the people who were literate in more than two languages.

CITIZENSHIP PATTERN

In the post-colonial era, the first population census conducted in 1970 included citizenship as one of the items in the questionnaire, and since useful information was obtained from it, the item was retained in the next two censuses. The citizenship item proved to be valuable in providing essential information on the distribution of the population by citizenship status as well as separate data relating to the characteristics of citizens and non-citizens in terms of other demographic and economic variables. An analysis of this type of census statistics is of considerable significance in enabling us to achieve a greater insight into the process and progress of nation-building in Singapore.

In the population census, the definition of citizenship was taken as the legal nationality of a person and it might be acquired by birth, registration, or naturalisation. In cases where a person was deemed to have dual nationality, the citizenship would refer to that preferred by him. Persons who had not acquired citizenship of any country or who voluntarily claimed to be stateless were classified as such, while those who were unable to specify their citizenship were classified as "Not Stated". Both these categories appeared under the heading of "Unknown" in the census tables.

According to the above principle, the population was divided into three groups — Singapore citizens, permanent residents, and non-residents. Permanent residents refer to those who have been granted permanent residence in the country under the existing immigration regulations, and those who claim permanent residence status by virtue of their long stay in Singapore. With regard to the proof of actual citizenship status, Singapore citizens would include holders of Singapore citizenship certificates, Singapore passports, Singapore birth certificates, and red Singapore identity cards. Permanent residents refer to holders of foreign passports with entry or re-entry permits issued by the Immigration Department as well as those residents with blue Singapore identity cards. Non-residents would cover foreign students studying in Singapore, temporary visitors on social visit pass, work permit holders, and employment pass holders and their dependants, if any.

The distribution of the population according to the above threefold classification is laid out in Table 3.8. The number of Singapore citizens enumerated in 2000 amounted to 2,973,091, up by 377,848 or 14.6 per cent as compared with the 2,595,243 enumerated in 1990. This is lower than the 18.3 per cent recorded during 1980–90 and the 17.0 per cent during the 1970–80. The growth in the citizen population was engendered mainly by persons becoming citizens by birth and, to a very limited extent, by permanent residents upgrading to the status of citizens. The slackening in the growth of citizens during the latest intercensal period may be attributed to the declining number of births and the slow take-up rate of citizenship by permanent residents. The strict citizenship laws at that time have remained basically unaltered during these years.

In sharp contrast, the number of permanent residents went through some wild swings. From an initial figure of 138,785 in 1970, the number of permanent residents dropped by 50,940 or 36.7 per cent to touch 87,845 in 1980, but rose again by 22,027 or 25.1 per cent to reach 109,872 in 1990. Thereafter, it shot up by 290,118 or 164.1 per cent to reach 295,118 in the latest census held in 2000.

TABLE 3.8
Distribution of Population by Citizenship Status and Sex, 1970–2000

Citizenship Status	1970	1980	1990	2000	Intercensal Increase (%)		
					1970–80	1980–90	1990–00
Both Sexes							
Singapore Citizens	1,874,778	2,194,280	2,595,243	2,973,091	17.0	18.3	14.6
Permanent Residents	138,785	87,845	109,872	290,118	-36.7	25.1	164.1
Non-residents	60,944	131,820	311,264	754,524	116.3	136.1	142.4
Total	2,074,507	2,413,945	3,016,379	4,017,733	16.4	25.0	33.2
Males							
Singapore Citizens	962,773	1,118,359	1,313,546	1,491,890	16.2	17.5	13.6
Permanent Residents	68,036	40,652	56,513	138,403	-40.2	39.0	144.9
Non-residents	31,318	72,749	147,717	*	132.3	103.1	*
Total	1,062,127	1,231,760	1,517,776	*	16.0	23.2	*
Females							
Singapore Citizens	912,005	1,075,921	1,281,697	1,481,201	18.0	19.2	15.6
Permanent Residents	70,749	47,193	53,359	151,715	-33.3	13.1	184.3
Non-residents	29,626	59,071	163,549	*	99.4	176.9	*
Total	1,012,380	1,182,185	1,498,603	*	16.8	26.8	*

* Not available.

In sharp contrast, the number of non-resident or foreign citizens rose sharply by 116.3 per cent, from 60,944 in1970 to 131,820 in 1980. This intercensal increase gathered momentum to reach 136.1 per cent during 1980–90, and 142.4 per cent during the latest intercensal period 1990–2000. Consequently, the number of non-residents was raised sharply from a mere 60,944 in 1970 to 754,524 in 2000. The rapid expansion in foreign citizens should not come as a surprise, considering the sustained high economic growth and the worsening shortage of local labour consequent on the accelerated fertility decline in the past. The inflow of foreign workers gathered momentum as more sectors of the economy continued to experience severe labour shortages. Many of these foreign workers were relatively unskilled who were hired on short-term work permits and did not qualify to become permanent residents. Of course, many of these workers were not interested in acquiring permanent resident status since their main aim was to earn the high wages to support their families back home. The greater dependence of the Singapore economy on foreign labour has resulted in the proportion of non-residents to the total population rising from 2.9 per cent in 1970 to 5.5 per cent in 1980, 10.3 per cent in 1990, and finally to 18.8 per cent in 2000.

Table 3.8 also shows some interesting differences between the males and females. During the first intercensal period 1970–80, the number of Singapore citizens grew faster among the females (18.0 per cent) than among the males (16.2 per cent). This slower growth among the male Singapore citizens was again recorded during the second period 1980–90 and the latest period 1990–2000. Among the permanent residents, greater changes were experienced by the males. During the period 1970–80, the number of male permanent residents decreased by 40.2 per cent, greater than the decrease of 33.3 per cent registered by their female counterparts. When an upturn occurred during the period 1980–90, the increase was much greater among the male permanent residents (39.0 per cent) than among the female permanent residents (13.1 per cent). But during the latest period 1990–2000, the position was reversed, with males recording a lower increase than the females. Less clear-cut changes were experienced by non-residents whose numbers fluctuated according to the demand for foreign workers and alterations in the rules governing the admission of such workers. During the period 1970–80, the number of male non-residents grew by 132.2 per cent, compared with the 99.4 per cent recorded by the female foreign citizens. In sharp contrast, the period 1980–90 witnessed a much steeper increase in the female non-residents (176.9 per cent) than the male foreign citizens (103.1 per cent). The faster growth in the female group was due mainly to the admission of more women from the Philippines to work as domestic maids. In the 2000 Census, the non-resident population has not been made available by sex.[8]

The above changes have resulted in a shift in the population according to citizenship status. In 1970 Singapore citizens accounted for 90.4 per cent of the total population, permanent residents 3.6 per cent, and non-residents 2.9 per cent. This pattern underwent significant shifts in the next thirty years; the corresponding proportions in 2000 were 74.0 per cent, 4.7 per cent and 18.8 per cent respectively. The fall in the Singapore citizen group was a reflection of the greater dependence on foreign workers and the desire to attract more foreigners to settle permanently in Singapore following the introduction of some pronatalist policies in 1987.

According to Table 3.9, the three main races recorded fairly similar changes in the number of Singapore citizens during the period 1970–80, with the Chinese increasing by 17.8 per cent, the Malays by 15.8 per cent, and the Indians by 14.5 per cent. Another common feature experienced by these three races was the decrease in their number of permanent residents, amounting to 35.9 per cent for the Chinese, 32.6 per cent for the Malays, and 48.8 per cent for the Indians. Furthermore, these races recorded an increase, though at very different rates, in the number of non-residents, the most mobile among the three citizenship classifications. The largest increase of 140.7 per cent was registered by the Chinese and the smallest increase of 13.8 per cent by the Indians, with a moderate increase of 70.4 per cent by the Malays.

A more diverse pattern of changes was displayed by the figures for the eighties. The rate of growth in the number of Singapore citizens during the period 1980–90 was quite different for the three races, with 16.2 per cent for the Chinese, 21.6 per cent for the Malays, and 36.2 per cent for the Indians. In the case of permanent residents, the Chinese recorded a huge increase of 70.0 per cent while the Indians had a minor increase of 5.5 per cent. In contrast, the Malays recorded a reduction of 53.9 per cent in their permanent residents. The largest increase in the number of non-residents was witnessed by the Indians with 243.7 per cent, followed closely by "Others", with 231.7 per cent. The non-residents component among the Chinese grew at a lower rate of 119.1 per cent,

TABLE 3.9
Distribution of Population by Citizenship Status and Race, 1970–2000

Citizenship Status	1970	1980	1990	2000	Intercensal Increase (%)		
					1970-80	1980-90	1990-00
Chinese							
Singapore Citizens	1,478,200	1,740,862	2,023,138	2,284,617	17.8	16.2	12.9
Permanent Residents	73,246	46,954	46,954	220,762	-35.9	70.0	370.2
Non-residents	28,420	68,421	149,905	*	140.7	119.1	*
Total	1,579,868	1,856,237	2,252,700	*	17.5	-21.4	*
Malays							
Singapore Citizens	264,361	306,027	372,192	441,737	15.8	21.6	18.7
Permanent Residents	33,647	22,691	10,464	11,896	-32.6	-53.9	13.4
Non-residents	13,371	22,790	25,344	*	70.4	11.2	*
Total	311,379	351,508	408,000	*	12.9	16.1	*
Indians							
Singapore Citizens	112,683	128,969	175,680	214,642	14.5	36.2	22.2
Permanent Residents	28,208	14,435	15,227	43,149	-48.8	5.5	183.4
Non-residents	9,864	11,228	38,593	*	13.8	243.7	*
Total	145,169	154,632	229,500	*	6.5	48.4	*
Others							
Singapore Citizens	19,534	18,422	24,233	32,093	-5.7	31.5	32.4
Permanent Residents	3,684	3,765	4,524	14,311	2.2	20.2	216.3
Non-residents	14,875	29,381	97,443	*	97.5	231.7	*
Total	38,093	51,568	126,200	*	35.4	144.7	*

* not available.

and the corresponding growth rate for the Malays was extremely small, at 11.2 per cent.

In the nineties, the three main races continued to display the same pattern of growth in the number of Singapore citizens. The lowest growth was again recorded by the Chinese with 12.9 per cent and the highest by the Indians with 22.2 per cent. The Malays occupied an intermediate position of 18.7 per cent. The declining births was responsible for the slower growth in Singapore citizens among the Chinese. The permanent residents also displayed the same differential growth rate among the three main races. The extremely high growth of 370.2 per cent was registered by the Chinese, followed by the slower growth of 183.4 per cent recorded by the Indians. The Malay permanent residents, which has been shrinking, managed to experience a small increase of 13.4 per cent during the latest intercensal period. Unlike the other two races which have received newcomers from China and the Indian sub-continent, and also from the West, the Malays have received fewer newcomers from Malaysia and Indonesia.

Among the 2,595,243 Singapore citizens enumerated in 1990, some 321,116, or 12.4 per cent, were born outside the country and acquired their citizenship after satisfying certain stringent conditions mentioned earlier. A few of these foreign-born citizens could have been born overseas to Singapore citizens and became citizens by birth, while a few of the local-born citizens were born of permanent residents and became citizens by registration. Among the 109,872 permanent residents in 1990, about 18,513, or 16.8 per cent, were born in Singapore to most probably parents who were permanent residents at the time of their birth. They were relatively young — for example, 13,509, or 73.0 per cent, were below the age of 21 compared with the corresponding figure of only 11.3 per cent for those born overseas.

Notes

1. M.V. Del Tufo, Malaya, *A Report of the 1947 Census of Population, 1957* (London: Crown Agents, 1949).
2. Victor Purcell, *The Chinese in Southeast Asia* (London: Oxford University Press, 1951), p. 305.
3. C.B. Buckley, *An Anecdotal History of Old Times in Singapore* (Singapore: Fraser and Neave Ltd., 1902), p. 320.
4. Saw Swee-Hock, "Errors in Chinese Age Statistics", *Demography* 4, no. 2 (1967).

5. Eddie C.Y. Kuo and Jon S.T. Quah, *Religion in Singapore: Report of a National Survey* (Singapore: Ministry of Community Development, 1988).
6. Eddie C.Y. Kuo and Long Chee Kiong, *Religion in Singapore* (Singapore: Department of Statistics, 1995).
7. Leow Bee Geok, *2000 Census of Population, Demographic Characteristics*, Statistical Release No. 1 (Singapore: Department of Statistics, 2001).

4

Migration

Until August 1965 Singapore and Peninsular Malaysia were treated as a single unit governed by common laws in matters relating to migration, and persons entering one territory could proceed to the other without any restriction at all. These two countries have been important areas of migration since the establishment of British colonial rule in the early nineteenth century. The large and sustained immigration was engendered by the demand for labour in the public works and agricultural plantations, by the good prospects for trade and commerce, and by the law and order attendant on British rule. Such forces of attraction, coupled with liberal immigration policies, were reinforced by equally strong repelling forces in the immigrants' countries of origin. Natural calamities, political upheavals, poverty and population pressure were the decisive factors that induced the immigrants to leave their countries.

There were essentially three main streams of immigration into Singapore before World War II, namely, the northern stream from China, the western stream, from the Indian sub-continent, and the less important southern stream from the then Dutch East Indies. In the early days, the immigrants from these regions would usually leave their families behind and come to Singapore not as permanent settlers but as "birds-of-passage", sending regular remittances home, making occasional visits and eventually returning to their countries after acquiring some wealth, or on retirement. In the course of time, however, an increasing number remained permanently, although the transient character of the population persisted for many decades until the outbreak of war in Singapore in late 1941. Since then, the Japanese occupation and the subsequent strict immigration control have put an end to large-scale immigration, while at the same time the pre-war immigrants were increasingly regarding Singapore as their permanent home.

CHINESE MIGRATION

While Chinese contacts with Singapore date back to ancient times, it was after the establishment of British rule on the island in the early nineteenth century that marked the beginning of a long period of continuous Chinese migration. Despite the opposition of the Chinese Government to the immigration of its nationals to overseas territories, thousands of Chinese managed to come into the country during the first half of the nineteenth century.[1] By far the largest group were those who came to work as labourers in the pepper and tapioca farms and the gambier and sugar-cane plantations.

By the mid-nineteenth century, the immigration of Chinese had evolved into a well-organised system.[2] Potential immigrants were recruited in South China, particularly Kwangtung and Fukien provinces, by a returned immigrant known as *kheh thau* (headman), or by a professional recruiter. The *kheh thau* usually carried out the recruiting in his own village among persons known to him, and accompanied his *sin kheh* (new recruits) to Singapore where he handed them over to a particular employer for whom he acted as an agent. As for the professional recruiter, he accompanied or sent his recruits to lodging-houses at the Chinese ports from which they were shipped to Singapore. On arrival, the recruits were met by an agent of the lodging-houses in Singapore, and eventually handed over to employers or labour contractors. The lodging-house owners acted as brokers, raking considerable profit from the recruitment and distribution of the immigrant labourers.

Whichever of the two methods the immigrants came by, they had their passage and other expenses paid for them by their employers who later recovered the amount from them, and they were therefore in debt on arrival. The system of Chinese immigration at that time was known to suffer from many evil practices, such as ill-treatment and exploitation. The first attempt at protecting and regulating Chinese immigration was made on 23 March 1877 when the colonial government enacted the Chinese Immigration Ordinance 1877. Under this Ordinance, a Chinese Protectorate Office was established in 1877. Conditions on board ships were improved, depots for receiving immigrants were set up, and recruits were licensed.[3]

A more important outcome was the emergence of Chinese indentured immigrants who signed formal contracts according to the provisions of the Ordinance in return for protection from the law. However, a large number of immigrants still preferred not to sign contracts, remaining legally free but still in the clutches of their employers as long as their debts remained.[4] In the 1880s, the proportion of indentured immigrants to total Chinese immigrants was slightly above 20 per cent, but by the 1910s it had fallen below 10 per cent. The original aim of introducing formal contracts to protect the immigrants was not achieved, and public opinion against the indentured system was also becoming more vocal in China. This led to the colonial government enacting the Labour Contracts Ordinance 1914 by which Chinese indentured immigration was abolished from 30 June 1914.[5]

The banning of indentured Chinese labour left the government with almost no legislation to deal with Chinese immigration, and for more than a decade the Chinese were free to enter the country. It was in 1928 that the Immigration Restriction Ordinance 1928 was introduced by the government to control immigration whenever the influx of immigrants threatened to bring about unemployment or economic distress.[6] This ordinance was first used in the World Depression when a monthly quota on adult Chinese male immigrants was imposed on 1 August 1930. From an initial figure of 6,016 per month, the quota was gradually reduced to 1,000 during the last five months of 1932. No quota was placed on the immigration of Chinese women and children under twelve years old.[7]

The Ordinance did not prove to be entirely satisfactory because it could only be resorted to in emergencies and did not provide any control over immigrants once they had landed. It was therefore replaced by the Aliens Ordinance 1933 which came into force on 1 January 1933 and transferred all functions concerning Chinese immigration from the Chinese Protectorate Office to the new Immigration Department.[8] The new legislation allowed the government to regulate the entry of aliens and to register and control alien residents in the country. From 1 April 1933, the quota system of restricting adult Chinese male immigrants was continued under the Aliens Ordinance until the outbreak of World War II in December 1941. The immigration of Chinese women and children continued to be exempted from any restriction up to 1 May 1938 when a quota on Chinese women was imposed to ease the unemployed situation at that time.[9] Immigration of Chinese was of course at a complete standstill during the Japanese Occupation from December 1941 to September 1945.

INDIAN MIGRATION

Contacts between the Indian sub-continent and the Malay Archipelago go far back into ancient times when traders from both regions visited one another's seaports. From the early seventh century such trading relations were reinforced by cultural and religious influences from India through the Hindu Empire of Srivijaya in Sumatra, which lasted from AD 600 to AD 1,000.[10] The movement of traders, missionaries and settlers between the two regions continued into the periods of European domination of the Straits of Malacca, but on a somewhat spasmodic and meagre scale. Following the establishment of British rule in Singapore in the nineteenth century, the immigration of Indians became officially countenanced and organised. Over the years, Indian immigration gradually evolved into several distinct forms according to the needs and conditions prevailing in the country.

One of the earliest forms of Indian immigration was the inflow of convicts, introduced soon after the founding of the Straits Settlements of Singapore, Malacca and Penang by the East India Company with its governing body located in Bengal. The convicts constituted a cheap and ready supply of labour to the government in the construction of essential public works, such as roads, railways, bridges, canals, wharves and government buildings. After completing their sentences, they were repatriated to India, but a few were allowed to remain behind to seek new jobs and a fresh start in life. But convict immigration received much publicity and criticism while it lasted; it was finally prohibited after 1860 and those already here were repatriated to India by 1873.[11]

Indian indentured immigration appeared to have existed in the early nineteenth century, but it was not until 1872 that it was legalised and controlled by laws introduced by the Indian Government.[12] From 1884, it was brought under the control and protection of regulations in Singapore. Immigrants imported under indenture were mainly employed in the cultivation of tapioca, tea, coffee and sugar-cane and in government departments dealing with the railway and public works. Notwithstanding the protection accorded by the law, a decreasing proportion of Indians came under this system owing to the lack of freedom in selecting and changing jobs. The diminishing usefulness of the system, the preference of the immigrants to the other systems, and the renewed public agitation against the system led to the government eventually banning Indian indentured immigration in December 1910.[13]

Another form of Indian immigration was known as the *kangany* system whereby the employers would send their own agent or *kangany* to India to recruit labourers. The *kangany*, usually a labourer already employed in the plantation, undertook to recruit workers from his village in India in return for a certain fee from his employer. But he advanced money to defray the expenses incurred by the recruits, who were willing to come but too poor to finance their own passage, and recovered the amount from their monthly wages. In most cases, the first month's wage was not sufficient to settle the debt completely so that the immigrants became the *kangany's* debtors from the outset, and hence subject to possible exploitation. Such immigrants, unlike the indentured ones, were legally not bound to serve their employer for a definite period, though they had to sign a promissory note for the advances made to them. The system was almost free from any restrictions until 1884 when *kangany* recruiters were required to be licensed.[14] In 1908 the system ceased to exist, having been modified and transformed under the assisted immigration system.

To increase the supply of labour in the early twentieth century, the government passed the Tamil Immigration Fund Ordinance 1907 by which the Indian Immigration Committee was constituted to manage the Indian Immigration Fund.[15] The fund, to which employers had to contribute, was used to finance the importation of Indian labourers. The Committee was responsible for regulating the flow of assisted immigrants by varying the number of recruiting licences and the recruiting allowance, or subsidy. Under the supervision of the Committee, Indian immigration evolved into two distinct types — recruited and non-recruited. Regardless of whether the immigrants came on their own or through licensed *kangany* recruiters, their expenses for the journey from India were met by the fund. These assisted immigrants were free from any debt and could change their job subject to one month's notice.

Apart from the above types of Indian immigration, there were the independent immigrants who were not subject to any government control. Such immigrants usually came on their own initiative and through their own financial means and arrangements. The years following the World Depression witnessed an increasing proportion of Indians coming in as independent immigrants, mainly to avoid the one week's detention at the quarantine camp.[16] This form of immigration was sharply curtailed from 15 June 1938 when the Indian Government's ban on the emigration of unskilled labourers to Singapore was imposed.[17] It may be recalled that at this time too, the other forms of Indian immigration had ceased to exist so that the only group of Indians to continue coming into the country after this date were independent immigrants other than the labouring class. The movement of Indian migration was completely halted by the outbreak of war on 8 December 1941, and remained at a standstill until the end of the Japanese Occupation in September 1945.

MALAY MIGRATION

Contacts between Singapore and the numerous islands in the Indonesian archipelago date back to ancient times. The earliest recorded contacts were with the Srivijaya Empire (AD 600–1000), the capital of which was situated at Palembang in south Sumatra. Since then, there has been a continuous stream of settlers, labourers, traders and others from various parts of the archipelago into Singapore. While the main features of Chinese and Indian immigration during the nineteenth and twentieth centuries stand out quite clearly, Malay immigration in the same period is less easy to study, owing to the paucity of official British colonial documentation. More information was in fact available from Dutch sources pertaining to the Netherland Indies government.[18]

The movement of indentured immigrants from Indonesia into the country was governed by regulations introduced by the Government of the Netherland Indies. In 1887, the Netherland Indies Government prohibited the emigration of skilled and unskilled labour outside the country, but in special cases the Governor General could lift the ban if the recruitment took place in Java and Madura.[19] Permission was therefore given to some emigrants from these regions to proceed to Singapore. The first official attempt at regulating and protecting indentured labour was made in 1909 when the Netherland Indies Labour Protection Enactment was put into force. This legislation was used to regulate the movement of indentured labour into Singapore and Peninsular Malaysia and to protect the workers by stipulating certain working and living conditions.

Indonesian indentured immigration outlived Chinese or Indian indentured immigration by many years partly because of the preference of the Dutch authorities for this system and partly because the relatively small numbers involved meant that abuses received little or no publicity. At the request of the Dutch authorities in 1927, and after protracted negotiations, Indonesian indentured immigration was finally abolished in 1932 when the Netherland Indies Labour Protection Enactment was abrogated. Another difference is that there was no government machinery instituted in Singapore to organise and promote immigration from the Indonesian archipelago. Nevertheless, there was movement of people from the various parts of Indonesia into Singapore over the years to work and trade. On account of their racial, religious and cultural similarities, the Indonesian immigrants mixed and intermarried freely with the local Malays. This process of assimilation has been ongoing so that the distinction between the two groups is now almost non-existent, and hence both are collectively known as Malays.

GROWTH OF FOREIGN-BORN POPULATION

In the preceding discussion on migration no statistical data were presented because of the absence of any migration statistics for Singapore. The statistics that are available pertain to the whole of Singapore and Peninsular Malaysia combined, and there is no way of separating the figures for these two territories since immigrants entering one territory could freely move to the other. Even after immigration control between the two countries was imposed in August 1965, migration statistics for Singapore were not made readily available to the public. The only source of migration statistics is from the series of population censuses, which provide data on the country of birth, and hence the foreign-born population who had migrated into the country at one time or another.

The census figures of the foreign-born population indicate the stock position of the immigrants at the various census dates compared to the dynamic position that can be revealed directly by migration statistics compiled from applications submitted by prospective immigrants. The census data are therefore defective to the extent that they do not take into account immigrants who died during the intercensal period as well as those who moved in and out of the country during the period. Another problem is that the data do not distinguish between those foreigners who came to Singapore to settle permanently and those who entered the country to study or to work on a short-term basis, returning to their home country in due course. A further complication is that some foreigners in the latter category may be granted permission to stay permanently in Singapore. Such inherent limitations must be borne in mind in interpreting the figures given in Tables 4.1 and 4.2.

The figures in Table 4.1 show the exact number of foreign-born population residing in the country in the various census years from 1921

TABLE 4.1
Growth of Foreign-Born Population, 1921–1980

Year	Foreign-Born Population	Percentage of Total Population	Intercensal Increase	
			Number	Percentage
All Races				
1921	301,913	72.2	—	—
1931	358,291	64.2	56,378	18.7
1947	411,716	43.9	53,425	14.9
1957	515,751	35.7	104,035	25.3
1970	530,883	25.6	15,132	2.9
1980	527,153	21.8	-3,731	-0.7
Chinese				
1921	240,673	76.4	—	—
1931	268,607	64.2	27,934	11.6
1947	308,225	42.3	39,618	14.7
1957	349,372	32.0	41,147	13.3
1970	369,447	23.4	20,075	5.7
1980	366,172	19.7	-3,275	-0.9
Malays				
1921	26,763	49.9	—	—
1931	17,879	27.5	-8,884	-33.2
1947	41,264	36.3	23,385	130.8
1957	72,671	36.9	31,407	76.1
1970	76,377	24.5	3,706	5.1
1980	69,065	19.6	-7,312	-9.6
Indians				
1921	24,571	76.0		
1931	41,770	82.2	17,199	70.0
1947	47,966	66.7	6,196	14.8
1957	79,446	61.3	31,480	65.6
1970	64,043	44.1	-15,403	-19.4
1980	57,967	37.5	-6,076	-9.5

to 1980. The changes in the figures given in the first column of the table are caused by three factors, namely, arrivals, departures and deaths among the foreign-born population during the intervening census years. A total of 301,913 foreign-born persons were living in Singapore in 1921, and this number rose consistently at every census up to 1970 when it stood at 530,883. It edged down slightly to 527,152 in 1980.

What is more important is that the clear uptrend in the foreign-born population over the years confirms the continuous movement of people into Singapore noted earlier. The increase recorded at nearly every population census suggests that the inflow of people must have been extremely large to even compensate for the loss caused by departures and deaths occurring among the foreign-born population during the intercensal periods. In fact, the dominance of immigration in the demographics of the country was clearly reflected in the very high proportion recorded in 1921. As natural increase became a more important factor of population growth, the proportion fell to 64.2 per cent in 1931 and 43.9 per cent in 1947. The downtrend continued in the post-war years.

When looking at the figures for the three main races shown also in Table 4.1, the earlier discussion on migrational trends among these races should be kept in mind. The number of foreign-born Chinese increased steadily from 240,673 in 1921 to 369,447 in 1970, after which it remained nearly the same at 366,172 in 1980. From the high of 76.4 per cent, the proportion of foreign-born Chinese to their total population declined steadily to 19.7 per cent in 1980. In the pre-war years, the foreign-born Chinese came mainly from China, but after the war they came from Malaysia, and more recently from Indonesia, Hong Kong and Taiwan.

The number of foreign-born Malays increased more rapidly in the earlier years, multiplying almost threefold from 26,763 in 1921 to 72,671 in 1957. It then grew very slowly to 76,377 in 1970, and even began to decline thereafter to reach 69,065 in 1980. In the early post-war years, many Malays from the various parts of Peninsular Malaysia came to Singapore to seek better employment and the more exciting city life, but in recent years this movement has ceased and some Singapore Malays have even moved north across the Causeway. As observed earlier, the inflow of Malays was not as large as the other two races and hence the proportion of foreign-born Malays to their total population stood at the low level of 49.9 per cent in 1921. This proportion fell to 36.3 per cent in 1947, and then rose to 36.9 per cent in 1957 because of the greater inflow of Malays from Peninsular Malaysia in the early post-war years. Interestingly enough, this proportion was even higher than the corresponding proportion of 32.0 per cent recorded by the Chinese. This higher Malay proportion persisted into 1957 and 1970.

A more rapid growth in the number of foreign-born Indians is revealed by the figures given in Table 4.1. The number increased by slightly more than threefold from 24,571 in 1921 to 79,446 in 1957. With the repatriation of some Indian workers, who were not Singapore citizens or permanent residents, back to India after the closure of the British Military Base in the 1960s, the number of foreign-born Indians was brought down to 64,043 in 1970. The number continued to shrink to 57,967 in 1980. Like the Chinese, the Indians also had a very high proportion of foreign-born persons, amounting to 76.0 per cent in 1921. But this proportion slowly declined to 61.3 per cent in 1957 and 37.5 per cent in 1980. Consequently, the proportion of foreign-born population was by far the highest among the Indians.

In the 1990 and 2000 Population Censuses, the tabulation of local-born and foreign-born was applied to the resident population but not to the total population, which also includes the non-resident population.[20] The figures laid out in Table 4.2 in respect of foreign-born resident population are therefore not comparable with the figures in Table 4.1 showing the foreign-born total population. In a way, the figures in Table 4.2 provide a more faithful picture of immigration flows into Singapore because they do not include the rather transient non-resident

TABLE 4.2

Growth of Foreign-Born Population, 1990–2000

Year	Foreign-Born Resident Population	Intercensal Increase		Percentage of Resident Population
		Number	Percentage	
All Races				
1990	412,475	—	—	15.2
2000	563,429	150,954	36.6	17.5
Chinese				
1990	319,610	—	—	15.2
2000	436,756	117,146	36.7	17.6
Malays				
1990	38,239	—	—	10.0
2000	35,689	−2,550	−6.7	8.5
Indians				
1990	48,229	—	—	25.3
2000	74,270	26,041	54.0	30.9

population entering the country to work on a temporary basis rather than to settle permanently.

The number of foreign-born persons among the resident population was enumerated as 412,475 in the census held in 1990. The number was pushed up by 150,954 or 36.6 per cent to reach 563,429 in the latest census taken in 2000. As a result, the proportion of foreign-born persons in the resident population was lifted from 15.2 per cent to 17.5 per cent. The increase in the foreign-born population has emerged even though some attrition due to deaths has taken place. It is quite clear that the latest intercensal period has received a net gain in migrational flow.

Marked variations in the growth of the foreign-born resident population existed among the three main ethnic groups. The number of foreign-born persons among the Chinese resident population rose from 319,610 in 1990 to 436,756 in 2000, up by 117,146 or 36.7 per cent. The population of foreign-born persons in this community managed to edge up slightly from 15.2 per cent to 17.5 per cent.

The Malays, on the other hand, saw their foreign-born population shrink by 6.7 per cent from 38,239 to 35,689 during the same period. This shrinkage may be attributed mainly to deaths occurring during the intercensal period and partly to the outflow of foreign-born Malay residents to neighbouring countries. There has also been very little movement of Malays from these countries into Singapore to work and settle permanently. The proportion of foreign-born population in this community in fact fell from 10.0 per cent to 8.5.

A somewhat different pattern was exhibited by the Indian resident population, which saw their foreign-born component being boosted up by 54.0 per cent from 48,229 to 74,270 during the same period. There is a greater tendency for the highly-qualified Indian newcomers to take up permanent resident status, and eventually Singapore citizenship. The proportion of foreign-born in this community recorded a hefty rise from 25.3 per cent to the high of 30.9 per cent.

BIRTHPLACE OF FOREIGN-BORN POPULATION

For more information about migration in Singapore, we will refer to Table 4.3 showing the distribution of foreign-born persons by country of birth. It should be mentioned that the figures can be employed to depict broad trends only since, for instance, a person born in India could have migrated to Singapore via Malaysia where he first entered much earlier.

TABLE 4.3
Distribution of Foreign-Born Population by Country of Birth, 1947–1980

Country of Birth	1947	1957	1970	1980
	Number			
Malaysia	44,878	128,548	187,192	233,162
China, Hong Kong and Taiwan	282,088	278,755	243,682	189,262
India, Pakistan, Bangladesh and Sri Lanka	44,723	69,124	50,876	42,379
Indonesia	27,654	25,683	26,947	27,113
Others	12,301	13,641	22,186	35,236
Total	411,644	515,751	530,883	527,152
	Percentage			
Malaysia	10.9	24.0	35.3	44.2
China, Hong Kong and Taiwan	68.5	24.0	35.3	44.2
India, Pakistan, Bangladesh and Sri Lanka	10.9	13.4	9.6	8.0
Indonesia	6.7	5.0	5.1	5.1
Others	8.0	2.6	4.2	6.7
Total	100.0	100.0	100.0	100.0

Furthermore, there were immigrants who died in Singapore and were not captured by the census figures showing the stock position at the various census dates.

Bearing in mind the above limitations, the figures suggest that the primary source of immigration during the post-war years has been the neighbouring country of Malaysia. The number of migrants born in Malaysia increased dramatically from 44,878 in 1947 to 233,163 in 1980. With no similar development experienced by those born in other countries, this has resulted in the rising predominance of the Malaysian-born group, snowballing from 10.9 per cent in 1947 to 44.2 per cent in 1980. Most of the non-resident persons were short-term guest workers from Thailand, the Philippines and the Indian sub-continent and foreign professionals from Europe, America, Japan and Australia.

Another important development concerns the decline in the number and proportion of persons born in China, Taiwan and Hong Kong. The drop in the number from 282,088 to 189,262 during the years 1947–80 was due to the cessation of immigration from China as a result of the establishment of the People's Republic of China in October 1949. No doubt there was some inflow from Taiwan and Hong Kong during these years, but this could not compensate for the depletion of the number born in these territories by mortality among the relatively older migrants who had come to Singapore prior to the outbreak of World War II. The proportion of those born in these three regions in Singapore, among the total foreign-born persons, was consequently pushed down to 35.9 per cent in 1980 from the high of 68.5 per cent in 1947. More significantly, this group of foreign-born persons, expressed in terms of the total population in Singapore, constituted only 7.8 per cent in 1980 compared with 30.1 per cent some three decades earlier.

The other traditional source of migration, the Indian sub-continent, continued to provide new migrants during the first intercensal period, when the number increased from 44,723 to 69,124 during the years 1947–57. In these early years, when Singapore was a British colony, immigration from this region was still unrestricted. The immigration control imposed in the late fifties and the repatriation of Indian workers from the British Military Base brought the number down to 50,876 in 1970. Since then it has declined further to 42,379 in 1980. Unlike the other two racial groups, the Indians experienced an up-down movement in the proportion of foreign-born persons to the total foreign-born population, moving up from 10.9 per cent to 13.4 per cent in 1957, and then down to 8.0 per cent in 1980. An interesting feature of Table 4.3 refers to the sustained growth in the foreign-born persons among the minority group designated as "Others". The figures for the group show a clear uptrend, increasing slowly from 12,301 in 1947 to 13,691 in 1957 and then more rapidly to 35,236 in 1980.

A more recent picture of migration is reflected in Table 4.4, showing the country of birth of foreign-born resident population in 1990 and 2000. In the two latest population censuses, the data for foreign-born persons are provided for the resident population only. As noted earlier, the exclusion of the transient non-resident population from the table would allow us to secure a better idea of migration trends and practices. It is a common practice nowadays for countries with a significant proportion of foreigners, particularly migrant workers, to present many series of the census statistics in terms of the more permanent segment of the population. For Malaysia, for example, the census statistics are mostly tabulated according to the citizen population.[21]

TABLE 4.4
Distribution of Foreign-Born Resident Population By Country of Birth, 1990–2000

Country of Birth	1990		2000		Intercensal Increase	
	Number	Percentage	Number	Percentage	Number	Percentage
Malaysia	194,929	47.3	303,828	53.9	108,699	55.8
China, Hong Kong and Taiwan	149,969	36.4	145,896	25.9	-4,093	-2.7
South Asia	35,164	8.5	58,293	10.3	23,129	65.8
Indonesia	21,454	5.2	29,314	5.2	7,860	36.6
Other Asian Countries	5,037	1.2	14,459	2.6	9,022	187.1
Others	5,922	1.4	11,659	2.1	5,737	96.9
Total	412,475	100.0	563,429	100.0	150,954	36.6

The foreign-born resident population citing Malaysia as their birth place rose steeply from 194,929 in 1990 to 303,828 in 2000, up by 108,699 or 55.8 per cent. Their proportion to the total foreign-born resident population was enhanced from 47.3 per cent to 53.9 per cent. The strengthening of the dominance of this group of foreign-born persons reflects the close connection between Singapore and Malaysia in terms of family ties across the causeway. The flow of few migrants from China, Hong Kong and Taiwan, coupled with the reduction of the original immigrants due to death, led to a drop in this group of foreign-born persons from 149,969 to 145,876 during the same ten-year period. This gives a decline of 4,098 or 2.7 per cent, and a fall in the proportion from 36.4 per cent to 25.9 per cent. But this group of foreign-born persons still continues to maintain their second position. The resident population born in the South Asian countries, the other traditional source of migrants, increased sharply by 65.8 per cent from 35,164 to 58,293, with share of the total foreign-born resident population rising slightly from 8.5 per cent to 10.3 per cent.

More comprehensive information about the foreign-born component of the resident population has been provided in the latest population census held in 2000.[22] Among the 563,429 foreign-born resident population enumerated in the census, there were 436,756 (77.5 per cent) Chinese, 74,270 (13.2 per cent) Indians, 35,689 (6.3 per cent) Malays, and 16,714 (0.3 per cent) belonging to a variety of minority people. A further classification of these ethnic groups according to their country of birth is depicted in Table 4.5. Whilst these detailed figures can give us a greater insight into the dynamics of immigration, we should be mindful that they represent the stock position as at the census date of 30 June 2000. What this implies is that the foreign-born persons, who entered the country before the census date and were still alive or still staying in the country, have become permanent residents or even Singapore citizens by the time of the census date.

The negligible inflow of migrants from China after World War II has continued to leave its imprint on the Chinese resident population classified according to their country of birth. The latest census held in 2000 revealed that among the 436,756 Chinese foreign-born residents, no less than 258,406 or 59.2 per cent were born in the neighbouring state of Malaysia. This is quite unlike the situation in the early days when the majority of the Chinese originated from China. The diminishing importance of the China-born residents has continued in

TABLE 4.5
Distribution of Foreign-Born Resident Population By Country of Birth and Race, 2000

Country of Birth	Chinese	Malays	Indians	Others
	Number			
Malaysia	258,406	28,184	15,317	1,921
China, Hong Kong and Taiwan	145,428	—	119	329
South Asia	142	257	57,350	544
Indonesia	21,858	6,797	380	275
Other Asian Countries	5,187	253	465	8,555
European Countries	1,417	29	240	3,001
USA and Canada	2,205	26	139	1,044
Others	2,114	143	256	1,045
Total	436,756	35,689	74,270	16,714
	Percentage			
Malaysia	59.2	79.0	20.6	11.5
China, Hong Kong and Taiwan	33.3	—	0.2	2.0
South Asia	0.0	0.7	77.2	3.3
Indonesia	5.0	19.0	0.5	1.6
Other Asian Countries	1.2	0.7	0.6	51.2
European Countries	0.3	0.1	0.3	18.0
USA and Canada	0.5	0.1	0.2	6.2
Others	0.5	0.4	0.3	6.3
Total	100.0	100.0	100.0	100.0

recent years, falling to second place in 2000 with 145,428 or 33.3 per cent. Way down third place was occupied by Indonesia where some 21,858 or 5 per cent of the Chinese foreign-born residents reported as their place of birth. Other smaller groups refer to the thousands of Chinese resident population born in other countries in Asia, Europe, Canada and the United States. These recent newcomers tend to communicate in English rather than Chinese, and have no real obstacles in mingling with the English-speaking populace and in integrating with the predominantly Chinese environment.

A rather unbalanced pattern of the country of birth was underlined by the figures for the Malays and Indians shown in Table 4.5. As expected, Malaysia emerged as the main source of migration for the

Malay population. No less than 28,184 or 79.0 per cent of the Malay foreign-born population was born in Malaysia. Indonesia occupied a very poor second position, with only 6,797 or 19.0 per cent born in the country. A similar two-country dominance was indicated by the Indian foreign-born resident population with regard to their third place. About 28,184 or 79.0 per cent were born in South Asia, and a smaller group of 15,317 or 20.6 in Malaysia. Unlike China, closed to outflow of migration for almost half a century, people from South Asia were still able to migrate to Singapore. Moreover, many newer Indian migrants, though from South Asia, came to Singapore via western countries where they were educated and worked for some years.

YEAR OF FIRST ARRIVAL

The above analysis of the data on country of birth appears to confirm that the flow of immigrants, whether for permanent settlement or temporary employment, did not cease completely during the period when Singapore had its own instrument of immigration control as an independent state. It is also evident that the more selective and controlled type of immigration resulted in immigrants coming from countries other than the traditional sources of China and the Indian sub-continent, as had occurred on a large-scale in the pre-war years. Additional information on the year of first arrival of foreign-born persons will throw further light on the changing pattern of immigration. There are, however, some limitations in using these statistics to measure migration flow. The figures do not take into account immigrants who died in the country and also those who returned to their own country or moved to another country before the census date.

It should be reminded that the data given in Table 4.6 pertain to the foreign-born resident population and not to the foreign-born total population because figures for the latter have not been released in the last two censuses. However, the non-resident population not included in the table refers more to newcomers on temporary work permits or employment passes rather than potential immigrants to Singapore. In this respect, the figures for resident population should provide a better idea of migration trends than those for the total population.

Among the total 412,475 foreign-born resident population enumerated in 1990, a much larger number of 300,906 or 73.0 per cent entered Singapore after World War II, in contrast to the smaller number of

TABLE 4.6
Distribution of Foreign-Born Resident Population
By Year of First Arrival, 1990–2000

Year of First Arrival	1990	2000	Intercensal Change
Before 1941	90,566	51,609	−38,957
1941–1945	21,003	20,012	−991
1946–1950	52,385	40,721	−11,664
1951–1955	45,878	38,511	−7,367
1956–1960	49,546	42,977	−6,569
1961–1965	25,703	25,422	−282
1966–1970	25,725	28,215	+2,490
1971–1975	29,089	31,007	+1,918
1976–1980	27,134	33,887	+6,753
1981–1985	24,720	34,385	+9,665
1986–1990	20,722	59,623	+38,901
1991–1995	—	91,523	+91,523
1996–2000	—	65,540	+65,540
Total	412,475	563,429	+150,954

111,569 who came in before the war. Though this pattern was affected by death among the older arrivals, it indicates that Singapore has continued to receive a significant inflow of immigrants during the postwar period. This tendency was in fact reinforced in the 2000 census when 491,808 or 87.3 per cent came into the country after the war. The detailed figures show that the volume of arrival for the early postwar years fluctuated from one five-year period to another, touching the low of 25,422 in 1961–65. After that, an uptrend became apparent as the number arriving during each period went up consistently to reach the high of 91,523 in 1991–95.

The number of foreign-born resident population arriving in a five-year period will be subjected to some changes in the future. Firstly, the original number will obviously be depleted by deaths and possibly by out-migration. Secondly, it can be enlarged by existing non-resident population and also by newcomers becoming permanent residents. The number of foreign-born resident population will remain unaltered if existing permanent residents become Singapore citizens because this would represent a mere shift in citizenship status within this population. An increase in the number from one census to another within a particular five-year period of arrival can be taken to mean a net inflow of migration.

We can therefore conclude that the positive figures in the column showing intercensal change in Table 4.6 would indicate an addition to the foreign-born resident population arriving during the five-year period on account of net inward migration movement. The negative figures, on the other hand, would indicate that the number of non-resident population or newcomers becoming permanent residents was not adequate to compensate for attrition due to deaths and emigration. It may be observed that a drop in the number of foreign-born resident population arriving every five-year period was recorded up to 1965. The decrease amounted to only 991 during 1941-45, when migration was at a very low level during the Japanese occupation. It jumped to 11,664 in the very next period 1946-50. After that a turnaround occurred, and the increase was swelled progressively from 2,490 in the period 1966-70 to 91,523 in the early nineties.

An evaluation of the separate figures for the four ethnic groups, shown in Table 4.7, will give a better understanding of migration trends. Similar figures from the 2000 census have not been published. The foreign-born Chinese residents who entered Singapore prior to 1946 amounted to 93,781, or 29.3 per cent, while those entering since 1946 reached 225,879, or 70.7 per cent. The largest number, 38,415, appear to have arrived during the five-year period 1946-50 when some of them came from China just before the emergence of the People's Republic in October 1949. Thereafter, Singapore received Chinese immigrants from primarily Malaysia and to a lesser extent Indonesia, Hong Kong and Taiwan, but the number slackened to 66,051 during the ten-year period 1951-60 and tumbled to 38,633 during 1961-70. The latter phenomenon was due to the small volume of movement from Malaysia when Singapore was a component state from 9 July 1963 to 9 August 1965. In the seventies, Chinese immigration picked up momentum again and reached 46,304, but fell back again to 36,476 in the eighties.

A different pattern of arrival was experienced by the foreign-born Indian residents. Only 16.4 per cent of the 48,229 arrived in Singapore before 1946, and this was due to their stronger tendency to return to the Indian sub-continent to spend their retirement years. Again unlike the Chinese, the post-war uptrend in Indian arrivals continued a few years longer and reached a peak of 16,229 during the years 1951-60. The number dropped steeply to 6,952 during the sixties and then more

TABLE 4.7
Distribution of Foreign-Born Resident Population by Year of First Arrival and Race, 1990

Year of First Arrival	Total	Chinese	Malays	Indians	Others
			Number		
Before 1931	33,094	29,292	1,927	1,675	250
1931–1940	57,472	49,073	3,772	4,244	383
1941–1945	21,003	15,416	3,355	1,967	265
1946–1950	52,385	38,415	6,980	6,490	500
1951–1960	95,425	66,051	12,363	16,229	782
1961–1970	51,428	38,633	5,221	6,952	622
1971–1980	56,223	46,304	2,258	5,991	1,400
1981–1990	45,445	36,476	2,093	4,681	2,195
Total	412,475	319,610	38,239	48,229	6,397
			Percentage		
Before 1931	8.0	9.1	5.0	3.5	3.9
1931–1940	13.9	15.4	9.9	8.8	6.0
1941–1945	5.1	4.8	8.8	4.1	4.1
1946–1950	12.7	12.0	18.3	13.5	7.8
1951–1960	23.1	20.7	32.3	33.6	12.2
1961–1970	12.5	12.1	13.7	14.4	9.7
1971–1980	13.6	14.5	6.6	12.4	21.9
1981–1990	11.0	11.4	5.5	9.7	34.3
Total	100.0	100.0	100.0	100.0	100.0

slowly to 4,681 during the eighties. The pattern of arrival of the Malays was quite similar to that of the Indians just outlined here, except that there was a much greater inflow of the former group during the early post-war years. It should be remembered that the Malays came from not only Malaysia but also Indonesia.

RECENT MIGRATION

The slackening rate of population increase caused by the persistently below-replacement fertility since 1975 has made it necessary for immigration policies to be relaxed to attract foreigners into Singapore to contribute to the maintenance of a high level of economic expansion and to the growth of the population when they become permanent residents, and subsequently citizens. In addition to this general relaxation, special schemes were introduced to attract certain categories of foreigners, for example, the professional and skilled workers migration scheme to give permanent residence to those coming from Hong Kong. Under this scheme, the number of Hong Kongers granted permanent residence in Singapore was some 31,000 in 1991, and 33,000 in 1992, but from this group only about 4,700 have actually taken up residence in Singapore. In more recent years, the emphasis of the immigration policy has been to attract foreign talent from all over the world, particularly Asians working in the West.[23]

The normal practice is for foreigners to be issued in the first instance with an employment pass, then permanent resident status after a few years, and citizenship eventually. In special cases, a foreigner may be offered permanent resident status at the very outset. On the other hand, not all employment pass holders would apply for permanent residence, and again not all permanent residents choose to become citizens. It is not uncommon for some permanent residents to refuse to apply for Singapore citizenship, preferring to retain their original passport and citizenship. Apart from the minimum statutory requirements, there could be voluntary delay on the part of the newcomers in taking up permanent residence, and of permanent residents in becoming citizens. It should be noted that the dependents of these newcomers may also become permanent residents and citizens, and thus contribute to the growth of the population. It is necessary to draw a distinction between the group of foreigners who are allowed to become a part of the resident population and the other group of transient foreigners admitted on short-term work permits to be employed in unskilled jobs, such as domestic maids and construction labourers. These transient workers are not allowed to marry Singapore citizens and to apply for permanent resident status, and must return to their country of origin after working for a number of years.

Some information on recent immigration is given in Table 4.8, which shows the number of foreign-born Singapore citizens and foreign-born permanent residents separately for the1980 and 1990 Censuses according to the year they first came to the country. Similar figures from the census held in 2000 have not been made available. It may be observed that in mid-1980 the number of foreign-born citizens who arrived prior to 1931 was 56,517 but by mid-1990 the number had fallen to 32,108. The loss of 24,409 represents those who died or left the country during the

TABLE 4.8

**Foreign-Born Resident Population by Citizenship Status and
Year of First Arrival, 1980–1990**

Year of First Arrival	Singapore Citizens			Permanent Residents		
	1980	1990	Intercensal Change	1980	1990	Intercensal Change
Before 1931	56,517	32,108	−24,409	2,160	986	−1,174
1931–1940	79,021	55,726	−23,295	3,490	1,746	−1,744
1941–1945	24,706	19,886	−4,820	1,898	1,117	−781
1946–1950	52,484	49,195	−3,289	5,852	3,190	−2,662
1951–1955	42,214	41,376	−830	9,408	4,503	−4,905
1956–1960	34,195	42,842	+8,647	14,858	6,704	−8,154
1961–1965	13,712	21,360	+7,648	9,696	4,343	−5,352
1966–1970	9,723	18,810	+9,087	10,052	6,915	−3,137
1971–1975	5,556	17,494	+11,938	11,905	11,595	−310
1976–1980	942	11,879	+10,937	9,958	15,255	+5,297
1981–1985	—	6,939	+6,939	—	17,784	+17,784
1986–1990	—	3,501	+3,501	—	17,221	+17,221

ten-year intercensal period. This depletion of the older foreign-born citizens mainly by death took place among those who came to the country before 1955. On the other hand, there was always an increase among those who came after this year through an infusion of post-war immigrants who took up citizenship during the intercensal period. It should be pointed out that the dip in the number of foreign-born citizens who arrived during 1941–45 was due to the Japanese Occupation when the only new arrivals were from Peninsular Malaysia.

A greater understanding of recent migration can be obtained by examining the figures for permanent residents, also shown in Table 4.8. The loss in the number of permanent residents during the intercensal period among those who came during the same period was due not only to death and emigration but also to upgrading to citizenship status. This accounts for the loss occurring even among those who came as late as 1975. Obviously, many immigrants with permanent resident status decided to take up Singapore citizenship during the intercensal period. The figures also reveal that at mid-1990 there were some 17,221 permanent residents who came during 1986–90, and another 17,784 who came during 1981–85. Some of these newer immigrants did not have the

necessary minimum residential qualification to become citizens, while
others might require more time to arrive at the important decision of
taking up Singapore citizenship.

In the absence of accurate and comprehensive statistics on recent
migrational movements in Singapore, some additional data have been
included in Table 4.9 to provide a broad picture of migrational trends
based on changes in the resident population. Since the resident population
refers to mid-year estimates, the figures for resident migration are for
twelve-month periods from mid-year to mid-year. The resident population
can only grow through the addition of births and new permanent residents,
and depletion through deaths and outflow of existing permanent residents
and citizens. One important point to note is that the newcomers had
actually entered Singapore earlier than that indicated in the table because
of the time-lag involved in acquiring permanent resident status and
citizenship.

TABLE 4.9

**Resident Population, Natural Increase and
Net Migration, 1990–2006**

Mid-Year	Resident Population		Natural Increase	Migration Increase
	Number	Increase		
1990	2,735,900	—		
1991	2,795,400	59,500	37,259	22,241
1992	2,852,100	55,700	34,813	20,887
1993	2,906,500	55,900	35,379	20,021
1994	2,961,400	54,900	31,521	23,379
1995	3,014,600	53,200	32,816	20,384
1996	3,067,800	53,200	32,363	20,837
1997	3,121,100	53,300	32,006	21,294
1998	3,174,800	53,700	31,249	22,451
1999	3,221,900	47,100	27,809	19,291
2000	3,263,209	41,309	29,036	12,273
2001	3,319,100	55,891	29,828	36,063
2002	3,378,300	59,200	24,622	34,578
2003	3,437,300	59,000	23,483	35,517
2004	3,486,900	49,600	21,158	28,442
2005	3,553,500	66,600	21,467	45,133
2006	3,608,500	55,000	22,358	32,642

According to the data given in Table 4.9, there was a continuous reduction in the number of natural increase, falling from 37,259 to 22,358 during the seventeen-year period. A continuous rise in the number of deaths, coupled with a general reduction in the number of births, has contributed to the downtrend in natural increase. Apart from natural increase, the resident population has always been augmented by the net inflow of migrants, amounting to some 22,241 during the twelve-month period from mid-1990 to mid-1991. This net inflow has managed to prevail at almost the same level during the 1990s, and to even assume an upward trend in the new millennium. The high of 45,133 was in fact recorded during the twelve months from mid-2004 to mid-2005.

It would appear that recent changes in immigration policies have succeeded in generating a fairly regular surplus of migration. In turn, this has guaranteed the resident population to grow without any interruption by an annual amount well above the 50,000-level. The position is quite sanguine as evidenced by the granting of citizenship to about 12,900 in 2005 and 6800 in January–June 2006 as against only 7,600 in 2004.23 The big challenge in the future is to ensure a greater inflow of foreigners to compensate for the slowdown in natural increase of the local population.

EMIGRATION

Viewed from the perspective of population growth, the more important consideration is the volume of net migration which refers to the difference between immigration and emigration. Among the well-known reasons for people leaving Singapore are children cannot cope with the second language, sons not wanting to serve national service, following foreign spouses back to their country of origin, not returning home after tertiary education overseas, leaving for better jobs not available locally, and escaping from the cramped and fast pace of life to a more relaxed lifestyle in a bigger country. For these, and other personal reasons, the external movement of people out of Singapore has always taken place over the years, but the precise nature of this type of movement is almost impossible to capture because of the paucity of statistics.

The only information available are those data concerning the number of Singaporeans renouncing their citizenship in order to take up another citizenship. However, there are some Singaporeans who can still retain their citizenship because the country of adoption practises dual citizenship. In other instances, a permanent residence status is good enough for them to reside forever in their newly-adopted country. Encouraging immigration should also be accompanied by measures to prevent emigration and to lure back Singaporeans studying and working overseas.

Notes

1. Victor Purcell, *The Chinese in Southeast Asia* (London: Oxford University Press, 1951).
2. A more detailed account is given in W. L. Blythe, "Historical Sketch of Chinese Labour in Malaya", *Journal of the Malayan Branch of the Royal Asiatic Society* 20, Part 1 (June 1947).
3. R.N. Jackson, *Immigrant Labour and Development of Malaya* (Kuala Lumpur: Government Printer, 1961).
4. C.W.C. Parr, *Report of Protector of Chinese 1914* (Singapore: Government Press, 1915).
5. Straits Settlements, *Report of Protector of Chinese 1914* (Singapore: Government Press, 1915).
6. Norman Parmer, *Colonial Labour Policy and Administration* (New York: Association for Asian Studies, 1960).
7. Straits Settlements, *Report of Protector of Chinese, 1932* (Singapore: Government Press, 1934).
8. Straits Settlements, *Report of the Immigration Department, 1933* (Singapore: Government Press, 1935).
9. Straits Settlement and Federated Malay States, *Report of the Immigration Department 1938* (Singapore: Government Press, 1940).
10. D.G.E. Hall, *A History of Southeast Asia* (London: Macmillan, 1958).
11. Straits Settlements, *Annual Report on the Administration of the Straits Settlements, 1860–1861*.
12. J. Geoghegan, *Note on Emigration from India* (Calcutta: Government Press, 1873).
13. Straits Settlements and Federated Malay States, *Report on Indian Immigration, 1910* (Singapore: Government Press, 1912).
14. N.E. Marjoribanks and A.K.G. Ahmad Tambi Marakkaya, *Report on Indian Labour Emigration to Ceylon and Malaya* (Madras: Government Press, 1917).
15. Parmer, op. cit.
16. Malaya, *Report of the Labour Department, 1938* (Singapore: Government Press, 1940).
17. Ibid.
18. Tungku Shamsul Bahrin, "Indonesian Labour in Malaya", *Kajian Ekonomi Malaysia* 2, no. 1, (June 1965).
19. *Proceedings of the 24th Session of the National Labour Conference* (Geneva, 1937).

20. Lau Kak En, *1990 Singapore Census of Population, Statistical Release 1: Demographic Characteristics* (Singapore: Department of Statistics 1992 and Leow Bee Giok, *2000 Singapore Census of Population, Statistical Release 1: Demographic Characteristics* (Singapore: Department of Statistics, 2001)

21. Saw Swee-Hock, *The Population of Malaysia* (Singapore: Institute of Southeast Asian Studies, 2007).

22. Leow Bee Geok, op cit.

23. "Singapore needs people with range of talents", *Straits Times*, 24 August 2006.

5

Mortality Trends and Differentials

The size and structure of the population at any given time are determined by the interaction of migration, mortality and fertility in the immediate past. While a previous chapter has dealt with migration, this chapter will be devoted to a discussion of mortality trends and differentials among the major races. A general survey of mortality trends from the late 1870s, when death statistics were first made available, will be presented first, followed by a more thorough analysis for the years after World War II. An attempt will also be made to examine the changing position regarding differentials in mortality among the three main races.

GENERAL MORTALITY TRENDS

In examining the long-term mortality trends we ought to be careful in interpreting the death statistics for the early years because they were probably subject to the progressive improvement in the vital registration system. The doubtful accuracy of population estimates used in the computation of the death rates may cast further doubt on the reliability of these rates. Another problem encountered in the analysis of mortality trends is that the annual death statistics of the early period were affected by violent fluctuations resulting from sporadic epidemics and frequent external displacement and replacement of the population caused by local economic depressions and booms. In view of these difficulties, the figures will be presented in terms of quinquennial years, which will enable us to trace the general direction of mortality trends.

In Table 5.1 are given the figures pertaining to the annual average deaths and the crude death rates for quinquennial years from 1878 onwards. The population denominator employed in the computation of

TABLE 5.1

Annual Average Deaths and Crude Death Rates, 1878–2005

Period	Annual Average Deaths	Crude Death Rate
1878–80	3,095	23.9
1881–85	4,818	32.9
1886–90	6,278	37.3
1891–95	6,771	35.4
1896–00	8,847	39.4
1901–05	11,349	47.1
1906–10	11,721	43.1
1911–15	12,078	37.6
1916–20	13,023	35.2
1921–25	13,206	29.1
1926–30	16,031	29.0
1931–35	12,722	23.1
1936–40	14,787	21.5
1941–45	29,166	35.6
1946–50	12,733	13.0
1951–55	11,472	9.6
1956–60	10,369	6.9
1961–65	10,208	5.7
1966–70	10,578	5.3
1971–75	11,578	5.3
1976–80	12,128	5.2
1981–85	13,118	5.1
1986–90	13,529	4.7
1991–95	14,638	4.5
1996–00	15,552	4.0
2000–05	15,860	3.8

the crude death rate is taken as the average of the five mid-year populations in each given five-year period. An examination of the rates shows that they passed through certain fairly noticeable phases.

The first phase covers the various five-year periods in the nineteenth century during which the crude death rate showed no clear signs of declining, generally fluctuating between the level of 33 and 40 per thousand population. There are grounds for suggesting that the rise in the late 1870s was engendered by an improvement in the registration of deaths and did not necessarily reflect an increase in the actual level of mortality. The exceptionally heavy mortality, as underlined by the high death rate, may be attributed to bad housing, insanitary surroundings, malnutrition, inadequate medical facilities, and unhealthy superstitious practices.

The second phase covers the first four decades of the twentieth century during which time a predominantly downward trend in the crude death rate became apparent. From the very beginning of this period, a continuous and marked decline in the crude death rate was noticeable, but the extent of reduction seemed to vary considerably from one period to another. Towards the end of this phase, the rate was brought down to a moderate level of 21.5 per thousand population in 1936–40, slightly less than half of what it was in the beginning. The mortality decline, as reflected by the downtrend in the rate, might be attributed to advances in medical science and the efforts of the health authorities towards constant improvement in hygiene and sanitation by which a wide range of infectious and epidemic diseases like malaria, typhoid and dysentry were brought under control. Other contributory factors were an improvement in the education of the community, particularly with regard to hygiene and health, and the rise in the general standards of living as reflected in better food, clothing and housing.

At the end of the above phase, the continuous decline was suddenly interrupted by the Japanese Occupation, during which mortality suddenly took a turn for the worse. The conditions prevailing at that time may be best seen in the following abstract from the *Report of the Medical Department.*[1]

> The civil population was exceedingly undernourished, malaria was rampant, beri-beri and other conditions due to malnutrition affected a considerable number of inhabitants of the island. Although the Japanese had done a certain amount of medical work, a great deal of important preventive and curative treatment had been grossly neglected.

In the absence of accurate population data, a very rough estimate of the crude death rate for the period 1941–45 is about 36 per thousand population.

An idea of the major causes of death is presented in Table 5.2. One principal cause was beri-beri, as a result of deficient diets overloaded with tapioca and potato carbohydrates. Indeed, the daily meals of the population during the war years consisted of sweet potatoes and tapioca, mixed occasionally with a little rice. A meal comprising rice solely was

TABLE 5.2
Principal Causes of Death, 1941–1945

Causes of Death	1941	1942	1943	1944	1945
	Number of Deaths				
Beri-beri	636	2,817	2,004	6,749	6,659
Infantile convulsion	1,769	4,280	3,166	4,562	3,080
Pneumonia	1,432	2,383	2,077	4,249	2,373
Respiratory Tuberculosis	1,791	2,172	2,282	3,338	2,764
Dysentry	394	2,248	460	2,977	1,719
Malaria	274	1,036	680	1,886	2,771
Total Deaths from all causes	15,978	29,833	21,936	42,751	35,330
	Percentage of Total Deaths				
Beri-beri	4.0	9.4	9.1	15.8	18.8
Infantile convulsion	11.1	14.3	14.4	10.7	8.7
Pneumonia	9.0	8.0	9.5	9.9	6.7
Respiratory Tuberculosis	11.2	7.3	10.4	7.8	7.8
Dysentry	2.5	7.5	2.1	7.0	4.9
Malaria	1.7	3.5	3.1	4.4	7.8

a rare treat, certainly benefiting a big celebration. The two other worsening causes of death were dysentry, resulting from deficient and improper diets, and malaria, from the neglect of systematic anti-malarial work and the shortage of quinine medicine. The heavy mortality experienced during the war years was therefore caused by the lack of preventive and curative facilities, absence of normal public health measures, and chronic malnutrition as a result of acute food shortages. We should also not forget that there were some unregistered deaths of causes not encountered during peace time — for example, fatalities resulting from active combat, guerrilla warfare, and execution by the Japanese *Kempetei*.

The fourth and most recent phase covers the post-war period which experienced a rapid decline in mortality. With the return of peace-time conditions after the war, the crude death rate was reduced dramatically from about 35.0 per thousand mid-year population in 1941–45 to 13.0 in 1946–50. It continued to fall fairly rapidly to 9.6 in 1951–55, and then slowly reached 3.8 in 2000–05. A more detailed analysis of mortality during these post-war years is presented in the following section.

POST-WAR MORTALITY TRENDS

One of the most spectacular demographic changes that occurred in many parts of the world during the years after World War II was the rapid decline in mortality and its consequent effect on the rate of population growth. The progress made in reducing mortality has been particularly impressive in developing countries, not excluding Singapore, where improved living conditions and new medical and public health amenities introduced soon after the Japanese Occupation engendered a marked downward shift in the level of mortality. Though the post-war downtrend in overall mortality appeared to have been disclosed by the crude death rate, it is necessary to examine this mortality decline in terms of more reliable indices. In this respect, we have presented the infant mortality rate, the neo-natal mortality rate and the maternal mortality rate for similar five-year periods from 1946 to 2005 in Table 5.3. It is unfortunate that we do not have the necessary statistics to compute these three rates for the five-year period 1941–55 which coincided with the Japanese Occupation. These rates must have been exceptionally high during the war years judging from what we have said earlier about overall mortality during this period, and must have registered a sharp decline in the first post-war period 1946–50.

The infant mortality rate, defined as the number of deaths under one year of age per thousand live-births, is generally accepted as a good index of mortality conditions prevailing in the country. It is not affected by differences in the age composition of the population as in the case of the crude death rates. The past sixty years have witnessed a continuous reduction in the infant mortality rate, which was brought down from 82.1 per thousand live-births in 1946–50 to 4.7 in 1991–95, and then to 2.6 in 2000–05. The annual rate for the latest year 2006 stood at the record low of 2.5, which compares very favourably with that for Japan, Australia and Sweden.

The level of infant mortality can be further examined in terms of its two main components, namely, neonatal mortality and post-neonatal mortality. Neonatal mortality refers to deaths during the first four weeks and post-neonatal mortality to deaths during the remainder of the first year after birth. The latter is attributed to exogenous causes and is more amenable to environmental and medical controls, while the former is due to endogenous factors which respond to these controls only up to a point. This is reflected by the figures in Table 5.3 where the reduction in the neonatal mortality rate has been usually smaller than that recorded

TABLE 5.3
Infant Mortality Rate, Neonatal Mortality Rate, and Maternal Mortality Rate, 1946–2005

Period	Infant Mortality Rate (IMR)	Neonatal Mortality Rate (NMR)	Maternal Mortality Rate (MMR)	Percentage Decline		
				IMR	NMR	MMR
1946–50	82.1	32.6	2.5	—	—	—
1951–55	62.9	28.2	1.4	23.4	13.5	44.0
1956–60	39.7	18.5	0.7	36.9	34.4	50.0
1961–65	29.6	18.6	0.4	25.4	1.6	42.9
1966–70	23.2	15.7	0.4	21.6	13.7	0.0
1971–75	18.3	13.1	0.2	21.1	16.6	50.0
1976–80	12.3	9.2	0.1	32.8	29.8	50.0
1981–85	9.8	7.1	0.1	20.3	22.8	0.0
1986–90	7.3	5.1	0.1	25.5	28.2	0.0
1991–95	4.7	2.8	0.1	35.6	45.1	0.0
1996–97	3.6	2.1	0.1	23.4	25.0	0.0
2001–05	2.6	1.5	0.1	27.8	28.6	0.0

by the infant mortality rate in the various five-year periods. For the whole period 1946–2005, the neonatal mortality rate was lowered from 32.6 per thousand live-births in 1946–50 to 1.5 in 2001–05, a reduction of 95 per cent, compared with the 97 per cent registered by the infant mortality rate. This has resulted in a narrowing of the gap between the two rates, with neonatal mortality being now only 42 per cent lower than infant mortality, compared with 60 per cent at the beginning.

Much more rapid strides were made in the saving of lives among mothers if we examine the movement of the maternal mortality rate, which is defined as the number of deaths caused by childbirth per thousand total live-births and still-births. As can be observed in Table 5.3, the rate was brought down at a relatively faster speed by about 44 per cent, from 2.5 in 1946–50 to 1.4 in 1951–55, and another impressive decline of 50 per cent to 0.7 in 1956–60. Not surprisingly, in 1957 the Kethering Shield was awarded by the National Baby Welfare Council of Great Britain to the Singapore Ministry of Health in recognition of the good work done in the rural areas for maternal and child welfare and, in particular, for the excellent facilities available for both ante-natal and post-natal care.[2] By the late seventies, maternal mortality had been reduced to the lowest possible level of 0.1 per thousand live-births and still-births.

An idea of the extent and nature of decline in mortality for the entire age range may be observed in Table 5.4, which shows the age-specific death rates for five three-year periods centred around the five census years. The reason for presenting the rates in terms of a three-year period instead of a single calendar year is to minimise the

TABLE 5.4
Age-Specific Death Rates, 1947–2005

Age Group	1947	1957	1970	1980	1990	2005
			Rates			
0*	85.74	42.54	20.50	11.86	6.25	2.53
1–4	17.90	4.62	1.30	0.70	0.37	0.22
5–9	2.93	1.24	0.48	0.27	0.23	0.13
10–14	1.95	0.89	0.42	0.35	0.23	0.13
15–19	3.43	1.05	0.82	0.66	0.36	0.29
20–24	5.65	1.42	1.03	0.89	0.61	0.54
25–29	7.61	1.66	1.25	0.99	0.70	0.64
30–34	9.12	2.38	1.30	1.06	0.84	0.68
35–39	10.73	3.57	2.23	1.65	1.15	0.93
40–44	12.97	5.48	3.63	2.63	1.85	1.30
45– 49	16.49	8.49	5.83	4.83	3.20	2.09
50–54	21.27	12.73	10.03	8.54	5.82	3.62
55 and over	56.81	55.22	46.82	36.95	29.93	21.46
			Percentage Decline			
0*	—	50.4	51.8	42.1	47.3	59.5
1–4	—	74.2	71.9	46.2	47.1	40.5
5–9	—	57.7	61.3	43.8	14.8	43.5
10–14	—	54.4	52.8	16.7	34.3	43.5
15–19	—	69.4	21.9	19.5	45.5	19.4
20–24	—	74.9	27.5	13.6	31.5	11.5
25–29	—	78.2	24.7	20.8	29.3	8.6
30–34	—	73.9	45.4	18.5	20.8	19.0
35–39	—	66.7	37.5	26.0	30.3	19.1
40–44	—	57.7	33.8	27.5	29.7	29.7
45–49	—	48.5	31.3	17.2	33.7	34.7
50–54	—	40.2	21.2	14.9	31.9	37.8
55 and over	—	2.8	15.2	13.7	19.0	28.3

* Infant mortality rate.

fluctuations in these rates caused by the random fluctuations in the annual death statistics from year to year. Besides indicating mortality decline at the various ages in the past, the rates demonstrate the considerable variations in mortality spanning the entire age range. In conformity with observations made in other countries, mortality in Singapore is very high in the first few years of life and decreases rapidly to the lowest level in the teenage group of 10–14, and then begins to rise gradually until the early forties after which it rises progressively faster until the last survivors of the generation are extinguished. Such a pattern prevails in the country irrespective of the general level of mortality at the five different time-periods.

The data presented in Table 5.4 point to a fairly substantial, though expectedly not uniform, decline in mortality at the various age groups. In the first period 1947–57, the mortality decline was most pronounced in the age groups below 45 years, with reductions ranging from 50 to 78 per cent, followed by smaller reductions in the older groups aged 45 and over. The progressively slower speed of decline among the old age groups can be seen to occur in subsequent intercensal periods. The resistance to decline among these older age groups may be attributed to what is commonly known as the generation factor — that is, deaths at old age are essentially caused by degenerative ailments which are not so readily amenable to medical science.

So far we have not answered the important question on the precise extent of reduction in the overall level of mortality that has taken place during the various intercensal periods. To perform this task satisfactorily, we will employ the age-specific death rates given in Table 5.4 to compute the age standardised death rates for the five census years. In computing these rates, the population by age enumerated in the 1990 census is used as the standard population. The rates, shown below, are not influenced by differences in the age composition of the population in the four census years, and can therefore be employed to measure changes in overall mortality.

Year	Standardised Rate	Percentage Decline
1947	15.84	—
1957	10.16	35.9
1970	7.70	24.2
1980	5.95	22.7
1990	4.59	22.9

The rates reveal that a fall of 35.9 in overall mortality was registered in the first intercensal period 1947–57, 24.2 per cent in the period 1957–70, 22.7 per cent in the period 1970–80, and 22.9 per cent in the latest period 1980–90. This confirms what was observed earlier in that there was an acceleration in overall mortality decline in the early post-war years. After the spectacular achievement in the early years, it is not surprising that mortality decline has slackened in recent years.

In one respect, the post-war mortality decline may be considered as a continuation of the downward trend experienced in the days before World War II, and in another, as part of the unprecedented rapid decline witnessed in almost every underdeveloped or developing country. Underlying these achievements in the post-war years are many general and specific factors the relative importance of which is difficult to assess. By and large, they may be grouped into two broad categories. The first of these is associated with the progress in economic and social development, and the consequent rise in the standards of living which exert a strong influence on the health conditions of the community. In simple terms, the more relevant components of rising standards of living are better food, clothing, housing and education. The second group covers technological advances, particularly in the field of medical and biological research and in the sphere of public health and sanitary measures. The beneficial results of these advances are spread directly by health authorities among the masses to prevent or cure diseases as well as to raise the standard of hygiene and sanitation.

MORTALITY DIFFERENTIALS

The main type of mortality differentials that would be of some interest to us would be the differences in the levels of mortality among the three main races in the early post-war years. Nowadays, the mortality differences among these races are quite negligible. Table 5.5 gives the rates for infant mortality, neonatal mortality, and maternal mortality for four selected years at intervals of six years.

In 1946, the highest infant mortality rate (140.5) was experienced by the Malays and the lowest (82.3) by the Chinese, with the Indian rate (94.5) slightly higher than the latter. These relative positions of the three races have remained the same throughout the period from 1946 to 1964, though the gap between the Malays and the other two races underwent certain changes. A widening of this gap followed the relatively slower

TABLE 5.5

Some Mortality Rates for Three Main Races, 1946–1964

Race	1946	1952	1958	1964
	Infant Mortality Rate			
Chinese	82.3	62.3	35.3	26.6
Malays	140.5	120.0	85.5	42.0
Indians	94.5	66.2	40.3	30.4
	Chinese = 100			
Malays	171	193	242	158
Indians	115	106	114	114
	Neonatal Mortality Rate			
Chinese	36.8	30.0	17.0	18.9
Malays	55.4	39.5	29.0	22.8
Indians	38.7	35.4	17.6	19.7
	Chinese = 100			
Malays	151	132	171	121
Indians	105	118	104	104
	Maternal Maternity Rate			
Chinese	*	1.6	0.6	0.3
Malays	*	2.0	1.7	1.0
Indians	*	1.8	0.2	0.4
	Chinese = 100			
Malays	*	125	283	333
Indians	*	112	33	133

decline in the Malay rate up to 1958; in 1946 the Malay rate stood at about 70 per cent higher than the Chinese rate and the position continued to worsen so that by 1958 the Malay rate was as much as 142 per cent higher. The next six years were noteworthy for the relatively sharper decline in the Malay rate which led to a marked narrowing of the gap to only about 58 per cent in 1964. Curiously enough, similar tendencies can be seen if we compare the Malay rate with the Indian rate. This is because the Indian rate has remained fairly stable at about 14 per cent above the Chinese rate.

Smaller differences in mortality during the first four weeks of life seem to exist among the three races judging from the figures for neonatal mortality rate also shown in Table 5.5. This may be taken to mean that the three races were subjected to greater differences in post-neonatal mortality rates than in infant mortality rates. What this amounts to is that the variations in infant mortality rates among the races are to a large extent engendered by exogenous factors, and hence mortality for the Malay infants under one year old has been less receptive to environmental and medical controls. The somewhat less satisfactory health conditions of the Malays are also reflected in the figures for the maternal mortality rate given in the same table.

The unfavourable mortality conditions that prevailed among the Malay community in the early post-war years can be explained in terms of a few interdependent factors. Firstly, the proportion of the population residing in less urbanised areas of the main island and in the neighbouring tiny islands in those days was far larger for the Malays (49.0 per cent) than for the Chinese (34.9 per cent), or the Indians (35.6 per cent). This was significant because in these places the medical and public health facilities were less adequate, and the environment was less satisfactory with regard to modern standards of personal hygiene and sanitation owing to the paucity of basic services, such as piped water, proper drainage and a good sewerage system.

The second factor, which was particularly responsible for the much higher mortality among children, is associated with nutritional deficiencies of the Malay diet as a result of poverty and food habits. These deficiencies tend to weaken the children and render them more susceptible to fatal diseases.[3] It has also been explained that a larger proportion of the Malay mothers gave birth at an extremely early age and these adolescent and childhood pregnancies probably carried additional risks of death to the infants.[4] Finally, some authorities seem to attribute the higher Malay mortality to superstitious practices involving *pawangs* and *bomohs*, and hence not relying on modern medical facilities.[5] In this connection, one must also take into consideration the fact that these medical and public health facilities were not only inadequate but also not within easy reach of the Malays, especially those living on the smaller islands at that time.

In addition to maternal mortality mentioned earlier, it would be instructive to examine the differences in the rates of the other major causes of death among the three main races. While the reasons given above might offer an explanation for some of the differences in the cause-specific rates, the differences themselves might in turn confirm the validity of the reasons offered. The extremely high Malay rate of

190.4 per 100,000 population for the first group of causes listed in Table 5.6 was to a large extent due to the greater number of ill-defined and unknown causes. A relatively larger proportion of the Malay deaths in those days were certified by non-medical personnel, most of whom were police officers. The major causes which were responsible for the greater mortality of the Malays were infections contracted by the new-born, pneumonia and, most importantly, the group of illnesses embracing gastritis, duodenitis, enteritis and colitis.

On account of their divergent social, cultural and economic backgrounds, the three races exhibit a completely different pattern in the cause of death. Leaving out the first group on the list from our comparison, the foremost causes of death were cancer among the Chinese, compared to infections among the new-born of the Malays, and diseases of the heart among the Indians. The next important causes were diseases of the heart among the Chinese, pneumonia among the Malays, and infections among the new-born of the Indians. In fact, the causes of death never seemed the same if we go down the line in descending order of importance to the third, fourth, and fifth places, and so on. What this means is that each cause of death afflicted the three races to different extents.

TABLE 5.6

Selected Causes of Death for Three Main Races, 1963

(Rate: Number of Deaths per 100,000 Population)

Selected Causes	Chinese	Malays	Indians
1. Senility without mention of psychosis, ill-defined and unknown causes	91.4	190.4	51.3
2. Cancer	89.9	25.7	43.8
3. Diseases of the heart	50.9	38.9	91.0
4. Infections of newborn	48.8	65.8	57.7
5. Pneumonia	39.4	60.0	34.2
6. Tuberculosis of respiratory system	41.9	20.1	22.6
7. Gastritis, duodenitis, enteritis and colitis, except diarrhoea of newborn	9.1	49.0	15.0
8. Motor vehicle accidents	11.4	8.0	13.0
9. Suicide amd self-inflicted injuries	10.8	1.2	4.1
10. Syphilis and its sequelae	2.6	0.4	4.1
11. Dysentery	1.5	2.4	2.7

Over the years, the three major races experienced a steady decline in mortality brought about by the rapid social and economic development that took place in the city-state. More specifically, the mortality decline was engendered by improved medical and public health amenities, better housing through government-subsidised apartments, modern sanitation and sewerage system, and improved diets with rising income. Nowadays, the level of mortality among the races is not only very low, but the differences between them are no longer significant. In 1997, the infant mortality rate was 3.2 for the Chinese, 5.0 for the Malays and 4.6 for the Indians. In the same year, the neonatal mortality rate for these three races were 2.3, 2.6 and 2.3, respectively.

CAUSES OF DEATH

An important aspect of the analysis of mortality trends is the examination of the changes in the pattern of the causes of death that accompanied the declining mortality phase in the post-war years. One inevitable difficulty encountered in the study of the causes of death is the multifarious number, and hence the problem of devising a sensible method of grouping them into a few manageable categories to suit our purpose. The statistics on causes of death are presented in three different classifications. The most detailed classification is based on an international categorisation of diseases, with 999 separate causes of death and using a three-digit code.[6] The statistics have also been presented according to an A List with 56 broad causes, and a B List with 57 broad causes. Since our intention is to look at the very broad trends and patterns, we have arranged the more important causes of death into 12 main groups, as shown in Table 5.7.

The absolute figures given in the table can provide an idea of the relative importance of the 12 groups at any point in time, but not the trend in the incidence of each of these broad causes of death during the post-war years. We have therefore included in the lower portion of the table the cause of death rate, which is defined as the number of deaths per 100,000 mid-year population. These rates underline the role played by certain causes of death in the general mortality decline discussed earlier. The most remarkable achievement was the battle against tuberculosis, which was reduced quickly from 174.3 per 100,000 population in 1947 to 51.9 in 1957, and thereafter less rapidly to touch the low of only 3.7 in 1990. The other important achievements were in the fight against pneumonia, which fell from 132.1 in 1947 to 39.5 in

TABLE 5.7
Principal Causes of Death, 1947–1990

Causes	1947	1957	1970	1980	1990
	Number				
1. Diseases of the heart	403	782	1,792	2,777	3,385
2. Cancer	306	769	1,896	2,561	3,027
3. Cerebrovascular disease	159	448	1,091	1,447	1,666
4. Pneumonia	1,239	1,034	847	1,129	1,191
5. Suicides	121	147	185	271	354
6. Diabetes mellitus	30	62	134	319	332
7. Motor vehicle accidents	66	164	280	250	246
8. Other accidents	265	254	308	122	200
9. Congenital anomalies	247	142	154	185	189
10. Diseases of the liver	79	123	198	189	182
11. Tuberculosis	1,635	751	458	240	113
12. Asthma	87	164	164	82	101
	Rate				
1. Diseases of the heart	43.0	54.1	86.4	115.0	112.2
2. Cancer	32.6	53.2	76.9	106.1	100.3
3. Cerebrovascular disease	16.9	31.0	50.2	59.9	55.2
4. Pneumonia	132.1	71.5	40.8	46.8	39.5
5. Suicides	12.9	10.2	8.9	11.2	11.7
6. Diabetes mellitus	3.2	4.3	6.5	13.2	11.0
7. Motor vehicle accidents	7.0	11.3	13.5	10.4	8.2
8. Other accidents	28.2	17.6	14.8	5.1	6.6
9. Congenital anomalies	26.3	9.8	7.4	7.7	6.3
10. Diseases of the liver	8.4	8.5	9.5	7.8	6.0
11. Tuberculosis	174.3	51.9	22.1	9.9	3.7
12. Asthma	9.3	11.3	7.9	3.4	3.3

NOTE: Rate refers to number of deaths per 100,000 population.

1990, and congenital anomalies which dropped from 26.3 to 6.3 during the same period. The incidence of deaths caused by accidents, other than motor-vehicle accidents, was also brought down appreciably from 28.2 in 1947 to 6.6 in 1990. From the initial level of 9.3 in 1947, the rate of asthma deaths was lowered to 3.3 towards the end of the period.

Though mortality from most causes followed a downward path as the decline in general mortality continued unabated during the post-war years, there are a few striking exceptions. Death rate attributed to diseases of the heart rose from 43.0 per 100,000 population in 1947 to 112.2 in 1990, while the rate for all types of cancer increased from 32.6 to 100.3 during the same period. Another pronounced rise was recorded in the rate for cerebrovascular disease or stroke, which moved up from 16.9 to 55.2 per 100,000 persons in these years. There is a common link underlying these rising tendencies in the sense that they are often associated with a quicker pace of life and changing lifestyles in a society undergoing rapid economic and social changes. This is in conformity with the experiences of developed countries in the West which witnessed the same upward tendencies in these causes of death in the declining mortality phase.[7] However, one minor exception was the death rate for motor-vehicle accidents, which did not rise significantly on account of government restraint on car ownership, an improved road system and accident prevention efforts on the part of the traffic police. It is also gratifying to note that the suicide death rate did not register any marked uptrend, hovering between 9 and 13 per 100,000 population.

The above changes in varying dimensions and directions have resulted in a completely different pattern in the relative importance of the various causes of death. The new pattern that has emerged may be easily seen in Table 5.7 where the causes have been listed in descending order according to the 1990 figures. The two principal causes of death in 1990 were heart disease, with 3,385 deaths, or a rate of 112.2 per 100,000 population, and cancer with 3,027 deaths, or a rate of 100.3. The next two principal causes were comparatively less dominant, and they were cerebrovascular disease and pneumonia, with rates of 55.2 and 39.5 per 100,000, respectively. Between them, these four major causes accounted for 9,269 deaths in 1990, about 66.7 per cent of the total deaths occurring in that year.

A comparison of the figures at the two ends of the period will reveal that heart diseases moved up from third place in 1947 to first place in 1990, and cancer from third to second place. A much more pronounced shift was recorded by cerebrovascular diseases, shooting up from seventh to third place. Pneumonia, which occupied fourth position in 1990, had in fact gone down from second place. Of greater significance was the drop in tuberculosis, from being the number one killer in 1947 to eleventh place at the end of the period. In many respects, the shift in the relative positions of the causes of death over the years has necessitated a constant review of the priorities in allocating finance, medical facilities, and personnel to combat diseases afflicting the population.

It would be interesting to examine in some detail the two dominant causes of death by looking at the separate data for the different types of heart disease as well as cancer. Among the 3,029 cancer deaths in 1990, 737, or 24.3 per cent, were trachea, bronchus and lung cancer; 364, or 12.0 per cent, stomach cancer; 317, or 10.5 per cent, liver and intrahepatic bile ducts cancer; and 265, or 8.7 per cent, colon cancer. Among the 3,385 deaths from diseases of the heart, no less than 1,757, or 51.9 per cent, were due to acute mycocardial infarction, and 889, or 26.3 per cent, to other forms of ischaemic heart disease.

One pertinent question concerns the accuracy of the information on causes of death which are certified by certain persons as stipulated by law. In some countries, a very small proportion of deaths are examined and certified by persons with some medical knowledge, and this imposes a severe limitation on the usefulness of the data on causes of death. In Singapore, the law requires a death to be certified by a doctor, coroner or an inspecting officer who may be either a hospital assistant or a police officer. Among the 12,381 deaths registered in 1951, 6,181, or 50 per cent, were certified by doctors, 1,031, or 8 per cent, by coroners, 2,684, or 22 per cent, by inspectors of the dead, and 2,485, or 20 per cent, by police officers. By 1990, considerable improvement in the certification of cause of death was achieved, with the corresponding percentages being 77 per cent, 19 per cent, 4 per cent, and 0 per cent. No less than 96 per cent of the deaths in Singapore are now examined and certified by doctors and coroners, the most reliable persons to perform this important task. The 4 per cent certified by inspectors of the dead are also fairly reliable since they have the same medical knowledge and are familiar with the names of the various diseases. A negligible proportion of deaths are certified by police officers who may not have the prerequisite background knowledge to perform the task satisfactorily.

LIFE EXPECTANCIES

By far the most sophisticated technique for measuring overall mortality is by means of a life table based on a closed cohort of persons who are assumed to be subject throughout their life to the death rates of the period. Table 5.8 presents the figures for life expectancy at birth by sex for the total population and for each of three main races.[8] Although these figures are for the four census years 1957, 1970, 1980 and 1990, the death statistics used in the construction of the life tables are in fact the average of a three-year period centred around each of the census years.

TABLE 5.8
Life Expectancy at Birth by Sex and Race, 1957–1990

Race	1957	1970	1980	1990	Increase					
					1957–70		1970–80		1980–90	
					Years	%	Years	%	Years	%
Male										
All Races	60.5	65.9	68.9	71.4	5.4	8.9	3.0	4.6	2.5	3.6
Chinese	60.9	66.3	69.4	72.1	5.4	8.9	3.1	4.7	2.7	3.9
Malays	56.9	66.4	68.6	71.2	8.5	14.9	3.2	4.9	2.6	3.8
Indians	62.9	65.2	65.3	66.4	2.5	4.0	0.1	0.2	1.1	1.7
Female										
All Races	66.6	72.2	74.3	76.2	5.6	8.4	2.1	2.9	1.9	2.6
Chinese	67.9	73.2	75.1	77.1	5.3	7.8	1.9	2.6	2.0	2.7
Malays	58.7	66.8	70.5	73.6	8.1	13.8	3.7	5.6	3.5	5.0
Indians	61.4	67.8	70.1	72.1	6.4	10.4	2.3	3.4	2.0	2.9

The life expectancy at birth serves as a good indicator of the overall level of mortality and hence the general health conditions of the population under investigation.

It is to be noted that in Table 5.8 the figures are presented for each sex separately because the life table is always computed for each sex separately on account of the difference in the pattern of mortality over the age range between the two sexes. If we wish to obtain a single figure for the life expectancy at birth for both sexes combined, we usually take the average of the two figures for the two sexes. According to this simple procedure, the life expectancy at birth for the total population in 1957 was 63.6 years, and 13 years later in 1970 it was raised by 5.5 years, or 8.6 per cent, to reach 69.1 years. The improvement continued in the seventies when the life expectancy rose to 71.6 years in 1980, an increase of 2.5 years, or 3.6 per cent. The following decade witnessed a further rise of 2.2 years, or 3.1 per cent, bringing the life expectancy to 73.8 years in 1990. As expected, both Singapore men and women have shared this slackening of the rise in life expectancy at birth as it moved towards a higher level. There is, however, an interesting difference in that Singapore men have recorded a faster rise in life expectancy than Singapore women, the former registering a rise of 10.9 years, or 18.0 per cent, compared with 9.6 years, or 14.4 per cent, for the latter during the whole period from 1957 to 1990. According to computation made by the Department of Statistics, the life expectancy at birth for men has reached 76.0 years in 2000 and 77.7 years in 2005, while that for women went up to 80.0 in 2000 and 81.6 in 2005.[9]

The progress made by the three main races may also be observed in Table 5.8. Among the males, Malay men recorded the greatest improvement of 8.5 years, or 14.9 per cent, during first period and Indian men the least improvement of not more than 2.5 years, or 4.0 per cent. As for Chinese men, their life expectancy at birth was raised by 5.4 years, or 8.9 per cent. This relative speed in the rise of life expectancy continued to prevail in the second period 1970–80. The persistently slow progress made by Indian men was most probably due to the erosion of the traditional custom of Indian men residing in Singapore as long as they were working, and returning to the Indian sub-continent on termination of employment, retirement, or serious ill health. This resulted in increasingly more retired or seriously ill men among this community remaining in Singapore, and hence causing the retardation in further improvement in their life expectancy at birth.

The above explanation appears to be consistent with the figures for female life expectancy at birth. The largest gain of 8.1 years, or 13.8 per cent, was experienced by Malay women during 1957–70, but it was the Chinese women who recorded the smallest improvement of 5.3 years, or 7.8 per cent. A greater improvement of 6.4 years or 10.4 per cent was recorded by Indian women. This relative speed in the rise in female life expectancy persisted into the second period 1970–80, and again in the latest period 1980–90.

The differences in the speed of progress in life expectancy at birth recorded by the various sex-race components of the population have resulted in some changes in the present position regarding differentials in life expectancy between the two sexes as well as among the three principal races. In 1990, Singapore women were enjoying a life expectancy at birth of 76.2 years, which was 4.8 years, or 6.7 per cent, higher than the 71.4 years recorded by Singapore men. This gap between the sexes is now much smaller than before, having been narrowed from 7.8 per cent in 1980, 9.6 per cent in 1970, and 10.1 per cent in 1957. In the main, this narrowing of the sex differentials may be attributed to the faster improvement in life expectancy at birth among Singapore men in the postwar years.

The figures in Table 5.8 also provide an idea of the sex differentials in life expectancy at birth among the three main races. In 1990, Chinese women were enjoying a life expectancy at birth of 77.1 years, some 5.0 years, or 6.9 per cent, longer than the 72.1 years enjoyed by Chinese men. This gap has narrowed in the last three decades or so. Malay women also enjoyed a longer life expectancy at birth than Malay men, at 73.6 years and 72.1 years, respectively. But there is a distinct difference in that the gap has always been somewhat smaller than the Chinese, at 3.4 per cent in 1990, 2.8 per cent in 1980, 2.1 per cent in 1970, and 3.2 per cent in 1957. Besides, there appears to be no clear-cut narrowing or widening of this gap during the period under consideration.

A more interesting pattern of sex differential in life expectancy at birth was exhibited by the Indians. Indian men enjoyed a longer life expectancy at birth than their female counterparts in 1957.[10] This unique feature may be partly explained in terms of the longer life expectancy of Indian men being caused by their stronger tendency to return to the Indian subcontinent in the early days, as mentioned earlier. The higher life expectancy of Indian men seems to be a distinctive feature of the peoples from the Indian sub-continent, as illustrated by the following figures for the Indian population in Peninsular Malaysia, Sri Lanka, Pakistan and India.[11]

Country	Males	Females
India, 1951–60	41.9	40.6
Pakistan, 1962	53.7	48.8
Sri Lanka, 1962	61.9	61.8
Peninsular Malaysia Indians, 1957	58.3	57.7

But in all these cases, the figures were below or in the early sixties, and the experience of Singapore Indians suggests that the universal phenomenon of higher female longevity at birth would emerge as mortality improves to a point equivalent to expectancy at birth around the mid- or late sixties.

Notes

1. Singapore, *Annual Report of the Medical Department, 1946* (Singapore: Government Printer, 1947).
2. Singapore, *Report of the Medical Department, 1957* (Singapore: Government Printer, 1959).
3. Malaya, *Report of the Medical Department 1957* (Kuala Lumpur: Government Printer, 1958).
4. T.A. Lloyd Davies and R. Mills, "Young Mothers in Singapore", *The Medical Journal of Malaya* (1958).
5. See, for instance, T.E. Smith, *Population Growth in Malaya* (London: Oxford University Press, 1952).
6. This detailed classification is based on the Mortality Tabulation List of the Ninth (1975) Revision of the International Classification of Diseases.
7. United Nations, *Population Bulletin*, no. 6 (New York: Department of Economic and Social Affairs, 1963).
8. The 1957 figures are obtained from Saw Swee-Hock, *Singapore Population in Transition* (Philadelphia: University of Pennsylvania Press, 1970), and the 1970 and 1980 figures from Saw Swee-Hock, "Increasing Life Expectancy in Singapore During 1969–1981", *Singapore Medical Journal* 25, no. 2 (April 1984).
9. Singapore, *Population Trends 2006* (Singapore: Department of Statistics, 2006).
10. See also M.A. El-Badry, "Higher Female Than Male Mortality in Some

Countries of South Asia: A Digest", *Journal of the American Statistical Association* 64, no. 328 (December 1969).

11. The figures are obtained from the *Demographic Yearbook* (New York: United Nations); and Saw Swee-Hock, *The Population of Peninsular Malaysia* (Singapore: University Press, 1988).

6

Marriage Trends and Patterns

An integral part of the study of the population of any country is an investigation of nuptial trends and patterns because the formation and dissolution of marital unions have an important bearing on the level of fertility. We may regard marriage as an event that marks the beginning of the potential period of childbearing and marital dissolution as the end of this period. This is particularly true in a country like Singapore where the modern form of consensus unions among persons who have never been married according to either legal or customary rites is rarely practised. An analysis of marriage trends and patterns will be presented in this chapter, while the next chapter will be devoted to the related issues of divorce trends and patterns.

In some countries, the study of nuptial trends is handicapped by a paucity of data compiled from a non-compulsory system of registering marriages and divorces. This is true in the case of Singapore for the period prior to 1961 when not all the different types of marriages solemnized according to the various customs and religions were required by law to be registered as in the case of births and deaths. In this chapter, we will therefore present only a brief account of marriages for this early period, but a more detailed analysis for the last three decades when more comprehensive marriage statistics were compiled and published.

MARRIAGE CUSTOMS AND LAWS

The great diversity of religions that was observed in an earlier chapter necessarily implies that it is quite impossible to introduce any common legislation to govern the different types of marriages taking place in the country. It was only natural that over the years separate laws were put in place to regulate marriages solemnised according to the various religious and customary rites. From the late nineteenth century, there existed three distinct legislations regulating marriages solemnised in the country, but in 1961 the two governing non-Muslim marriages were replaced by a new one which introduced the compulsory registration of these marriages.

Prior to September 1961, the two legislations regulating non-Muslim marriages were the Christian Marriage Ordinance 1940 and the Civil Marriage Ordinance 1940. The former ordinance was enacted to repeal the previous ordinance of 1899, and came into force on 1 January 1941.[1] This ordinance was meant for couples, one or both of whom professed the Christian religion, to contract Christian marriages and to have them registered accordingly. Christian marriages were solemnised by ministers or pastors in churches or other places and registered with the Registry of Marriages. Such marriages were by law monogamous and hence offered some protection to the woman against her husband taking secondary wives.

The Civil Marriages Ordinance 1940 came into force on 1 January 1941 and repealed the previous ordinance of 1899.[2] This ordinance was meant for couples, except when both were Muslims, to contract civil marriages if they wished to do so. Civil marriages could be solemnised by the Registrar of Marriages or authorised persons according to customary rites, but all such marriages must be registered with the Registry of Marriages. The main advantage of registering these marriages was that the law accorded some protection since they tended to be monogamous in nature. But some couples at that time still preferred to marry outside the provision of the ordinance, and the registration of marriages in Singapore therefore remained incomplete for a very long time.

As part of an election promise in 1959, the People's Action Party (PAP) government enacted the Women's Charter 1961 which came into force on 15 September 1961 and repealed both the Christian and Civil Marriage Ordinances.[3] From this date onwards, all persons, except when both are Muslims, must marry under the provision of this new legislation which requires such marriages to be monogamous and to be registered with the Registry of Marriages. The twofold significance of this new development was that thenceforth polygamy among non-Muslims was prohibited and registration of all marriages solemnised in Singapore became compulsory and complete.

Marriages under the Women's Charter can be solemnised by the Registrar in the Registry of Marriages or by authorised persons such as priests. Justices of Peace and community leaders in churches, temples, and community centres. Both parties must be at least 18 years of age, but a special licence to marry may be granted to a female party under 18 years. If any one party is a Muslim, the couple may contract a marriage under the Charter. Until 1967, non-Muslim marriages conducted according to customary rites were still recognised, but the enactment of the Women's Charter (Amendment) Act 1967 on 2 June 1967 specifically stipulated that only marriages contracted with a certificate issued by the Registry in accordance with the provisions of the Charter would be regarded as valid.[4] The actual ceremony could still be held according to religious or customary rites. It was also stipulated that from the same date, a man who married under the Charter could not convert to Islam and assert his right of taking up to three more wives.

The oldest piece of legislation introduced in the country to regulate marriages refers to that meant for persons who profess the Islamic faith to marry according to Muslim law.[5] Such Muslim marriages are now solemnised under the provision of the Administration of Muslim Law Act, which came into force on 1 July 1968.[6] This Act repealed the earlier Muslim Ordinance 1957, which had in turn replaced the very old ordinance of 1880.[7] The Act stipulates that when both parties are Muslims they must marry under Muslim law, but if only one party is a Muslim, they may choose to have their marriage conducted under the Women's Charter. The groom must be at least 18 years of age and the bride at least 16, although in exceptional circumstances permission may be granted to a man or woman below the minimum age to marry. The most striking feature of Muslim marriages is that Muslim law permits polygamy by which the husband may take up to four wives at any point in time provided he accords them equal treatment.

According to the Act, it shall be lawful for the *wali* (guardian) of the woman to be wedded to solemnise the marriage according to Muslim law. Any *Kadi* or *Naib Kadi* may solemnise a marriage when requested by the *wali* of the woman, or where there is no *wali* or where a *wali*, on grounds which the *Kadi* does not consider satisfactory, refuses his consent to the marriage. In all these cases, the *Kadi* is required to conduct a full inquiry in order to satisfy himself that there is no lawful obstacle to the marriage according to Muslim law or the Act. The marriage shall be solemnised in the *daerah masjid* (district mosque) in which the bride ordinarily resides, but the *Kadi* may permit the marriage to be solemnised elsewhere. All Muslim marriages must be registered with the *Kadi* or *Naib Kadi* who must send a copy of the certificate of marriage to the Registrar of Marriages within one week of the date of registration.

There are special rules governing cases where the husband wishes to exert his right of polygamy. A polygamous marriage shall not be solemnised if the man is married to any person other than the other party to the intended marriage except by a *Kadi*, or by the *wali* of the woman to be wedded with the written consent of the *Kadi*. Before solemnising the marriage or giving his written consent, the *Kadi* must satisfy himself after inquiry that there is no lawful obstacle according to Muslim law or the Act to such a marriage. The practice of polygamy among Muslim men in Singapore is, however, quite rare nowadays.

MARRIAGE TRENDS

Before focusing our attention on marriage trends, it would be useful to comment on certain problems underlying the marriage statistics compiled in Singapore. Whilst all Muslim marriages solemnised in the country have always been registered, the registration of non-Muslim marriages was made compulsory only as late as 1961. What this means is that our analysis of overall marriage trends in Singapore has to be confined to the last four decades only. However, the annual number of Muslim marriages, without any classification by various characteristics, is available as far back as 1921.[8]

Another problem concerns the difference between the statistics compiled according to date of registration and date of occurrence or solemnisation of the marriage, since delayed registration exists to some extent among marriages solemnised according to the Women's Charter. The statistics obtained according to the date of registration have to be adjusted to convert them according to a date of occurrence. This is done by using a table giving the marriages registered in a particular year according to the year of occurrence.[9] The sum of all the marriages whose registration was delayed from previous years plus the marriages actually registered in that particular year will give us the statistics according to date of occurrence, as shown in column one of Table 6.1. No adjustment to Muslim marriages is made as they are automatically registered with the Registry of Marriages on the day of the solemnisation.

In the process of converting the annual data from the date of registration to the date of occurrence, it was ascertained that most of the

TABLE 6.1

Marriages and General Marriage Rate by Type of Marriages, 1961–2006

Year	Non-Muslim Marriages	Muslim Marriages	All Marriages	General Marriage Rate
1961	5,140	1,560	6,700	7.2
1962	5,687	1,483	7,170	7.5
1963	6,568	1,690	8,258	8.4
1964	7,370	1,698	9,068	8.8
1965	8,290	1,922	10,221	9.6
1966	9,427	1,911	11,338	10.3
1967	9,518	1,894	11,412	10.1
1968	9,612	1,971	11,583	9.8
1969	10,682	1,972	12,654	10.3
1970	12,343	2,272	14,615	11.5
1971	12,729	2,471	15,200	11.6
1972	15,194	2,662	17,856	13.1
1973	22,249	2,823	25,072	17.7
1974	23,100	2,895	25,995	17.7
1975	18,813	3,233	22,046	14.5
1976	17,711	2,946	20,657	13.2
1977	17,017	3,163	20,180	12.5
1978	17,645	3,109	20,754	12.5
1979	17,443	3,677	21,120	12.3
1980	18,573	4,032	22,605	13.7
1981	20,234	4,429	24,663	14.5
1982	18,270	4,822	23,093	13.2
1983	17,465	4,594	21,813	12.2
1984	20,446	4,494	24,940	13.6
1985	18,903	4,563	23,466	12.6
1986	15,690	4,385	20,075	10.5
1987	18,939	4,465	23,404	12.0
1988	20,052	4,801	24,853	12.5
1989	18,868	4,794	23,662	11.6
1990	19,577	4,762	24,339	11.5
1991	20,386	4,806	25,192	11.7
1992	21,117	4,724	25,841	11.8
1993	20,700	4,606	25,306	11.3
1994	20,251	4,411	24,662	10.8
1995	20,562	4,412	24,974	10.7
1996	19,940	4,171	24,111	10.2
1997	21,305	4,367	25,672	10.6
1998	18,979	4,135	23,114	9.4
1999	21,566	4,087	25,653	10.2
2000	18,555	4,011	22,566	8.8
2001	18,284	4,001	22,285	8.6
2002	19,258	3,941	23,199	8.7
2003	18,098	3,871	21,969	8.1
2004	18,095	4,098	22,193	8.0
2005	19,043	3,950	22,993	8.1
2006	19,761	3,945	23,706	8.1

delayed registration pertained to marriages solemnised before the 1967 amendment to the Women's Charter, which made marriages according to customary rites void if they were not registered with the Registry of Marriages. This in effect resulted in many marriages before this date being registered only after the amendment and also in almost all marriages contracted after this cut-off point being registered immediately. What this means is that the difference between the figures given in Table 6.1 and the figures according to the date of registration is significant for the years prior to 1967 but negligible thereafter. For instance, out of 9,427 marriages solemnised in 1966, some 1,078, or 11.5 per cent, were cases of delayed registration, compared with only 31 out of 9,612 in 1968.

The number of Muslim marriages displayed a steady uptrend until the early 1980s, increasing from 1,560 in 1961 to 2,272 in 1970, to 3,163 in 1977 and to a peak of 4,822 in 1982. Thereafter, it fell in most years to reach 4,385 in 1986 and then rose again to the peak of 4,806 in 1991, after which it underwent a clear downturn to touch the low of 3,945 in 2006. In contrast, the number of non-Muslim marriages contracted under the Women's Charter recorded a steeper but shorter upward movement, rising from 5,140 in 1961 to a peak of 23,100 in 1974. The movement after that was rather irregular, moving down in the next few years and fluctuating quite widely until 2005 when it stood at 19,043. An extremely low number of 15,690 marriages was recorded in 1986, probably because this was the Tiger Year in the Chinese calendar, an inauspicious time for Chinese to marry. The total number of marriages in Singapore moved up quite quickly during the first fourteen years from 1961, with 6,700, to 25,995 in 1974, but it went down and up a few times within the range of 20,000 and 25,000 until the end of the eighties, and then within the narrow range of 23,000 and 26,000 in the nineties. Since then it fluctuated around 22,000, but went up to 23,706 in 2006.

It is difficult to derive a good measure of the incidence of marriage in Singapore owing to the inadequacy of data. Strictly speaking, the index must relate to the group of persons exposed to the possibility of marriage, and they would refer to persons, except those already married, aged 15 and over. But such a denominator is only available in a population census year. Instead, the general marriage rate, defined as the number of marriages per thousand mid-year population aged 15 and over, is employed to provide a rough idea of marriage incidence in the country. The rate is based on the total population for the years up to 1978, but on the resident population from 1980 onwards. According to the rate given in

Table 6.1, the marriage incidence was raised from 7.2 marriages per thousand population aged 15 and over in 1961 to a peak of 17.7 in 1973 and 1974, and then it seemed to fluctuate within the range of 10.5 and 13.5. The dip to a low of 10.5 in 1986 was, as noted earlier, caused by the Tiger Year. The rise in marriage rate in 1997 was due to couples rushing to marry to avoid paying the new $5,000 deposit introduced in May under the Fiance/Fiancee Scheme for Housing and Development Board apartments.[10] From 2,000 onwards, the general marriage oscillated just above the 8.0 level.

The data laid out in Table 6.2 for the three main races require some explanation. The figures for the Malays are identical to the number of Malays contracting Muslim marriages, while those for the Indians are obtained by adding those Indians contracting Muslim marriages and those contracting marriages under the Women's Charter. The Chinese figures are identical to the Chinese contracting marriages under the Women's Charter. It was assumed that the small number of Muslim marriages classified as "Others" did not include any Chinese marriages. Similarly, it was assumed that the "Others" category in the Women's Charter table did not include Malay marriages. These two assumptions would in no way mar our interpretation of the information presented in Table 6.2. The same adjustment used to convert the figures by date of registration to date of occurrence mentioned earlier was also applied to these figures.

The number of Chinese marriages increased continuously from 5,178 in 1961 to 13,937 in 1972, and then shot up to 20,828 in 1973, and 21,312 in the following year. It dropped immediately to 17,277 in 1975 and hovered generally below this level right through the seventies. There was an abnormally larger number registered in 1973 and 1974 caused by "couples who were previously married under customary rites having their marriage legally registered at the registry, following the government's announcement in 1973 that marriages solemnised under customary rites after 1st June 1967 were deemed to be illegal".[11] The conversion of the figures to the date of occurrence had failed to eliminate the full impact of the announcement, and this can only be attributed to many couples reporting the day when they registered their previously-solemnised marriage rather than the original day as the date of solemnisation of their marriage.

In view of the recent greater public interest on marriages generated by the direct action of the government in encouraging marriages among

TABLE 6.2

Marriages and General Marriage Rates for
Three Main Races, 1961–2006

Year	Number of Marriages			General Marriage Rate		
	Chinese	Malays	Indians	Chinese	Malays	Indians
1961	5,178	1,356	469	7.1	5.2	6.6
1962	5,624	1,211	364	4.2	4.8	2.9
1963	5,901	1,324	371	4.2	5.1	2.8
1964	6,623	1,354	395	4.6	5.1	3.1
1965	7,421	1,546	379	5.2	5.6	2.8
1966	8,487	1,547	444	5.8	5.3	3.3
1967	8,548	1,529	470	6.7	5.2	3.4
1968	8,631	1,584	535	5.6	5.3	3.8
1969	9,508	1,568	462	6.1	5.1	3.3
1970	11,105	1,865	670	7.0	6.0	4.6
1971	11,452	1,954	788	11.2	11.3	8.5
1972	13,937	2,132	817	13.1	11.8	8.7
1973	20,828	2,229	959	18.9	11.8	9.9
1974	21,312	2,311	1,284	18.7	11.8	12.9
1975	17,272	2,522	1,010	14.6	12.3	9.9
1976	16,033	2,266	1,123	13.2	10.6	10.7
1977	15,455	2,488	1,081	12.3	11.2	10.0
1978	15,979	2,412	1,143	12.4	10.5	10.3
1979	15,744	2,895	1,184	11.9	12.2	10.4
1980	16,756	3,192	1,240	12.3	13.0	10.7
1981	18,298	3,494	1,346	13.2	13.8	11.3
1982	16,503	3,791	1,311	11.6	14.5	10.8
1983	15,377	3,657	1,408	10.7	13.6	11.4
1984	18,255	3,496	1,491	12.5	12.8	11.9
1985	16,747	3,576	1,581	11.3	12.8	12.0
1986	13,824	3,415	1,316	9.1	12.0	10.3
1987	16,904	3,545	1,364	11.0	12.2	10.5
1988	17,861	3,787	1,373	11.4	12.8	10.4
1989	16,629	3,763	1,463	10.5	12.5	11.0
1990	17,113	3,718	1,475	10.3	13.6	10.0
1991	17,929	3,724	1,483	10.5	13.4	9.8
1992	18,762	3,658	1,325	10.8	13.0	8.6
1993	18,297	3,487	1,362	10.3	12.3	8.7
1994	17,688	3,381	1,267	9.8	11.7	7.9
1995	17,981	3,270	1,276	9.8	11.2	7.7
1996	17,247	3,033	1,335	9.2	10.2	7.8
1997	18,764	3,197	1,211	9.8	10.6	6.3
1998	16,086	3,021	1,249	8.3	9.8	6.8
1999	18,694	2,919	1,095	9.3	9.3	5.8
2000	15,742	2,806	1,065	7.8	8.8	5.5
2001	15,155	2,913	1,037	7.4	9.0	5.2
2002	16,113	2,837	1,073	7.8	8.5	5.2
2003	14,417	2,749	857	6.8	8.1	4.0
2004	14,299	2,816	860	6.6	8.1	3.9
2005	15,535	2,542	962	7.1	7.1	4.1
2006	16,063	2,472	924	7.2	6.8	3.8

the better-educated singles, the marriage figures have attracted more attention in recent years. Chinese marriages did not exhibit any clear trend in the eighties, swinging widely between a high of 18,298 and a low of 15,377. There was, however, an abnormal dip to 13,824 in 1986, which could only be due to this year being the Tiger Year in the Chinese calendar, apparently inauspicious for the Chinese to get married. In the nineties, there was less fluctuation in Chinese marriages, with the figure staying always above 17,000 but below 19,000, except during the Tiger Year in 1998 when the number dipped to 16,086. In recent years, there was a further reduction in Chinese marriages, being lowered to only 14,299 in 2004, but recovered in the next two years to reach 16,063 in 2006.

By comparison, a clearer trend was displayed in the number of Malay marriages, which moved up from below the 2,000 level in 1961–71, to below the 3,000 level from 1972 to 1979, and to below the 4,000 level from 1980. However, since the nineties, the number of Malay marriages has been declining, staying well below 3,000 in the last few years. A more irregular trend was experienced by Indian marriages. The number oscillated below 500 during the first decade and then climbed up to a high of 1,284 in 1974. It then declined in the next few years, perked up more decisely to a peak of 1,581 in 1985, but edged down again in recent years. The government warning issued in 1973 seemed to have also affected Indian marriages which surged in 1974. The number of Malay marriages was not affected since Muslim marriages are registered on the day of solemnisation by the *Wali* or *Kadi*.

The Chinese marriage rate in general increased from 4.1 per thousand population aged 15 and over in 1961 to 13.1 in 1972, after which it shot up to 18.9 in 1973 and 18.7 in 1974 for the same reasons stated earlier. Thereafter, it seemed to have fluctuated around 11.0 per thousand until the early nineties, and remained a shade above 7.0 in recent years. The Malay rate moved up in most years from 5.2 in 1961 to the peak of 14.5 in 1982 and remained above 12.0 until the early nineties. It has also fallen somewhat in recent years. From the low level of 3.6 in 1961, the Indian rate generally increased to reach 12.9 in 1974 and then hovered between 10.0 and 12.0 until 1991. Thereafter, it fell in most years to touch the low of 3.8 in 2006. The rather low marriage rate of the Indians in the early years could be due to the practice of Indian men returning to the Indian sub-continent to get a bride. More often than not, the Malays have experienced the highest marriage rate and the Indians the lowest rate, with the Chinese occupying an intermediate position.

AGE AT FIRST MARRIAGE

An analysis of the average age at first marriage of women and men can be considered as a central piece in the study of nuptiality trends and patterns in any country. The age at marriage marks the beginning of marital formation on a permanent basis for the majority of the population, even though some may end up in divorce or separation. The age at first marriage of women is recognised as one of the important factors that determine the level of fertility and hence the rate of population growth. The experience of many developing countries has demonstrated that a very low marital age of women has been the major factor responsible for a high level of fertility, particularly in situations where contraceptive use is negligible. An upward shift in this low marital age is usually followed by a decline in fertility. In fact, the raising of the minimum marital age for women through legislation has been resorted to by some developing countries as part of their overall strategy in trying to bring down the level of fertility.

The average age at first marriage for men and women computed from registration data is presented in Table 6.3. It may be observed that this average age for non-Muslim men remained almost stationary at slightly above 28 years from 1961 to 1967, and then went down continuously to a low of 27.1 in 1976. The downtrend was arrested and the average age went up in the next two decades to reach 29.8 years in 1996 and finally to 31.1 years in 2005. The average age for Muslim men was generally unchanged at above 27 for the first few years, and after that it followed a slow downtrend to reach a low of 25.7 in 1973. It remained stationary at slightly above 26 for the next decade and rose rapidly from 26.1 in 1984 to 28.2 in 1997, and oscillated slightly around 28.0 years in recent years. The net effect of these diverse trends is that the average age at marriage of all Singapore men did not display any significant changes, generally staying slightly above 27 until 1974 and below this age until 1983. A slow rise was noticeable when it climbed to 29.3 in 1996, and finally edged up to 30.5 in 2006.

As for the women, the trend in their average age at first marriage seems more simple. The average age for non-Muslim women hovered slightly above 24 right up to 1977 and thereafter advanced steadily to 27.4 years in 2005. Muslim women exhibited an even more clear-cut trend, with their average age rising continuously from 19.7 in 1961 to 25.3 in 1997, after which it stayed just below 25 until today. The net outcome was that the average for all Singapore women was also raised,

TABLE 6.3

Average Age at First Marriage by Type of Marriages and Sex, 1961–2006

Year	Male			Female		
	Non-Muslim Marriages	Muslim Marriages	All Marriages	Non-Muslim Marriages	Muslim Marriages	All Marriages
1961	27.7	27.0	27.0	23.7	19.7	22.0
1962	28.8	27.2	27.2	23.9	19.7	22.6
1963	27.9	27.5	27.3	24.1	19.5	22.7
1964	28.1	27.1	27.4	24.1	19.8	22.9
1965	28.1	26.5	27.3	24.2	19.9	23.0
1966	28.1	26.3	27.3	24.3	20.0	23.1
1967	28.1	26.4	27.3	27.3	20.3	23.1
1968	27.9	26.1	27.2	24.1	20.5	23.1
1969	27.9	26.4	27.2	24.2	20.9	23.2
1970	27.8	26.2	27.1	24.1	21.0	23.3
1971	27.7	25.8	26.9	24.0	21.1	23.1
1972	27.6	26.9	24.2	24.2	21.3	23.3
1973	27.7	25.7	27.0	24.1	21.4	23.3
1974	28.0	25.8	27.3	24.2	21.8	23.4
1975	27.1	26.0	26.4	23.9	22.0	23.2
1976	27.1	26.3	26.3	24.0	22.5	23.2
1977	27.3	26.1	26.6	24.2	22.6	23.4
1978	27.4	26.1	26.7	24.4	22.6	23.6
1979	27.5	26.0	26.7	24.4	22.8	23.7
1980	27.4	26.0	26.7	24.5	23.0	23.8
1981	27.5	26.1	26.1	24.6	23.0	24.2
1982	27.7	26.2	26.9	24.8	23.2	24.0
1983	27.8	26.0	26.9	24.9	23.1	24.1
1984	28.0	26.1	27.2	25.2	23.3	24.2
1985	28.0	26.3	27.2	25.3	23.5	24.4
1986	28.3	26.6	27.4	25.5	23.8	24.7
1987	28.5	26.8	27.7	25.8	24.0	25.8
1988	28.6	27.2	27.9	25.8	24.4	25.1
1989	28.8	27.1	28.0	26.0	24.3	25.2
1990	29.0	27.2	28.2	26.2	24.4	25.4
1991	29.1	27.4	28.3	26.3	24.4	25.4
1992	29.3	27.7	28.6	26.4	24.7	25.6
1993	29.5	27.9	28.8	26.6	24.9	25.8
1994	29.7	27.9	28.9	26.6	24.9	25.8
1995	29.7	28.1	28.9	26.6	25.0	25.9
1996	29.8	28.1	29.3	26.8	25.0	26.0
1997	29.6	28.2	28.8	26.7	25.3	26.0
1998	29.4	28.0	29.1	26.3	24.7	26.0
1999	29.4	27.9	29.2	26.5	24.8	26.2
2000	30.5	27.9	30.1	26.6	24.6	26.3
2001	29.8	27.9	29.5	26.7	24.3	26.3
2002	29.8	27.9	29.5	26.8	24.7	26.4
2003	30.0	28.0	29.7	27.0	24.7	26.7
2004	30.4	28.2	30.1	27.3	24.9	26.9
2005	31.1	28.3	30.7	27.4	24.9	27.0
2006	30.9	28.2	30.5	27.5	25.1	27.2

but less rapidly, from 22.2 in 1961 to 27.2 in 2006. Older data for Christian and civil marriages suggest that the average age at first marriage of non-Muslim women had commenced to move upwards much earlier than 1961 compared with that for Muslim women.

Among the factors contributing to the rise in the marriage age of women was the normalisation of the sex ratio at marriageable ages in the early post-war years, thus allowing men to marry older women rather than much younger women. In more recent years, couples tended to postpone their marriage until they were able to secure a subsidised government apartment under the Fiance/Fiancee Scheme for public housing.[12] The other reasons were the pursuit of higher educational qualifications, the emphasis on one's working career to be economically secure before marrying, and the emergence of attitudes favouring later marriages in the context of a society undergoing rapid modernisation.

The diverse trends in marriage age exhibited by women and men during these years have a considerable impact on the age difference between the bride and groom. In 1961 the non-Muslim men were marrying women who were 4 years younger than themselves, but this gap narrowed to 3.7 years in 1970, 2.9 years in 1980 and 2.8 years in 1991, and thereafter widened slowly to 3.4 years in 2006. Among Muslims, the age gap started widely at 7.3 years and narrowed quickly to 2.8 in 1990, mainly because of the sharp rise in the average female marriage age. After that, the gap widened to 3.1 in 2006.

MARRIAGE CHANGES BY AGE

The incidence of marriage naturally varies considerably among the different ages within the main marriage age range. The pattern of variation can best be examined in terms of the age-specific marriage rates, which may be defined as number of marriages in a specific age group per thousand unmarried population in the same age group. It is customary to calculate the rates for each sex separately in view of the significant differences between the age pattern of the two sexes. In Table 6.4, we have presented the rates compiled by the Department of Statistics for quinary age groups from age 15 to 44 for each sex separately.[13] These rates have been computed on the basis of the resident and not the total population.

One clear feature revealed by the figures refer to the reduction of marriage incidence in the first two age groups. From 1980 to 2005, the

TABLE 6.4
Age-Specific Marriage Rates by Sex, 1980–2005

Age Group	Male						Female					
	1980	1985	1990	1995	2000	2005	1980	1985	1990	1995	2000	2005
Rates												
15–19	1.7	1.2	1.2	1.2	1.7	1.0	18.4	15.2	11.0	7.5	7.4	4.5
20–24	49.9	43.8	35.1	29.3	23.7	17.2	110.5	95.5	84.8	70.1	54.3	38.2
25–29	140.1	110.3	107.6	113.1	104.0	83.7	136.5	111.8	133.0	135.7	133.0	111.5
30–34	138.0	109.8	96.4	108.0	98.3	103.5	74.3	62.6	69.1	76.5	69.8	68.4
35–39	106.3	83.2	68.5	70.8	64.5	76.0	43.6	33.4	36.6	37.3	32.4	31.1
40–44	62.8	54.5	41.6	54.8	43.8	53.5	22.0	18.5	14.7	16.9	17.2	14.6
Percentage Change												
15–19		−29.4	−29.4	0.0	+41.7	−41.2		−17.4	−27.4	−29.1	−1.7	−39.2
20–24		−12.2	−12.2	−16.5	−19.1	−27.6		−13.6	−11.2	−17.3	−22.5	−29.7
25–29		−21.2	−2.4	+5.1	+5.1	−19.5		−18.1	+18.1	+2.0	−2.0	−16.2
30–34		−20.4	−12.2	+12.0	−9.0	+5.3		−15.7	+15.7	+10.7	−8.8	−2.0
35–39		−21.7	−17.7	+3.4	+3.4	+17.8		−23.4	+23.4	+1.9	−13.1	−4.0
40–44		−13.2	−14.5	+31.7	−20.1	+22.1		−15.9	−15.9	+15.0	+1.8	−15.1

rates for the men was reduced from 1.7 per thousand summarised male resident population to 1.0 in the youngest age group 15–19, and from 49.9 to 17.2 in the second age group 20–24. Similarly, the rates for the women was brought down from 18.4 to 4.5 and from 1105 to 38.2 in the two corresponding age groups. In the other three age groups above age 24, no clear trend over the years can be discussed, being subjected to up-down movement. Still, these three age groups have experienced a clear decrease in the rates by the end of the twenty-five year period.

A casual glance at the figures given in Table 6.6 confirms the different pattern age-specific marriage rates displayed by each sex. The 1980 figures show that the female rate rises steeply from 18.4 per thousand female resident population to the peak of 136.5 in the 25–29 age group, after which it falls to only 22.0 in the 40–44 age group. In contrast, the rate for the men starts at a lower rate of 1.7 in the 15–19 age group, rises to the peak of 140.1 in the 25–29 age group, and declines slower in the next three age groups. By the end of the period in 2005, the peak marriage rate for the women occurred in the 25–29 age group as compared to the men's rate peaking in the older age group 30–34. Another clear difference is that the rates for the two young age groups have been consistently higher for the women than for the men, while the reverse position have always prevailed in the two old age groups above age 34. The differential pattern between the two sexes may be attributed to the older age at which men marry.

INTERRACIAL MARRIAGES

A study of interracial marriages among the diverse ethnic and religious groups in Singapore is of considerable importance not only in its possible impact on certain facets of the demographics of the country, but also in the area of racial assimilation within the context of building a more cohesive society. Opportunities for racial intermingling do exist in the ethnically-mixed public housing estates, educational institutions, workplaces and recreational centres, and have been facilitated by the wide use of the English language. Marriages between persons of different ethnic origins are identified in the registration system and presented in both the non-Muslim and Muslim marriage statistics. The figures for the combined total number of interracial marriages for these two types for the years 1961 to 2005 are presented in Table 6.5. The application of the previously-described procedure to convert the data from

TABLE 6.5

Interracial Marriages and Interracial Marriage Rate, 1961–2006

Year	Number	Rate	Year	Number	Rate
1961	333	4.9	1984	1,564	6.3
1962	361	5.1	1985	1,518	6.5
1963	451	5.5	1986	1,406	7.0
1964	425	4.8	1987	1,475	6.3
1965	508	5.0	1988	1,732	7.0
1966	505	4.5	1989	1,673	7.1
1967	538	4.7	1990	1,908	7.8
1968	527	4.6	1991	1,913	7.6
1969	659	5.2	1992	1,976	7.6
1970	675	4.6	1993	2,031	8.0
1971	788	5.2	1994	2,169	8.8
1972	783	4.4	1995	2,250	9.0
1973	873	3.5	1996	2,272	9.4
1974	908	3.5	1997	2,290	8.9
1975	1,050	4.8	1998	2,496	10.8
1976	1,069	5.2	1999	2,706	10.5
1977	1,038	5.1	2000	2,724	12.1
1978	1,093	5.3	2001	2,814	12.6
1979	1,149	5.4	2002	2,842	12.1
1980	1,240	5.5	2003	2,515	11.4
1981	1,359	5.5	2004	2,763	12.4
1982	1,465	6.3	2005	3,424	14.9
1983	1,467	6.7	2006	2,821	11.9

registration date to occurrence date yielded very little difference between the two sets of figures, and as a matter of convenience the registered figures will be used here. The rate is expressed as a percentage to the total number of marriages.

Except for some minor ups and downs, the number of interracial marriages moved upwards during the last four decades from 333 in 1961 to 2,724 in 2000. It moved up rapidly in the new millenium to reach the all-time high of 3,424 in 2005, but fell in the very next year to 2,821. It increased by slightly more than twofold in the first decade, about half in the second decade, and a quarter in the third decade. Despite the faster rise in the absolute number in the earlier years, the rate of growth of interracial marriages has remained almost at the same level for the first two decades, oscillating around 5 per cent. Incidentally, the lower rate recorded in 1973 and 1974, in the absence of a corresponding drop in the absolute number, serves as a further confirmation that many of the marriages had their date of solemnisation wrongly stated as 1973 or 1974. A steady rise in the level of interracial marriages occurred in the eighties when the rate increased from 5.5 in 1980 to 7.1 in 1989, followed by a faster uptrend in the nineties when it reached 10.5 in 1999. It was pushed up further in recent years to 14.9 in 2005. It would appear that the past stabilised state of relations among the difference races is now giving way to a very gradual advance in the level of assimilation, but this is still way behind the creation of a melting-pot situation of mixed races.

We will proceed a step further in our study of interracial marriages in Singapore by examining the data for each of the major ethnic groups shown in Table 6.6. Among the non-Muslim grooms taking partners outside their own race in 2006, there were 1,242 Chinese, 52 Malays, 255 Indians, 89 Eurasians, and 544 Caucasians. The last

TABLE 6.6

Distribution of Grooms and Brides Contracting Interracial Marriages by Type of Marriage and Race, 2006

Race	Non-Muslim Marriages	Muslim Marriages	Total	Interracial Marriages Rate
Grooms				
Chinese	1,242	77	1.319	7.6
Malays	52	503	555	22.5
Indians	255	265	520	36.0
Eurasians	89	14	103	*
Caucasians	544	50	594	*
Others	263	290	553	*
Brides				
Chinese	779	104	883	5.1
Malays	184	549	733	22.9
Indians	96	175	271	22.7
Eurasians	57	5	62	*
Caucasians	49	8	57	*
Others	1,280	358	1,638	*

* not available

group was of course made up of quite heterogeneous European peoples, such as English, French, Germans and Italians not identified separately in the annual statistics. A somewhat different racial composition was displayed by the figures for Muslim grooms. Not surprisingly, the largest number of such Muslim grooms were Malays (503) who are the dominant group in the Muslim community. The second largest group of Muslim grooms consisted of 265 Indians, mostly Pakistanis, Bangladeshis, and Indian Muslims. Another difference was the small number of Chinese (77), Eurasian (14) and Caucasian (50) men contracting interracial Muslim marriages.

The women contracting interracial non-Muslim marriages in 2006 came from a more diverse racial background, with 779 Chinese, 184 Malays, 96 Indians, 57 Eurasians and 49 Caucasians. The remaining 1,280 were from a wide range of other minority races. In contrast, the number of women from the "Others" groups contracting interracial Muslim marriages amounted to no more than 358. There was a high concentration of Malay women (549) and Indian women (175), which is a reflection of the well-known fact that Islam has been an important factor in influencing the higher level of mixed marriages among the Indians and Malays, the two predominant groups in the Muslim community. On the other hand, Christianity cuts across all ethnic groups in Singapore, and this is one of the reasons for the wider racial dispersion of persons contracting non-Muslim marriages in Singapore.

In order to measure the incidence of men and women from the main ethnic groups contracting interracial marriages, we have computed an interracial marriage rate for the two types of marriages combined. This rate, shown in Table 6.6, is defined as the proportion of men (or women) in a particular ethnic group contracting interracial marriages to the total number of men (or women) in the same ethnic group marrying in the year. For example, in 2006 there were 1,319 Chinese men contracting interracial marriages out of a total of 17,382 (1,319 plus 16,063 unmixed marriages), and this gives a rate of 7.6 per cent. This rate can also be employed to measure the relative incidence of interracial marriages between the two sexes in a particular ethnic group.

The male rates show that the lowest incidence of interracial marriages occurred among Chinese men, with only 7.6 per cent, and the highest among Indian men with 36.0 per cent, while the intermediate position was occupied by Malay men with 22.5 per cent. A different relative position prevailed among the women of these three races, with 5.2 per cent for Chinese women, 22.7 per cent for Indian women, and 22.9 per cent for Malay women. The overall incidence of interracial marriages for the mixed group of other races designated as "Others" was extremely high, with 77.1 per cent for the men and 77.8 per cent for the women. The willingness to marry outside one's race appears to vary conversely with the size of the population because the small supply of marriageable persons from one's own community in a small population is one of the important factors determining mixed marriages. This will naturally be reinforced by a common religion such as Christianity, and hence the extremely high incidence of mixed marriages among the minority races known collectively as "Others". Incidentally, it is not possible to compute the interracial marriage rate for the Eurasians and Caucasians separately because figures for persons from these two groups contracting non-mixed marriages are included in the "Others" category.

The availability of statistics for the bivariate distribution of grooms and brides according to the six ethnic groupings enables us to examine the racial combinations of interracial marriages. Out of the total of 2,446 persons contracting interracial non-Muslim marriages in 2006, the most popular combination was the 356 Caucasian grooms and Chinese brides, followed by the 130 Indian grooms and Chinese brides. The third position was taken up by the 122 Chinese grooms and Malay brides, and fourth by the 58 Eurasian grooms and Chinese brides. It should also be mentioned that there were 1,038 Chinese grooms who married women collectively classified as "Others" (excluding Eurasians and Caucasians). The 1,199 interracial Muslim marriages in 2006 were dominated by two combinations: 199 Indian grooms with Malay brides, and 126 Malay grooms with Indian brides. Religion was not a serious obstacle in this type of interracial marriages since almost all these Indians practised the same Islamic faith as the Malays. A poor third position was occupied by the 76 Malay grooms with Chinese brides, and a close fourth by the 56 Chinese grooms with Malay brides. The above highlights of the racial combinations provide a clearer picture of the dynamics of interracial marriages which can only become more common and diverse in a modern cosmopolitan city-state.

MARRIAGE PATTERNS

Among the 23,706 marriages solemnised in 2006, 19,761, or 83.4 per cent were non-Muslim marriages conducted under the Women's Charter, and 3,945, or 16.6 per cent, were Muslim marriages held under the

Administration of Muslim Law Act. No less than 16,063, or 81.3 per cent, of the non-Muslim marriages were contracted by Chinese couples, 759, or 3.8 per cent by Indian couples, and 494, or 2.5 per cent, by couples from the other races. The remaining 2,445, or 12.4 per cent, were mixed marriages contracted by couples not from the same ethnic group. Muslim marriages were dominated by Malay couples amounting to 2,472, or 62.7 per cent, and Indian couples numbered some 165, or 4.2 per cent. Even the 1,199 interracial marriages were contracted primarily by persons belonging to these two ethnic groups. Only 109 marriages were contracted by couples from the other races.

It was noted earlier that marriages registered under the Women's Charter can be conducted in the Registry of Marriages as well as in churches, temples, and other places. This is to allow couples to choose to have their marriages solemnised in accordance with their own religious or customary rites. However, the Registry was a popular place for couples to solemnise their marriage, accounting for 5,420, or 27.4 per cent, of the total in 2006. The other non-Muslim marriages took place in churches (1,678), Hindu temples (138) and Chinese temples (133), while 5,883 were solemnised by grass-root leaders and 2,067 by Justices of the Peace in other locations. One should be careful in not equating these figures with the religious affiliations of the couples.

The religious faith of the couples can in fact be identified more precisely by the figures for the bivariate distribution of grooms and brides according to religion, presented in Table 6.7. The table reveals that in the same year there were 2,674 Christian couples contracting marriages under the Women's Charter, which may be taken to mean that nearly half of these marriages were held in the Registry rather than churches. There were 567 Hindu couples and most of them married in the Registry rather than in Hindu temples. Buddhist couples were by far the biggest religious group contracting non-Muslim marriages, and they amounted to 6,538, or 33.1 per cent, of the total registered in 2006. There were, of course, couples without any religion at all — by no means a negligible figure as 2,845 couples declared no adherence to any religion at the time of marriage. As for Muslim couples, we have already seen that 3,945 marriages were registered under the Administration of Muslim Law Act in 2006. It should be noted that the stipulation requiring couples marrying under this legislation to be both Muslims has resulted in the common practice whereby the non-Muslim partner becomes a Muslim convert prior to tying the marriage knot.

TABLE 6.7
Bivariate Distribution of Non-Muslim Marriages by Religion of Grooms and Brides, 2006

Religion of Grooms	Religion of Brides						
	Buddhism	Christianity	Taoism/ Confucianism	Hinduism	Other Religions	No Religion	Total
Buddhism	6,538	525	362	4	139	1,021	8,589
Christianity	474	2,674	90	52	88	544	3,922
Taoism/Confucianism	367	102	877	2	33	232	1,613
Hinduism	41	90	9	567	60	14	783
Other Religions	88	77	15	18	203	71	472
No Religion	744	523	160	6	106	2,845	4,384
Total	8,252	3,991	1,513	649	629	4,727	19,761

Apart front the above marriages contracted by couples belonging to the same religion, the figures also disclose inter-religious marriages conducted under the Women's Charter. Out of the 3,922 Christian men marrying in 2006, 2,674, or 68.2 per cent, selected partners who were also Christian, and the others had taken partners professing other religions or no religion at all. As for Christian women, 2,674, or 67.0 per cent, married men with the same religion. In the case of Buddhists, 2,051, or 23.9 per cent of the 8,589 Buddhist men married outside their own religion, and so did 1,714 or 20.8 per cent of the 8,252 Buddhist women. The corresponding figures for Hindus were 82, or 12.6 per cent, of the 649 women. It would appear that among the Christians and the Buddhists, the women were more prepared to marry persons not professing their own religion, but the reverse position prevailed among the Hindus.

With regard to the pattern of marital status, 85.2 per cent of the grooms and 87.2 per cent of the brides contracting non-Muslim marriages in 2006 were singles marrying for the first time. There were more divorced persons than widowed persons among those who remarried, with 2,693 divorced men and 234 widowed men. Similarly, there were 2,628 divorced women and 151 widowed women among those remarrying. Persons who lost their spouses through death were generally quite advanced in age and had less desire to remarry, while divorced persons, besides being younger, often took steps to dissolve their marriage in order to remarry another person. Marriage between bachelors and spinsters was of course the most dominant combination, accounting for 15,299, or 77.4 per cent, of the total non-Muslim marriages in 2006. The other combinations were extremely insignificant — for example, the second most popular combination — that between male divorcees and spinsters — numbered no more than 1,791, and the third — between bachelors and female divorcees — numbered 1,457.

In view of the higher level of divorce incidence experienced by the Muslim community, we can expect remarriage to be more common among persons contracting marriages under the Administration of Muslim Law Act. Out of the 3,945 grooms in 2006, there were 2,935 bachelors, or 74.4 per cent, marrying for the first time and 1,010, or 25.6 per cent, remarrying. The corresponding figures for brides were 2,918, or 74.0 per cent, and 1,025, or 26.0 per cent. Divorced persons contracting Muslim marriages were more conspicuous, with 910 grooms or 23.1 per cent, and 941 brides or 23.9 per cent. A unique feature of the marital pattern of Muslim marriages is the possibility of married men remarrying since Islamic law permits a man to have up to four wives under certain stringent conditions. However, there were only 11 married men contracting Muslim marriages in 2006, with 5 marrying spinsters, 4 marrying divorced women, and 2 marrying widows. Polygamy is seldom practised by Muslim men in Singapore.

Apart from marriages between bachelors and spinsters being the principal combination in Muslim marriages (2,553, or 64.7 per cent), the second position was occupied by marriages between male and female divorcees with 535, or 13.6 per cent. The third position was taken up by bachelors marrying female divorcees with 362, or 9.2 per cent, followed closely by marriages between male divorcees and spinsters with 339, or 8.6 per cent. The conspicuous presence of divorced persons in these marital status combinations was a clear manifestation of the higher divorce rate prevailing among the Muslim population.

Since the introduction of an eugenic population policy in 1984 to improve the quality of the population, considerable attention has been focused on the educational background of persons marrying. The reason for this interest is centred on the premise that the intelligence of children depends on nature rather than nurture, and hence highly-educated mothers tend to produce intelligent children. There was some concern about highly-educated women remaining single on account of their reluctance to marry, among other reasons, men with lower educational attainment. A fuller discussion of the eugenic policy will be presented in a subsequent chapter dealing with population policies and programmes.

Out of the total number of grooms marrying in 2005, 32.0 per cent had tertiary education, 31.2 per cent had post secondary such as GCE "A" level and diplomas, 27.9 per cent had secondary, and 8.9 per cent primary or no education. The educational qualification of brides was somewhat lower, with only 31.0 per cent with tertiary education and 30.3 per cent with post secondary education, 31.6 per cent with secondary education, and 7.0 with primary or no education. Clearly, this educational pattern of grooms and brides was a reflection of the educational pattern of the population in general as determined by the past educational system in the country. A more instructive aspect of this educational pattern is the question of persons marrying upwards or downwards, which can be demonstrated by figures for the bivariate distribution of grooms and brides according to educational qualification. These figures have been utilised in Table 6.8 to show the percentage of

TABLE 6.8
Percentage Distribution of Groom and Bride by Education, 2005

Education of Groom/Bride	Bride's Education Compared with Groom's			Groom's Education Compared with Bride's		
	Lower	Same	Higher	Lower	Same	Higher
No Education	—	16.7	83.3	—	2.0	98.0
Primary	5.0	37.7	57.3	0.4	35.9	63.7
Secondary	17.5	52.9	29.6	14.2	47.8	38.0
Post Secondary	40.6	32.1	27.3	28.9	36.7	34.4
Tertiary	35.5	64.5	—	30.7	69.3	—

grooms or brides marrying partners with the same, lower, or higher educational qualification.

The study of grooms and brides marrying downwards or upwards has been conducted in many countries, but assumed special significance in Singapore in the mid-1980s when the reluctance of higher-educated women to marry men with lower educational qualification was cited as the main cause for some of these women remaining single and hence not producing intelligent children. According to Table 6.8, 64.5 per cent of the grooms in 2005 with tertiary education married women with the same educational qualifications and another 35.5 per cent married women with lower qualifications. This contrasts sharply, with the position of tertiary brides, with only 30.7 per cent marrying men with lower educational attainment. Similarly, 40.6 per cent of grooms with secondary education married women with lower education, but a lower 28.9 per cent of brides with secondary education married men with lower education. The greater reluctance on the part of highly-educated women to marry downwards can also be seen to exist in many other countries. However, this tendency is quite insignificant among those with primary education, most probably because of the negligible distinction in social status between such poorly educated persons and those with no educational qualifications.

Notes

1. Singapore, *Christian Marriages Ordinance 1940*, No. 10 of 1940 (Singapore: Government Printers, 1940).

2. Singapore, *Civil Marriages Ordinance 1940*, No. 9 of 1940 (Singapore: Government Printers, 1940).

3. Singapore, *Women's Charter 1961*, No. 18 of 1961 (Singapore: Government Printers, 1961).

4. Singapore, *Women's Charter (Amendment) Act 1967* (Singapore: Government Printers, 1967).

5. Ahmad bin Mohamad Ibrahim, "Development in Marriage Laws in Malaysia and Singapore", *Malaya Law Review* 2, no. 2 (December 1970).

6. Singapore, *Administration of Muslim Law Act 1966* (Singapore: Government Printers, 1966).

7. Singapore, *Muslim Ordinance 1957*, No. 25 of 1957 (Singapore: Government Printers, 1957).

8. The number of Muslim marriages for the early years is obtainable directly from the Registry of Muslim Marriages.

9. See, for example. Table 67 in *Report on the Registration of Births and Deaths and Marriages, 1970* (Singapore: Government Printing Office, n.d.).

10. New Paper, 10 June 1997.

11. Singapore, Report on the *Registration of Births and Deaths and Marriages, 1973* (Singapore: Singapore National Printers, n.d.).

12. *Straits Times*, 16 June 1997.

13. Singapore, *Population Trends 2006* (Singapore: Department of Statistics, 2006).

7

Divorce Trends and Patterns

In this chapter we will examine marital dissolution so as to complete our account of nuptiality trends and patterns. Divorce, the final outcome of irreconcilable marital discord, is seen to create social problems for the families concerned and for the community at large. It is also common to view a high divorce rate in a society like Singapore as a sign of diminishing family stability and weakening Asian cultural and social values. Not surprisingly, a rising trend in divorce incidence often generates considerable public concern and debate. From the demographic point of view, changes in the divorce incidence would have some impact on the level of fertility since a breakup in marriage will effectively reduce the period of reproductive life of the woman.

The study of divorce in some countries is often handicapped by a paucity of statistics owing to the absence of an ongoing system of registering divorce cases and compiling statistics from such cases. Though records of divorce cases have been kept by the relevant authorities in Singapore, it was not until the early eighties that the Department of Statistics launched a project to compile divorce statistics on a regular basis. Two separate sets of divorce statistics are compiled nowadays: Muslim divorce statistics from the register of divorces administered by the Shariah Court, and non-Muslim divorce statistics from the records of divorce case files maintained by the High Court Registry. The two sets of annual statistics, along with some data for the years 1980–83, are made available in the annual publication entitled *Statistics on Marriages and Divorces* for the year 1984 onwards.[1] These statistics do convey an accurate picture of divorce trends and patterns in Singapore since marriages and their dissolution are effected within the legal framework of the country; marriages and divorces by consensus outside the law are not legally recognised.

DIVORCE CUSTOMS AND LAWS

The marital dissolution of non-Muslim marriages is not handled by the Registry of Marriages but by the High Court in accordance with specific sections of the Women's Charter. In instances where the divorce petition is contested, the court would arrive at a decision after hearing the submissions presented by both the parties concerned. If the petition is uncontested, only the party seeking the divorce will be called upon to present the submissions. When the petition is successful, the court grants a decree nisi, which will finally dissolve the marriage when it is converted into a decree absolute after three months, or after a shorter period if the court so orders. During the intervening period, either party may show why the decree nisi should not be made absolute, such as by reason of its having been obtained by collusion or by reason of material facts not having been brought before the court. The particulars pertaining to the divorce eventually approved are kept in the records of the High Court, which provide the raw data for compiling the divorce statistics.

The conditions under which a divorce may be granted are spelt out in the relevant sections of the Women's Charter.[2] In the first place, petitions for a divorce may not be submitted, except in special cases, during the first three years of marriage. This is aimed at discouraging persons from contracting ill-considered marriages and ensuring that marital dissolution is not readily employed to solve matrimonial problems in the early years. The court may, however, allow a petition on the ground that the case is one of exceptional hardship suffered by the petitioner, or exceptional depravity on the part of the respondent. In exercising its discretion, the court has to take into account the interests of the children of the marriage and any reasonable chance of reconciliation between the parties before the end of the three-year period. The court may also refer the differences between the parties to a Conciliation Officer.

After three years, a divorce petition may be submitted to the court under any one of the following common grounds:

1. that the spouse had committed adultery and the petitioner finds it intolerable to live with the respondent;
2. that the spouse had behaved in such a way that the petitioner cannot reasonably be expected to live with the respondent;
3. that the spouse had deserted the petitioner for a continuous period

of at least two years immediately preceding the presentation of the petition;

4. that both parties have lived apart for a continuous period of at least three years immediately preceding the presentation of the petition, and the respondent consents to a decree being granted; and

5. that both parties have lived apart for a continuous period of at least four years immediately preceding the presentation of the petition.

In addition to the above grounds, there is provision for either spouse to request the court for a decree of presumption of death and of divorce by proving that there exist reasonable grounds for supposing that the spouse is dead. If a spouse has continually been absent for seven years or more, and the other spouse has no reason to believe that he has been living within that time, this shall be prima facie evidence that he is dead.

The dissolution of Muslim marriages is governed by the law of Islam which has traditionally permitted divorce to be effected in four different ways.[3] First, the husband may divorce his wife by pronouncing *talak* three times in front of her at any time without the need for a witness to be present. If he pronounces one or two *talak* only, his wife is considered divorced but may not remarry another person for a period of one hundred days. During this period, known as *iddah*, the husband is allowed to change his mind and to be reconciled with his wife. If there is no reconciliation, the divorce becomes final at the expiry of the period of one hundred days. The second method of divorce is known as *khuluk* by which a divorce is granted in cases where the wife seeks a divorce from a reluctant husband by offering him a sum of money or some property by way of compensation. The third method is known as *cerai taklik*, whereby conditions are attached to the marriage which, if contravened by the husband, entitles the wife to a divorce. By the fourth method, *fasakh* is granted where the wife seeks a divorce in cases where her husband deserts her and fails to maintain her, or where he is impotent or abjures Islam. The conditions and procedures for the above four methods are laid out in the relevant sections of the Administration of Muslim Law Act. Muslim divorce cases are finalised and registered in the Shariah Court, established under this Act on 24 November 1958.[4]

The registration of Muslim divorce is made compulsory by Section 102 of the Administration of Muslim Law Act. But Section 103(3) provides that a *Kadi* shall not register any divorce unless he is satisfied after an inquiry that both parties have consented thereto. Section 102(4) expressly prohibits a *Kadi* from registering any divorce with three *talak*, or a divorce in which he is not satisfied that both the parties have consented to the registration thereof. In these cases, the *Kadi* must refer the application to the Shariah Court which is empowered to make such decree or order as is lawful under Muslim law. Moreover, Section 47(1) allows a married woman to apply to the Court for a divorce in accordance with Muslim law, and the Court shall summon the husband and ascertain whether he consents to the divorce. If the husband, so consents, the Court shall cause him to pronounce a divorce, presumably the *talak* type.

Section 47(3) of the Act regulates the granting of a divorce to a married woman by redemption, or *khuluk*. The husband, who is summoned to the Shariah Court as a result of the wife applying for a divorce, may not agree to divorce the wife but both parties may agree to a divorce by *khuluk*. In this case, the Court may assess the amount that the wife must pay to her husband, taking into account the status and means of the parties, and shall thereupon cause the husband to pronounce a divorce by redemption. On payment of the amount so assessed and the prescribed fees, the divorce is registered in the Court.

Section 48 of the Act sets out the granting of divorce, known as *cerai taklik*, to a married woman as a result of the breach of a condition agreed to at the time of or after the marriage. Any lawful condition may be included. Section 48(1) provides that a married woman may, if entitled in accordance with Muslim law to a divorce because of the breech of the terms of a written *taklik*, apply to the Court to declare that such a divorce has taken place. Section 45(2) stipulates that the Court shall examine the written *taklik* and make the necessary enquiries to determine the validity of the divorce. If the Court is satisfied that the divorce is valid in accordance with Muslim law, the divorce is confirmed upon payment of the prescribed fees.

The conditions under which a married woman may apply to the Court for a decree of *fasakh* are spelled out in Section 49 of the Act. A wife is entitled to apply for a decree of *fasakh* on any one or more of the following grounds: (1) that her husband has neglected or failed to provide for her maintenance for a period of three months, (2) that her husband has been sentenced to imprisonment for a period of three years or more, (3) that her husband has failed to perform, without reasonable cause, his marital obligations for a period of one year, (4) that her husband is impotent, (5) that her husband is insane or is suffering from some chronic or incurable disease, (6) that her husband treats her with cruelty, and (7) on any other ground which is recognised as valid for the dissolution of marriage by *fasakh* under Muslim law. Besides summoning the husband, the Court is required to record the sworn statement of the woman and at least two witnesses. If the Court is satisfied that the woman is entitled to a decree of *fasakh* in accordance with one or more of the above conditions, the divorce is granted and registered accordingly.

Since one of the main reasons for introducing the Administration of Muslim Law Act is to control the incidence of divorce among the Muslim community, Section 50 of the Act empowers the Shariah Court to try and reconcile the parties seeking a divorce. Before making an order or decree for any of the four types of divorce, the Court may appoint, in accordance with Muslim law, two arbitrators or *hakam* to act for the husband and wife respectively. Preference would be given to close relatives of the parties who would have knowledge of the circumstances underlying the case. The Court may give instructions to the *hakam* with regard to the conduct of the arbitration, and they must conduct it according to these instructions and Muslim law. If they are unable to agree or if the Court is not satisfied with their conduct in the arbitration, it may remove them and appoint other *hakam* in their place. The *hakam* are expected to do their utmost to bring about a reconciliation between the parties and, if successful, shall report the reconciliation to the Court. If the parties refuse to be reconciled, the *hakam* may decree a divorce and report it to the Court. Apart from the appointment of the *hakam* to effect a reconciliation, the officials in the Shariah Court provide reconciliatory services to parties seeking a divorce.

The procedures for handling cases in the Shariah Court are quite institutionalised by now. A spouse or couple desiring to seek a divorce must first supply certain basic particulars of the husband and wife in a standard Intake Form. Arrangements are then made for the parties concerned to appear before one of the three Muslim social case workers employed by the Shariah Court. It is the duty of the case worker to investigate the divorce case thoroughly and to try his very best to effect a reconciliation between the husband and wife. If reconciliation is not feasible, he would refer the case to the *Kadi* of the Shariah Court. If the two parties agree to a divorce, the *Kadi* will grant the couple a divorce and register it accordingly. If the *Kadi* is unable to grant a divorce on account of disagreement between the two parties, he is obliged to refer the case to a hearing of the Shariah Court presided over by its President. The divorce granted during the hearing of the Court would also be registered immediately.

DIVORCE TRENDS

The study of divorce trends is handicapped by the lack of time-series data on non-Muslim divorces since the official compilation and publication of the statistics started only in the early 1980s. In Table 7.1 the non-Muslim statistics for the years 1980–97 refer to the official figures published by the Department of Statistics while those for 1960–71 were compiled from Tai,[5] those for 1972–77 were estimated by Wong and Kuo,[6] and those for 1978 and 1979 were kept by the Department of Social Welfare. The compilation of the early statistics by the scholars from the divorce files kept in the High Court was extremely laborious and difficult because these files contained all petitions for divorces and annulments with different outcomes, such as granted, rejected, withdrawn and pending. Another problem is that since the derivation of the divorce rate had to be related to the marriage figures, as will be explained shortly, the rate cannot be computed for the years prior to 1961 when marriage registration was not compulsory.

The number of non-Muslim divorces stood at only 57 in 1961 and 58 in 1962, most probably because divorce proceedings under the Women's Charter were still new to couples with marital discord and perhaps to their lawyers too. In 1963, the number increased almost twofold to reach 108, and then rose moderately to be doubled again in 1973 when it stood at 203. This was followed by a continuous upswing, with the number touching 1,046 in 1980, 2,178 in 1990, and the high of 4,696 in 2005. On the other hand, because of the good efforts of the Shariah Court, the number of Muslim divorces was even halved in the 1960s, reducing from 401 in 1961 to 200 in 1968. After that, the downtrend reversed and the number edged up slowly to 505 in 1980, 972 in 1990, and finally to 1,873 in 2005. The combined effect of the two movements in the total number of divorces in Singapore was that there was no clear trend in the first seven years, fluctuating between 410 and 540. From the low of 352 in 1968, it moved up to 1,551 in 1980, 3,150 in 1990, 4,943 in 2000, and finally to 6,649 in 2006.

To obtain a good idea of the incidence of divorce, it is necessary to derive a rate expressed in terms of the married population, sub-divided into the non-Muslim component and the Muslim component. Such

TABLE 7.1

Divorces and Divorce Rate by Type of Divorces, 1961–2006

Year	Number of Divorces			Divorce Rate		
	Non-Muslim	Muslim	Total	Non-Muslim	Muslim	Total
1961	57	401	458	10.9	257.1	67.6
1962	58	447	505	10.3	301.4	70.9
1963	108	430	538	16.7	254.4	66.1
1964	132	324	456	18.3	190.8	51.3
1965	105	366	471	12.7	190.4	46.1
1966	113	301	414	12.0	157.5	36.6
1967	157	374	531	16.5	197.5	46.6
1968	152	200	352	15.8	101.5	30.4
1969	151	244	392	14.1	123.7	31.1
1970	182	219	401	14.8	96.4	27.4
1971	181	241	422	14.2	97.5	27.8
1972	204	254	458	13.4	95.4	25.7
1973	208	278	486	9.4	98.5	19.4
1974	317	311	628	13.7	107.4	24.2
1975	358	304	662	19.0	94.0	30.0
1976	375	300	675	21.2	101.8	32.7
1977	593	377	970	34.9	119.2	48.1
1978	570	357	927	32.3	114.8	44.7
1979	772	515	1,287	44.3	140.1	61.0
1980	1,046	505	1,551	56.4	125.2	68.7
1981	1,228	614	1,842	65.8	138.6	74.8
1982	1,306	536	1,842	71.0	111.2	79.3
1983	1,358	711	2,069	77.8	154.8	93.8
1984	1,391	637	2,028	68.0	141.7	81.3
1985	1,310	738	2,048	69.3	161.7	87.3
1986	1,485	786	2,271	94.6	179.2	113.1
1987	1,543	796	2,339	81.5	178.2	99.9
1988	1,643	893	2,536	81.9	186.0	102.0
1989	1,634	907	2,541	86.6	189.2	107.4
1990	2,178	972	3,150	111.3	204.1	129.4
1991	2,792	1,021	3,813	137.0	212.4	151.4
1992	2,565	1,002	3,567	121.5	212.1	138.0
1993	2,602	1,224	3,826	125.7	265.7	151.2
1994	2,503	1,082	3,585	123.6	245.3	145.4
1995	3,127	983	4,110	152.1	222.8	164.6
1996	3,368	1,088	4,456	168.9	260.8	184.8
1997	3,475	1,212	4,687	163.1	277.5	182.6
1998	3,924	1,465	5,389	206.7	354.3	233.1
1999	3,521	1,563	5,084	163.3	382.4	198.2
2000	3,336	1,607	4,943	179.8	400.6	219.0
2001	3,491	1,347	4,838	190.9	336.7	217.1
2002	4,006	1,532	5,538	208.0	388.7	238.7
2003	4,188	2,105	6,293	231.4	543.8	286.4
2004	4,192	1,855	6,047	231.7	452.7	272.5
2005	4,696	1,873	6,569	246.6	474.2	285.7
2006	4,705	1,944	6,649	238.1	492.8	280.5

figures are only available from the population censuses conducted at
long intervals of ten years. In the absence of relevant figures on an
annual basis, it is not possible to derive the annual rate based on this
desirable denominator. As an alternative, we have compiled the rate by
expressing the number of divorces in any year per thousand marriages
occurring in the same year. The marriage figures included in the previous
chapter have therefore been utilised to calculate the three divorce rates
shown in Table 7.1. This measure has been generally accepted though it
may create a spurious relationship because the number of divorces
granted in any year comes from not only marriages in that year but also
marriages in previous years.

The non-Muslim divorce rate was only 10.2 per thousand marriages
in 1961 and 10.3 in 1962, but went up quickly to 18.3 in 1964. After that,
the rate dropped slightly and remained low until 1975 when it rose to
19.0 in that year. From the mid-seventies, a definite trend was recorded,
with the rate advancing steadily to 56.4 in 1980 and then staying above
the 80-level until 1989. In recent years, it shot up to 111.3 in 1990, 179.8
in 2000, and then to the all-time high of 246.6 in 2005. Except for some
temporary increases in certain years, the Muslim divorce rate experienced
a downtrend from 1961 to 1975 when the rate was brought down from
257.1 to 94.0. For the rest of the period, the rate seemed to climb up
slowly in most years until the mid-eighties and then more positively to
reach the high of 265.7 in 1993. It took a downtrend in the next two
years, but quickly went up again to 277.5 in 1997 because the Shariah
Court was clearing divorce cases more quickly.[7] Thereafter, it moved up
to 492.8 in 2005. The overall divorce rate in Singapore was reduced from
67.6 in 1961 to the low of only 19.4 in 1973, but after that it rose steadily
to 113.1 in 1986, levelled off in the next three years, and advanced
steeply to 129.4 in 1990 and the high of 285.7 in 2005.

At the beginning of the period in 1961, the incidence of Muslim
divorces was about twenty-five times that of the non-Muslim divorces.
As the former was kept under control, with the incidence nowadays still
staying below that prevailing in the early 1960s and the former increasing
by eight or nine times, the gap between the two types has narrowed
dramatically. The extremely wide gap that existed in the early 1960s has
been narrowed to less than twice in recent years. What this means is that
although the impact of Muslim divorce on the overall incidence in
Singapore has been weakening fast, it is still a major determinant of the
overall incidence nowadays.

Mention was made earlier regarding the availability of statistics on the total number of Muslim marriages and divorces obtainable for the year 1921 onwards. In Table 7.2, the figures for the years prior to 1957 were obtained directly from the Registrar of Muslim Marriages and for the years 1957 to 1960 from the *Annual Report of Births, Deaths, Marriages and Persons.*[8] The figures confirmed the extremely high incidence of divorce that had prevailed in the past among the Muslim community: one marriage in two ended up in marital dissolution. It was, of course, this unsatisfactory state of affairs that led to the establishment of the Shariah Court in November 1958.

The incidence of Muslim divorces remained at the high level of 492.7 per thousand marriages in 1958 as the Shariah Court could only start operating towards the end of the year. But the effectiveness of the various sections concerning divorce in the Administration of Muslim Law Act and the work of the Shariah Court was evidenced by the sudden drop in the Muslim divorce rate to 272.7 in 1959, and also by the general downtrend in subsequent years. In part, the great improvement in the level of divorce was a manifestation of the positive response of the Muslim community to the work of the Court, thereby enabling the community to enjoy the benefits that come with greater marital stability. A point of interest is the higher than usual divorce rate (667.5) registered during the war years 1941–45 when extremely

TABLE 7.2

Muslim Marriages, Divorces and Divorce Rate, 1921–1960

Period	Muslim Marriages	Muslim Divorces	Muslim Divorce Rate
1921–25	10,946	6,173	564.0
1926–30	12,609	6,941	550.5
1931–35	10,454	6,070	580.6
1936–40	10,684	5,966	558.4
1941–45	12,468	8,322	667.5
1946–50	13,995	7,459	533.0
1951–55	12,732	7,021	551.4
1956	2,414	1,074	444.9
1957	2,303	1,192	517.6
1958	2,332	1,149	492.7
1959	2,116	577	272.7
1960	1,814	574	316.4

deprived and precarious conditions prevailing at that time must have brought forth, among other things, additional discord and dissolution. On the other hand, there appeared to be a slight marriage boom during the post-war period 1945–50 when the number of Muslim marriages was at the high of 13,995.

The extremely high divorce incidence among Muslims prior to the setting up of the Shariah Court may be attributed to various conditions in Malay life.[9] First, a divorce could be effected quite easily under the old Muslim Ordinance of 1880 because the religious authorities failed to be strict with couples seeking divorce and did not provide much conciliatory services. Secondly, in those days there were no strong social sanctions against divorce, and divorces carried little social stigma of any kind. In fact, divorce appeared to be culturally accepted and remarriage of divorced persons was expected and encouraged. Thirdly, the economic obstacles to divorce were not very strong, as the divorced woman readily derived financial support from her close kin, her children were easily taken care of by her relatives or given away for adoption, and remarrying was not an expensive affair. Finally, the predominantly urban Muslim population was quite mobile, resulting in many cases of desertion on the part of a spouse.

It would be interesting to see in what way the recent resurgence in both the non-Muslim and Muslim divorce rates has affected the three principal communities in Singapore. Fortunately, there are adequate statistics for the years 1980–2006 for us to examine this important question. The figures depicted in Table 7.3 are derived on the same basis as that for marriages by race in the previous chapter; it was assumed that the "Other" category does not include Malay divorces in the non-Muslim divorce statistics, and similarly, Chinese divorces in the Muslim statistics. The divorce rate for each of the races is based on the respective marriage figures in Table 6.2 as the denominator. The errors entailed in the assumption is very negligible since the figures in the "Other" category is extremely small. For instance, in 1991 there were only 13 "Other" non-Muslim divorces and 6 "Other" Muslim divorces.

Table 7.3 indicates that the recent deterioration in marital harmony was experienced by every one of the three major communities. From 1980 to 2006, Chinese divorces increased steadily from 926 to 3,942; Malay divorces from 380 to 1,460; and Indian divorces from 94 to 428. During the same period, the fastest upward movement in the incidence of divorce was recorded by the Indians, with the rate pushed up by 515

TABLE 7.3

Divorces and Divorce Rate for Three Main Races, 1980–2006

Year	Number of Divorces			Divorce Rate		
	Chinese	Malays	Indians	Chinese	Malays	Indians
1980	926	380	94	55.3	119.0	75.3
1981	1,103	472	109	60.3	135.1	81.0
1982	1,136	432	96	68.8	114.5	73.2
1983	1,209	549	115	78.2	150.1	81.7
1984	1,243	505	103	68.1	144.5	69.1
1985	1,125	579	136	67.2	162.9	89.6
1986	1,290	619	143	93.3	180.7	108.7
1987	1,321	639	131	78.1	179.4	96.0
1988	1,443	714	129	80.8	188.5	94.0
1989	1,429	712	141	85.9	189.2	96.4
1990	1,920	762	197	112.2	204.9	133.6
1991	2,502	801	184	139.6	215.1	124.1
1992	2,232	790	223	119.0	216.0	168.3
1993	2,293	996	203	125.3	285.6	149.0
1994	2,161	912	219	122.2	269.7	172.8
1995	2,689	803	276	149.5	245.6	216.3
1996	2,838	933	306	164.6	307.1	229.2
1997	2,998	1,015	283	159.8	317.5	233.7
1998	3,346	1,141	367	208.0	377.7	293.8
1999	2,897	1,183	280	155.0	405.3	255.7
2000	2,714	1,131	269	172.4	403.1	252.6
2001	2,882	1,015	265	190.2	348.4	255.5
2002	3,235	1,145	326	200.8	403.6	303.8
2003	3,425	1,640	357	237.6	596.6	416.6
2004	3,350	1,425	319	234.3	506.0	370.9
2005	3,967	1,481	368	255.4	582.6	382.5
2006	3,942	1,460	428	245.4	590.6	463.2

per cent from 75.3 to 463.2 per thousand marriages. The second fastest was experienced by the Malays, with the rate moving up by 396 per cent from 119.0 to 590.6, and the slowest by the Chinese which saw this rate rising up by 344 per cent from 75.3 to 245.4. Another noteworthy point shown in the table is that the Malays have always suffered the greatest breakdown in married life, while the least breakdown was experienced by the Chinese. The Indians occupied an intermediate position, but nearer to that of the Chinese, and even lower in 1991. The upswing in divorce incidence in Singapore has naturally generated some public debate and concern because of the adverse impact on the children of broken homes and the undesirable consequences of single parenthood, especially for the women.[10] The resurgence of marital instability among all religious and ethnic groups in the country underlines the pervasiveness of the factors contributing to this instability. It is generally believed that this is the price that a country must pay in the process of moving towards a more developed and open society, exposed to the influences of events happening in other parts of the world.

The recent rise in the rate of divorce in Singapore may be attributed to changing values attached to marriage and family life. For one thing, couples nowadays expect to attain greater happiness from their married life, and when this fails to materialise, they are more willing to seek divorce as a solution to their unhappy marriage. At the same time, there is a weakening in the role of the family in terms of economic, social, religious, recreational, and protective functions that used to be an integral part of family life. Many of these functions are gradually being taken over by educational institutions, religious organisations, community centres, recreational centres, and clubs. A decline in social and moral values has also been gathering pace with the breakup of the traditional extended kinship system and the rapid social and economic progress based on an open modernised economy. However, there still exist many forces that tend to hold the family together in Singapore, compared with many industrialised countries in the West where the divorce rate is very much higher.

DEMOGRAPHIC BACKGROUND OF DIVORCEES

Among the 4,696 non-Muslim divorces in 2005, no less than 3,967, or 84.5 per cent, were among Chinese couples, 299, or 6.4 per cent among Indian couples, and 37, or 0.8 per cent among couples from the minority groups. The remaining 342 or 7.3 per cent were among couples who had contracted interracial marriages. There are no figures for the Malays because Muslims cannot marry and divorce according to the provisions of the Women's Charter. As for the 1,873 Muslim divorces in 2005, there were 1,481 or 79.1 per cent among Malay couples, 69 or 3.7 per cent among Indian couples, and 8 or 0.2 per cent among couples from the minority groups. Interracial divorces accounted for as many as 315 or 16.8 per cent of the total Muslim divorces.

Couples contracting interracial marriages have to overcome certain inherent problems arising out of the differences in ethnicity and sometimes even religion.[11] Some of the more important problems are the conflict of values held by spouses from different cultural backgrounds, difficulties encountered with family members from both sides, and obstacles created by certain sections of society antagonistic towards such marriages. Such deleterious influences have been weakened over the years by rapid social and economic changes moving generally in the direction of modernisation and globalisation, engendering a gradual emergence of a new set of social and cultural values that are more conducive to interracial marriages.

An examination of the age patterns of male and female divorcees in 2006 is presented in Table 7.4. Among the male divorcees affected under the Women's Charter, about 6.6 per cent were under the age of 30, 42.2 per cent within the age group 30–39, and 51.2 per cent aged 40 and over. The non-Muslim female divorcees were much younger, with the three corresponding percentages standing at 16.7 per cent, 45.2 per cent, and 38.1 per cent. The resultant average age at the time of divorce was 40.6 years for non-Muslim male divorcees, and 37.1 years for the female counterparts. This is, of course, a reflection of the fact noted in the preceding chapter that when couples marry, the bride is almost always younger than the groom.

The same pattern of younger divorcees among the women than men also prevailed among couples divorced under the provisions of the

TABLE 7.4
Percentage Distribution of Divorcees by Type of Divorce and Sex and Age Group of Divorcees, 2006

Age Group	Male			Female		
	Non-Muslim	Muslim	Total	Non-Muslim	Muslim	Total
Under 30	6.6	19.5	10.4	16.7	32.7	21.3
30–39	42.2	38.1	41.0	45.2	36.9	42.8
40–49	30.7	30.2	30.6	23.6	22.9	23.4
50 & over	20.5	12.2	18.0	14.5	7.5	12.5
Total	100.0	100.0	100.0	100.0	100.0	100.0
Average Age	40.6	38.2	39.5	37.1	35.1	36.3

Administration of Muslim Law Act. Some 19.5 per cent of the Muslim male divorcees were under the age of 30, 38.1 per cent were between the ages of 30 and 39, and 42.4 per cent were aged 40 and over. In contrast, about one-third (32.7 per cent) of their female counterparts were under the age of 30, and about 30.4 per cent were aged 40 and above. The average age of Muslim male divorcees was 38.2 years, compared with 35.1 years for the female divorcees. Another noteworthy feature is that Muslim couples had their marriages dissolved at a relatively earlier age than the non-Muslim couples. It can be surmised that among other things, young Muslim couples seemed to be less able to cope with the responsibilities and pressures of early married life and parenthood.

Since there is a close association between race and religion in Singapore, it would be of some interest to examine the distribution of divorcees by religion. We can only do this for non-Muslim divorces, but not for Muslim divorces which must be effected under the Islamic law. Couples contracting marriages under the Woman's Charter can belong to different religions, and hence we have to scrutinise the data for male divorcees and female divorcees separately. Among the 4,188 non-Muslim male divorcees in 2003, 40.6 per cent were Buddhists, 10.9 per cent Christians, 2.2 per cent Taoists/Confucianists, and 4.0 per cent Hindus. As for their female counterparts, the four corresponding figures were 38.8 per cent, 11.5 per cent, 2.7 per cent and 3.7 per cent. It is also possible to have divorcees under the Women's Charter with no religion at all, and this was so for 17.6 per cent of the female divorcees and 24.5 per cent of the male divorcees, a reflection of the common tendency for women to be more religious then men. After 2003, the non-Muslim statistics according to the religion of divorcees ceased to be published.

MARITAL BACKGROUND OF DIVORCEES

Having obtained an idea of the demographic background of divorcees, we will proceed to look at their marital background so as to secure a better appreciation of the dynamics of divorce in Singapore. The first aspect that we will examine is the marital status of the divorcees at the time of marriage, as shown in Table 7.5. In this table, there are figures in the "married" row for Muslim male divorcees but not for Muslim female divorcees because according to Islamic law only men may practise polygamy. As for non-Muslim divorces, there are no "married" figures for both the males and females since all non-Muslim marriages must be

TABLE 7.5

Percentage Distribution of Divorcees by Type of Divorce and Sex and Previous Marital Status of Divorcees, 1984 and 2005

Previous Marital Status	Non-Muslim		Muslim	
	1984	**2005**	**1984**	**2005**
Male				
Single	97.2	80.5	87.9	79.8
Divorced	2.2	5.8	9.7	19.8
Widowed	0.6	0.5	1.6	0.1
Married	—	—	0.8	0.3
Not Stated	—	13.2	—	—
Total	100.0	100.0	100.0	100.0
Female				
Single	98.5	80.9	84.3	76.5
Divorced	1.1	5.5	12.9	23.3
Widowed	0.4	0.4	2.8	0.2
Not Stated	—	3.2	—	—
Total	100.0	100.0	100.0	100.0

monogamous. From 2004 onwards, statistics for the previous marital status of non-Muslim divorces have not been published.

The distribution of non-Muslim male divorcees in 1984 according to their marital status at the time of marriage was 97.2 per cent single, 2.2 per cent divorced, and 0.5 per cent widowed. By 2003, there was a drop in the proportion of singles to 80.5 per cent, while the proportion who were divorced was raised to 5.8 per cent. Similar shifts were experienced by the non-Muslim female divorcees during the same period, with the proportion of singles falling from 98.5 per cent to 80.9 per cent, and the proportion divorced moving up from 1.1 per cent to 5.5 per cent. The proportion of widowed persons at the time of marriage has remained somewhat stable over the years.

More significant changes were recorded by the Muslim divorcees. The figures for Muslim males show that the proportion divorced shot up from 9.7 per cent in 1984 to 19.8 per cent in 2005 compared to the drop in the proportion of singles at marriage from 87.9 per cent to 79.8 per cent, and the proportion widowed from 1.6 per cent to 0.2 per cent. Similar shifts were experienced by the Muslim female divorcees, with the proportion divorced expanding from 12.9 per cent to 23.3 per cent, and both the proportion of singles at marriage and widowed registering a reduction. It would appear that Muslim marriages involving at least one divorcee are exposed to a greater risk of marital discord, apart from the fact that this risk has been clearly on the uptrend in recent years. Since Muslim men are permitted to have more than one wife, we have in fact married men as a previous marital status, but the proportion of married men has fallen from 0.8 per cent in 1984 to 0.3 per cent in 2005.

A better way of analysing the relationship between previous marital status and Muslim divorces is to look at the divorce rate for the separate categories in marital status. In 2005, the divorce rate for Muslim men who were single at the time of marriage was 506 per thousand bachelors contracting Muslim marriages, compared with 21 for those widowed and 419 for those divorced. A similar pattern seemed to exist among the women, with the three corresponding rates standing at 490, 36 and 317 per thousand. However, there is no doubt that Muslim men and especially Muslim women whose marriages were dissolved at least once before are likely to have greater difficulties in forming a lasting relationship in a subsequent marriage.

Another aspect of the marital background of divorcees meriting some attention is the age at marriage. The majority of the non-Muslim male divorcees in 2005 were married between the ages of 25 and 29, with 42.2 per cent. This was closely followed by 26.5 per cent between the ages of 20 and 24, and 29.8 per cent for those aged 30 and over, and 1.5 per cent for those aged under 20. In contrast, the age at marriage of non-Muslim divorced women was concentrated in the younger age group 20–24, with 45.5 per cent followed by 28.9 in the older age group 25–29. Almost the same pattern seems to exist among the Muslim couples who divorced in 2005, with a much higher proportion of female divorcees having married under the age of 20. The proportion of those marrying under the age of 20 amounted to 4.7 per cent for the Muslim male divorcees and 19.5 per cent for their female counterparts.

It may be observed that among both the non-Muslim and Muslim divorcees a very much higher proportion of female divorcees than male divorcees married at very young ages. The most likely explanation may be the inability of the young wives to cope with the problems and pressures confronting their married life. Most of the young wives were still socially and emotionally immature and found it difficult to adjust to married life. In addition to those who had a premarital pregnancy, the other young wives also tended to have children at an early age and to have to face the additional burden of parenthood. Relatively more of the young wives came from low educational and poor economic backgrounds, and their adjustment to being wife and mother was further exacerbated by financial difficulties.[12]

For a better understanding of the pattern of divorce, we will examine the data given in Table 7.6 in respect of the number of years the couples stayed married before they were divorced. For non-Muslim marriages, the risk of a marital breakdown was the greatest during the second five years of married life, followed by the second greatest risk occurring during the third five years of married life. In sharp contrast, the risk of Muslim marriages ending up in divorce was the greatest during the first five years of married life, and this risk was reduced rapidly as the marriages last longer. The average duration of the whole group of divorced Muslim couples was 9.5 years in 2006, compared with the corresponding figure of 11.9 years for non-Muslim couples. It may be recalled that under the Women's Charter couples cannot petition for a divorce if they have been married for less than three years, but there is no such restriction in the case of Muslim marriages. The shorter marriage

TABLE 7.6

Percentage Distribution of Divorcees by Type of Divorce and Marriage Duration, 1984 and 2006

Years of Duration	Non-Muslim		Muslim	
	1984	2006	1984	2006
Under 5	8.3	13.2	36.6	33.6
5–9	45.3	36.3	28.3	27.1
10–14	21.6	19.7	18.6	15.4
15–19	12.2	11.1	7.3	10.2
20–24	7.1	8.3	5.5	6.7
25 and over	5.4	11.3	3.6	7.0
Total	100.0	100.0	100.0	100.0
Average Duration	11.6	11.9	9.0	9.5

duration of Muslim marriages is another consequence of the relatively higher divorce incidence among the Muslim community.

The distribution of the number of dependent children under age 21 at the time of marital dissolution is presented in Table 7.7 for 1984 and 2003. Similar statistics are no longer made available from 2004 onwards. A substantial proportion of couples whose marriages broke down did not have any children at all; they comprised 32.7 per cent of non-Muslim couples and 29.0 per cent of Muslim couples in 1984. These two percentages were raised to 52.2 and 32.1 respectively in 2003. One of the reasons for these childless couples to dissolve their marriage was of course the inability to produce children. Furthermore, some childless couples were more prepared to resort to divorce for other reasons since there were no children to bind them together. The increasing tendency for childless couples to dissolve their marriage contract has naturally led to a fall in the proportion of couples with children during the same period, moving down steeply from 67.3 per cent to 47.8 per cent in the case of non-Muslim divorces, and slightly, from 71.0 per cent to 67.9 per cent for Muslim divorces.

In spite of the above changes, there is still a greater chance for couples with children than those without to resort to divorce as a final solution to their marital dissension. Among the non-Muslim divorced couples in 2003, about 26.1 per cent had one dependent child and 16.9 per cent had two dependent children. A small group of 4.3 per cent had three dependent children, while slightly less than 1 per cent had four or

TABLE 7.7

Percentage Distribution of Divorcees by Type of Divorce and Number of Dependent Children, 1984 and 2003

Number of Dependent Children	1984			2003		
	Non-Muslim	Muslim	Total	Non-Muslim	Muslim	Total
0	32.7	29.0	31.6	52.2	32.1	45.5
1	30.9	29.4	30.4	26.1	26.3	26.2
2	25.8	22.1	24.6	16.9	22.1	18.6
3	8.3	11.6	9.4	4.3	13.7	7.4
4 and over	2.3	7.9	4.0	0.5	5.8	2.3
Total	100.0	100.0	100.0	100.0	100.0	100.0

more. Among the Muslim divorced couples, about the same proportion had one child (26.3 per cent) and two dependent children (22.1 per cent). A much larger proportion (13.7 per cent) had three dependent children and a conspicuous proportion (5.8 per cent) had four or more dependent children. The hearing of divorce proceedings in respect of couples with dependent children are of course more complicated since the question of child custody and visiting rights has to be resolved.

REASONS FOR DIVORCE

We have observed the differences in the procedure for seeking a divorce under the Women's Charter and the Administration of Muslim Law Act and also in the legal grounds for divorce as laid down in these two legislations. The statistics in respect of legal grounds for divorce are compiled and published in two different formats for the two types of marriages, and they cannot be combined to give the overall position for Singapore. It is therefore necessary for us to present two separate accounts of the reasons for marital dissolutions, and this might even be preferred since the two types of marriages are exposed to somewhat different influences and divorce procedures.

It would be useful to comment on the reliability of the statistics for the causes of divorce compiled from the divorce case files kept by the High Court and from the register of divorces maintained in the Shariah Court. First, the divorces are tabulated according to one cause of divorce as stated officially in the case files or the register. In practice, there are usually many reasons that lead the petitioners to take the final step to seek a dissolution of their marriage, and at best the legal ground appearing in the statistical tables may be considered as the principal reason. Secondly, there is always the possibility that the reported ground for divorce may not necessarily reflect the underlying reason for the marital breakdown. The petitioners may decide to choose to write down the reason which would be most adequate for the purpose of securing the divorce in the High Court or the Shariah Court and which would engender the least personal pain and public embarrassment.

The data given in Table 7.8 were compiled according to the main grounds for petitioning for a divorce under the Women's Charter, as described earlier. It would appear that the relative importance of individual grounds has changed in recent years. The proportion of decrees granted for adultery was reduced from 8.5 per cent in 1984 to 2.1 per cent in

TABLE 7.8

Percentage Distribution of Non-Muslim Divorces by Reason for Divorce, 1984–2006

Year	Adultery	Desertion	Unreasonable Behaviour	Separation	Other Reasons	Total
1984	8.5	19.3	—	61.2	11.0	100.0
1985	8.6	19.1	—	58.5	13.8	100.0
1986	8.3	14.8	—	60.7	16.2	100.0
1987	6.9	14.8	—	61.3	17.0	100.0
1988	6.9	13.7	—	57.8	21.6	100.0
1989	6.4	9.7	—	58.0	25.9	100.0
1990	6.3	8.6	—	59.2	25.9	100.0
1991	4.9	8.3	24.3	62.5	0.0	100.0
1992	5.6	7.3	31.6	55.5	0.0	100.0
1993	4.3	5.5	28.6	61.6	0.0	100.0
1994	3.9	4.7	33.9	57.5	0.0	100.0
1995	4.6	5.2	35.6	54.6	0.0	100.0
1996	4.2	4.7	37.0	54.0	0.1	100.0
1997	3.7	4.2	38.0	54.1	0.0	100.0
1998	3.4	3.7	40.8	51.9	0.2	100.0
1999	2.6	3.5	44.8	48.1	1.0	100.0
2000	3.4	0.0	43.1	50.7	2.8	100.0
2001	2.2	0.0	41.8	45.9	10.1	100.0
2002	2.2	0.0	45.4	49.6	2.8	100.0
2003	2.2	0.0	48.7	46.9	2.2	100.0
2004	1.8	1.8	46.0	50.3	0.1	100.0
2005	1.9	2.1	47.0	48.9	0.1	100.0
2006	2.1	1.6	48.7	47.5	0.0	100.0

2006. A much greater reduction in the proportion of decrees granted for desertion was recorded during the same period, being lowered from 19.3 per cent to 1.6 per cent. No clear trend was registered by the proportion for separation, oscillating around 60 per cent in the early years and thereafter down slightly to 54.1 per cent in 1997, and finally to 47.5 per cent in 2006. As a result of the diminished importance of the first two reasons in the eighties, the proportion for all the other grounds for divorce has moved up from 11.0 per cent in 1984 to 25.9 per cent in 1990. Thereafter, this figure has become very negligible with the introduction of a new ground known as "Unreasonable Behaviour", which accounted for 24.3 per cent in 1991, and rose to 48.7 per cent in 2006. Notwithstanding the recent changes, separation has remained as the most popular reason used by spouses seeking a divorce under the

Women's Charter because it is an anodyne ground for divorce proceedings. The other major reason has been unreasonable behaviour.

Information about the party to whom the divorce was granted under the Women's Charter throws further light on the nature of marital dissolution. In 2005 about two-thirds of the divorce proceedings were instituted by the wife. Looking at the legal grounds for these proceedings, proportionately more husbands (3.9 per cent) than wives (1.3 per cent) petitioned on the ground of desertion. The same is true in the case of separation which was cited by 64.3 per cent of the husbands and 42.4 per cent of the wives, and also in the case of adultery mentioned by 4.0 per cent of the husbands and 3.6 per cent of the wives.

As Table 7.9 shows, the most common ground used by Muslim couples to obtain a divorce in 2006 was personality differences of the

TABLE 7.9
Percentage Distribution of Muslim Divorces
by Reason for Divorce, 1984–2006

Year	Infidelity	Desertion	Inadequate Maintenance	Assault	Personality Difference	Other Reasons	Total
1984	14.9	6.6	14.3	2.0	39.9	22.3	100.0
1985	12.7	9.3	13.6	2.2	38.5	23.7	100.0
1986	10.9	6.6	22.0	2.8	36.8	20.9	100.0
1987	12.2	6.4	17.3	4.8	28.0	31.3	100.0
1988	11.9	3.8	21.6	4.4	31.4	26.9	100.0
1989	17.9	2.9	17.6	4.6	33.5	23.5	100.0
1990	16.8	3.5	17.2	6.8	32.5	23.2	100.0
1991	17.7	3.6	16.0	4.1	34.1	24.5	100.0
1992	19.8	3.0	14.5	4.7	37.8	20.2	100.0
1993	16.8	4.3	16.1	6.0	42.3	14.5	100.0
1994	15.6	1.9	17.4	3.5	46.8	14.8	100.0
1995	8.0	3.8	8.9	3.5	52.2	23.6	100.0
1996	0.9	2.6	0.4	0.4	91.9	3.8	100.0
1997	12.3	5.5	2.7	0.4	40.0	14.1	100.0
1998	9.7	8.9	2.3	0.3	30.4	48.4	100.0
1999	6.9	7.2	3.9	0.7	35.4	45.9	100.0
2000	8.6	8.3	4.0	1.5	28.4	49.2	100.0
2001	9.1	3.3	14.9	0.7	38.2	33.8	100.0
2002	16.7	1.4	5.9	3.3	39.8	32.9	100.0
2003	15.7	1.0	3.0	2.3	42.7	35.3	100.0
2004	18.6	1.8	16.6	1.9	29.9	31.2	100.0
2005	18.2	2.5	15.1	1.8	29.2	33.2	100.0
2006	16.9	3.3	14.5	4.0	21.6	39.7	100.0

marriage partners, which was cited by 21.6 per cent of the couples. Infidelity appeared to be the second major problem as 16.9 per cent of the divorces were granted on this ground. The next cause of divorce was inadequate maintenance, which was the root of the trouble for 14.5 per cent of the marital dissolutions. This was followed by assault, with 4.6 per cent, and desertion, with 3.3 per cent. The "Other Reasons" mentioned in the table would include drinking, gambling, drug taking, mental illness, in-law problems, and polygamy. Polygamy on the part of the husband is a minor cause of divorce (0.6 per cent in 1989) because it is practised on a very small scale.

The time series data given in the same table reveal a slight shift in the pattern of grounds of divorce in recent years. The two causes which have assumed lesser importance are desertion and personality difference, the former falling from 6.6 per cent in 1984 to 3.3 per cent in 2006, and the latter from 39.9 per cent to 21.6 per cent during the same period. Infidelity rose in relative importance in the early nineties, falling in the nineties, but rose again in recent years. The exceptionally high proportion of 91.9 per cent citing personality differences recorded in 1996 has made it difficult to evaluate the changes at that time. There seems to be collection and recording errors in the compilation of statistics in that year.

A greater understanding of the breakdown of Muslim marriages is underlined by the statistics cross-classified by reason of divorce and petitioner given in Table 7.10. It may be recalled that the three types of

TABLE 7.10
Percentage Distribution of Muslim Divorces
by Reason for Divorce, 2005

Reason	Husband	Wife	Joint	Total
Personality Differences	45.3	19.3	41.7	29.2
Infidelity	17.6	19.9	11.7	18.2
Inadequate Maintenance	1.4	23.4	4.5	15.1
Neglect/Irresponsibility	10.4	15.4	2.3	12.2
Nagging/Complaining	2.7	0.7	25.9	4.8
Other Reasons	22.6	21.3	13.9	20.5
Total	100.0	100.0	100.0	100.0

Muslim divorce which can be granted to a wife are known as *khuluk*, *cerai taklik* and *fasakh*, while the one granted to a husband is known as *talak*. In addition, the Shariah Court has the authority to hear and grant a divorce by mutual consent to a couple submitting a joint petition. Among the total number of divorces granted in 2005 slightly less than two-thirds (60.0 per cent) were petitioned by the wife and about one-quarter (25.8 per cent) by the husband. Less than one-fifth (14.2 per cent) of the divorces were jointly petitioned by the couples. Judging from similar time series information, this pattern has not changed very much in recent years.

Some interesting differences in the cause of divorce may be observed to exist among the three types of petitioners. Among the husbands granted divorce in 2005, the most common cause given was personality differences with 45.3 per cent, followed by infidelity with 17.6 per cent. The third position was taken up by neglect/irresponsibility with 10.4 per cent, and fourth by nagging/complaining with 2.7 per cent. The other reasons identified as inadequate maintenance, drug rehabilitation centre (DRC) or imprisonment, and assault are relatively unimportant. The four most important reasons cited by the wives were inadequate maintenance (23.4 per cent), infidelity (19.9 per cent), personality differences (19.3 per cent), and neglect/irresponsibility (15.4 per cent). Compared to the husbands, very few wives (only 0.7 per cent) cited nagging/complaining as the cause of divorce. In the case of joint petitions, about 41.7 per cent of the divorces were granted on the ground that the marriage had failed due to personality differences. This was followed by nagging/complaining (25.9 per cent) and infidelity (11.7 per cent).

Notes

1. *Singapore, Statistics on Marriages and Divorces 1984* (Singapore: Department of Statistics, n.d.).
2. Sections 84 and 94 of the Women's Charter.
3. M. B. Hooker, *Islamic Law in South-East Asia* (Kuala Lumpur: Oxford University Press, 1984); and Mohamed Din bin Ali, "Malay Customary Law and Family", *Intisari* 2, no. 2 (1965).
4. For a good account of the Shariah Court, see Judith Djamour, *The Muslim Matrimonial Court in Singapore* (London: Athlone Press, 1966).
5. Tai Ching Ling, "Divorce in Singapore", in *The Contemporary Family in Singapore*, edited by Eddie C. Y. Kuo and Aline K. Wong (Singapore: Singapore University Press, 1979).

6. Aline K. Wong and Eddie C. Y. Kuo, eds. *Divorce in Singapore* (Singapore: Graham Brash, 1983).

7. *Straits Times*, 20 May 1998.

8. Singapore, *Report on the Registration of Births and Deaths, Marriages and Persons* (Singapore: Government Printing Office, n.d.).

9. Djamour, op. cit.

10. See, for instance, "Shariah Court Works to Help Troubled Couples", *Straits Times*, 15 November 1988; and "Divorce: A Malay Worry", *Sunday Times*, 12 March 1989.

11. Wong and Kuo, op. cit.

12. Saw Swee-Hock, "Muslim Divorce Trends and Patterns in Singapore", *Genus* 48, no. 2 (1992).

8

Fertility Trends and Differentials

In Singapore there was the emergence of government concern at various times on certain aspects of the demography of the country and the subsequent implementation of government measures that had a direct or indirect impact on the future course of population trends. In the area of fertility, we have included the next two chapters to present a detailed account of government measures first introduced in the mid-1960s to encourage a reduction in fertility and the recent adjustment of the antinatalist policy to encourage more births. The effect of government measures will be touched upon in this chapter on fertility trends and differentials.

A general survey of fertility trends up to 1946 and a more thorough appraisal for the post-war period when comprehensive data became available will be presented. The complete absence of vital statistics make it impossible to cover the period prior to 1878, and even the information published during the first few decades after this period is grossly lacking in detail and reliability. The analysis of fertility differentials during the post-war period will be confined to the three main races who display marked differences explainable in terms of their divergent social, cultural, and economic development.

GENERAL FERTILITY TRENDS

In examining the general trends in fertility, we can go as far back as 1878 when birth statistics from the vital registration system were first made available. Even so, the births for the pre-war years were not tabulated according to the age of mothers, and hence the superior fertility indices such as the gross reproduction rate (GRR) and the total fertility rate

(TFR) cannot be calculated. What we can derive is the crude birth rate defined as the number of births per thousand population. In utilising the statistics, we have also decided to present the births and the computed crude birth rate in Table 8.1 in terms of five-year periods in order to remove the somewhat erratic annual fluctuations and to enable us to focus our attention on the long-term movements. The population denominator adopted to calculate the rates refers to the average of the five mid-year populations in each given period.

TABLE 8.1
Annual Average Births and Crude Birth Rates, 1876–2005

Period	Annual Average Births	Crude Birth Rates
1878–80	835	6.5
1881–85	2,201	15.0
1886–90	2,770	16.4
1891–95	3,310	17.3
1896–00	3,835	17.1
1901–05	5,113	21.2
1906–10	6,051	22.3
1911–15	7,693	23.9
1916–20	9,819	26.5
1921–25	13,418	29.5
1926–30	18,991	34.3
1931–35	22,280	40.5
1936–40	31,643	45.9
1941–45	29,897	36.5
1946–50	43,738	44.8
1951–55	53,693	47.8
1956–60	61,877	41.0
1961–65	58,476	33.4
1966–70	48,595	24.2
1971–75	45,650	20.8
1976–80	40,517	17.2
1981–85	41,906	16.8
1986–90	46,753	17.3
1991–95	49,386	15.1
1996–00	45,981	11.9
2001–05	38,872	9.2

The movement in the annual average number of births during the sixty-year period before World War II was clearly upwards without any break. Ignoring the statistics for the first period 1878–80, which were not reliable, the average number of births rose steadily from 2,201 in 1981–85 to 9,819 in 1916–20 and then rapidly to 31,643 in 1936–40. Except for a dip in 1896–1900, the crude birth rate also experienced a similar long-term trend; it went up very slowly from 15.0 in 1881–85 to 26.5 in 1916–20, and then relatively faster to reach the high of 45.9 in 1936–40. The continuous uptrend in the crude birth rate in Singapore from an initially low level seems to be in direct contrast to the experience of most European countries when the trend during the same period was predominantly downward from an initially high level.[1] But, while the downward movement in these countries was the result of a genuine fall in fertility, the upward trend in Singapore was caused not so much by a rise in fertility as by a gradual improvement in the completeness of birth registration and by a normalising of the sex ratio noted earlier. These two reasons were repeatedly emphasised by the Registration-General in his early reports.

For example, the 1886 report states: "I am still of the opinion, however, that birth registration in this settlement is far from being as thorough as one would wish to see it, and that many, especially among the Chinese, omit to register the births of their children ... either from ignorance or for the purpose of evading vaccination. We cannot, therefore, accept the figures above as being very accurate. Even making allowance for the disproportion known to exist between male and female... a high birth rate could certainly be shown if we had at hand the material wherewith to work the ordinance properly".[2] The extremely low birth rate of 6.5 in the first period 1878–80 must be due to incomplete registration during the experimental years of registering births. However, the other factor began to exert a greater influence over time, especially during the 1930s when the sex ratio improved significantly.

A reversal in the uptrend occurred during 1941–45 when a drop in the annual average number of births and the crude birth rate was recorded. The former fell from 31,643 in 1936–40 to 29,897 in 1941–45 and the latter from 45.9 to 36.5 over the same period. The explanation for the rather low birth rate during the Japanese Occupation lies in the postponement of marriages and/or births on account of the extremely difficult economic and social conditions at that time. The recovery after the war was almost immediate and the crude birth rate went up to

44.8 in the first post-war period 1946–50 and rose further to peak at 47.8 in 1951–55. The subsequent decline in the crude birth rate engendered by a genuine decline in fertility will be discussed in greater detail in the next section.

FERTILITY TRANSITION

After World War II, the number of births rose year after year, from 43,045 in 1947 to a peak of 62,495 in 1958. The crude birth rate remained exceptionally high, above 45 per thousand population up to 1954, after which it began to fall. An interesting question naturally arises whether the latter phenomenon marks the beginning of a change in the level of fertility. There is evidence to show that the drop in the crude birth rate, which attracted considerable attention at that time among those connected with the private family planning movement, was caused entirely by a reduction in the proportion of women in the reproductive ages, brought about by the entry of a relatively smaller number of women than usual into the reproductive age range. This smaller cohort of women, resulting from the low birth rate and high infant mortality during the war years 1941–45, would by 1957 have consisted of women within the ages of 13 to 16. This, coupled with the increasing proportion of women born after this cohort, caused the proportion of women of reproductive age to the total population to be lowered from 23.0 per cent in 1947 to 21.7 per cent in 1957.

That the level of fertility was not reduced at all may be seen in the figures for the total fertility rate (TFR) shown in Table 8.2. This rate is defined as the average number of children produced by each woman during her whole reproductive period. It is a reliable measure of fertility level, being unaffected by changes in the sex-age structure of the population. After moving downwards from 6.55 in 1947 to 6.18 in 1951, the rate went up again to reach the all-time high of 6.56 in 1957. The extremely high fertility rate prevailing during the first post-war decade or so may be attributed to attitudes and beliefs which were deeply embedded in the cultural and religious traditions prevalent at that time.

First, there was the interaction of the lower mean age at first marriage of women, the high marriage rate and the larger proportion ultimately married. At that time, women were expected to marry early; marriage was universal; and celibacy found little social acceptance among the people. Secondly, the average size of a family was very large,

TABLE 8.2
Birth, Crude Birth Rate and Total Fertility Rate, 1947–1975

Year	Number of Births	Crude Birth Rate	Total Fertility Rate	Annual Change (%)		
				Births	CBR	TFR
1947	43,045	45.9	6.55	—	—	—
1948	44,450	46.3	6.46	+3.3	+0.9	−1.4
1949	46,169	47.2	6.42	+3.9	+1.9	−0.6
1950	46,371	45.4	6.20	+0.4	−3.8	−3.4
1951	48,116	45.0	6.18	+3.8	−0.9	−0.3
1952	51,196	45.4	6.30	+6.4	+0.9	+1.9
1953	54,548	45.8	6.47	+6.6	+0.9	+2.7
1954	57,028	45.7	6.52	+4.6	−0.2	+0.8
1955	57,812	44.3	6.39	+1.4	−3.1	−2.0
1956	60,892	44.4	6.54	+5.3	+2.3	+2.3
1957	61,757	42.7	6.56	+1.4	−3.8	+0.3
1958	62,495	41.1	6.39	+1.2	−3.8	−2.6
1959	62,464	39.4	6.14	0.0	−4.1	−3.9
1960	61,775	37.5	5.80	−1.1	−4.8	−5.5
1961	59,930	35.2	5.46	−3.0	−6.1	−5.9
1962	58,977	33.7	5.26	−1.6	−4.3	−3.7
1963	59,530	33.2	5.17	+0.9	−1.5	−1.7
1964	58,217	31.6	4.95	−2.2	−9.6	−4.3
1965	55,725	29.5	4.62	−4.3	−6.7	−6.7
1966	54,680	28.3	4.42	−1.9	−4.1	−4.3
1967	50,560	25.6	3.95	−7.5	−9.5	−10.6
1968	47,241	23.5	3.50	−6.6	−8.2	−11.4
1969	44,561	21.8	3.15	−5.7	−7.2	−10.0
1970	45,934	22.1	3.10	+3.1	+1.4	−1.6
1971	47,088	22.3	3.06	+2.5	+0.9	−1.3
1972	49,678	23.1	3.07	+5.5	+3.6	+0.3
1973	48,269	22.0	2.81	−2.8	−4.8	−8.5
1974	43,268	19.4	2.37	−10.4	−11.8	−15.7
1975	39,948	17.7	2.08	−7.7	−8.8	−12.2

which was partly a manifestation of the tradition of desiring large families among all the races. Among the many and varied factors favouring large families were the desire for male heirs, deep-rooted religious injunctions, and the Asian form of extended family and kinship system. Lastly, the people in general did not practise family planning to such a significant extent as to influence fertility level. The idea of reducing mortality level through medical and public health measures had long been accepted by the masses, but the notion of taking concrete steps to space as well as to limit the number of children ultimately produced was something new and revolutionary in the minds of the public at that time.

While the decade up to 1957 was dominated by a very high level of fertility that remained fairly stable, the period following was equally noteworthy for the sustained decline in fertility. As can be observed from the total fertility rate in Table 8.2, the decline in fertility commenced in 1958, some ten years after family planning services were made available by the Family Planning Association. The initial fall of 2.6 per cent in that year was edged up and sustained at the moderate reduction of less than 6 per cent per annum in most years until 1966. During the second year of the national programme in 1967, the decline gathered momentum with a fall of 10.6 per cent, and continued to do so at an accelerated reduction rate of 11.4 per cent in 1968 and 10.0 per cent in 1969.

The next few years saw the fertility decline slackening dramatically to 1.6 per cent in 1970 and 1.3 per cent in 1971, and subsequently coming to a virtual halt in 1972 when a small rise of 0.3 per cent was recorded. The most plausible explanation for these adverse trends is that the women, who had earlier become acceptors of family planning during the first four years of the national programme to space their children, were now beginning to produce their postponed births. The fertility increase in 1972, coupled with the upturn in the number of births and the crude birth rate between 1970 and 1972, was viewed with some anxiety and concern by the government and led to the tightening of old incentive and disincentive measures and the introduction of new ones to reinforce the population control programme.

After the postponed births had been translated into actual births and as the population control programmes were strengthened, fertility decline continued at a rapid pace, with a drop of 8.5 per cent in 1973. Although this decline was not as precipitous as that experienced between 1967 and 1969, its significance in the context of the prevailing low fertility level can hardly be over-emphasised. This noteworthy achievement was soon eclipsed by the spectacular fall of 15.7 per cent in 1974, followed by another impressive reduction of 12.2 per cent in the following year, pushing the total fertility rate to 2.08 in 1975. This is slightly below the rate of 2.15 which is the level required to ensure that the population will

FIGURE 8.1

Total Fertility Rate and Births, 1947–2006

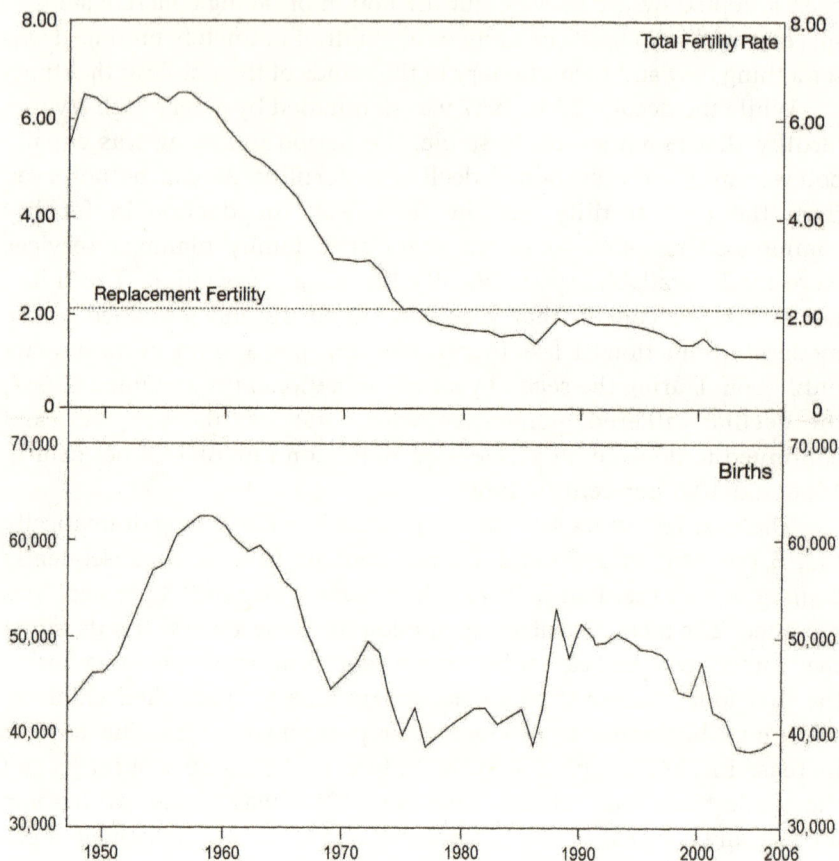

just replace itself in the future. It is estimated that according to current mortality experience, the total fertility rate will approximate 2.15 when the net reproduction rate is exactly 1.00.

The spectacular performance achieved by Singapore in the area of fertility transition from a high to replacement level in the last eighteen years may be traced to a combination of factors, some of which are interdependent. The commencement of fertility decline in 1958 was triggered off by the rising age at first marriage of women and reinforced by the reduction in the proportion of women ultimately married. In addition, there was the catalytic role played by the private family planning programme which had been providing not only clinical services to new and old acceptors, but also educational and motivational activities to create the general acceptance of family planning for almost ten years prior to the decline of fertility in 1958. The downward movement in fertility was maintained and accelerated in the late 1960s by the introduction of the effective government family planning programme in 1966.

The remarkable fertility decline during 1973–75, following the earlier slowdown, was due to the adoption of measures beyond family planning. By far the most important of these measures was the legalisation of induced abortion to make it available to pregnant women on a restrictive basis in 1970 and subsequently on demand in 1975. There was also the simultaneous legalisation of voluntary sterilisation to make ligation and vasectomy available to women and men on a somewhat restrictive basis in 1970 and on demand in 1975. Furthermore, the early 1970s witnessed the introduction of incentive and disincentive measures in the areas of maternity leave, accouchement fees, income tax, housing and education aimed at promoting the two-child family and sterilisation. A comprehensive account of the development of the population control programme in Singapore will be presented in the next two chapters.

We must not forget the interaction of cultural, social and economic forces that have come into play during the whole process of fertility transition since 1958. There are the cultural and social variables experienced in terms of modernisation, higher educational attainment, changing attitudes towards the value of children and family size, the breakdown of the extended family system, and the increasing scarcity of domestic help. Consideration should also be given to the impact of rapid economic progress, as reflected in a higher standard of living and greater participation of women in the labour force. The enhanced labour force participation tended to encourage single women to postpone marriage or remain permanently unmarried, and to induce married women to space or terminate their childbearing. Finally, we must mention the role of the government in Singapore in the complex process of fertility transition. As observed in the previous chapter, there was great political will on the part of the PAP government in the implementation of a strong and comprehensive population control programme. The fertility transition from high to replacement level was completed within 18 years in Singapore, a much shorter time-period than that taken by Japan, South Korea, Taiwan, and Hong Kong.

FERTILITY CHANGES BY AGE

An analysis of the pattern of fertility declines over the various reproductive age groups is presented in Table 8.3. In calculating the age-specific fertility rates, the relatively small number of female births to women under 15 and above 49 years has been included in the 15–19 age group and the 45–49 age group respectively. The small number of births with the age of mothers not stated has been prorated to the relevant five-year age groups according to the known age distribution of the mothers. It has been established that among the countries of the world there are three basic patterns of fertility according to age: the early-peak type in which fertility is highest at ages 20–24, the late-peak type in which peak fertility occurs at ages 25–29, and the broad-peak type characterised by maximum and nearly uniform fertility levels in the age groups 20–24 and 25–29.[3] The figures show that the age pattern of fertility in Singapore resembled that of the broad-peak type prior to the commencement of fertility decline, after which it shifted to the late-peak type and has remained so ever since, notwithstanding the profound changes in the rates.

TABLE 8.3
Age-Specific Fertility Rates, 1947–1975

Age Group	1947	1952	1957	1962	1967	1972	1975
				Rates			
15–19	101.8	89.2	78.0	52.5	35.8	25.7	16.9
20–24	314.1	331.6	302.7	247.4	195.4	138.3	102.2
25–29	333.8	309.8	354.6	291.6	246.1	219.5	154.7
30–34	269.7	254.7	289.5	230.3	166.7	140.1	95.0
35–39	196.3	184.9	194.8	156.0	95.9	66.6	36.3
40–44	83.3	80.7	81.3	64.7	42.8	21.1	10.0
45–49	10.6	10.1	11.8	9.1	7.7	3.0	1.2
			Percentage Change				
15–19		−12.4	−12.6	−32.7	−31.8	−28.2	−34.2
20–24		+5.6	−8.7	−18.3	−21.0	−29.2	−26.1
25–29		−7.2	+14.5	−17.8	−15.6	−10.8	−29.5
30–34		−5.5	+13.6	−20.4	−27.6	−16.0	−32.2
35–39		−5.8	+5.4	−19.9	−38.5	−30.6	−45.5
40–44		−3.1	+0.7	−20.4	−33.8	−50.7	−52.6
45–19		−4.7	+16.8	−22.9	−15.4	−61.0	−60.0

Prior to the commencement of fertility decline in 1958, there was a minor shift in the pattern of fertility spanning all age groups. During the first five-year period 1947–52, a small increase in fertility rate was recorded by the quinary age group 20–24, and an equally minor decrease was recorded by the other three age groups between 25 and 49. A more significant change can be seen in the pronounced drop of 12.4 per cent registered in the teenage group 15–19. This tendency continued into the next period 1952–57 when this youngest age group again experienced the largest reduction, amounting to 12.6 per cent. A drop was also recorded in the next age group 20–24, while a rise was experienced by the five older age groups. By and large, these were relatively minor shifts in the pattern that did not affect very much the overall level of fertility and were less significant than the new developments that emerged after 1957.

During the first five-year period of fertility decline from 1957 to 1962, a reduction ranging from 18 per cent to 23 per cent was recorded by the age groups from 20 onwards. As for the teenage group 15–19, a much steeper fall of some 32.7 per cent was experienced. The greater reduction among the youngest age group appears to be different from the pattern observed in Western Europe[4] and Taiwan[5] where the decreases during the initial phase of fertility transition were concentrated among women in the older age groups. Considerable significance may be attached to this difference in the initial path towards lower fertility. The women who were having fewer children at the young age were likely to have fewer children when they became older, thus affecting the fertility of the older age groups in the years ahead. Moreover, the somewhat equal decreases at the second age group upwards would mean that the population would grow more slowly in the long run because of the increasing average length of the new generation.

The more pronounced decline experienced by women in the youngest age group, coupled with the large decline they had experienced prior to the onset of overall fertility decline in 1958, suggests that the fertility decline in Singapore, in the absence of illegitimate births, was triggered off mainly by a rise in the average age at first marriage. According to the population census data, the median age group at first marriage of women had risen from 19.8 years for the cohort marrying during 1946–50 to 20.2 for the cohort marrying during 1951–55, 21.4 for the cohort marrying during 1956–60, and 22.5 for the cohort marrying during 1961–65.[6] According to data from the registration of marriages, the average age at first marriage of women went up from 22.2 years in 1961 to 23.0 years in 1965.[7] As mentioned in the previous chapter, the trend towards later marriage was caused by, among other things, women achieving higher educational attainment and greater participation in the labour force. Moreover, the minimum age of marriage for both bride and groom under the Women's Charter was raised from 16 to 18 years with effect from September 1961, and a few years later, in 1966, the minimum age for girls marrying under the Muslim law was raised from 15 to 16.

FIGURE 8.2

Age-Specific Fertility Rates, 1947–77

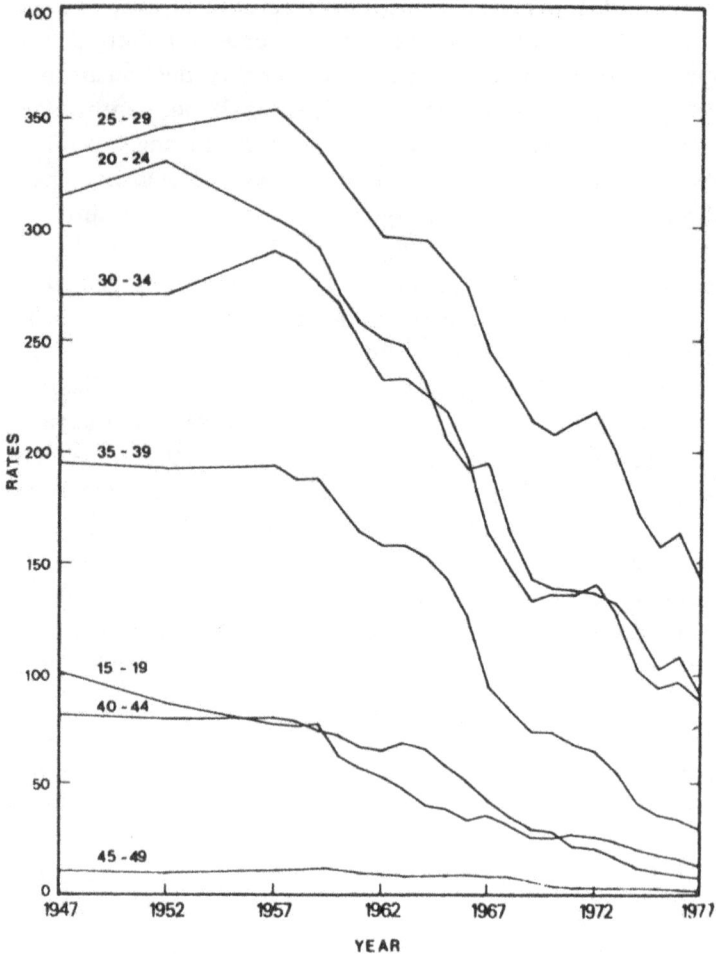

The subsequent levelling off in the rise in marriage age and the extensive use of birth control to limit family size after the introduction of the government family planning programme in 1966 caused the pattern of fertility declines to take on a new direction whereby the older women were experiencing a larger reduction. Signs of this tendency began to emerge during the period 1962–67 when women in the two age groups between 35 and 44 experienced a larger reduction of 38.5 per cent and 33.8 per cent respectively. The swing towards larger decreases among the older groups not only continued but became more pronounced after 1967 when the emphasis of the population control programme was aimed at the high parity women who were to be found in the older age groups. Indeed, during the period 1967–72 the greatest reduction of 61.0 per cent was recorded by the oldest age group 45–49, and the second largest of 50.7 per cent by the second oldest age group. The relatively larger reductions in the older age groups were not only maintained but reinforced during the next period 1972–75.

Another aspect of the changes in fertility at various ages may be illustrated by considering the relative contribution of each age group to gross total fertility. This contribution is measured by adding the fertility rate for each age group and determining the percentage of the rate for each age group to the total. These percentages are displayed in Table 8.4 for four specified calendar years. The relative contribution of women in the youngest age group declined continuously during the period under

TABLE 8.4
Relative Contribution of Each Age Group to
Gross Total Fertility, 1947–1975

Age Group	1947	1957	1967	1975
15–19	7.8	5.9	4.5	4.1
20–24	24.0	23.1	24.7	24.5
25–29	25.5	27.0	31.1	37.2
30–34	20.6	22.1	21.1	22.8
35–39	15.0	14.8	12.1	8.7
40–44	6.4	6.2	5.4	2.4
45–49	0.8	0.9	1.0	0.3
Total	100.0	100.0	100.0	100.0

consideration, moving down from 7.8 per cent at the beginning to 4.1 per cent in 1975. As for the women in the second age group 20–24, their relative contribution to total fertility remained somewhat stable, oscillating within the narrow range of 23.1 to 24.5 per cent.

The situation near the end of the childbearing period was quite different. Women aged 45 to 49 experienced a minor rise in their relative contribution during the first two decades up to 1967, and thereafter declined steeply to reach the negligible level of 0.3 per cent in 1975. Women in the second oldest age group 40–44 recorded a sustained reduction in their relative contribution, decreasing from 6.4 per cent in 1947 to 2.4 per cent in 1975. A similar diminution in their relative contribution was experienced by women aged 35 to 39; their contribution was reduced from 15.0 per cent to 8.7 per cent during the same period. The relative contribution to gross total fertility by women in the 30–34 age group rose from 20.6 per cent in 1947 to 22.1 per cent in 1957, dipped to 21.1 per cent in 1967 and rose again to 22.8 per cent by the end of the period. By far the most notable change was the persistent rise in the relative contribution of women aged 25 to 29 from 25.5 per cent in 1947 to 37.2 per cent in 1975. On the whole, greater changes in the relative contribution of women occurred towards the end of the period.

The above changes in the relative contribution of women at various ages have resulted in the initial greater spread of the total fertility becoming more concentrated in essentially the three age groups between 20 and 34. Compared with the 70.1 per cent in 1947, these groups contributed no less than 84.5 per cent of the total fertility in 1975, with women between the ages of 25 to 29 alone accounting for more than a third of the total fertility. It should be emphasized that this concentration of fertility within the peak reproductive years took place during the entire period of fertility transition when a reduction was experienced by all other age groups, and was only brought about by the greater reduction at the young age group during the initial phase of decline and subsequently by the much greater reduction at the older age groups during the later phase. The concentration of fertility in an increasingly narrow portion of the reproductive period, that was observed to have occurred in Singapore, is one of the principle characteristics of declining fertility in a country. The position where childbearing takes place over a much shorter segment of the reproductive age span is typical of a country like Singapore where fertility is at replacement level.

FERTILITY CHANGES BY BIRTH ORDER

To obtain a better understanding of the nature of fertility transition, we will examine the changes in fertility rates by birth order or parity, as depicted in Table 8.5. Unlike age-specific fertility rates which were available from the early post-war years, the gross total fertility rates by birth order can be calculated only from 1967 onwards since the statistics for births classified by birth order were first compiled in that year.[8] This has restricted our study of fertility changes by birth order to the later phase of the period of fertility transition. The gross total fertility rate of a given birth order shown in the table is obtained by adding the age-specific fertility rates for births of that order calculated for quinary age groups from age 15 to 49. This form of measurement is superior to the general fertility rate by birth order because it isolates the influence of changes in the age composition of women within the reproductive age range, and it thus serves our purpose better in view of the recent changes in the age structure of Singapore women.

According to the figures for the annual percentage change displayed in the lower half of Table 8.5, there was a fall in the rates for all the birth orders in 1968 and 1969 when double-digit declines in overall fertility were recorded. In both years, the extent of the fall in the rate became progressively larger with the advance of parity from the first to the sixth orders, and hovering at around 20 per cent in the higher birth orders. The slackening in the speed of decline in overall fertility in 1970 (1.6 per cent) was related to the upturn in the rates for the first to fourth orders after moving downwards in previous years and also to the much diminished reduction for the fifth and higher orders. This general pattern of changes was repeated in 1971 when overall fertility slackened further (1.3 per cent), with some variation however. This time only the first three birth orders experienced a downward trend in the rates, but the extent of reduction was appreciably larger. In 1972, when the overall fertility rate edged up by 0.3 per cent, the general pattern of changes in the previous year was maintained, but with a much greater rise for the first order and a lesser reduction for the fifth and higher orders. The halt in the rapid fertility rate decline in the last three years was mainly due to the appearance of births previously postponed by the bigger group of women who became acceptors of the government programme to space their children.

In 1973 when the overall fertility rate resumed its downward trend, the fall in the rates not only became more substantial at the

TABLE 8.5
Gross Total Fertility Rates by Birth Order, 1967–1975

Birth Order	1967	1968	1969	1970	1971	1972	1973	1974	1975
					Rates				
1	164.4	153.1	146.1	148.0	155.3	163.3	165.6	163.6	134.5
2	143.0	133.0	128.9	132.2	139.6	143.3	138.1	123.2	128.1
3	107.0	98.7	96.4	98.3	103.5	105.2	95.3	76.9	73.7
4	86.4	71.5	64.6	65.8	65.6	64.5	57.9	43.3	34.4
5	70.7	58.4	47.5	45.1	40.6	41.1	32.5	22.7	17.0
6	59.3	48.1	37.0	34.1	29.3	26.8	21.0	13.7	9.8
7	50.8	39.2	30.0	28.5	22.7	19.6	14.8	8.8	5.7
8	38.7	32.0	25.1	22.0	16.1	14.7	11.0	6.5	4.1
9	28.3	22.9	17.8	15.7	12.4	10.1	8.0	4.3	2.9
10 and over	50.0	39.7	31.5	26.5	20.0	18.4	13.2	7.9	4.8
			Annual Percentage Changes						
1		−6.9	−4.6	+1.3	+4.9	+7.1	+1.4	−1.2	−17.8
2		−7.0	−3.1	+2.6	+5.6	+2.7	−3.6	−10.8	+4.0
3		−7.8	−2.3	+2.0	+5.3	+1.6	−9.4	−19.3	−4.2
4		−17.2	−9.7	+1.9	−0.2	−1.7	−10.2	−25.2	−20.6
5		−17.4	−18.7	−5.1	−10.0	−1.2	−20.9	−30.2	−25.1
6		−18.9	−23.1	−7.8	−14.1	−8.5	−21.6	−34.8	−28.5
7		−22.8	−23.5	−5.0	−20.4	−13.7	−24.5	−40.5	−35.2
8		−17.3	−21.6	−12.4	−26.8	−8.7	−25.2	−40.9	−36.9
9		−19.1	−22.2	−11.8	−21.0	−18.5	−20.8	−46.3	−32.6
10 and over		−20.6	−20.7	−15.9	−24.5	−8.0	−28.3	−40.2	−39.2

higher birth orders, but also penetrated the second and third orders again. By 1974, when the post-war record of 15.7 per cent reduction of the overall fertility rate was registered, even the first order underwent a downturn although by a small margin of 1.2 per cent. Equally noteworthy was the larger reduction experienced by the second order (10.8 per cent), third order (19.3 per cent), and fourth order (25.2 per cent) compared with those in previous years. In the fifth and sixth orders, the reduction was about one-third, and for the higher orders it was extremely pronounced, exceeding 40 per cent. The Gregorian calendar year 1974 coincided with the Chinese lunar calendar year designated by the tiger as the zodiac sign, and this Chinese year of the Tiger is believed by some Chinese couples to be an inauspicious time for producing children.[9] This accounts for the much larger reduction

FIGURE 8.3

Gross Total Fertility Rates by Birth Order, 1967–77

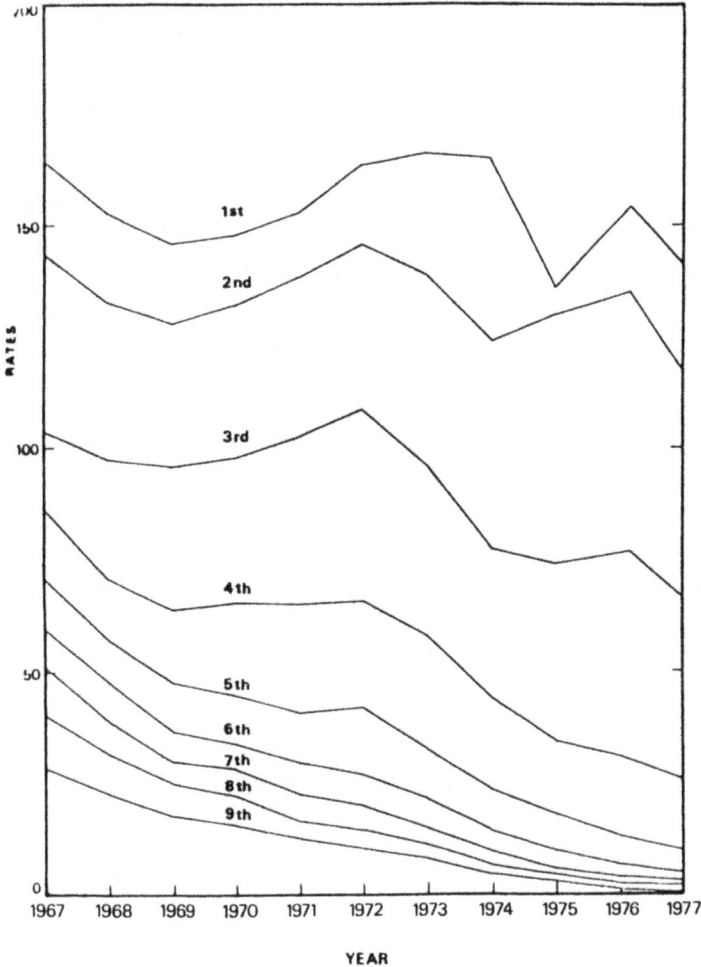

than usual in the rates for the second and higher orders, and of course for the record reduction in overall fertility.

The completion of fertility transition in 1975 when fertility was brought down to slightly below replacement level may be attributed solely to the spectacular decline of 17.8 per cent recorded by the first birth order since the decreases in the other orders were not as large as those experienced in the previous year. This dip in the rate for the first order is directly related to the steep rise in the proportion of nulliparous women undergoing abortion, from 7 per cent in 1974 to 20 per cent in 1975.[10] It was in 1975 that induced abortion was first made available to women on demand with the enactment of the Abortion Act 1975, which repealed the more restrictive Abortion Act 1970. What this means is that without the complete liberalization of induced abortion in 1975, the attainment of replacement fertility would most probably have been delayed by one or two years.

The above changes in the rates for the various birth rates have resulted in a shift in the relative contribution of each birth order to gross total fertility. This relative contribution can be obtained by adding the rate for each birth order and calculating the percentage of the rate for each order to the total. The computed percentages are exhibited in Table 8.6 for three selective years. The relative contribution by the first order births enlarged from one-fifth in 1967 to one-fourth in 1971, and finally to one-third in 1975 when replacement fertility rate was attained. Similarly, the relative contribution of the second order births was enhanced during the same period, advancing from 17.9 per cent in 1967 to 23.1 per cent in 1971 and 30.9 per cent in 1975. This is not surprising since the aim of the population control programme was to inculcate a two-child family norm.

TABLE 8.6

Relative Contribution of Each Birth Order to Gross Total Fertility, 1967–1975

Birth Order	1967	1971	1975
1	20.6	25.7	32.4
2	17.9	23.1	30.9
3	13.4	17.1	17.8
4	10.8	10.8	8.3
5	8.9	6.7	4.1
6	7.4	4.8	2.4
7	6.4	3.8	1.4
8	4.8	2.7	1.0
9	3.5	2.0	0.7
10 and above	6.3	3.3	1.2
Total	100.0	100.0	100.0

The third birth order witnessed a moderate improvement in its relative contribution from 13.4 per cent in 1967 to 17.1 per cent in 1971, and thereafter a very minor rise to 17.8 per cent in 1975. The relative contribution by the fourth order births remained stable at 10.8 per cent between 1967 and 1971, and was later pushed down to 8.3 per cent in 1975. A clearcut position was displayed by the fifth and higher birth order; their relative contribution was consistently lowered over the years.

FERTILITY TRENDS AMONG MAIN RACES

Our study of the remarkable fertility transition that occurred in Singapore would not be complete if we do not proceed a step further by investigating the changes in the levels and patterns of fertility encountered by the three main races in the country. In doing this, we will plunge immediately into the heart of the matter by examining the total fertility rate, which is the best measure for comparing fertility trends among different population groups. In examining the total fertility rates laid out in Table 8.7, it is important to bear in mind that, considering the race composition of the population, changes in the Chinese rate would have a far greater impact on the overall fertility trends in Singapore than changes in the Malay or the Indian rate.

A close examination of the figures given in the table will reveal that diverse fertility trends were experienced by the major races before and after the onset of overall fertility decline in 1958. Prior to 1958, the fertility of the Indians was moving generally downwards, with the total fertility rate lowered from 9.80 in 1947 to 7.24 in 1957. On the other hand, the fertility of the Malays followed an upward movement, increasing from 5.74 in 1947 to 6.28 in 1957. A fairly constant fertility, reflected by the total fertility rate remaining at about 6.50, was displayed by the Chinese. This unchanging fertility level of the majority race was responsible for the overall fertility in Singapore remaining persistently high during the first decade or so after World War II. In the same way, the onset of overall fertility decline in Singapore in 1958 was caused by the decline in the Chinese fertility that year. The fertility of both the Malays and the Indians commenced to move downwards a few years later.

The downward trend in the Chinese fertility after 1958 was sustained at a fairly constant speed right up to 1966, with the annual decline

TABLE 8.7
Total Fertility Rates for Three Main Races, 1947–1975

Year	Chinese	Malays	Indians	Annual Change (%)		
				C	M	I
1947	6.58	5.74	9.80			
1948	6.66	4.98	8.67	+1.2	−13.2	−11.5
1949	6.57	5.29	7.96	−1.4	+6.2	−8.2
1950	6.32	5.02	7.82	−3.8	−5.1	−1.8
1951	6.27	4.95	7.75	−0.8	−1.4	−0.9
1952	6.35	5.35	7.77	+1.3	+8.1	+0.3
1953	6.56	5.75	6.93	+3.3	+7.5	−10.8
1954	6.55	6.18	7.05	−0.2	+7.5	+1.7
1955	6.40	6.08	6.96	−2.3	−1.6	−1.3
1956	6.54	6.25	6.99	+2.2	+2.8	+0.4
1957	6.55	6.28	7.24	+0.2	+0.5	+3.6
1958	6.22	6.48	7.45	−0.5	+3.2	+2.9
1959	5.92	6.61	7.40	−4.8	+2.0	−0.7
1960	5.65	6.53	7.44	−4.6	−1.2	+0.5
1961	5.23	6.57	6.98	−7.4	+0.6	−6.2
1962	4.96	6.67	6.89	−5.2	+1.5	−1.3
1963	4.84	6.73	6.77	−2.4	+0.9	−1.7
1964	4.57	6.69	6.69	−5.7	−0.6	−1.2
1965	4.17	6.21	6.33	−8.8	−7.2	−5.4
1966	4.04	5.97	6.39	−3.1	−3.9	+0.9
1967	3.66	5.37	5.61	−9.4	−10.1	−12.2
1968	3.28	4.46	4.45	−10.4	−16.9	−20.7
1969	3.00	3.65	3.96	−8.5	−18.2	−11.0
1970	3.03	3.50	3.19	+1.0	−4.1	−19.4
1971	3.01	3.31	3.18	−0.7	−5.4	−0.3
1972	3.03	3.33	3.16	+0.7	+0.6	−0.6
1973	2.80	2.91	2.64	−7.6	−12.6	−16.5
1974	2.34	2.48	2.32	−16.4	−14.8	−12.1
1975	2.07	2.14	1.96	−11.5	−13.7	−15.5

hovering around 5 per cent in most years. The decline was enlarged to 9.4 per cent in 1967, 10.4 per cent in 1968, and 8.5 per cent in 1969, reflecting the success of the newly-introduced government programme in recruiting family planning acceptors. As some of these acceptors began to produce children, postponed earlier because of spacing, the decline in fertility halted, and rose by 1.0 per cent in 1970, fell slightly by 0.7 per cent in 1971, and rose again by 0.7 per cent in 1972. With a new equilibrium reached following the birth of postponed babies, the fertility decline gathered momentum again to chalk up 7.6 per cent in 1973, the all-time high of 16.4 per cent in the Chinese Tiger year in 1974, and 11.5 per cent in 1975.

The upward trend in the Malay fertility after World War II continued well into 1963 when the total fertility rate peaked at 6.73. The delayed start of the fertility decline among the Malays may be attributed to many factors, the chief of which is the incidence of divorce. Many studies have shown that the higher divorce rate, with its attendant marital instability, tends to depress fertility in some Muslim populations, and any sudden marked reduction in divorce will lead to a temporary rise in fertility as more births would be forthcoming from a more stable family life structure.[11] We have observed in a previous chapter the exceptionally high incidence of divorce among Muslims during the years up to 1958, and thereafter the very sharp drop following the establishment of the Shariah Court to, among other things, curb Muslim divorces. This created greater marital stability among the Malays and hence a rise in their fertility. As the effect of the divorce downturn faded and as the norms favouring larger family size were weakened by social and economic

FIGURE 8.4

Total Fertility Rates for Three Main Races, 1947–1975

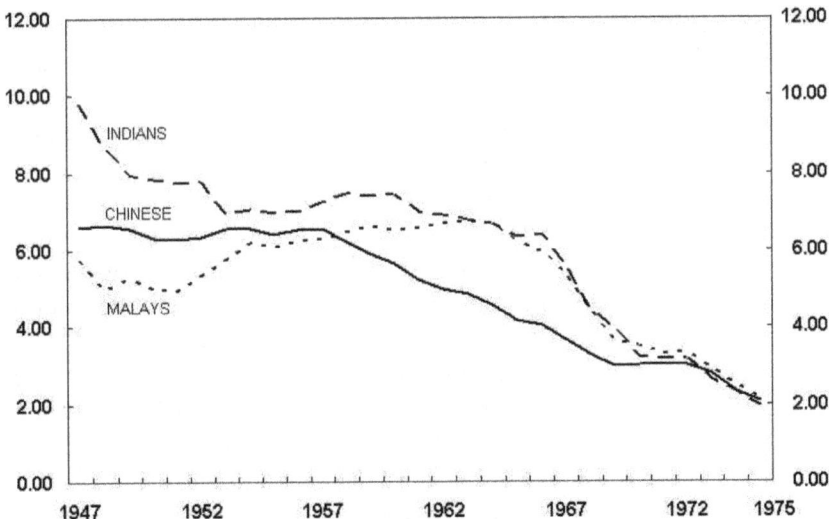

progress, the Malay fertility rate began to descend in 1964 and continued until replacement fertility was attained in 1975.

A delay, though a shorter one, in the start of fertility decline was also experienced by the Indians. After some up-down movements above the high level of 7.00 during the post-war years, the total fertility rate of the Indians showed a clear downward trend from 1961 onwards. In comparison with that of the Chinese, the fertility decline of the Indians was rather slow and gathered speed only after government family planning services were made available after 1966. In fact, the greatest reduction ever recorded among the three main races was that of the Indian fertility, which was slashed by 20.7 per cent in 1968. Even the second largest decrease was registered by the Indians, with a fall of 19.4 per cent in 1970.

The three main races have displayed not only some major differences in their fertility transition, but also some striking similarities. First, they have responded positively to the introduction of government family planning services in the late 1960s, as evidenced by their common experience of an accelerated fertility decline in these years. Secondly, a significant proportion of them practised birth control during the initial years of the government programme for the purpose of spacing their children, and hence the subsequent production of postponed births depressed their fertility in the early 1970s. Thirdly, the emergence of other measures beyond family planning in the early 1970s had a similar impact on the three races when fertility tumbled again after 1972. Fourthly, regardless of the timing of the onset of the fertility decline in the past, they managed to attain replacement fertility simultaneously in 1975.

The earlier onset of fertility decline among the Chinese, even prior to the national family programme, appeared to be consistent with the experience of Chinese populations in Malaysia, Hong Kong, and Taiwan.[12] In these countries there was early and substantial fertility decline among the Chinese even prior to, or without, a government programme. Another common experience of the Chinese population wherever they were is the sustained fertility decline until replacement level is attained. While the Chinese population in Peninsular Malaysia is very near to replacement level, the Chinese in Hong Kong attained this level in 1980 and the Taiwanese in 1983. It is also interesting to note that the Japanese had successfully achieved replacement fertility in 1957, and the South Koreans in 1985.

FERTILITY DIFFERENTIALS

In Singapore, the process of racial assimilation has taken place on such a minor scale that each of the main races still retain its own basic traits as determined by diverse religious and cultural backgrounds. The earliest racial integration was known to have occurred among the two largest communities when some Chinese men, faced with a lack of women of their own race, took Malay women as their wives. These Straits-born Chinese, or Babas, adopted Malay customs, language, attire and food, but very rarely the Islamic religion. Being mostly followers of Buddhism and Taoism, their marriages and childbearing behaviour conformed closely to that of the Chinese community. In the course of time, their offspring took spouses mainly from among the Chinese and this early racial intermingling soon vanished. A more enduring case refers to the Muslims originating from the Indian sub-continent, who have assimilated with the Malays through a common religion and/or intermarriage. Such Indians have become fully integrated with the Malay community, but the vast majority of Indians have not assimilated under such conditions. With almost no significant racial integration, the three main races have always exhibited some interesting and important differences in their fertility levels and patterns.

The differences in the fertility level of the three races are analysed in Table 8.8 which reproduces the total fertility rates for selected years. As was mentioned earlier, the total fertility rate is a reliable measure of fertility and is therefore a suitable index for the purpose of studying fertility differentials. In the early post-war year of 1947, the highest fertility registered was for the Indians with a rate of 9.80, some 49 per cent higher than the rate of 6.58 recorded by the Chinese. The lowest fertility was experienced by the Malays with 5.74, about 13 per cent lower than the Chinese rate. From 1960 onwards, the Chinese were experiencing the lowest fertility, and from 1970 onwards the highest fertility was recorded by the Malays. By 2006 the fertility level of the Malays was about 187 per cent higher than that of the Chinese, while the Indian fertility was only about 17 per cent higher than the latter.

The exceptionally high Indian fertility in the early post-war years was most probably caused by a post-war baby-boom resulting partly from postponement of marriage and partly from postponement of births. However, the fact that the two post-war censuses recorded a higher proportion of married women in 1957 than in 1947 suggests that the primary factor was the postponement of births during the difficult times

TABLE 8.8

Total Fertility Rates for Three Main Races, 1947–2006

Year	Chinese	Malays	Indians	Chinese = 100	
				M	I
1947	6.58	5.74	9.80	87.2	148.9
1950	6.32	5.02	7.82	79.4	123.7
1955	6.40	6.08	6.96	95.0	108.8
1960	5.65	6.53	7.44	115.6	131.7
1965	4.17	6.21	6.33	148.9	151.8
1970	3.03	3.50	3.19	115.5	105.3
1975	2.07	2.14	1.96	103.4	94.7
1980	1.66	2.04	1.93	122.9	116.3
1985	1.50	2.11	1.94	140.7	129.3
1990	1.67	2.70	1.93	163.5	115.6
1995	1.53	2.53	1.75	165.4	114.4
2000	1.45	2.45	1.62	167.0	111.7
2006	1.11	2.07	1.30	186.5	117.1

under the Japanese regime. Compared with the other two races, the Indians had a better reason to postpone their childbearing since it is generally known that the war years exerted a greater disruptive influence on the family life of the community. In particular, the forced movement of Indian labourers to work on the construction of the Siam-Burma "death" railway resulted in many cases of separation of Indian spouses. It is not unexpected that more Indian babies than usual were born in the immediate post-war years when family life became normal once again with the return of peacetime conditions and with the reunion of Indian men with their wives.

BELOW-REPLACEMENT FERTILITY

It may be recalled that the population control programme was introduced in the mid-sixties with the sole objective of lowering the level of fertility so as to reduce the rate of population growth as part of the national development plan to raise the standard of living of the people. As it became apparent that this objective would be achieved by the seventies, attention was focused on the wider issue of the maximum size of the population that Singapore could accommodate in the future. The extremely small land area with no endowment of natural resources must necessarily imply that Singapore cannot allow its population to grow indefinitely into an unmanageable figure that can threaten the very existence of the island Republic. It is not surprising that in 1974 the government announced the adoption of the national demographic goal of stabilising the population in the future.[13]

In order to achieve the long-term demographic goal, it is necessary to fulfill two conditions concerning fertility in accordance with stationary population theory. The first condition requires the lowering of fertility to the replacement level of a two-child family and the second condition entails the maintenance of fertility at this level indefinitely. In Singapore, the first condition was realised in 1975 when fertility fell for the first time to replacement level. But the second condition has never been fulfilled because, instead of proceeding henceforth along a horizontal path, fertility has moved well below this point for the past thirty-two years. It would be instructive to examine the causes and consequences of below-replacement fertility since the mid-seventies.

It would appear that the immediate target of working towards fertility moving down to replacement level was generally recognised as a necessary condition for achieving the long-term goal of a stationary population. However, there is evidence to suggest that there was a failure to appreciate the importance of holding fertility at this level indefinitely in the future. It was this lack of understanding of the absolute necessity to fulfill the second condition in the context of a stationary population theory that below-replacement fertility has been allowed to prevail in Singapore. The need to hold replacement fertility constant was first mentioned in the 1977 Report of the Singapore Family Planning and Population Board when it stated: "With Replacement Level attained in 1975, the broad policy of the National Family Planning and Population Board Programme during the Third Five-Year Plan is to maintain fertility at this level".[14] This statement of the objective of the 1976-80 plan was merely repeated every year in the annual report of the Board right up to 1982 without any concrete and effective action being taken to relax or eliminate the existing strong anti-natalist measures in order to encourage fertility to move back to replacement level.

In fact, the extremely low fertility rate recorded a few years before 1975 had already sent a clear signal that in a short time fertility would touch replacement level, and it would have been timely and necessary to take action immediately to reverse the strong antinatalist measures.

Worse still, after the attainment of replacement level in fertility in 1975, these measures were left unaltered for more than a decade. It should have been obvious that the continuation of these measures would surely depress fertility to well below the replacement level, and that was what actually happened in the past thirty-two years. One should not forget that the other broad group of social and economic factors favouring small family norms continue to exert a strong influence on the reproductive behaviour of most women. What it implies is that the presence of these factors will most probably inhibit any significant rise in fertility even if the government were to adopt a non-interventionist policy by abolishing all the anti-natalist measures.

The need for fertility policy changes was also made known on a few occasions. The importance of making policy changes was first made public by this author in a paper delivered in December 1979 at a seminar on "Singapore Towards the Year 2000" organised by the National Academy of Science and the Singapore Science Centre. After presenting some facts and figures, the following statement was made "... the persistence of fertility well below replacement level during the past four years, and most probably in the next few years, should be taken as a fair warning of the need to conduct a thorough review of our population policies relating to induced abortion, voluntary sterilisation, and incentive and disincentive measures".[15] This public call to review and change the strong antinatalist policies was repeated in his book *Population Control for Zero Growth in Singapore*, published in early 1980.

It was not until the mid-eighties that the government began to take serious notice of the sustained movement of fertility below replacement level and the undesirable consequences that would emerge from this trend. After careful consideration of the views of the public and the submission of the Inter-Ministerial Population Committee, the government finally introduced in early 1987 some major changes to the population control programme with the aim of encouraging women to produce more children. The possible impact of these changes, discussed in detail in Chapter 10, should be borne in mind when we interpret the figures for the more recent years given in Table 8.9.

It is important to note that the total fertility rates for Singapore and the three main races for the years 1990–2006 are based on the female resident population and not the female total population in the reproductive age groups from 15 to 49. This method was used because the figures for the latter population have not been made available. But the birth statistics

TABLE 8.9
Annual Births and Total Fertility Rate, 1975–2006

Year	Number of Births	Total Fertility Rate	Annual Changes (%)	
			Birth	TFR
1975	39,948	2.08	—	
1976 (D)	42,783	2.11	+7.1	+1.4
1977	38,369	1.82	−10.3	−13.7
1978	39,441	1.80	+2.8	−1.1
1979	40,778	1.79	+3.4	−0.6
1980	41,219	1.74	+1.1	−2.8
1981	42,250	1.72	+2.5	−1.1
1982	42,654	1.71	+1.0	−0.6
1983	40,585	1.59	−4.9	−7.0
1984	41,556	1.61	+2.4	+1.3
1985	42,484	1.62	+2.2	+0.6
1986 (T)	38,379	1.42	−9.7	−12.3
1987	43,616	1.64	+13.6	+15.5
1988 (D)	52,957	1.98	+21.4	+20.7
1989	47,669	1.79	−10.0	−9.6
1990	51,142	1.88	+7.3	+5.0
1991	49,114	1.78	−4.0	−5.3
1992	49,402	1.77	+0.6	−0.6
1993	50,225	1.79	+1.7	+1.1
1994	49,554	1.76	−1.3	−1.7
1995	48,635	1.73	−1.9	−1.7
1996	48,577	1.73	−0.1	0.0
1997	47,333	1.68	−2.6	−2.9
1998 (T)	43,664	1.54	−7.8	−8.3
1999	43,336	1.54	−0.8	0.0
2000 (D)	46,997	1.68	+7.8	+0.9
2001	41,451	1.48	−11.8	−11.9
2002	40,760	1.45	−1.7	−0.2
2003	37,485	1.32	−8.0	−9.0
2004	37,174	1.31	−0.8	−0.8
2005	37,492	1.31	+0.9	0.0
2006	38,217	1.33	+1.9	+1.5

(T) = Tiger year; (D) = Dragon year.

used in the computation refer to births produced by the total population and not the resident population since the birth statistics classified by five-year age groups of resident mothers have never been published in the *Report on the Registration of Births and Deaths.* The Statistics Department, with access to unpublished data, has released figures for the total fertility rate in respect of the resident population of Singapore only.[16] For example, the total fertility rate of this resident population released by the Department for 2005 was 1.25 as compared to our 1.31 based on birth statistics for the total population.

After the unprecedented decline during the years up to 1975, the overall fertility in Singapore has continued to proceed downwards below replacement level. The figures reveal that from the slightly below-replacement level of 2.08 in 1975, the total fertility rate edged up to 2.11 in the very next year but after that it moved generally downwards to touch the low of 1.31 in 2004. The few exceptions to this downtrend was engendered by the influence of the Tiger and Dragon years in the Chinese calendar and the effect of the major population policy changes in 1987 and 2004.

The sharp drop of 12.3 per cent in the total fertility rate in 1986 coincided with the inauspicious Tiger year for Chinese couples with respect to producing babies. Bearing in mind this unique influence in 1986, it is not surprising that the recovery was immediate in the following year when the rate moved up by 15.5 per cent to the level of 1.64. The great upsurge of 20.7 per cent, which brought the rate to the high of 1.98 in 1988, was caused by the relaxation of some old antinatalist measures and the introduction of some limited pronatalist measures in early 1987. However, the upsurge was also partly due to 1988 coinciding with the auspicious Dragon year for Chinese births. As the rush to take advantage of the new incentives, financial or otherwise, diminished and the influence of the Dragon year ran its course, the total fertility rate fell again by about 9.2 per cent to 1.79 in 1989.

The next two years witnessed less violent fluctuations in the total fertility rate because the other animals in the Chinese zodiac calendar have no influence on the Chinese in terms of producing babies. In 1990, the rate was raised by 5.0 per cent to 1.88, but this rise may be attributed partly to the utilisation of the female resident population, instead of the female total population, to calculate the total fertility rate for 1990, and the years that followed. In the following year, the rate was lowered by 5.3 per cent to 1.78 and remained at about this level until 1996. The important point is that the 1987 policy changes arrested the downward trend in fertility for a few years only and have not succeeded in pushing it back to the replacement level of 2.15. The persistence of below-replacement fertility in Singapore should not come as a surprise in view of the failure of many countries to raise their fertility back to replacement level by means of government measures.[17]

As the effect of postnatalist measures began to be overwhelmed by the socio-economic factors influencing the reproductive behaviour of women, the somewhat stationary fertility at above the level of 1.70 could no longer be sustained. A reduction of 2.9 per cent was recorded in 1997, bringing the total fertility rate to 1.68. This was immediately followed by a more significant decline of 8.3 per cent in 1998 when the rate was

FIGURE 8.5

Annual Births and Total Fertility Rate, 1970–2006

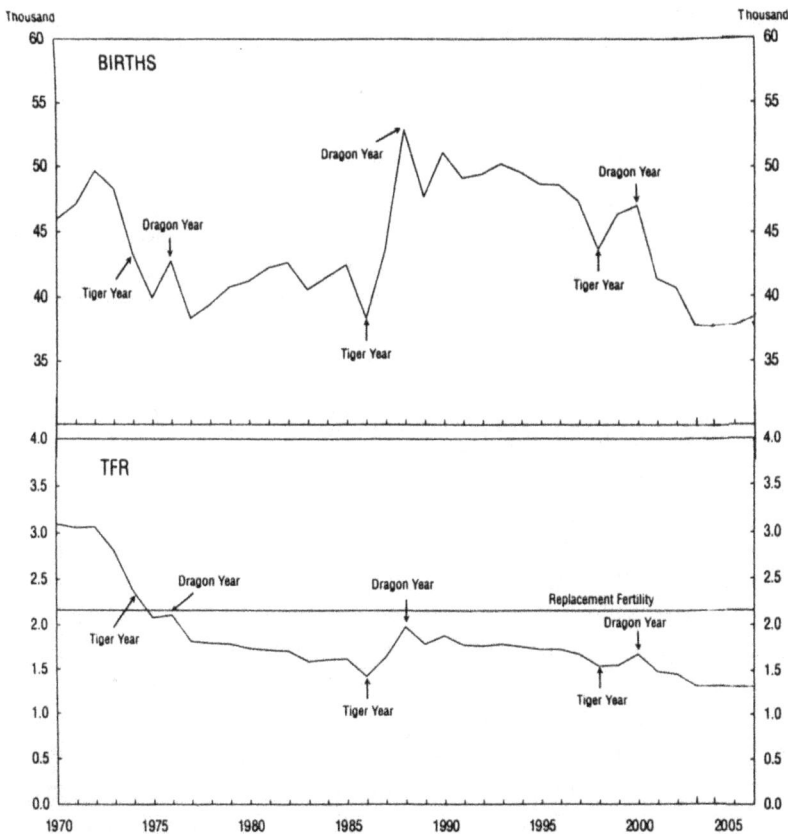

pushed down to the low of 1.54. Again, the Tiger year in the Chinese calendar coinciding with 1998 was surely responsible for the sharp fertility decline. Having registered this steep fall, fertility remained at the same level in the following year, but rose by 0.9 per cent in the Chinese Dragon year in 2000. This moderate rise, as compared to the much bigger upturn in the previous Dragon year in 1988, may be taken as a reflection of the waning influence of the Chinese animal year in the reproductive behaviour of the Chinese population.

In aboslute terms, the number of births was pushed down to 43,664 in 1998 from 47,333 in 1997, but was uplifted from 43,336 in 1999 to 46,997 in the latest Chinese Dragon year of 2000. Thereafter, the number went down continuously to bottom at the all-time low of 37,174 in 2004, with the corresponding total fertility rate standing at only 1.31. The widespread concern about this exceptionally low fertility resulted in the introduction of a comprehensive set of pronatalist measures in August 2004. Though it is still too early to say whether these measures would be effective, the decline in the number of birth was arrested as reflected in the slight rise to 37,492 in 2005 and 38,217 in 2006. The level of fertility was stabilised in 2005 at 1.31, and even went up to 1.33 in 2006.

It may be recalled that the three main races managed to reach replacement fertility at the same time in 1975, and it would be interesting to see what happened to their fertility trends after this remarkable achievement. In Table 8.10 are given the figures for the total fertility rates of the three main races. The Chinese fertility edged up to the target of replacement level equivalent to 2.15 in the Dragon year in 1976, after falling slightly below this level in the previous year. But this was only a flash in the pan as it resumed its downward trend immediately, to reach the low of 1.45 in 1983. Thereafter, a minor rise was recorded when the Chinese fertility moved up to 1.46 in 1984 and 1.50 in 1985. But this gentle uptrend was abruptly broken by the Tiger year which caused the Chinese fertility to shrink by 16.0 per cent and to reach the low of 1.26 in 1986. It recovered by 17.5 per cent to 1.48 in the following year and then shot up by 27.0 per cent to reach 1.88 in the Dragon year of 1988. It took an immediate downturn to 1.60 in the following, a pronounced drop of 14.9 per cent. The spectacular decline in 1988, as noted earlier, was partly due to the pronatalist measures introduced in 1977. From thenceforth, the Chinese fertility followed a downward path, with a huge reduction of 11.6 per cent recorded in the Tiger year of 1998 and a rise of almost magnitude equivalent to 11.5 per cent in the Chinese Dragon year of 2000. Since then, the Chinese fertility has fallen to the

TABLE 8.10

Total Fertility Rates for Three Main Races, 1975–2006

Year	Chinese	Malays	Indians	Annual Change (%)		
				C	M	I
1975	2.07	2.14	1.96	—	—	—
1976 (D)	2.15	1.91	1.85	+3.9	−10.7	−5.6
1977	1.81	1.88	1.69	−15.8	−1.6	−8.6
1978	1.78	1.84	1.80	−1.7	−2.1	+6.5
1979	1.77	1.85	1.88	−0.6	+0.5	+4.4
1980	1.66	2.04	1.93	−6.2	+10.3	+2.7
1981	1.62	2.09	1.94	−2.4	+2.5	+0.5
1982	1.60	2.11	1.96	−1.2	+1.0	+1.0
1983	1.45	2.06	1.91	−9.4	−2.4	−2.6
1984	1.46	2.10	1.95	+0.7	+1.9	+2.1
1985	1.50	2.11	1.94	+2.7	+0.5	−0.5
1986 (T)	1.26	2.05	1.89	−16.0	−2.8	−2.6
1987	1.48	2.16	1.95	+17.5	+5.4	+3.2
1988 (D)	1.88	2.31	2.11	+27.0	+6.9	+8.2
1989	1.60	2.40	2.18	−14.9	+3.9	+3.3
1990	1.67	2.70	1.93	+4.4	+12.5	−11.5
1991	1.56	2.65	1.86	−6.6	−1.9	−3.6
1992	1.55	2.62	1.94	−0.6	−1.1	+4.3
1993	1.57	2.57	1.97	+1.3	−1.9	+1.5
1994	1.53	2.56	1.85	−2.6	−0.4	−6.1
1995	1.53	2.53	1.75	0.0	−1.2	−5.4
1996	1.51	2.53	1.79	−1.3	0.0	+2.3
1997	1.46	2.50	1.77	−3.3	−1.2	−1.1
1998 (T)	1.29	2.44	1.75	−11.6	−2.4	−1.1
1999	1.30	2.44	1.62	+0.8	0.0	−7.4
2000 (D)	1.45	2.45	1.62	+11.5	+0.4	0.0
2001	1.22	2.48	1.61	−15.9	+1.2	−0.6
2002	1.20	2.33	1.61	−1.6	−6.0	0.0
2003	1.09	2.17	1.45	−0.9	−6.9	−9.9
2004	1.08	2.14	1.38	−0.9	−1.4	−4.8
2005	1.09	2.11	1.30	+0.9	−1.4	−5.8
2006	1.11	2.07	1.30	+1.8	−1.9	0.0

(T) = Tiger year; (D) = Dragon year

rock-bottom of 1.08, just slightly more than half the replacement level. The 2004 pronatalist measures appeared to have prevented the Chinese fertility from drifting further downhill in the next two years when it advanced by 0.9 per cent in 2005 and 1.8 per cent in 2006.

Since the Tiger and Dragon years have such an important impact on not only the fertility level but also the marriage incidence, a more detailed analysis of the phenomenon is presented below:

Year	Chinese Marriages	Annual Changes in Chinese Gross Total Fertility Rate (%)			
		1st Order	2nd Order	3rd Order	4th Order
1984	18,255	−2.7	+6.5	−0.7	−7.6
1985	16,747	+3.9	−0.9	−5.5	−11.3
1986	13,824	−8.1	−20.3	−16.2	−25.6
1987	16,904	−2.8	+29.3	+35.2	+29.7
1988	17,861	+24.7	+23.5	+48.4	+28.9

The 16 per cent decline in Chinese fertility during 1986, the Tiger year, was related to the corresponding pronounced drop in the gross total fertility rates for the first to the fourth order. One would expect the Chinese fertility in the following year to recover to above the level prevailing prior to 1986 because of the postponed births occurring in 1987, but this did not happen as the total fertility rate went up to only 1.48, which was still below the 1985 figure of 1.50. This is because the upturn took place at the second order (29.3 per cent), third order (35.2 per cent) and fourth order (29.7 per cent), but failed to do so in the first order with only a small rise of 2.8 per cent. This failure to bounce back may be attributed directly to the dip in Chinese marriages in the Tiger year, resulting in a smaller number of first order births than usual in the following year. The Dragon year in 1988 saw the Chinese fertility go up by the all-time high of 27.0 per cent to reach 1.88, and this was caused by the sharp rise in the first to the fourth order births.

The path taken by the Malay fertility was by comparison more simple and clearcut. After reaching replacement level in 1975, the Malay fertility continued to proceed downwards to the lowest level of 1.84 in 1978, after which it crept up steadily back to the replacement level of 2.16 in 1987. In response to the population policy changes introduced at

FIGURE 8.6

Total Fertility Rates for Three Main Races, 1975–2006

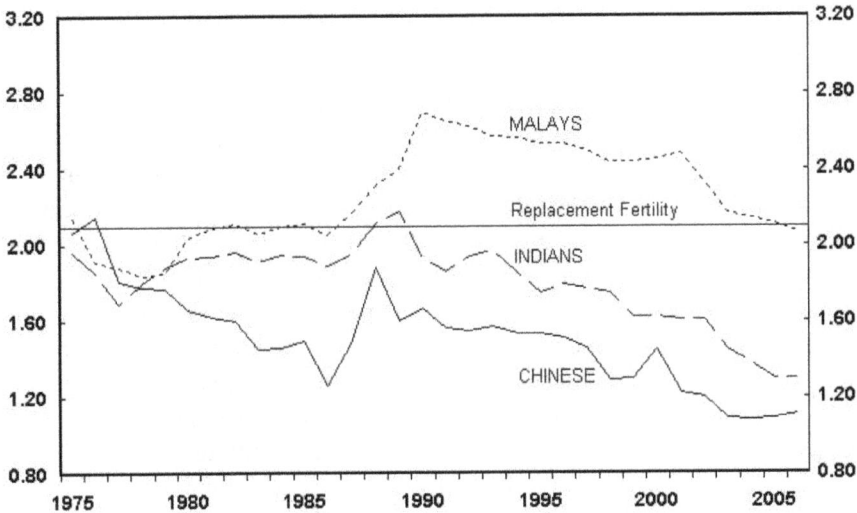

the beginning of 1987, the Malay fertility went up more decisively above replacement level for a few years to touch the peak of 2.70 in 1990. It immediately turned around, and drifted downwards to finally reach the below-replacement level of 2.07 in 2006. This downtrend was interrupted again by the policy changes implemented in 1998, resulting in a temporary upsurge of 0.8 per cent in 1999 and 11.5 per cent in 2000, but not by the changes made in 2004 as the downward path continued after this year. The Malay community appeared to have responded quite positively to the pronatalist policies introduced in 1987 and 1998, but not to the most latest policies made in 2004.

The movement of the Indian fertility, after going slightly below replacement level in 1975, was less pronounced and dramatic. The Indian fertility continued to move down after 1975 and quickly reached its lowest level of 1.69 in 1977, after which it took an upward turn in general but still hovered below replacement level right up to 1987 when it stood at 1.95. It then moved up to 2.11 in 1988 and 2.18 in 1989 as a result of the postnatalist measures introduced in 1987. But this upward trend was interrupted as it declined immediately to 1.93 in 1990, and continued to move down without any interruption to reach the all-time low of 1.30 in 2006. Clearly, the pronatalist measures have exerted the least influence on the reproductive behaviour of the Indian community.

BIRTH SHORTFALL BELOW-REPLACEMENT LEVEL

We will now proceed to examine to what extent the annual number of births produced by women in 1975 and thereafter was not adequate to ensure that the population would be able to replace itself in the future. An idea of this birth shortfall is presented in Table 8.11. The estimated annual number of births in the third column has been calculated on the assumption that the age-specific fertility rates corresponding to a total fertility rate (TFR) of 2.15 and a net reproduction rate 1.00 would prevail. What we have done is to scale up the age-specific fertility rates for each year so that the resultant TFR would be equal to 2.15 and to apply these adjusted rates to the mid-year female population in the various reproduction age groups to give us the estimated births.

The figures show that a TFR of 2.37 in 1974 yielded 43,268 births, giving an excess of 4,194 over the 39,074 births produced at the replacement fertility level of 2.15. In 1975, the TFR of 2.08 yielded 39,948 births, about 755 or 1.9 per cent short of the number required to ensure that the population would be replacing itself in the future. The existence of this birth shortfall not only persisted but also became more significant over the years. From the first year of 1.9 per cent in 1975, the birth shortfall rose consistently to touch the high of 25.3 per cent in 1983. It fell to 22.2 per cent in the following year, but immediately worsened to 24.0 per cent in 1985 and 30.9 per cent in the Chinese Tiger year of 1986. Not surprisingly, the birth shortfall quickly improved to 23.0 per cent in the following year and to only 6.7 per cent in the Dragon year of 1988, by far the smallest shortfall during the whole thirty-two years of below-replacement fertility. Of course, this remarkable improvement may be attributed partly to the emerging influence of the pronatalist incentives provided in 1987.

The percentage of birth shortfall immediately went up to 16.7 per cent in 1989 and remained generally below the 20-level until 1997. From thenceforth, the birth shortfall took a turn for the worse, with the percentage jumping to 27.7 per cent in the Tiger year of 1998 and also in the following year. There was a temporary improvement in the Dragon year of 2000 when the shortfall fall back to 21.1 per cent, only to follow by more discouraging events. The birth shortfall not only

TABLE 8.11

Annual Births According to Actual Fertility and Replacement Fertility, 1974–2006

Year	Actual Fertility		TFR = 2.13	Birth Shortfall	
	TFR	Births	Births	Number	Percentage
	(1)	(2)	(3)	(4)	(5)
1974 (T)	2.37	43,268	39,074	+4,194	+10.7
1975	2.08	39,948	40,703	755	1.9
1976 (D)	2.11	42,783	43.035	252	0.6
1977	1.82	38,364	44,788	6,424	14.3
1978	1.80	39,441	46,521	7,080	15.2
1979	1.79	40,779	48,887	8,108	16.6
1980	1.74	41,217	50,235	9,018	18.0
1981	1.72	42,250	52,176	9,926	19.0
1982	1.71	42,654	53,576	10,924	20.4
1983	1.59	40,585	54,316	13,731	25.3
1984	1.61	41,556	54,174	12,618	22.3
1985	1.62	42,484	55,900	13,416	24.0
1986 (T)	1.42	38,379	55,532	17,153	30.9
1987	1.64	43,616	56,661	13,045	23.0
1988 (D)	1.98	52,957	56,739	3,782	6.7
1989	1.79	47,669	57,252	9,583	16.7
1990	1.88	51,142	57,944	6,802	11.7
1991	1.78	49,114	60,087	10,973	18.3
1992	1.77	49,402	59,448	10,046	16.9
1993	1.79	50,225	59,765	9,540	16.0
1994	1.76	49,554	59,968	10,414	17.4
1995	1.73	48,635	59,874	11,239	18.8
1996	1.73	48,577	59,808	11,231	18.8
1997	1.68	47,333	60,011	12,678	21.1
1998 (T)	1.54	43,664	60,392	16,728	27.7
1999	1.54	43,336	59,537	16,207	27.7
2000 (D)	1.68	46,997	59,579	12,582	21.1
2001	1.48	41,451	59,152	17,701	29.9
2002	1.45	40,760	60,035	19,275	32.1
2003	1.32	37,485	60,269	22,784	37.8
2004	1.31	37,174	60,318	23,144	38.4
2005	1.31	37,492	60,960	23,468	38.5
2006	1.33	38,217	61,680	23,463	38.0

(T) = Tiger year; (D) = Dragon year.

FIGURE 8.7
Annual Births According to Actual Fertility and
Replacement Fertility, 1974–2006

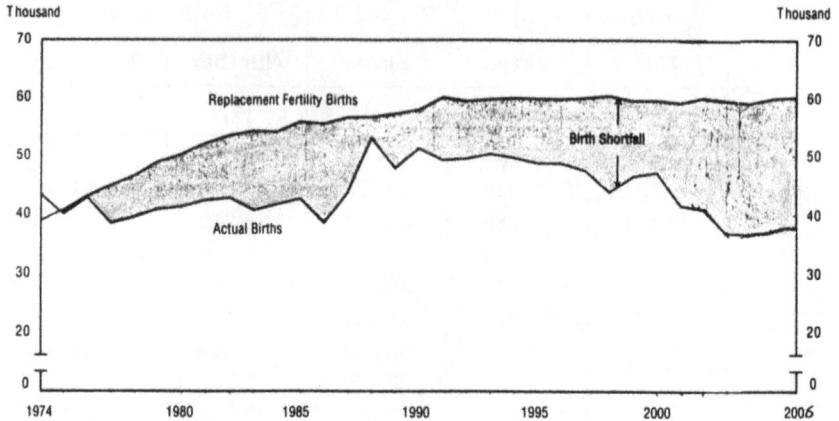

moved back to the higher level of 29.9 per cent in 2001, but continued to worsen until it stood at the level of 38 per cent nowadays. The persistent presence of birth shortfall is the result of the limited effectiveness of government pronatalist measures in the context of the stronger influence of socio-economic factors in determining reproductive behaviour. In this respect, the government has now recognised that the promotion of immigration is the only way of replenishing the people to ensure the continued growth of population in the years ahead.

Notes

1. United Nations, *Recent Trends in Fertility in Industrialized Countries*, ST/SOA/ Series A, Population Studies No. 29 (New York: Department of Economic and Social Affairs, 1958).
2. Straits Settlements, *Annual Report on the Registration of Births and Deaths 1886* (Singapore: Government Printer, n.d.).
3. United Nations, *Conditions and Trends in Fertility in Industrialized Countries*, Population Bulletin No.7, ST/SOA/Series N/T (New York: Department of Economic and Social Affairs, 1976).
4. United Nations, *Recent Trends in Fertility in Industrialized Countries*, ST/SOA/ Series A/27 (New York: Department of Economic and Social Affairs, 1968).
5. Taiwan, *1973 Taiwan Demographic Fact Book*, p. 69.

6. P. Arumainathan, *Singapore: Report on the Census of Population, 1970* (Singapore: Department of Statistics, 1973), Vol. 1, p. 66.
7. Singapore, *Report on the Registration of Births and Deaths, and Marriage, and Persons, 1961 and 1965* (Singapore: Government Printing Office, n.d.).
8. Singapore, *Report on the Registration of Births and Deaths and Marriages, 1967* (Singapore: Government Printing Office, n.d.).
9. Saw Swee Hock, *Population Control for Zero Growth in Singapore* (New York: Oxford University Press, 1980).
10. Ibid.
11. Saw Swee-Hock, "Muslim Fertility Transition: The Case of the Singapore Malays", *Asia-Pacific Population Journal* 4, no. 3 (September 1989).
12. Saw Swee-Hock, *The Population of Peninsular Malaysia* (Singapore: Singapore University Press, 1988); and R. Freedman and A. L. Adiokha, "Recent Fertility Decline in Hong Kong", *Population Studies* 22 (July 1968).
13. Chua Sian Chin, "Speech by Mr Chua Sian Chin, Minister for Health and Home Affairs, at the World Population Conference, Bucharest, Romania, 19–30 August 1974", *Singapore Public Health Bulletin* 15 (January 1975).
14. SFPPB, *Annual Report of the Singapore Family Planning and Population Board* (Singapore, 1977).
15. Saw Swee-Hock, "Too Little Land, Too Many People", in *Singapore Towards the Year 2000*, edited by Saw Swee-Hock and R. S. Bhathal (Singapore: Singapore University Press, 1981).
16. Singapore, *Population Trends 2006* (Singapore: Department of Statistics, 2006).
17. Paul Demeny, "Pronatalist Policies in Low-Fertility Countries: Patterns, Performance, and Prospects", *Population and Development Review* 12 (1986): 335–58.

9

Family Planning, Abortion and Sterilisation

Population policies refer to those adopted by a government to influence the course of population trends and patterns in the country.[1] Some examples are immigration policies regulating the inflow of foreigners into the country, mortality policies affecting the general health of the people, population distribution policies governing the movement of people within the country, and fertility policies affecting the reproductive behaviour of the population. There are two types of fertility policies — those designed to encourage childbearing and those meant to discourage childbearing. Those policies adopted by the government to persuade people to produce more children in order to raise the rate of population growth are known as pronatalist policies, while those meant to do the exact opposite are known as antinatalist policies.

In Singapore, the government adopted a strong antinatalist stance in the mid-sixties and introduced a comprehensive population control programme over the years to accelerate the decline in fertility and hence the rate of population growth. The programme consisted of four major components: government family planning, induced abortion, voluntary sterilisation, and incentives and disincentives aimed at reducing fertility.[2] The rapid decline in fertility to replacement level in 1975 and the continuation of fertility below this level led to major changes in the programme in 1987 in order to encourage more births. Before this, some eugenic measures were introduced in 1984 to improve the quality of the population.

PRIVATE FAMILY PLANNING PROGRAMME

Birth control as a means of spacing children and limiting family size has long been practised by couples in Singapore on an individual basis, sometimes with the advice of doctors and friends and the use of family planning literature. The idea of providing family planning services to the masses was discussed probably in the thirties, culminating in the suggestion for the establishment of a family planning society in the leading article of an English newspaper in 1938.[3] But nothing positive came out of this recommendation and it was not until a decade later that such a society was formed.

The need for providing family planning services to the general public was debated again immediately after World War II when the country was confronted with widespread social and economic problems, particularly food shortages. The Social Welfare Department, with the assistance of voluntary workers, set up numerous food centres to feed the starving population, especially the children. The voluntary workers assisting in the scheme were convinced that feeding the hungry children would not solve the problem and a better solution was to help parents plan their family size according to their means. In response to their request, the Municipal Council agreed in May 1949 to permit its infant welfare clinics to provide family planning services once a week in three of the five clinics.[4] This fell short of the work envisaged and the group of volunteers, mainly doctors and social workers, gathered together on 22 July 1949 to form the Family Planning Association (FPA).

The primary aim of the Association was to provide family planning services to the masses to help them avoid unplanned childbearing, and thus to improve the health of the mothers and the general welfare of the family. The objects of the Association as incorporated in its constitution were as follows:[5]

1. To educate the people in family planning and to provide facilities for scientific contraception so that married people may space or limit their families and thus promote their happiness in married life and mitigate the evils of ill-health and over-crowding;
2. To advocate and promote the establishment of family planning centres at which, in addition to advice on scientific contraception, women can obtain advice on and, when necessary, treatment for any or all of the following:
    a. involuntary sterility
    b. minor gynaecological ailments
    c. difficulties connected with the marriage relationship.
3. To encourage the production of healthy children who would be an

asset to the nation, provided that their parents have the health and means to give them a reasonable chance in life.

4. To examine some other problems as are relevant to the above, and to take such action as may be considered advisable.

The Association commenced work after office hours in three clinics, located in the private dispensaries of three of its members. This was followed shortly by another three clinics which opened at the Municipal Health Centres through the influence of the members of the Association who were in the municipality. By the end of the year, the Association had an agreement with the government to offer family planning services in the North Canal Out-Patient Dispensary. The demand for family planning services continued into 1950 when two clinics were opened at Municipal Health Centres and two at government Infant Welfare Centres in the rural districts. At the close of 1950, the Association was operating eleven clinics, nine in the municipal areas and two in the rural areas. The increase in the number of clinics at the end of each year is shown in Table 9.1. In the seventeen-year period 1949–65, the number of clinics increased from seven to thirty-four. After the government takeover of its clinics in January 1966, the Association continued to operate in three clinics until November 1968 when it was ordered by the government to close down.

In the early days, the Association, being a small voluntary body, had to overcome many major obstacles in connection with accommodation, manpower and finance. As mentioned above, the space needed to dispense family planning services was provided by its members, the municipality and the government in their clinics. During this time, the Association depended entirely on volunteers, mainly social workers, doctors, nurses and interpreters, to carry out the daily administrative work and to man the clinics. When the expanding number of clinics and patients became too large to handle, part-time employees were engaged in 1952, and this was soon followed by the recruitment of full-time staff. By far the most serious problem confronting the Association was finance, which directly determined the scope of the services provided. The money came from members' subscriptions, clinic receipts, annual government grants, and donations from the International Planned Parenthood Foundation (IPPF), the Asia Foundation and the Ford Foundation.

The growth of the private programme mounted by the Association can best be examined in terms of the annual number of women seeking

TABLE 9.1
Annual Number of Clinics, Acceptors and Visits, 1949–1968

Year	Number of Clinics	Acceptors			Total Visits	Average Visits Per	
		New	Old	Total		Clinic	Acceptor
1949	7	600	n.a.	n.a.	n.a.	n.a.	n.a.
1950	11	1,871	n.a.	n.a.	n.a.	n.a.	n.a.
1951	12	1,880	n.a.	n.a.	n.a.	n.a.	n.a.
1952	8	1,787	n.a.	n.a.	3,841	n.a.	n.a.
1953	9	2,302	n.a.	n.a.	5,548	n.a.	n.a.
1954	12	2,966	n.a.	n.a.	9,223	n.a.	n.a.
1955	14	2,850	n.a.	n.a.	10,072	n.a.	n.a.
1956	25	3,772	n.a.	n.a.	14,393	n.a.	n.a.
1957	29	3,820	n.a.	n.a.	18,443	n.a.	n.a.
1958	25	5,280	n.a.	n.a.	27,522	n.a.	n.a.
1959	27	5,938	9,235	15,173	34,445	1,276	2.3
1960	28	7,472	10,135	17,607	37,757	1,348	2.1
1961	30	8,070	11,472	19,543	43,724	1,457	2.2
1962	28	7,189	13,083	20,272	48,916	1,747	2.4
1963	31	8,429	15,006	23,435	60,194	1,942	2.6
1964	30	9,339	16,243	25,582	78,368	2,612	3.1
1965	34	9,845	17,109	27,054	103,986	3,058	3.8
1966	3	2,145	4,214	6,359	26,403	8,801	4.2
1967	3	1,349	n.a.	n.a.	22,643	7,548	n.a.
1968*	3	1,019	n.a.	n.a.	17,301	5,767	n.a.

n.a. not available.
* Up to 31 October 1968.

birth control services and their total attendance at the various clinics. The women may be considered as new acceptors or old acceptors, the latter referring to those who attended the clinics on a second and subsequent occasions. In the first two months of November–December 1949, some 600 new acceptors were recruited, and in the first full year of the Association's existence in 1950 a total of 1,871 new acceptors were registered. As indicated in Table 9.1, the annual number rose steadily over the years, reaching 5,938 in 1959 and finally 9,845 in 1965.

The sharp drop in the number of new acceptors in 1966 was caused by the government takeover of most of the clinics in January, leaving only three clinics to the Association. A good proportion of the new acceptors continued to attend the clinics after their first visit, and every year the number of old acceptors attending the clinics exceeded the number of new acceptors. For instance, in 1965 there were 17,109 old acceptors compared with the 9,845 new acceptors mentioned earlier. The total number of attendances made by all the acceptors rose dramatically, increasing from 3,841 in 1952 to 103,986 in 1965. All this meant an increasing workload for the Association and a possible impact on the course of fertility in Singapore.

In many respects, the Association was a pioneer organisation in the field of family planning in the local and international scene. It was one of the earliest to be established in Asia and was a founder member of the International Planned Parenthood Federation, which was founded in 1952. For some seventeen years it was the only organised agency in Singapore responsible for providing the much-needed family planning services to the people and by October 1968 a total of 87,921 new acceptors had been recruited. There is no doubt that the work of the Association was partly responsible for precipitating the decline in fertility in 1958 as well as for the continuous decline up to the time when the government took over its clinics in 1966. Its increasing educational as well as clinical activities over the years created the necessary infrastructure for widespread acceptance of family planning ideas and practice among the masses. In a way, voluntary efforts played a significant role in bringing about a climate favourable to the eventual introduction of a government programme.

GOVERNMENT FAMILY PLANNING PROGRAMME

By the late fifties, the Association found it increasingly difficult to cope with the seemingly insatiable demand for its services mainly because of inadequate funds. It is not surprising therefore that in its 1957 Annual Report the Association requested the then Colonial Government to take over "the responsibility for providing family planning services for the population".[6] This request was repeated on numerous occasions, even after the People's Action Party (PAP) government assumed office in mid-1957. Though the expansion of family planning activities was part of its election manifesto, the newly elected PAP government did not take over the Association's work because it had to deal with many social and economic problems of greater priority. But it continued to provide the annual grant, participated actively in the Association's family planning campaigns, allowed its Maternal and Child Health centres to be used for family planning purposes, and gave a valuable piece of land at nominal rent to the Association to build its headquarters.

Years later, the government appointed a three-man Review Committee, on 13 March 1965, to look into the question of taking over the Association's clinics. The Committee's Report, submitted in June 1965, recommended the government takeover of all except three of the clinics. This led to the tabling of a *White Paper on Family Planning in Parliament* in September 1965, accepting not only the recommendations of the Committee, but also proposing the introduction of a national population policy.[7] The document spelt out in detail the various aspects of a national population policy which the PAP government would implement in order "to liberate our women from the burden of bearing and raising an unnecessarily large number of children and as a consequence to increase human happiness for all". Following the enactment in December 1965, of the Singapore Family Planning and Population Board Act 1965, the Singapore Family Planning and Population Board (SFPPB) was established in June 1966.[8]

The change in government policy from one of indirect participation to one of direct provider of family planning services was proclaimed a few weeks after the momentous political event of the separation of Singapore from Malaysia on 9 August 1965, and with the full knowledge that the newly independent state had to survive alone without the traditional economic hinterland. The separation highlighted the small area of Singapore and the economic difficulties of the tiny island state devoid of natural resources. This focused serious attention on the dire need to check the rapid population growth in planning for the social and economic development of the country. At that time, the crude birth rate was in the neighbourhood of 30 per thousand population and the annual rate of population increase was no less than 2.5 per cent.

The aims of the Board as stated in the 1965 Act were as follows:

1. To act as the sole agency for the promotion and dissemination of information pertaining to family planning in Singapore;
2. To initiate and undertake the population control programme;
3. To stimulate interest in demography in Singapore;
4. To advise the government on all matters relating to family planning and population control.

The establishment of the autonomous statutory board, invested with such important responsibilities, expressed full government endorsement of family planning with the prestige and authority that necessarily follow.

The Board was directly responsible to the Minister for Health and was composed of fifteen members, with seventeen ex-officio members drawn from government departments, two from the University of Singapore and six from among members of the public. The Chairman of the Board was the Deputy Director of Medical Services (Health). Various committees, such as the Executive Committee, the Research and Evaluation Committee, and the Training Committee helped in the implementation of the general policies formulated by the Board. The daily work was organised under six units: the Clinical Services Unit, the Cytology Unit, the Research and Evaluation Unit, the Information, Education and Communications Unit, the Training Unit, and the Administrative Services Unit. In addition to some 175 staff personnel of all grades stationed in the operational units, the Board drew heavily on the services of government officers in the Ministry of Health, especially those in the government clinics where family planning services were offered. The Board, unlike the Family Planning Association, had access to funds from the government, and was thus in a much better position to carry out its work.

The national programme operated by the Board was strongly integrated into the work of the Ministry of Health. The clinical services for family planning were offered in the forty-six Maternal and Child Health clinics and the six purely Family Planning clinics. These fifty-two clinics, strategically located in various parts of the island, provided family planning advisory and clinical services free of charge, and all contraceptives at nominal prices. There was also a mobile clinic, staffed by a doctor and nursing personnel, which visited certain places on request. The methods available at all the clinics were provided on a menu system, which included oral contraceptive pills, IUD, injectable contraceptives, spermicidal creamer tablets, diaphragms and condoms.

Apart from making family planning services readily available, the Board embarked on extensive educational campaigns to generate public awareness about the population problem and to stress the important need for family planning. The initial message of "Plan Your Family" appeared to have been widely publicised by 1968, so that the emphasis was shifted to "Singapore Wants Small Families", which became the

TABLE 9.2
Family Planning Acceptors and Acceptance Rate, 1966–1997

Year	Family Planning Acceptors	Acceptance Rate	Annual Change (%)	
			Acceptors	Rate
1966	30,410	79.4	—	—
1967	30,935	78.1	+1.7	-1.6
1968	35,338	84.9	+14.2	+8.7
1969	35,643	81.7	+0.9	-3.8
1970	24,230	53.1	-32.0	-35.0
1971	17,749	37.4	-26.7	-29.6
1972	17,666	35.7	-0.5	-4.5
1973	19,102	37.2	+8.1	+4.2
1974	18,292	34.3	-4.2	-7.8
1975	16,692	30.2	-8.7	-9.0
1976	17,674	31.0	+5.9	+2.6
1977	16,158	27.4	-8.6	-11.6
1978	15,192	25.0	-6.0	-8.8
1979	15,266	24.4	+0.5	-2.4
1980	15,009	23.4	-1.7	-4.1
1981	14,534	21.7	-3.2	-7.3
1982	14,651	20.7	+0.8	-4.6
1983	13,741	19.1	-6.2	-7.7
1984	12,481	16.9	-9.2	-11.5
1985	12,686	16.7	+1.6	-1.2
1986	11,460	14.7	-9.7	-12.0
1987	10,000	14.2	-12.7	-3.4
1988	7,412	10.4	-25.9	-2.7
1989	7,436	10.3	+0.3	-1.0
1990	6,535	9.0	-12.1	-12.6
1991	6,575	8.5	+0.6	-5.6
1992	5,581	7.4	-15.1	-12.9
1993	5,061	6.7	-9.3	-9.5
1994	4,716	6.2	-6.8	-7.5
1995	3,892	5.0	-17.5	-19.4
1996	3,500	4.5	-10.1	-10.0
1997	3,200	4.1	-8.6	-8.9

central theme in the following few years. This gave way to "Two-Child Families for Singapore" in 1972, and subsequently to "Boy or Girl — Two is Enough", which was meant to drive home the concept of the two-child family irrespective of the sex of the children.[9] The underlying objective

FIGURE 9.1

Family Planning Acceptors and Acceptance Rate, 1966–1997

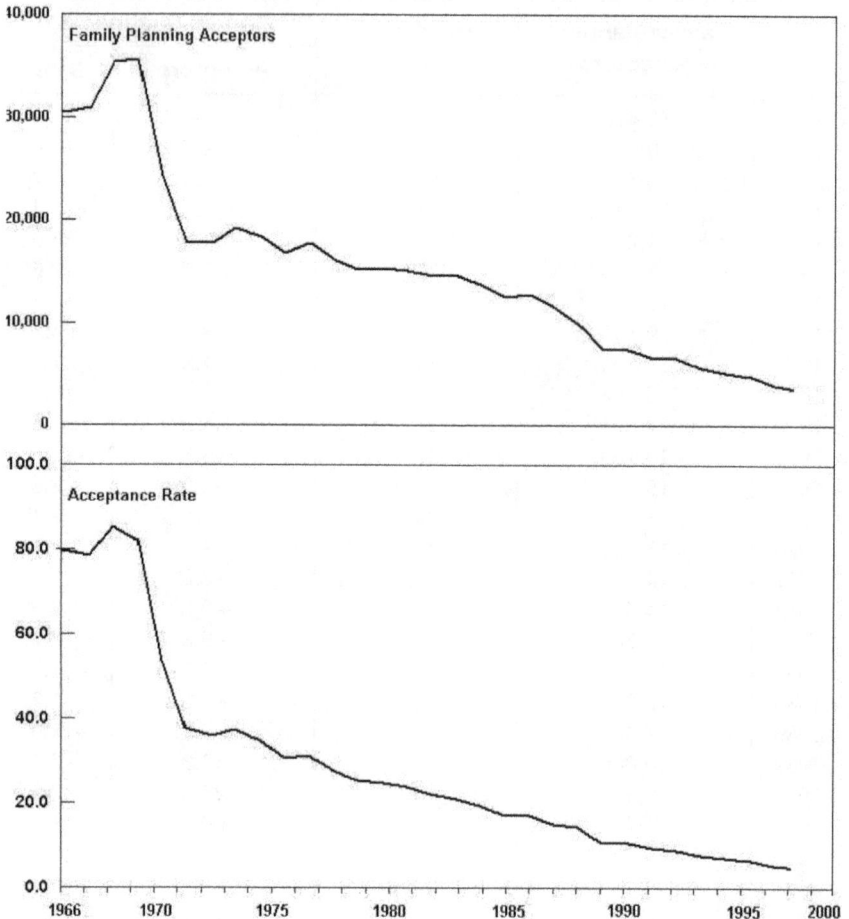

of the slogan was to reduce fertility to replacement level in order to stabilise the population in the future. Replacement fertility was attained in 1975, and the Board was eventually abolished in May 1986.

The work of the Board and the effectiveness of the national programme may be examined in terms of family planning acceptors and the acceptance rate. A family planning acceptor refers to a woman who visited any of the Board's clinics for the first time for the purpose of practising birth control. The acceptance rate is defined as the number of family planning acceptors registered during the year per thousand female population aged 15 to 44.[10] Although 1966 was essentially a year of planning and organising for the Board, there was a steady increase in the number of acceptors from 411 in January to 2,234 in December. For the whole year, the total of 30,410 acceptors were recruited, but some of these acceptors of the government programmes were in fact former patients of the Family Planning Association clinics, most of which were taken over by the Board. The number of acceptors hit a peak of 35,643 in 1969, after which it fell in most years and managed to reach only 3,200 in 1997. The low level of attendance at government family planning clinics may be attributed to the ability of couples to practise birth control on their own with the help of relevant printed materials and perhaps their doctor's advice.

INDUCED ABORTION

Before 1970, the procurement of abortion in Singapore, like many other member countries of the Commonwealth, was governed by laws based on legislation passed in the nineteenth century in Victoria England. It constituted a criminal act punishable under Section 312–316 of the Penal Code and could only be defended on the plea that abortion was caused in good faith to safeguard the life of the woman concerned. It is not surprising then that both the Association and the Board turned down numerous requests for induced abortion from their patients, even when the pregnancy was due to contraceptive failure. Soon after its establishment, the Board conducted a thorough review of the question of induced abortion in the context of the national population control policy: it was agreed that induced abortion should be made available as a complement to the family planning programme but not as an alternative to the other less drastic and preventive methods of family planning.

The findings of the review were submitted by the Board to the Health Ministry for consideration and in August 1967 the Ministry announced the intention of the government to legalise induced abortion. On 3 December 1968, the Health Minister introduced into Parliament, for the first reading, the Abortion Bill designed to reform and liberalise the laws. The publication of the eagerly-awaited details of the Bill generated widespread debate among the public and renewed criticisms from opponents of induced abortion. It is not surprising that Parliament referred the controversial Bill, together with the Voluntary Sterilisation

Bill, to a Select Committee in order to allow interested groups to air their views and propose amendments. The revised version of the Bill, with a few amendments, taking into account the Report of the Select Committee, was finally approved by Parliament on 29 December 1969, and came into force on 20 March 1970. It was agreed that the Abortion Act 1969 would initially operate for four years, but the Minister could extend it for a further year.[11] This implied that the effectiveness of the Act would be reviewed towards the end of the five-year period and consideration would be given by Parliament as to the desirability of continuing the legislation.

Under the Abortion Act, which was in many respects based on the 1967 Abortion Act passed by the British Parliament in October 1967, an eleven-member Termination of Pregnancy Authorisation Board was established to authorise the treatment to terminate pregnancy by registered medical practitioners under defined circumstances. These were spelled out in Section 5(2) of the Act:

(a) that the continuance of the pregnancy would involve serious risk to the life of the pregnant woman or serious injury to the physical or mental health of the pregnant woman;

(b) that the environment of the pregnant woman, both at the time when the child would be born and thereafter so far as is foreseeable, justifies the termination of her pregnancy (the expression "environment" in this paragraph includes the family and financial circumstances of the pregnant woman);

(c) that there is substantial risk that if the child was born it would suffer from such physical or mental abnormalities as to be seriously handicapped;

(d) that the pregnancy is the result of rape under Section 375 of the Penal Code or of incest under Section 376A of the Penal Code, or of unlawful carnal connection under paragraph (j) of subsection (1) of Section 128 of the Women's Charter, or of intercourse with an insane or feebleminded person.

Furthermore, under Section 5(3), a registered medical practitioner without the Board's authorisation may perform an abortion after consulting another registered medical practitioner if they were of the opinion that the termination of pregnancy was necessary on the ground indicated in Section 5(2)(a) above, provided that the abortion was carried out in a government hospital or in an approved institution. Section 5(5) provided that if the medical practitioner considered that such a treatment was immediately necessary to save the life of the patient, such treatment need not be carried out in a government hospital or an approved institution, and the second opinion of a medical practitioner is not required. In practice, most of the applications for abortion were authorised on the socio-economic grounds stated in Section 5(2)(b), which constituted the key component to the liberalised views and the most significant from the family planning point of view. However, there were certain safeguards, such as that the pregnant woman must be a Singapore citizen, the wife of a citizen or, alternatively, a resident for at least 4 months, and must not be more than 16 weeks pregnant for socio-economic reasons and more than 24 weeks for medical grounds.

As mentioned earlier, the Abortion Act 1969 was a temporary legislation which was subject to review before its expiry date in five year's time. Considering the satisfactory working of the Act in the past and the desire to have a comprehensive population control programme at that time, the government decided not only to continue with the Act but to liberalise it further so as to make induced abortion on demand possible and to make it a permanent fixture of the laws of Singapore. In October 1974, the new Abortion Bill was presented to Parliament, and, unlike the previous occasion, it attracted little public comment and less heated debate in Parliament. The Abortion Act 1974 was passed on 6 November 1974 and came into force on 27 December 1974, repealing the original Act.[12]

The Abortion Act 1974 introduced the principle of abortion on demand subject to certain safeguards by incorporating very liberalised laws and extremely simplified procedures governing its operation. Section 3(1) states: "Subject to the provisions of this Act, a person shall not be guilty of an offence under the law relating to abortion when a pregnancy is terminated by a registered medical practitioner acting on the request of a pregnant woman and with her written consent". Abortion for any pregnancy up to 24 weeks' duration can now be provided with her written consent, and the medical practitioner no longer has to be satisfied that any of the four grounds stipulated under Section 5(2) of the old Act exist. The procedures for a pregnant woman to obtain an abortion were thus simplified and streamlined. For example, the Termination of Pregnancy Authorisation Board was abolished and the qualifications required for a practitioner to perform abortions were relaxed. However, most of the original safeguards, such as Singapore citizenship or four-month residential requirement, were retained.

In the early eighties, an attempt was made to strengthen the control over doctors and institutions involved in the termination of pregnancy. The Abortion (Amendment) Act 1980[13] and the Abortion (Amendment) Regulations 1981[14] required all medical practitioners in private practice who wished to perform abortion to be authorised by the Health Ministry. The new legislation imposed further selective specialist qualification restrictions on physicians seeking approval to perform abortions, and stipulated that approval for institutions to perform abortions was renewable every two years. The latter was further tightened by the Abortion (Amendment) Regulations 1982 which limited the period of approval for an institution to only one year.[15] In spite of these changes, the laws and procedures governing induced abortion are so liberal and simplified that a woman can terminate her unwanted pregnancy quite easily, and cheaply too. Nevertheless, legalised abortion on demand has constituted a very insignificant component of the national population control programme in Singapore.

The laws governing abortion on demand have never been amended to make it more difficult for women to undergo abortion even when pronatalist measures were introduced since the 1980s in an attempt to raise the below-replacement fertility so that more births can be produced. What was implemented was the introduction of compulsory counseling by doctors before and after abortion with effect from 1 October 1987. But this compulsory counseling, to be provided by doctors authorised to perform abortions in government and private hospitals, is applicable to only women with at least one or two children and with at least some secondary education. Hopefully, this counseling will provide all the essential facts concerning abortion to the women to give them a chance to change their mind and to proceed with the pregnancy. For those who decide to opt for an abortion, counseling is provided once again by the doctors after the operation with the aim of preventing them from seeking repeat abortions in the future.

The data on the annual number of abortions performed according to the provisions of the Act since 1970 are presented in Table 9.3. A total of 1,913 abortions were performed during the last nine months or so in 1970, bearing in mind that the Act came into force on 20 March of that year. In the following year, the number rose to 3,407 and continued to increase steadily to 7,175 in 1974. With the complete liberalisation of the

TABLE 9.3

Abortions and Abortion Ratio and Rate, 1970–2006

Year	Number of Abortions	Abortion Ratios	General Abortion Rate	Annual Increase (%)		
				Number	Ratio	Rate
1970	1,913	41.6	4.2	—	—	—
1971	3,407	72.4	7.2	78.1	74.0	71.4
1972	3,806	76.6	7.7	11.7	5.8	6.9
1973	5,252	108.8	10.2	38.0	42.0	32.5
1974	7,175	165.8	13.5	36.6	52.4	32.4
1975	12,873	322.2	23.3	79.4	94.3	72.6
1976	15,496	262.2	27.1	20.4	12.4	16.3
1977	16,443	428.6	27.9	6.1	18.3	3.0
1978	17,246	437.3	28.4	4.9	2.0	1.8
1979	16,999	416.9	27.1	-1.4	-4.7	-4.6
1980	18,219	442.0	28.4	7.2	6.0	4.8
1981	18,890	477.1	28.2	3.7	1.2	1.4
1982	19,110	448.0	27.0	1.2	0.2	-4.2
1983	19,100	470.6	26.5	-0.1	5.0	-5.6
1984	22,190	534.0	30.0	16.2	13.4	13.2
1985	23,512	553.4	31.0	6.0	3.6	3.2
1986	23,035	600.1	29.6	-2.0	8.4	-4.5
1987	21,226	486.7	26.6	-7.9	-18.9	-10.1
1988	20,135	380.2	24.5	-5.1	-21.9	-7.9
1989	20,619	432.5	24.4	2.4	13.8	-0.4
1990	18,669	361.2	24.2	-9.5	-16.5	-0.8
1991	17,798	362.4	24.0	-4.7	0.3	-6.3
1992	17,073	345.6	22.7	-4.1	-4.6	-5.4
1993	16,476	328.0	21.7	-3.5	-5.1	-4.4
1994	15,690	316.6	20.5	-4.8	-3.5	-5.5
1995	14,504	298.2	18.8	-7.6	-5.8	-8.3
1996	14,000	288.2	18.0	-3.5	-3.4	-4.3
1997	13,500	281.3	17.1	-3.6	-2.4	-5.0
1998	13,838	315.5	17.2	2.5	12.2	0.6
1999	13,753	317.4	17.0	-0.6	0.6	-1.2
2000	13,734	292.2	16.9	-0.1	-7.9	-0.6
2001	13,140	317.0	16.2	-4.3	8.5	-4.1
2002	12,749	312.0	15.6	-3.0	-1.6	-3.7
2003	12,272	327.4	14.9	-3.7	4.9	-4.5
2004	12,070	324.7	14.5	-1.6	-0.8	-2.7
2005	11,482	306.3	13.7	-4.9	-5.7	-5.5
2006	12,032	314.8	12.0	+4.8	+2.8	-1.2

FIGURE 9.2

Annual Abortions and General Abortion Rate, 1970–2005

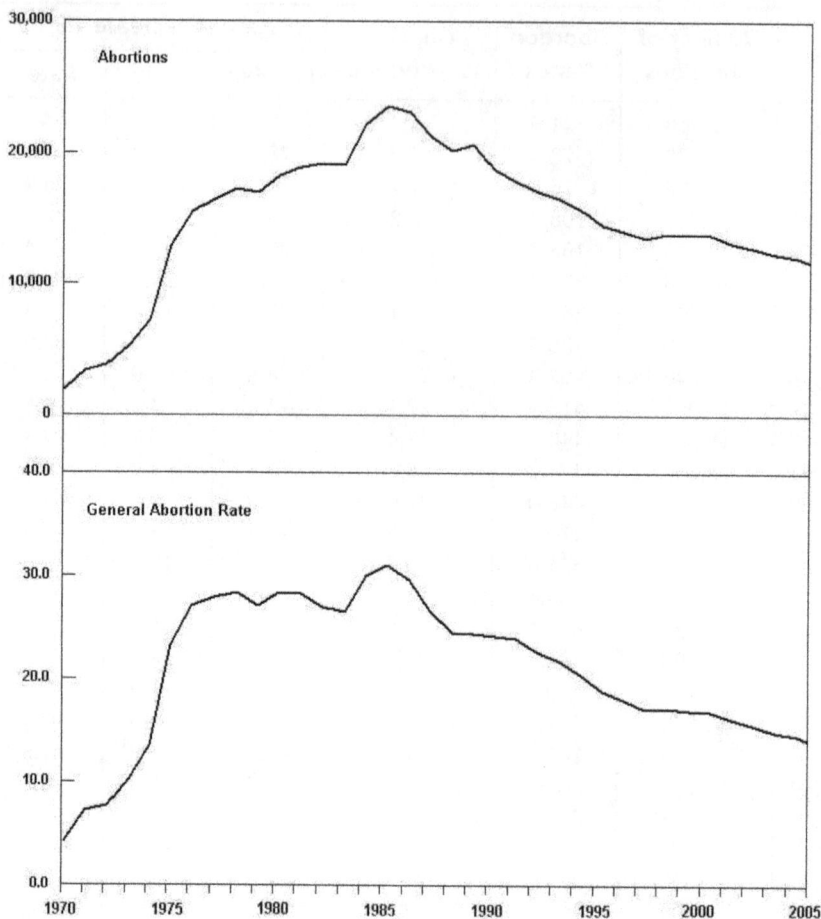

laws in early 1975, the figure shot up by 79.4 per cent to 12,873 in 1975, followed by a more moderate rise of 20.4 per cent in the following year. Thereafter, the number of abortions increased slowly and steadily until 1985 when it touched the record figure of 23,512. Since then, the rise has been arrested and a clear downtrend has emerged, with the number falling to 18,669 in 1990 and 13,500 in 1997. The recent reversal in the long-term trend was due to the 1987 changes in the population control programme to encourage more births, which included the introduction of compulsory pre-abortion and post-abortion counselling, and also to the more widespread practice of safe-sex through condoms to prevent AIDS (Acquired Immune Deficiency Syndrome).

Induced abortion in any particular year may be measured by the abortion ratio and the general abortion rate. The ratio refers to the number of abortions performed in the year per thousand live-births occurring in that year, while the rate expresses the number of abortions per thousand women in the reproductive age groups 15 to 44. As can be observed in Table 9.3, the ratio rose rapidly from 41.6 per thousand live-births in 1970 to 428.6 in 1977 and then more gradually to the peak of 600.1 in 1986, after which it commenced to fall to 361.2 in 1990, 281.3 in 1997, and finally to 306.3 in 2005. A somewhat similar trend was exhibited by the general abortion rate, which rose quickly from 4.2 in 1970 to 27.1 in 1976 and then slowly to the peak of 31.0 in 1985. Thereafter, it fell continuously to reach 24.2 in 1990, 17.1 in 1997, and finally to the low of 12.0 in 2006.

The clear downtrend in the incidence of abortion since the mid-1980s may be attributed to the introduction of pronatalist measures since that time. Interestingly, the descent in the general abortion rate from the second high of 31.0 in 1985 to only 12.0 in 2006 was interrupted in 1998 when the rate went up by 0 .6 per cent. The most likely explanation for this aberration is that 1998 concided with the Chinese lunar calendar designated by the Tiger, which is considered to be an unauspicious year to produce babies. An idea of the incidence of abortion in Singapore in the 1980s may be obtained by comparing the 1984 rate of 30.0 with the corresponding rate of 14.9 for France, 17.7 for Sweden, 21.5 for Japan, 31.0 for Hungary and 75.7 for Yugoslavia.[16]

VOLUNTARY STERILISATION

Voluntary sterilisation, which was not forbidden by law, was performed in the sixties in Kandang Kerbau Hospital and Toa Payoh Hospital. In those days, both the FPA and the SFPPB did not perform sterilisation, but referred the more deserving cases to these hospitals. When reviewing the abortion question in 1966, the Board also made a study of the laws and guidelines governing voluntary sterilisation. The outcome of its deliberation was that conditions were laid down for the performance of the operation through the legalisation of sterilisation.

In December 1968, the Voluntary Sterilisation Bill was presented to Parliament where it attracted little attention from members of the House and the general public. Although the Bill could have been passed easily by Parliament, it was also committed to the Select Committee that had been specifically set up to consider the more controversial Abortion Bill. The revised Voluntary Sterilisation Bill, which took into consideration the recommendations of the Committee, was eventually passed by Parliament on 29 December 1969.

Under the Voluntary Sterilisation Act 1969, which came into force on 20 March 1970, a five-member Eugenics Board was constituted to provide the necessary authority for registered medical practitioners to perform male and female sterilisation on medical, social and eugenics grounds in government hospitals and approved institutions.[17] Under Section 5(a) of the Act, the Board may authorise treatment of sexual sterilisation on any applicant of 21 years of age and over, if he or she has had at least three children and has the consent of the spouse. Sterilisation on persons under 21 years of age may only be done if they are afflicted with any hereditary form of recurrent illness, mental deficiency, or epilepsy.

The working of the Act was examined in the light of the experience in the first two years, and this led to some amendments aimed at making sterilisation as a method of birth control more readily available to men and women. Under the Voluntary Sterilisation (Amendment) Act 1972 which came into force on 12 May 1972, approval for sterilisation could now be given to applicants with only two instead of three living children and even to those with only one child under certain exceptional circumstances.[18] The mandatory interview before the Eugenics Board was dispensed with, and the waiting period for treatment after approval was granted was reduced from 30 days to 7 days.

As in the case of the Abortion Act, the Voluntary Sterilisation Act was supposed to be temporary and subject to review in five years' time. In desiring to have an effective population control programme, the government decided not only to continue with the Act but to further liberalise it and to make it a permanent feature of the laws of Singapore. Consequently, the Voluntary Sterilisation Act 1974 was passed by Parliament in November 1974 and came into force on 27 December 1974, repealing the original 1969 Act.[19] Under the provisions of the new Act, sterilisation may be obtained on request and would be purely a matter between the persons concerned and the doctors approved to carry out such procedures. Sterilisation is now available to persons without any children and can be performed at any time without waiting for days as long as all the necessary formalities have been completed.

Sterilisation, being one of the major components of the population control programme, was rigorously promoted by giving incentives to married women and men to undergo sterilisation. For instance, public sector employees were given one week's unrecorded leave immediately after undergoing tubal ligation or vasectomy. With effect from 1 April 1987, this one-week unrecorded leave was cancelled for those with one or more passes at Ordinary Level in the GCE examination, regardless of how many children they have.[20] The intention of this change was to discourage government employees, except the lowly-educated ones, from going for sterilisation and hence to continue to produce children in the future.

There was also the old antinatalist policy intended to encourage women or their husbands to undergo sterilisation by offering them lower accouchement fees in government hospitals. For B2 and C class wards, the fees would be waived if the woman patient or her husband underwent sterilisation within six weeks of the delivery of the baby. A modification of this scheme was put into effect on 1 April 1987 when the women warded in these lower wards could only have the fees waived if she or her husband went for the sterilisation operation after having the third of higher order births.[21] The change is meant to stop discouraging couples with only one or two children from having more children. Notwithstanding this change, the original antinatalist character underlying the policy still remained, but to a lesser extent because the fee waiver incentive is no longer available to couples producing their fourth or subsequent children.

Another change in the area of sterilisation is connected with the primary school registration system which was liberalised somewhat by extending priority to the third child in Phase 2C. The original intention of persuading married women or their husbands to undergo sterilisation was also modified. Phase 2D in the overall priority arrangement was meant for a child, one of whose parents has been sterilised before the age of forty and after the birth of the third or subsequent children.[22] The implication of this modification is that the parents can proceed to produce a fourth child without losing priority in the registration exercise under Phase 2D. The sterilisation incentive incorporated in the primary school registration system has been dismantled and no longer exist today.

FIGURE 9.3
Annual Sterilisations and Sterilisation Rate, 1970–2005

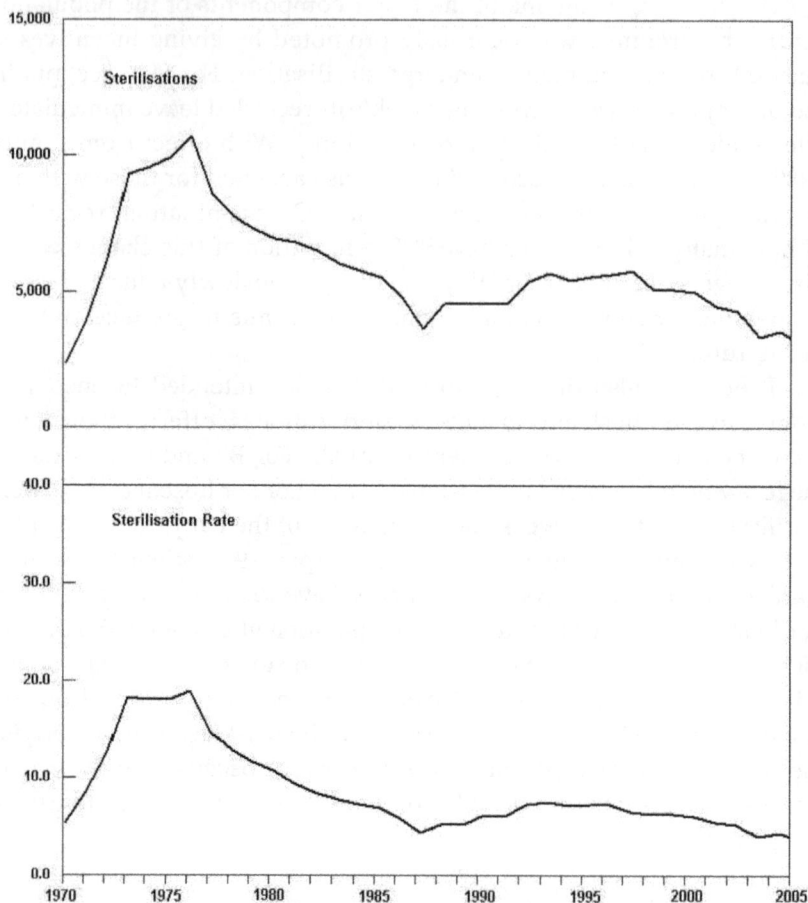

The final measure aimed at limiting sterilisation among couples was the introduction of compulsory pre-sterilisation counselling in October 1987 for women and men with only one or two children. We have observed that voluntary sterilisation in Singapore is on demand by women and men, even among those with only one or two children. This compulsory counselling is meant to change the mind of those women and men with fewer than three children, and hopefully additional children might be forthcoming in the future. These additional second or

TABLE 9.4
Male and Female Sterilisations, Sterilisation Ratio and Sterilisation Rate, 1970–2005

Year	Female Sterilizations	Male Sterilizations	Total	Sterilisation Ratio	Sterilisation Rate
1970	2,321	51	2,372	51.4	5.3
1971	3,871	99	3,970	84.1	8.4
1972	5,842	347	6,189	124.6	12.5
1973	8,964	374	9,338	193.6	18.2
1974	9,241	326	9,567	221.1	18.0
1975	9,495	453	9,948	249.0	18.0
1976	10,310	408	10,718	250.5	18.8
1977	8,236	351	8,587	223.8	14.6
1978	7,447	340	7,787	197.4	12.8
1979	6,768	495	7,263	178.1	11.6
1980	6,487	458	6,945	168.5	10.8
1981	6,312	486	6,798	160.9	9.4
1982	6,011	494	6,505	152.5	8.5
1983	5,571	456	6,027	148.5	7.7
1984	5,417	369	5,786	139.2	7.3
1985	5,233	251	5,490	129.2	6.9
1986	4,504	264	4,768	124.2	5.8
1987	3,524	128	3,652	83.7	4.4
1988	4,398	171	4,569	86.3	5.3
1989	4,367	172	4,539	95.2	5.2
1990	4,401	134	4,535	88.7	6.2
1991	4,697	163	4,560	92.8	6.1
1992	5,225	154	5,379	108.9	7.2
1993	5,549	128	5,677	113.0	7.5
1994	5,309	125	5,434	109.7	7.1
1995	5,410	152	5,562	114.4	7.2
1996	5,500	150	5,650	116.3	7.2
1997	5,600	160	5,760	118.8	6.5
1998	4,907	181	5,088	116.5	6.3
1999	4,889	191	5,080	117.2	6.3
2000	4,821	162	4,983	106.0	6.1
2001	4,280	170	4,450	107.4	5.4
2002	4,070	218	4,288	105.2	5.2
2003	3,127	206	3,333	88.9	4.0
2004	3,367	194	3,561	95.8	4.3
2005	2,825	247	3,072	81.9	3.7

third can of course enjoy the various financial and other benefits provided under the various incentive schemes.

Prior to the legalisation of voluntary sterilisation, the number of sterilisations performed in government hospitals amounted to 653 in 1967,1,057 in 1968, and 1,438 in 1969. With voluntary sterilisation put on a proper legal basis, the number increased moderately to 2,372 in 1970 and 3,970 in 1971. After the initial slow uptrend, it rose sharply to 6,189 in 1972 and to 9,338 in 1973, and then increased slowly to reach the all-time high of 10,718 in 1976; as the saturation effect came into play, it began to decrease continuously to 4,768 in 1986. The spectacular decline in the following year to 3,652 was caused by the pronatalist measures introduced at the beginning of 1987. But the impact of these measures was quickly diminished as the number bounced back to 4,569 in 1988, and remained at about this level up to 1991 and even rose in recent years to touch 5,760 in 1997. Thereafter, it took a clear downtrend, reaching the low of 3,072 in 2005, in response to the promotion of pronatalist measures.

The sterilisation ratio, also given in Table 9.4, confirms the recent trends in the incidence of sterilization. After attaining the all-time high of 250.5 in 1976, the sterilisation ratio decreased regularly to 124.2 in 1986, and then tumbled to 83.7 in the following year. Thereafter, it fluctuated around the 90-level until 1991 and then rose slowly to 118.8 in 1997, after which it went down to 81.9 in 2005. A similar trend was displayed by the sterilisation rate, which declined to the low level of 3.7 in 2005.

Notes

1. For a good discussion of population policies, see United Nations, *Determinants and Consequences of Population Trends* (New York: Department of Economic and Social Affairs, 1973).
2. A fuller account of the population control programme is given in Saw Swee-Hock, *Population Control for Zero Growth in Singapore* (New York: Oxford University Press, 1980).
3. *Straits Times*, 21 September 1938.
4. G.G. Thomson and T.E. Smith, "Singapore: Family Planning in an Urban Environment", in *The Politics of Family Planning in the Third World*, edited by T.E. Smith (London: Allen and Unwin, 1973).
5. *Fifth Annual Report of the Family Planning Association of Singapore* (Singapore, n.d.).

6. *Eighth Annual Report of the Family Planning Association of Singapore 1957* (Singapore: n.d.).
7. Singapore, *White Paper on Family Planning*, Command 22 of 1965.
8. Singapore, *Singapore Family Planning and Population Board Act* 1965, No. 32 of 1965.
9. *Annual Report of the Singapore Family Planning and Population Board, 1979* (Singapore: Eurasia Press, 1979).
10. United Nations, *Assessment of Acceptance and Effectiveness of Family Planning Methods*, Asian Population Studies No. 4 (Bangkok: Economic and Social Commission for Asia and the Pacific, 1968).
11. Singapore, *The Abortion Act 1969* (Singapore: Government Printer, 1969).
12. Singapore, *The Abortion Act 1974* (Singapore: Government Printer, 1974).
13. Singapore, *The Abortion (Amendment) Act 1980* (Singapore: Government Printer, 1980).
14. Singapore, *The Abortion (Amendment) Regulations 1981* (Singapore: Government Printer, 1981).
15. Singapore, *The Abortion (Amendment) Regulations 1982* (Singapore: Government Printer, 1982).
16. C. Tietze and S. K. Henshaw, *Induced Abortion: A World Review 1986*, 6th edition (New York: Alan Guttmacher, n.d.).
17. Singapore, The Voluntary Sterilization Act 1969 (Singapore: Government Printer, 1969).
18. Singapore, *The Voluntary Sterilization (Amendment) Act 1972* (Singapore: Government Printer, 1972).
19. Singapore, *The Voluntary Sterilization Act 1974* (Singapore: Government Printer, 1974).
20. *Straits Times*, 4 April 1987.
21. *Straits Times*, 6 March 1987.
22. *Straits Times*, 4 July 1987.

10

Fertility Policies and Programmes

With the view of strengthening the population control programme in the 1960s, the government introduced incentive and disincentive measures aimed at reducing the high level of fertility. When fertility continued below-replacement level from 1975 onwards, most of the antinatalist measures were abolished, and pronatalist measures were put in place to try to raise fertility from its extremely low level. An account of the development of these fertility policies and programmes will be presented in this chapter.

EARLY PROGRAMME

From the early sixties, the government was aware of the conflicting character of some of its policies with respect to the promotion of a small family norm within the context of a national population control programme. In introducing the Employment Act 1968, the government took the opportunity to abandon the old practice of granting paid maternity leave to working women irrespective of the number of children.[1] Under this Act, a female worker was entitled to paid maternity leave for four weeks before and four weeks after each confinement up to the third child only — a measure aimed at discouraging rather than prohibiting large families. Subsequently, paid maternity leave was further restricted to the first two confinements through a Ministry of Finance directive for the public sector and through the Employment (Amendment) Act 1973 for the private sector. In government service, female employees with more than two children could still be granted paid maternity leave prescribed by their doctors if they were sterilised after a delivery or abortion. Another way of promoting sterilisation was the granting of seven days unrecorded full-pay leave to male and female civil servants for the purpose of undergoing sterilisation.

In the area of public housing, some of the rules which had a tendency to encourage parents to produce more rather than fewer children were first changed in the late sixties. One rule stipulated that to qualify for public apartments the minimum household size had to be five, thus barring couples with no children or with fewer than three children from applying for them. In 1968, the Housing and Development Board (HDB) amended this rule to make such couples eligible for its apartments. A further relaxation was introduced in 1972 when two or more spinsters, one of whom must be at least 40 years old, were made eligible to apply to rent or buy such apartments.[2] In allocating the apartments on the point system, the HDB used to give points to those with larger families, but the rule was amended in August 1973 in such a way that family size would not be used to determine the priority for public housing. At the same time, the rule concerning subletting was revised to allow families with not more than three children to sublet their HDB and Jurong Town Corporation apartments under certain conditions; previously, subletting of any kind was prohibited.

Another disincentive aimed at discouraging large families was built into the accouchement fee charged in government maternity hospitals. For many years, the fee was fixed at a standard flat rate, but from 1 April 1969 it was raised to $50 for the fourth and subsequent child, with the fee of $20 remaining the same for the first three children. In the following year, this two-tier system was amended to $10 for the first child, $20 for the second, $50 for the third and $100 for the fourth or subsequent child. The next review of the fee took cognisance of the fact that government maternity hospitals were divided into three classes, A, B, and C. With effect from 1 August 1973, the government introduced a more comprehensive system with three different progressions of fees with advancing parity affixed to the three different classes. From the same date, the fees for patients in Classes B and C wards would be waived if the husband or wife underwent sterilisation within six months of the delivery of the child. The system of accouchement fees was adjusted many times over the years.

Another old practice which was inconsistent with the national population policy was the granting of tax relief to all children regardless of their parity. In October 1972, the tax relief for families with more than three children was revised by an amendment to the Income Tax Act. The amendment distinguished two different situations.[3] Taxpayers who had three or more children on or before 1 August 1973 were given a tax relief of $750 for the first child, $500 for the second and third, and $300 for the fourth and fifth. For those with fewer than four children after 1 August 1973, relief was fixed at $750 for the first and second child and $500 for the third. No deduction was allowed for the fourth or subsequent child born after this date.

The excessive demand for Primary One places in certain good schools necessitated the introduction of some kind of priority system in the annual registration exercise held in the middle of the year for children reaching the age of six before 1 January the following year. Incentives designed to promote small families and sterilisation were first introduced in the August 1973 registration exercise. Children who were either the first and second child of parents, one of whom had been sterilised after the birth of the first or second child, provided such sterilisation was performed before the age of 40, were accorded priority in Phase Two of the registration exercise.[4] In addition, children who were the only child were given greater priority, while children who were the fourth or subsequent child were given low preference.

Although the first incentive policy was introduced in 1968, most of the new measures and the reinforcing of old measures were effected only in the early seventies when the decline in the number of births and the crude birth rate halted and even showed an upward trend. This reversal forced the government to look beyond the family planning programme, legalised abortion and liberalised sterilisation for further measures to promote the two-child family norm. Thus, the wide range of incentives and disincentives became a vital component of the population control programme that aimed at attaining replacement fertility.

1984 PROGRAMME CHANGES

The year 1984 ushered in a new phase in the demographic history of Singapore when for the first time changes to the population control programme were designed to influence the qualitative aspect of the population. The government, believing that intelligence was determined mainly by nature rather than nurture, expressed concern about the lopsided procreation pattern in which the better-educated women were producing too few children and the lesser-educated too many children since it was feared that this would tend to lower the quality of the population.[5] The changes to the programme were therefore eugenic in nature and meant to encourage the better-educated women to produce more children and the lower-educated fewer children.[6]

The first change aimed at encouraging more births from better-educated women was announced in January 1984 in relation to the primary school registration exercise for children commencing school in January 1985. As noted earlier, antinatalist measures restricting priority to the first two children and to children with a sterilised parent had been incorporated in the registration exercise. To provide an incentive to the better-educated women to produce children, the various phases in the registration exercise were amended to provide priority to children in accordance with the educational level of their mothers. Children whose mothers had "an acceptable university degree or approved professional qualifications" were given greater priority in their choice of schools.

The announcement of the pronatalist eugenic policy provoked considerable public discussion, mainly on the grounds that it was unfair to give children of better-educated mothers an advantage over those of lesser-educated mothers. In the registration exercise of May 1984, a total of 157 children of graduate mothers were given priority under the amended scheme and the vast majority of the 4,000 or so children were still registered according to their schools of choice.[7] Apart from the extremely small number of children benefiting from the scheme, a great deal of unhappiness and resentment was generated as evidenced by letters to the press, opposition speeches in the December 1984 general election campaigns, and even, according to some political analyst, the considerable protest votes cast in the elections itself. The graduate mother scheme, as it came to be known, was therefore abolished and the old registration system was reinstated in the 1985 registration exercise for children going to school in January 1986.

The second pronatalist eugenic measure, announced in March 1984 in Parliament, was included in the existing enhanced child relief for specially-qualified women in their income tax return, which was originally intended to induce highly-educated women to remain or to re-enter the workforce.[8] Under the existing rule, specially-qualified working women were entitled to claim an additional 5 per cent of their annual earned income for each of their first three eligible children, apart from the normal child relief of $750 for the first two children and $500 for the third child which all working mothers can claim. This rule was amended to raise the enhanced child relief for specially-educated women to 5 per cent for the first child, 10 per cent for the second and 15 per cent for the third, subject to a maximum of $10,000 for each child. In addition, the eligibility for the enhanced child relief was enlarged from the original group of specially-qualified women to all working women with at least five passes at Ordinary Level in the General Certificate of Education (GCE) examination.

The amended enhanced child relief became effective for the income earned by the greatly enlarged group of better-educated women in 1984 and filed in the Year of Assessment 1985. The pronatalist eugenic measure has undoubtedly served to reinforce the original aim of the scheme in encouraging married woman with children to participate in economic activity in the context of a tight labour market in Singapore. It is probably less effective in inducing better-educated working women to produce more children because of the conflicting demands on their time and energy at home and at work. Other factors, such as the availability of good childcare centres, reliable domestic servants and relatives to take care of their children play an important role in determining whether they will produce more children. The financial gain accruing from the liberalised enhanced child relief is only one of the many considerations. Compared with the graduate mother scheme, this pronatalist eugenic policy did not encounter any serious opposition from the general public and has remained in operation.

The third pronatalist eugenic measure, aimed at single graduate women, was a completely new one, not based on the modification of any existing measure. The government expressed concern about the large proportion of single graduate women who should be married and produce children to contribute to the improvement of the quality of the population. This led to the establishment of the Social Development Unit (SDU) in the Finance Ministry in January 1984 to provide matchmaking services to single graduate officers in government departments, statutory boards, and some government-owned companies.

Unlike the other measures which were widely publicised, the activities of the Unit were conducted very discreetly. The low profile was adopted because of the very sensitive nature of government involvement in graduate matchmaking and the natural desire of the participants to protect their privacy. Gradually, more information about the work of the Unit was made known to the general public.[9] The activities of the Unit centred around getting the single graduate officers of both sexes together through its computer matchmaking service and through talks, courses, workshops, dances, parties, local outings, and overseas trips on a subsidised basis. The work of the Unit in assisting single graduates to marry so as to produce children is an integral part of the government strategy to improve the quality of the population.

Having implemented these incentive measures in early 1984 for the better-educated women to produce more children, the government announced in June 1984 the introduction of an antinatalist eugenic measure aimed at discouraging the poor and lesser-educated parents from having many children.[10] This antinatalist measure took the form of a $10,000 cash grant which is given under the following conditions:

a) The mother must be under 30 years of age and be sterilised after the first or second child;
b) Neither parent should have any GCE Ordinary Level passes;
c) Neither parent should earn more than $750 per month nor should the combined family income exceed $1,500;
d) Both parents must be Singapore citizens or permanent residents.

Under the scheme, the government would pay $10,000 into the mother's Central Provident Fund (CPF) account, and if she did not have one, an account would be opened and she would be allowed to withdraw the $10,000 plus the earned interest when she attained the age of 55 years. Alternatively, she had the option of using the money to purchase a Housing and Development Board (HDB) apartment under certain conditions. The cash grant was the first of its kind to be offered by the government as part of the national fertility policy. However, the scheme did not prove popular among the eligible couples, and only a small number took advantage of the scheme over the years. It would appear that couples are reluctant to stop at two, and more so at one, or do not consider the quantum of cash grant large enough.

Another antinatalist eugenic measure was announced at the same time as the above measure in June 1984, and it involved the modification of the system of accouchement fees. With effect from 1 March 1985, the fees were raised for the fifth and subsequent child in Class A and Class Bl and for the third child onwards for Class B2 and Class C (see Table 10.1). The changes have resulted in a common fee of $1,000 for the fifth and subsequent child delivered in all the four classes, $600 for the fourth child, and $400 for the third child delivered in the three lower classes. This is completely different from the old system which charged lower

TABLE 10.1

Changes in Accouchement Fees in Government Hospitals with Effect From 1 March 1985

Birth Order		Class A	Class B1	Class B2	Class C
1st child	no charge	$ 350	$ 200	$ 150	$ 100
2nd child	no charge	$ 450	$ 250	$ 200	$ 150
3rd child	old	$ 550	$ 400	$ 350	$ 300
	new	same	same	same	$ 400
4th child	old	$ 750	$ 600	$ 500	$ 500
	new	same	same	$ 600	$ 600
5th or subsequent child	old	$ 850	$ 700	$ 650	$ 600
	new	$1,000	$1,000	$1,000	$1,000

fees for the lower ward classes in respect of the same birth order. The underlying objective of the new fees was to discourage the poorer and presumably lesser-educated women from producing more children by imposing a relatively greater financial burden for delivering higher parity babies.

1987–89 PROGRAMME CHANGES

It was quite apparent some time before 1975 that the strong population control programme was no longer consistent with the national demographic goal of aiming for a stationary population in the future, and hence there was an urgent need to eliminate the antinatalist measures to raise fertility back to replacement level. Since this was not done, fertility has continued well below the replacement level, resulting in the worsening of the labour shortage, the acceleration of the population ageing process, and the real danger of the population actually declining in the early part of the next century.[11]

It was only in the mid-eighties that the government recognised the need to alter the national population policy and established a high-level Inter-Ministerial Population Committee to review the population control programme and to make recommendations accordingly. While the Committee was deliberating on the various aspects of the subject matter, there were some public discussions in the press.[12] After studying the recommendations of the Committee submitted in late 1986, the government announced on 1 March 1987 its decision to make major changes to the population control programme in order to encourage more births, and accordingly a new slogan was coined: "Have Three or More if You Can Afford It". Two types of changes were made, one involving the relaxation of some old antinatalist measures and the other concerning the introduction of some limited pronatalist measures. In both cases, the measures were designed to encourage women to produce more children up to the third or, at most, the fourth child.

Personal Income Tax

One method of making the old antinatalist measures less severe is to make changes to the rules governing personal income tax.[13] Under the old rule implemented in August 1973, the normal child relief was $750 for each of the first two children and $500 for the third child. Under this antinatalist schedule there was no relief for the fourth and subsequent children. A small modification was introduced whereby the relief of the third child was raised to $750 for the 1988 Year of Assessment. Parents submitting their tax returns in 1988 and subsequent years were able to claim this increased amount on their income earned in 1987. This increased relief is applicable to a third child existing at the time of announcement on 4 March 1987 as well as a third child from after this date. The effect of this change is rather negligible since the amount of increase was only $250 for the third child and more importantly, the zero relief for the fourth and subsequent child was retained.

It is therefore not surprising that the Minister for Finance, Mr Richard Hu, announced the further liberalisation of the above policy in his 1989 Budget Statement delivered in Parliament on 3 March 1989.[14] The normal child relief for personal income tax was doubled from $750 to $1,500 for the first, second and third child. A more notable change was the introduction of a new relief amounting to $1,500 for the fourth child born on or after 1 January 1988. This has the immediate impact of benefiting the parents of some 2,036 children of fourth order born in 1988.

The other modification to the personal income tax rule refers to the numerous changes to the enhanced child relief scheme announced by the Minister for Finance in his budget speech. The scheme, originally introduced in August 1978, serves the purpose of inducing mothers with special educational qualifications to remain in, enter or re-enter, the workforce. This scheme gives these women with at least five passes at Ordinary Level in the GCE examination and opted for separate assessment from their husbands to claim 5 per cent of their earned income for the first child, 10 per cent for the second child, and 15 per cent for the third child, subject to a maximum of $10,000 per child. This is in addition to their eligibility to claim the normal child relief.

The above scheme did not give working mothers the right to claim for their fourth and subsequent children. The Minister announced in Parliament a liberalisation of the existing scheme by extending the enhanced child relief to the fourth child born on or after 1 January 1988, but not backdated to the fourth child born before this date. The working mothers are eligible to claim relief for her new-born fourth child 15 per cent of her earned income, subject to the same maximum of $10,000. The other change announced by the Minister refers to the lowering of the educational qualification of the mothers from five passes to three passes at Ordinary Level in the GCE examination. With the change, working mothers possessing any three or four passes can claim enhanced child relief for the first three children born before 1 January 1988 and also for the fourth child born on or after this date. With effect from the 1990 Year of Assessment, the percentages of relief for the second, third, and fourth child were raised from 10, 15 and 15 per cent to 15, 20 and 25 per cent respectively.[15] The maximum claim for each child was also increased from $10,000 to $15,000.

In the longer term, the two modifications to the enhanced child relief scheme will result in a bigger group of working mothers being able to claim this relief for any child up to the fourth one born in 1988 and thereafter. The modifications have the advantage of reinforcing the two-fold objective of encouraging working mothers to remain in the workforce as well as to produce more children. These changes constitute a partial liberalisation of the antinatalist philosophy underlying the enhanced child relief scheme since it is not applicable to all children irrespective of birth order. Out of a total of 43,664 births born in 1988, some 700 or 0.2 per cent were from the fifth and higher order.

Tax Rebates

An important pronatalist measure was announced in the 1987 Budget Statement delivered by the Minister for Finance, Mr Richard Hu, in Parliament in March 1987.[16] This incentive refers to the granting of a special tax rebate from the 1988 Year of Assessment to couples who had their third child on or after 1 January 1987. In the following year, the rebate was extended to couples having their fourth child on or after 1 January 1988 to take effect from the 1989 Year of Assessment as declared by the Minister for Finance in Parliament in early 1988.[17] Finally, the rebate was extended to the second child born on or after 1 January 1990 on condition that the mother is below 31 years of age at the time of delivery. The amount of tax rebate is fixed at $20,000 for the third or fourth child, but it varies according to the age of the mother in the case of the second child as shown below:

Age of Mother of Delivery Date	Amount of Rebate ($)
Below 28	20,000
Below 29	15,000
Below 30	10,000
Below 31	5,000

The purpose of varying the amount of tax rebate according to age is to help mothers to bear the second child as early as possible.

The special tax rebate for each qualifying child can be utilised within a period of nine years from the Year of Assessment following the year of birth of the qualifying child. The rebates for the second, third and fourth children may be claimed consecutively within a cumulative period of 27 years. The rebate can be utilised to set-off against either the husband's or wife's account, and vice versa. Another feature of the tax rebate scheme is that if the working wife has opted for separate assessment, she is entitled to a further tax rebate equivalent to 15 per cent of her earned income in lieu of maternity leave not made available to mothers giving birth to the third or fourth child.[18] However, this rebate can only be employed to offset the wife's tax liabilities. Her earned income is defined to include income received from trade, business, profession, vocation or employment.

There are of course certain conditions attached to the granting of the special tax rebates. Only legitimate children or stepchildren are eligible for the tax rebate, and adopted children do not qualify the parents for the rebate. All the children must be Singapore citizens at the time of birth or within 12 months after birth to ensure that only families committed to the country can benefit from this pronatalist incentive. If the qualifying child is given up for adoption or the marriage is dissolved by divorce, the tax rebate will cease from the Year of Assessment following the year of divorce. The impact of this pronatalist policy should be more extensive and lasting as almost all parents with two, three or four children are tax payers, and thus stand to gain from this financial incentive every year until the fourth child starts working years later.

A different kind of pronatalist incentive linked to personal income tax refers to medical expenses incurred in childbirth. With effect from 1 January 1988, delivery and hospital expenses for a fourth child can be offset against the earned income of the parents, subject to a maximum of $3,000. The tax structure is such that this incentive will benefit mostly parents earning $2,000 or more per month. But the implementation date of 1 January 1988 implies that parents with an existing fourth child or expecting a fourth child on 4 March 1987 cannot benefit from this new policy. The financial incentive is confined not only to future births, but to the fourth child only and not to the third child. The influence of this policy will probably be not so significant as the amount of financial gain is relatively small and receivable on a one-off basis.

Primary School Registration

We have noted earlier the incorporation of antinatalist measures in 1973 in the annual registration of Primary One school children conducted in the middle of the year for them to commence schooling in January the following year. Over the years various changes were introduced in this annual registration exercise, and by 1986 some kind of priority was given to children of families with up to three children, except for one category in Phase 2C (see Table 10.2).

With effect from the registration exercise held in mid-1987 for children commencing Primary One education in January 1988, Phase 2C was amended as indicated in the table.[19] The extension of priority to the three-child family in the second category of Phase 2C has removed the remaining penalty imposed on the third child. Priority for a third child has already been accorded in all the other stages in the registration exercise.

TABLE 10.2
Amendment to Primary School Registration, 1987

Old System	New System
Phase 2C Second or third child whose brother/sister is studying in an affiliated school	Phase 2C No change
OR Child from a one-child or two-child family	OR Child from a one-child, two-child or three-child family

Use of Medisave

Medisave is a compulsory savings scheme introduced in April 1984 as an integral part of the Central Provident Fund (CPF). The scheme has been designed to help Singaporeans build up sufficient savings for their hospitalisation expenses, especially in their old age. Under the scheme, every employee contributes 6–8 per cent, depending on his age group, of his monthly salary to a special Medisave account. The savings can be withdrawn to pay the hospital bills of the account holder and his immediate family members.

The Medisave scheme could previously be employed to pay for medical expenses incurred in childbirth for the first two children only. This facility was extended on 1 March 1987 when payment of delivery and hospital charges for the third child can be made from the Medisave account. With effect from 1 January 1988, delivery and hospital expenses for a fourth child could be offset against the parents' earned income, subject to a maximum of $3,000. This liberalisation of the old antinatalist policy will make it easier for couples to have their third and fourth child by allowing them to use their savings in the Central Provident Fund (CPF) through the Medisave scheme. The impact of the changes was relatively insignificant as the quantum of financial gain was relatively small and given on a one-off basis.

Childcare Subsidy

It was recognised that not all working mothers have relatives such mothers or mothers-in-law or domestic maids to look after their young children at home, and even if they have such persons, they may still need to send their kids to childcare centres. A pronatalist financial incentive in the form of a childcare subsidy was therefore offered on 1 April 1987 to parents sending their young children to childcare centres.[20] For the purpose of administering this subsidy, the young children are subdivided into those aged 2 months to below 18 months and those aged 18 months to below 7 years. The government decided to pay a subsidy of $100 per month to working mothers for each of their first three pre-school children under 7 years of age placed in approved full-day childcare centres. If the child remains in the crèche for only half a day, the subsidy will be reduced to $50 accordingly. The subsidy was later raised to $150 for full-day childcare and $75 for half-day. At least one of the parents must be a Singapore citizen or permanent resident in order to qualify for the subsidy. By definition the childcare subsidy is applicable to children aged 18 months to less than 7 years old.

Public Sector Flexible Work

Apart from leave, the public sector took the lead in instituting flexible work to permit staff to look after their children and families. With effect from 1 April 1987, a new pronatalist measure was made available to women officers in the civil service with a child under six years of age to convert their full-time job into part-time work up to a maximum of three years.[21] The part-time officer must work 21 hours, equivalent to half of the normal week, and must spread this shortened hours over at least five days a week from Monday to Friday. Her monthly salary will be half that of a full-time officer and she will be entitled to one increment once in two years. The idea behind this policy is to make it easier for some of the married women to have their first child or additional children without having to cease working completely.

Public Sector Leave

Earlier on 6 March 1987, the Ministry of Finance had announced the introduction of a pronatalist policy linked to the granting of short unrecorded leave to working mothers in the public sector.[22] With effect from 1 April 1987, working mothers are entitled to take paid unrecorded leave to attend to their sick children. They can apply for such leave limited to five days for each child under six years of age up to the first three children. Every application must be supported by a medical certificate for the sick child. This special leave is addition to the normal leave and sick leave to which the mother is entitled.

Public Housing

In Singapore about 90 per cent of the population stay in apartments purchased from or rented from the Housing and Development Board (HDB). Some subsidised apartments are of course governed by a set of rules, including those concerning the sale of existing apartments to purchase bigger apartments. First of all, there was the rule saying that if the owners had stayed in the apartment for less than five years, they cannot sell the apartments in the open market at usually a higher price, but must sell it back to the HDB. There is another rule requiring the apartments to be sold back to HDB and not in the open market if they are second or third ones. As for the larger apartments the owners wishing to buy, the application would be placed in a queue to be processed on a first-come-first-served basis.

A new pronatalist incentive was implemented by HDB on 4 April 1987 in respect of the sale of an existing apartment to purchase a bigger one.[23] The rules were altered to make it easier for families with a third child born on or after 1 January 1987 to sell their three-room or larger apartment and buy a bigger one. They can jump the queue by backdating their application by three years, thus enabling them to buy the bigger apartment sooner. Moreover, they can sell their existing apartment on the open market even if they had resided in it for less than the required five years, and even if their apartment is a second or third one. Though this liberalised policy applies to couples with a third child, the HDB will also consider, on its own merit, couples with a fourth child wishing to take advantage of the new policy. This new policy making it easier for HDB dwellers to upgrade to larger apartments was formulated to enable them to accommodate more children.

The HDB has also revised other rules to give some pronatalist incentives to couples staying in its apartments. The first change refers to rules concerning the third child. If the mother's first pregnancy results in twins, the child born in the second pregnancy will be treated as the third child. If the third pregnancy results in twins, the couple can still benefit from the new policy though they have four children. The second change concerns divorcees who remarry. The number of children they are given custody of will be counted in the application of the new policy.

The implementation date of the new policy was backdated to 1 January 1987, and the benefits will be restricted to existing children born during 1 January to 4 March 1987, children due to be born, and children from future pregnancies. HDB couples with existing children born before 1987 cannot benefit from the new policy. Finally, although they are not given any direct financial incentives from the HDB or the government, they can in fact gain financially by selling their existing apartment in the open market rather than being compelled to sell back to the HDB.

2000 PROGRAMME CHANGES

The next major group of pronatalist measures were introduced in the new millennium following the traditional address by the Prime Minister, Mr Goh Chok Tong, in the National Day Rally held on 20 August 2000. Among other things, he said, "We must create a total environment conducive to raising a family. Our policy is to have three children or more if you can afford it".[24] It is important to emphasise that the somewhat restricted pronatalist policies are quite different from those completely pronatalist policies adopted in many European countries to raise the level of their below-replacement fertility.

Third Child Maternity Leave

We have taken note of the antinatalist policy introduced in the early seventies which restricts paid maternity leave of eight weeks of the first two children in the Employment Act.[25] Unpaid maternity leave of eight weeks is still available to mothers regardless of the birth order. The relaxation of this old antinatalist policy was announced by the Prime Minister, Mr Goh Chok Tong, in his address delivered in the National Day Rally held on 20 August 2000.

In discussing the issue of paid maternity leave for the third child, he said,

> "We must create a total environment conducive to raising a family. Our policy is to have three children or more if you can afford it .... We have to do something, even while recognising that getting married and having children are personal decisions .... Many Singaporeans have said

that the lack of paid maternity leave for the third child is an obstacle to having their third child. The Government will help reduce the obstacle to you being so."[26]

The key issue in giving paid maternity leave for the third child is the question of who is going to pay for the salary bearing in mind the necessity not to overburden the employers with additional costs.

Instead of taking unpaid maternity leave, working mothers can take eight weeks of paid maternity leave when they give birth to their third child with effect from 1 April 2001. Their employers are not required to incur any expenses because government will pay the cost of the maternity leave for the third child, subject to a maximum of $20,000. A system was put in place whereby the employers would continue to pay the usual salary to the working mothers, and claim for reimbursement from the Minister of Community Development and Sports, responsible for the administration of this scheme.[27]

To be eligible for the scheme, mothers who are employed or self-employed must fulfil certain conditions. The child's mother must be lawfully married to the child's father at the time of birth, the child must be a Singapore citizen, and the child must be the third live-birth of the mother. Stepchildren or adopted children are not eligible for the scheme and cannot be employed to reckon the birth order of the children in the family. To qualify for the scheme, the mother must have worked with the employer for at least 180 days prior to the birth of the child. There are, however, no eligibility criteria linked to the age or educational qualification of the working mothers.

If the working mother already has a first child and produces a pair of twins, she can only claim either the second or third child maternity leave, but not both. If she is already entitled to the second child maternity leave paid by the employer under the Employment Act, she will not be allowed to claim for the new third child maternity leave scheme. If a third child was born before the implementation date of 1 April 2001, she can only claim for the period of the maternity leave consumed on or after 1 April 2001. The amount receivable will be pro-rated according to the actual duration of the leave period covered by the scheme.

To enable the employer to pay the mother the usual payroll while she is on the third child maternity leave, she must submit a declaration form (Form ML1) to her employer at least one week prior to commencing her maternity leave. The employer will in turn submit a claim form

(Form ML2) to the Ministry of Community Development and Sports after the completion of the eight-week maternity leave, and this must be done within one month. The reimbursement of the amount paid to her will be deposited into the employer's bank account within three weeks for internet submission and four weeks for manual submission.

An important advantage of the scheme is that it allows self-employed mothers to participate in the scheme in order to compensate them for the loss of earnings during their maternity leave. They must not be actively engaged in their trade, business, profession or vocation during the maternity leave period and have suffered loss of income before they can submit their claim. They must submit the completed Form ML3 to the Ministry of Community Development and Sports, together with a six-month income and expenditure statement for the period preceding the maternity leave, the latest available year-end income and expenditure account declared for taxation, and certification of Registration of Business Company. Upon approval of the application, they will be reimbursed an amount equivalent to the average monthly net income earned in the 180 days before the maternity leave period.

Baby Bonus

By far the most important pronatalist policy promulgated by the Prime Minister in the 2000 National Day Rally was the baby bonus scheme. This scheme was put into effect on 1 April 2000 for parents producing a second or third child on or after this date. The scheme consists of a two-tier payment given annually by the government for a period of six years after the birth of the child. In the first tier, the government will give an outright cash gift, while in the second both the parents and the government will contribute to a co-savings account. The scheme has been structured in such a manner as to provide extra funds for the parents to use solely for the benefit of the children. The Family Services Department in the Ministry of Community Development and Sports is responsible for administering the baby bonus scheme.[28]

To be eligible for the baby bonus, the mother must be legally married to the child's father at the time of the child's birth or conception, the child must be a Singapore citizen, and the child must be the second or third child born alive to his mother. This means that step children or adopted children will not be entitled to the baby bonus, nor can they be counted to determine the birth order of the eligible children. Children born to Singaporeans overseas are entitled to the baby bonus when they take up Singapore citizenship. Multiple births such as twins, triplets and quadruplets are considered as separate births in reckoning the birth order of the children eligible for the baby bonus.[29]

The procedures adopted to administer the scheme are quite established and streamlined. It is not necessary for the parents to apply for the scheme since, based on birth registration records in the Registry of Births and Deaths, an invitation to participate in the scheme will be sent automatically by the Ministry of Community Development and Sports. The parents have the option to decline or accept the invitation by returning the completed Declaration Form. Under the first tier, the government will pay into the bank account of the parents a cash gift of $500 for the second child and $1,000 for the third child when the baby bonus application is approved. Thereafter, the cash bonus will be paid five times more on the first to the fifth anniversary of the opening of the bank account, bringing the total sum to $3,000 for the second child and $6,000 for the third child. The parents have the discretion to employ the cash gift to defray the costs and incidental expenses of the care and development of the child.

The second tier resembles a co-savings arrangement whereby the government will match dollar-for-dollar the annual amount the parents put into the child's Children Development Account (CDA) opened with the participating bank, DBS Bank. The parents may contribute any amount per year, but the matching payment by the government is subjected to a maximum of $1,000 for the second child and $2,000 for the third child. The matching contribution by the government will be made six months after the opening of the CDA, and subsequently every twelve months. The money can be employed to pay for the fees at approved institutions such as kindergartens, childcare centres and other pre-school programmes. Furthermore, the money can be used for all the children in the family and not just for the relevant second or third child. Any funds and interests remaining in the CDA when the child reaches seven years will be transferred to the Edusave account of the child.

A clearer picture of the baby bonus scheme is presented in Table 10.3 showing the numerical examples of the first tier and the second tier. For these two examples, it is assumed that the parents contribute the maximum of $1,000 for the second child and $2,000 for the third. The parents have money to spend for the benefit of the children to the amount of $2,500 per year from the entitlement of the second child, and

TABLE 10.3

Baby Bonus Scheme for the Second Child and the Third Child

Year	First Government Contribution ($)	Second Tier Parents' Contribution ($)	Second Tier Government Contribution ($)	Total ($)
		Second Child		
First	500	1,000	1,000	2,500
Second	500	1,000	1,000	2,500
Third	500	1,000	1,000	2,500
Fourth	500	1,000	1,000	2,500
Fifth	500	1,000	1,000	2,500
Sixth	500	1,000	1,000	2,500
Total	**3,000**	**6,000**	**6,000**	**15,000**
		Third Child		
First	1,000	2,000	2,000	5,000
Second	1,000	2,000	2,000	5,000
Third	1,000	2,000	2,000	5,000
Fourth	1,000	2,000	2,000	5,000
Fifth	1,000	2,000	2,000	5,000
Sixth	1,000	2,000	2,000	5,000
Total	**6,000**	**12,000**	**12,000**	**30,000**

$5,000 from the third child. The sum available will of course be less if the contributions from the parent are below the two maximum figures. The baby bonus scheme has been structured in such a manner that financial incentives are not given to parents producing the first child, and, more importantly, the fourth and subsequent children. It is a pronatalist policy of a limited kind, and different from those in other countries where restrictions on the utilisation of the money are not imposed.

Childcare Subsidy

A complementary scheme to childcare subsidy is the infant care subsidy given to working mothers who put their infants aged 2 months to 18 months old in childcare centres. The amount of subsidy is the same, but the fees for these infants are much higher than those for children aged

18 months to below 7 years. The working mothers have to spend very much more in sending their infants to the centres. Another difficulty confronting the mothers is the inadequate number of childcare centres taking care of infants since not all centres provide infant care services. Non-working mothers, ineligible for the two types of subsidies, have been clamouring for some financial assistance. The government finally conceded in January 2002 when a subsidy of $75 per month was given to non-working mothers who enrol their kids aged under 18 months or aged 18 months to below 7 years in childcare centres. Regardless of the type of subsidy, the government pays the money to the care centre, and the parents pay the difference between the subsidy they are entitled to and the full fee charged by the centre.

To overcome the shortage of care centres and the reluctance of some mothers to put their children in these centres, the Ministry for Community Development and Sports established the Family Day Care Service scheme for mothers with infant age 2 to 18 months.[30] Under this scheme the mothers can approach 10 childcare centres to matchmake nannies of their choice to take care of their kids on a full-day basis in the homes of the nannies. In most cases the parents have to take the kids to the nanny's home. The nanny is paid about $500 to $625 per month, and the childcare centres are paid up to $30,000 to cover the administration and other expenses incurred in providing the nanny matchmaking services.

Public Sector Flexible Work

Following the National Day Rally held in August 2000, it was announced on 28 August 2000 that government departments would be permitted to adopt flexible working hours for their staff.[31] The working hours of each employee can be adjusted within the framework of 42 hours per week without any loss in productivity and lapse in standard of service. Within these general guidelines, is it possible to come to an arrangement whereby an officer can work five days per week, but working long hours during the five days to clock a total of 42 hours. The departments must still operate a six-day week.

Public Sector Leave

The second category of pronatalist measures is related to the leave of employees in the public sector, which is easier to change since government has the authority to alter the working condition of civil servants. Soon after the National Day Rally speech by the Prime Minister, it was announced on 28 August 2000 by the Chairman of the Working Committee on Marriage and Procreation, Mr Eddie Teo, that a government employee will be permitted to take three days' paid marriage leave when he marries for the first time.[32] This special leave, effective from 1 October 2000, is meant to facilitate civil servants to get married. It was also declared that with effect from the same date, fathers in civil service will be allowed to take three days' paternity leave to look after their first three children. It is hoped that this pro-family measure will assist husbands to play a bigger role in raising their children.

Public Housing

An old Housing and Development Board rule required young couples to pay a 20 per cent down payment for the purchase of an apartment. With effect from 28 August 2000, the rule was relaxed to permit the down payment to be made in two stages, 10 per cent when the couple sign the agreement and the other 10 per cent when they take possession of the apartment. This will apply to first-time couples buying a four-room apartment from 1 October 2000. The husband or wife must be between 21 and 30 years of age. This relaxation of the HDB rule is meant to facilitate young couples to marry and start a family as soon as possible.

2004 PROGRAMME CHANGES

We have observed that on the basis of the recommendations of the Inter-Ministerial Population Committee, the government implemented a wide range of incentive measures in 1987 aimed at encouraging women to produce more children. This was subsequently followed by a few pronatalist measures announced by the Prime Minister in the National Day Rally held in August 2000. The effectiveness of all the measures has not been very encouraging mainly because they were formulated to loosen some of the old antinatalist measures and to introduce some limited pronatalist measures. Furthermore, the socio-economic factors favouring small family norms have continued to exert a strong influence in prolonging the movement of low fertility below the replacement level.

The government became extremely concerned about the continuous decline of the low fertility below the replacement level and the attendant

fall in the number of births from 46,997 in 2000 to the second low of
37,485 in 2003. In presenting his Budget to Parliament on 22 February
2004, the then Deputy Prime Minister and Finance Minister, Mr Lee
Hsien Loong, said:

> "Our existing measures are not enough. We must take a more
> comprehensive approach to solving this problem. We must encourage
> young people to marry and marry earlier, and make it easier for young
> couples to start and raise a family.... The approach must be both holistic
> and coherent, addressing parents' concerns from childbirth through the
> years of bringing up their children".[33]

In March 2004 the government established a Working Committee on
Population with Mr Eddie Teo, Permanent Secretary to the Prime
Minister's Office, as the Chairman. Other members of the Committee
were the permanent secretaries of several ministries and chiefs of some
statutory boards and government departments.[34] The Working Committee
was required to submit its findings to a five-member Steering Group on
Population chaired by Mr Lim Hng Kiang, Minister in the Prime Minister's
Office. The other members of this group consisted of Dr Yacoob Ibrahim,
Minister for Community Development and Sports, Dr Ng Eng Hen,
Acting Minister for Manpower, and two members of Parliament, Mrs
Lim Hwee Hua and Dr Amy Khor.[35]

In formulating the new package of pronatalist measures, the Steering
Group has benefited from extensive feedback from public emails,
telephone calls, letters to the press, media stories, and tripartite
consultation with employee and union representatives. By August 2004,
the Steering Group was able to complete its deliberations and submitted
its recommendations. The main features of the new package were made
known by the new Prime Minister, Mr Lee Hsien Loong, in his National
Day Rally held on 22 August 2004. More information was provided a few
days later in a press conference held by the Steering Group with all five
members engaged in a question-and-answer session. The details of the
new package were given in a press release and also in the websites of
relevant ministries, especially the Ministries of Community Development
and Sports, Manpower and Health.

The new package of measures seek to ease the burden, financial or
otherwise, of parenthood in promoting marriage, facilitating conception,
making child birth more affordable, increasing childcare options, giving
of financial support to raising children, and encouraging conducive

work-life situation. Some of the measures constitute a further relaxation of old antinatalist policies as well as a further strengthening of the limited pronatalist policies implemented earlier. The more important point to note is that the new package also contains a wide range of new pronatalist measures, some of which constitute a radical departure from traditional beliefs and practices. A discussion of these new pronatalist measures will be presented later while we start with the strengthening of the old pronatalist measures.

Use of Medisave

We have noted earlier that the use of Medisave for medical expenses incurred in childbirth was extended from the first two children to the first three with effect from 1 March 1987. Under the new Medisave maternity package, the use of Medisave for maternity purposes has been extended to women giving birth to their fourth child on or after 1 August 2004. Another concession is that Medisave can be utilised for the pre-delivery and delivery medical expenses incurred by women giving birth to the fifth and subsequent child provided the parents have a combined Medisave balance of at least $15,000 at the time of delivery.[36] This minimum balance is necessary to prevent premature depletion of the Medisave accounts of the parents so that they would have sufficient funds for future hospitalisation needs, particularly during their old age.

The Medisave maternity package has also been structured in such a manner as to assist couples with delivery expenses and pre-delivery medical expenses such as consultations and ultrasound. Under the new arrangement, parents are allowed to withdraw up to $450 more their Medisave to pay for the delivery and pre-delivery medical expenses of the fourth births born on or after 1 August 2004. This scheme can also be extended to similar expenses of the fifth and subsequent birth if the parent have a combined Medisave balance of $15,000 at the time of delivery. The reason for this minimum sum has been explained earlier.

Another liberalisation of the use of Medisave concerns the current practice of allowing it to be used to pay for expenses arising from assisted conception procedures, subject to a withdrawal limit of $4,000 per treatment cycle up to a maximum of three treatment cycles. To increase the ability of couples to undergo this type of treatment, the withdrawal limit has been raised to $6,000, $5,000 and $4,000 for the first, second and third treatment cycles respectively. Couples undergoing treatment on or after 1 August 2004 can benefit from this revised limits since they can use more Medisave and thereby reduce their out-of-pocket payment. However, the use of Medisave for assisted conception procedures is still restricted to a maximum of three treatment cycles as the success rates tend to fall sharply after the third cycle. The restriction is meant to prevent a large increase in the number of claimable cycles from rapidly depleting the Medisave funds meant primarily for future use in old age.

Extra Paid Maternity Leave

One of the antinatalist policies implemented in the early seventies to discourage women from producing too many children was the amendment to the Employment Act to restrict paid maternity leave of eight weeks to the first two children. In April 2001 this maternity leave scheme was relaxed to allow women to take eight-week maternity leave when they give birth to the third child, but their normal salary during this period was paid by the government instead of their employer. The maternity leave scheme was further relaxed in 2004 by extending maternity leave to working women giving birth to their fourth child and, more importantly, by lengthening the leave period from 8 weeks to 12 weeks for the first four births.[37] For the first two confinements, the employers will continue to pay for the 8-week maternity leave according to the Employment Act, and the government will pay for the extra 4 weeks subject to a maximum of $10,000. As for the third and fourth confinements, the government will fund the full 12 weeks with a cap of $30,000. The extra four weeks for the first and second birth and the full 12 weeks for the third and fourth birth are provided by an amendment of the Children Development Co-Savings Act enacted in Parliament on 21 September 2004. The amended Act also gives woman executives, managers, confidential staff, civil servants and statutory board employees the entitlement to the extended paid maternity leave.

In practice, the salary will continue to be paid to the mother by the employer for the duration of the extra maternity leave, and the employer will in turn claim reimbursement from the government. The employer is not required to pay above the capped amounts, though he can choose to do so voluntarily. The additional 4 weeks can be taken in a flexible manner over a period of 6 months from the birth of the child with the mutual agreement of the both the employee and employer. Otherwise, the 4-week leave has to be consumed as a block immediately after the first 8 weeks. The latest relaxation of maternity leave is aimed at encouraging working mothers to have more children by relieving some of their financial burden and by giving them more time to rest and take care of their newborn. Moreover, the option accorded to them to take the additional 4 weeks flexibly will give them more time to arrange for good infant care and ease back into the workplace.

In order to qualify for the government disimbursement through her employer under the enhanced maternity leave scheme, a female employee must fulfil the following requirements:

(a) Her child is a Singapore citizen at the time of birth, and must be born on or after 1 October 2004.
(b) She has not more than 3 children at the time of her confinement.
(c) She is lawfully married to the child's father at the time of child's conception or birth.
(d) She has worked for her employer for at least 180 days before the birth of the child.

Self-employed married women are also entitled to the government-paid maternity leave. In addition to satisfying requirements (a), (b) and (c), they must fulfil two other conditions. First, they must have been engaged in a particular business/trade/profession as vocation for at least 180 days before the birth of the child. Second, they have lost income as a result of not engaging in their trade, business, profession or vocation during the maternity leave period.

We have observed the ineligibility of adopted children to benefit form the mandatory 8-week paid maternity for the first two births under the Employment Act and from the government-paid third child maternity leave scheme discussed earlier. Similarly, adopted children do not qualify for the extra maternity leave scheme. As part of its pro-family gesture, the government decided to introduce a special scheme whereby it will fund up to 4 weeks of maternity leave for a mother who adopts a child on or after 1 August 2004 if the employer agrees to provide the leave on a voluntary basis. The funding is capped at $10,000, including CPF contributions, and she must satisfy the following conditions:

(a) She is married, widowed or divorced at the time of the child's adoption or naturalisaion.

(b) She must have fewer than 4 children, excluding adopted children and stepchildren.

(c) The adopted child is a Singapore citizen or becomes one at the time of adoption or naturalisation.

(d) The adoption and naturalisation process, where applicable, must be completed before the child reaches 6 months old.

(e) The leave is consumed before the child turns 6 months old.

According to the procedure put in place by the government, the female employee is required to submit a declaration form to her employer at least a week before she commences her maternity leave. She should reach an agreement before hand with her employer regarding the manner in which she would like to take the extra leave. Her employer will make an initial check to ensure that she qualifies for the benefit and seek reimbursement from the government later. She would continue to receive her salary from her employer throughout her maternity leave as if she had been working without any break. The employer would submit a claim to the government for reimbursement after the employee has completed her extra 4 weeks of maternity leave for the first or second birth and 12 weeks for the third or fourth birth.

CPF Top-Up Grant for HDB Apartments

Apart from the further relaxation of the above two old antinatalist measures, the government strengthened some of the limited pronatalist measures discussed in the previous chapter. We have noted a minor relaxation of the method of down payment for the purchase of an apartment for first-time couples with effect from 28 August 2000. The use of subsidised public housing to promote marriage among young Singaporeans was reinforced in August 2004 with the introduction of the CPF housing top-up grant scheme. Under this scheme, a married couple can apply to top-up the singles grant to family grant for the present apartment they wish to retain as their matrimonial apartment. As for the purchase of another resale apartment, they receive a top-up grant equivalent to the difference between the current family grant of $30,000 for existing apartment or $40,000 for resale apartment and the singles grant they have already received.

Under the singles grant scheme, the grant can be employed to pay the down payment, and if they is any balance left, it must be employed to reduce the mortgage loan. The singles grant cannot be used to offset the cash payment where the declared resale price exceeds the market valuation. To qualify for the singles grant scheme, the applicant must be a Singapore citizen, at least 35 years old and a single person who is unmarried, divorced or widowed.[38] The gross monthly household income must not exceed $3,000, and the applicant can only purchase up to a five-room apartment.

With the introduction of the CPF top-up grant scheme, an apartment owner who had received the singles grant before can apply to top-up the singles grant to a family grant for the current flat to be retained as a matrimonial apartment. The top-up grant can be used for lump-sum repayment or full redemption of the mortgage loan, but cannot be employed to pay the monthly instalments. If the top-up grant exceeds the outstanding mortgage loan, the applicant and the spouse can decide on the amount to be deducted from the respective amount each will receive to redeem the loan. If the top-up grant is more than enough to discharge the mortgage loan, the balance will be deposited into the applicant's or the spouse's CPF account. This unused amount of top-up grant can be used to purchase another HDB apartment in the future, or it can remain as part of the CPF money available for withdrawal under the CPF rules when the applicant or the spouse reaches 55 years of age.

The CPF top-up grant can also be employed to purchase another resale apartment with the spouse. The top-up grant derived from the difference between the singles grant and family grant will be deposited into the applicant's CPF account or the spouse's account, or both their accounts according to the approved proportions. The top-up grant can be used to pay the downpayment of the resale flat if the applicant does not have sufficient CPF savings. Any balance left must be utilised to reduce the mortgage loan. The top-up grant must not be used to offset the cash payment where the resale price exceeds the market valuation. If the applicant is purchasing a resale flat with a bank loan, the top-up grant will be treated as part of the applicant's or the spouse's CPF fund, which can be employed to pay for the CPF portion of the downpayment, but not the cash portion, or to reduce the mortgage loan.

Extending Baby Bonus to First and Fourth Child

In the previous chapter we have discussed the introduction of a limited pronatalist measure in April 2000 in the form of a baby bonus for the second and third child. To lighten further the financial burden of raising children, the baby bonus scheme has been extended to the first and fourth child born on or after 1 August 2004. Under the enhanced baby bonus scheme, the cash gift that parents can receive from the government amounts to $3,000 each for the first and second child, and $6,000 each for the third and fourth child. In addition, the co-savings arrangement will enable the parents to receive a maximum of $6,000 for the second child and a maximum of $12,000 for each of the third and fourth child from the government.[39] The co-savings arrangement does not apply to the first child. On the whole, the parents can expect to receive from the government a maximum sum of $3,000 for the first child, $9,000 for the second child, and $18,000 each for the third and fourth child.

In the 2000 baby bonus scheme, the cash gift from the government is paid to the parents in six annual instalments over a period of six years. The cash gift is now given out earlier in five equal instalments over a shorter period of 18 months from the birth of the child so that the parents can choose to use the cash for more immediate expenses consequent on the newborn. The cash gift for each entitled child is given within 3 weeks after the mother joins the scheme, and the subsequent cash contributions are provided when the child reaches 6, 12 and 18 months of age (see Table 10.4). The cash gift is deposited directly into the nominated bank account of the parents.

TABLE 10.4
Cash Gift Schedule

Age of Child	Birth Order	
	First & Second	Third & Fourth
Within 3 weeks after Joining the scheme	$750	$1,500
6 months	$750	$1,500
12 months	$750	$1,500
18 months	$750	$1,500
Total	$3,000	$6,000

The co-savings to be contributed by both the parents and the government are deposited in a special savings account opened for the child at any POSB branch. This account, also known as Children Development Account, recognises that the primary responsibility for providing for the child rests with the parents. The government will match dollar-for-dollar the amount of savings the parents contribute to their child's account. There are 6 co-savings periods, with the first period beginning with the opening of the account and ending on the last day of the month before the child's first birthday. Subsequent co-savings periods are of one year each and start from the child's month of birth. For each co-savings period, the parent's savings would be matched in the child's month of birth up to a maximum of $1,000 for the second child, and $2,000 for the third and fourth child (see Table 10.5). As mentioned earlier, there is no co-savings arrangement for the first child. The funds in the account may be employed to pay the fees of approved childcare centres, kindergartens and special schools. The funds can be used by all their children attending the approved institutions.

For a child to qualify for the baby bonus scheme, the following conditions must be fulfilled:

(a) born on or after 1 August 2004;
(b) is a Singapore citizen or becomes a Singapore citizen;
(c) is the first to fourth child born alive to the mother;
(d) the mother is lawfully married to the child's father at the time of the child's birth or conception.

An adopted child is also eligible for the baby bonus scheme if the adoption occurred on or after 1 August 2004. Furthermore, the adopted child must be less than 6 years old on or after 1 August 2004, a Singapore citizen, and the first and fourth child of the adoptive mother, divorcee or widower. Regardless of whether the child is adopted or the natural child

TABLE 10.5
Government Matching in A Co-savings Schedule

Age of Child	Birth Order	
	Second	Third & Fourth
1	Up to $1,000	Up to $2,000
2	Up to $1,000	Up to $2,000
3	Up to $1,000	Up to $2,000
4	Up to $1,000	Up to $2,000
5	Up to $1,000	Up to $2,000
6	Up to $1,000	Up to $2,000
Total	Up to $6,000	Up to $12,000

of the mother, stepchildren and children who are not Singapore citizens are not considered in the counting of birth order.

The baby bonus scheme was liberalised in March 2005 to allow parents to save more in one year and less in another, depending on what they can afford within the stipulated six-year period. In addition, they were allowed to use the co-savings to buy health insurance for the children or to pay for programmes for their disabled children with special needs. In August 2005, the scheme was further extended by raising the age limit for contribution to the Children Development Account from 6 to 18 years of age. Parents have 12 years more to contribute to the maximum amount matched by the government. The unused savings at the end of age 6 will be automatically transferred to the Child Post-Secondary Education Account once he starts primary school. The savings can be used to pay for the child's education in junior colleges, polytechnics and universities.

Increased Infant Care Subsidy

It may be recalled that the government has been providing a subsidy of $150 through childcare centres to working mothers who put an infant aged 2 months to below 18 months or a child aged 18 months to less than 7 years in a care centre. But the fee charged by the centre is very much higher for the infant than for the child. As part of the overall package of pronatalist incentives, the government increased with effect from 1 August 2004 the monthly subsidy for infant care from $150 to $400. This subsidy is available to an infant aged 2 years to below 18 months who is a Singapore citizen and belonging to the birth order from first to fourth.[40] This increased subsidy makes it more affordable and easier for working mothers to take care of their children by enrolling their infant in infant care programmes in licensed care centres.

The increased infant care subsidy is also available on a pro-rated basis for infants receiving less than a full-day care as shown in Table 10.6. It is to be noted that the subsidy has remained at $75 per full-day or half-day for non-working mothers. Single fathers who are divorced or widowed are also entitled to the infant care subsidy. The monthly subsidy according to the schedule shown in table is paid by the government to the care centres which will collect from the parent the subsidised fee equivalent to the difference between the full-fee and the government subsidy.

TABLE 10.6

Infant Care Subsidy Rates

Programme (Daily Care)	Working Mother	Non-working Mother
Full-day Care	$400	$75
Half-day Care	$200	$75
Flexible Programme Number of Hours Per Week	**Working Mother**	**Non-working Mother**
12 hours to 24 hours	$100	$25
Above 24 hours to 36 hours	$200	$50
Above 36 hours to 48 hours	$300	$75
Above 48 hours	$400	$75

Parenthood Tax Relief

One of the limited pronatalist measures discussed in the previous chapter refers to the special tax rebate which amounted to $20,000 for the third or the fourth child, and $5,000 to $20,000 for the second child of the mother depending on the age of the mother. This special tax rebate had been replaced by a more liberal parenthood tax rebate to take effect from the 2005 Year of Assessment.[41] As compared to the special tax rebate, the parenthood tax rebate has been liberalised in the following manner:

1. It does not have an age requirement for the mother to claim rebate for the second child as in the special tax rebate.
2. It has no time limit of 9 years for claiming the rebate as in the special tax rebate. It can be claimed any time until the rebate is fully utilised.
3. It does not require the child's elder siblings to be Singapore citizens as in the special tax rebate.

The new tax rebate system will provide parents with greater financial support for raising their children.

To qualify for the parenthood tax rebate, the mother must be legally married to the child's father, and the child must be a Singapore citizen at the time of birth or becomes one within 12 months thereafter. An adopted child is also entitled to the rebate, but must be legally adopted, a Singapore citizen at the time of adoption or becomes one within 12 months thereafter. However, the rebate is made available to a legitimate second, third or fourth child born to the family on or after 1 January 2004 or to a second child or fourth child legally adopted on or after 1 January 2004 while the claimant is married, divorced or widowed. The birth order of the children is based on the date of birth or the date of legal adoption in the case of adopted children. This means that an adopted child will be considered as the second child in the family even though the first child born to the family is younger.

The amount of rebates for the second, third and fourth child under the parenthood tax rebate as compared to that provided under old special tax rebate is presented in Table 10.7. The amount of rebate can be used by either parents or shared between parents in their filing of the income tax returns. Any unutilised rebate balance can be carried forward to future assessments until such time as the rebate is fully utilised. It is important to note that the parenthood tax rebate is only available to parents producing their second, third and fourth child. There is therefore no financial support under this scheme provided by the government to couples producing the first or fifth child and subsequent child. In this sense, the liberalised parenthood tax rebate is still considered as a limited type of pronatalist policy.

Working Mother's Child Relief

We have observed earlier the numerous changes made to the enhanced child relief and the further tax rebate which were designed to provide some financial assistance to working women with children to support. These two schemes have been replaced by the working mother's child

TABLE 10.7

Comparison of Rebates Under the Old and New Schemes

Birth Order	Parenthood Tax Rebate	Special Tax Rebate	
			Mother's Age
Second	$10,000	$20,000	Below 28
		$20,000	Below 29
		$20,000	Below 30
		$20,000	Below 31
Third	$20,000	$20,000	
Fourth	$20,000	$20,000	

relief with effect from the 2005 Year of Assessment.[42] This new relief scheme still retains the original two-fold aim of providing some financial support to working women to produce more children and to rejoin or continue to be part of the workforce after childbirth.

The quantum of tax relief given to working mothers varies according to the birth order of the child as shown below:

Birth Order	Percentage of Mother's Earned Income
First Child	5 per cent
Second Child	15 per cent
Third Child	20 per cent
Fourth Child	25 per cent

The total amount of relief for each child is capped at $25,000. Working women who are married women, divorcees or widows with children qualify for the relief. Unlike the parenthood tax relief, the working mother's child relief cannot be shared by the husband since it is specifically meant for working women.

A married, divorced or widowed working woman can claim the relief if the child is:

1. unmarried;
2. a Singapore citizen as at the end of the year preceding the Year of Assessment of claim;
3. the claimant's legitimate child, step child or legally adopted child;
4. both the age of 16 or receiving full-time education at any educational institution or is handicapped; and
5. is not receiving an annual income of more than $2,000 in that year.

Working women producing or adopting a fifth and subsequent child are not eligible for the working mother's child relief which is therefore only a limited type of pronatalist measure.

Two-Day Childcare Leave

One of the new pronatalist incentive introduced in 2004 is the 2 days of statutory childcare leave granted to each working parent provided by an amendment to the Employment Act passed in Parliament on 21 September

2004.[43] With effect from 1 October 2004, parents are entitled to take 2 days per year of this statutory employer-paid leave if they have at least a child under 7 years of age. The leave is granted on the basis of her parent and not per child, i.e., each parent can only take 2 days in a year even if there are more than one child under 7 years old in the family. However, parents have full flexibility to use this leave to spend time with their children for whatever purpose since it is not predicated on other conditions such as illness of the child. As part of the overall package of measures to support parenthood, the childcare leave somewhat allows working parents to take time off to care for their children without any loss of income and to achieve a more harmonious work-life environment.

The childcare leave is also made available to working parents with any stepchildren or legally adopted child below age 7.[44] The parents can be single, divorced or widowed, and they can be regular employees, fixed-term contract workers, or temporary or part-time employees. The important condition is that they must have worked for a period of no less than 3 months. Foreign workers are eligible for the childcare leave as long as they are covered under the Employment Act and meet the above requirements. In fact, foreign employees can take the childcare leave together with their annual leave to go back to their home countries to spend time with their children. Employees are required to submit an application to their employer and it can be refused if the employer believes that the leave will be used for purposes other than taking care of their children.

Lower Maid Levy

Faced with the non-availability of Singaporeans to work as domestic maids in private homes, families have to employ foreign maids from neighbouring countries. To control the total number of foreign maids working in Singapore, the government requires families to pay a monthly maid levy of $345 per foreign maid in addition to the salary that has to be paid to the maid. As part of the package of new pronatalist measures, the government reduced the monthly foreign domestic maid-levy to $250 for families with children aged less than 12 years of age, or with elderly person aged 65 and above.[45] This maid levy concession will make the employment of foreign maids more affordable for families who need help in providing full-time domestic care for young children or elderly persons at home.

With effect from 1 August 2004, an employer will be eligible for a lower levy rate per month for each foreign domestic worker if any one of the following conditions is fulfilled:

(a) the employer or spouse has a child below the age of 12 years who is a Singapore citizen staying in the same household as the employer; or

(b) the employer or co-residing spouse is a Singapore citizen aged 65 years or above; or

(c) the employer has a parent, parent-in-law, grandparent or grandparent-in-law aged 65 years or above who is a Singapore citizen staying in the same household as the employer.

The employer is eligible for levy concession for up to a maximum of two foreign domestic maids at any one time subject to the conditions being met. The employers will be notified by the Ministry of Manpower of the lower levy bill which they will receive in September or October 2004. It should be mentioned that employers need not be working in order to qualify for the lower maid levy, but the need for maids would be greater in families with both parents working. In February 2005, the levy for maids looking after children or elderly was further reduced to $200.

Grandparent Care-Giver Relief

It is not unusual for grandparents to help in taking care of grandchildren, especially when both parents are working. A new pronatalist measure was announced in August 2004 to recognise the important role played by grandparents in childcare by implementing a grandparent caregiver relief of $3,000 for working mothers to claim this relief from the 2005 Year of Assessment if their parents or parents-in-law look after their children aged not more than 12 years. A working mother, whether married, divorced or widowed, can claim the relief if she satisfies the following conditions:[46]

1. Her parent or parent-in-law taking care of children must not be working as employee or self-employed person receiving income during the Year of Assessment claim.

2. The parent or parent-in-law must be staying in Singapore.

3. The child must be a Singapore citizen aged 12 years or younger.
4. The child must be a legitimate child, stepchild or legally adopted child.
5. The claimant is the only person claiming the relief in respect of one particular parent or parent-in-law.

Once the claimant applies for the relief on the basis that her mother is taking care of her children, her siblings cannot submit another claim even though her mother has been taking care of her nephews and nieces. If her mother takes care of her children and her father takes care of her sister's children, both she and her sister are entitled to submit a claim each. Her husband is not allowed to share the relief in his income tax submission since it is meant for working mothers. She can claim the grandparent care-giver relief in respect of her mother in addition to the parent relief because they are for different objectives. Furthermore, if she has a domestic maid in addition to her mother to care for her children, she can claim both the lower foreign maid levy as well as the grandparent care-giver relief.

Five-Day Working Week

One of the major issues confronting working parents with young children is the difficulty of having more time to spend with their children during the weekend when they are required to work more than 5 days a week. The clamour for a 5-day working week in the civil service has been made on umpteen occasions, but the government has always refused to accede to this request. In the meantime, a few government departments and statutory boards have installed their own alternate-week system where employees take a Saturday off one in two weeks, with business as usual on Saturdays manned by about half the staff strength. For the private sector there is a wider variety of working week practices adopted in the different sectors of the economy as determined by the nature of the business of each company.

In June 2003, the Remaking Singapore Committee recommended, among other things, the adoption of a 5-day working week in the civil service.[47] This recommendation was promptly rejected by the government, but was subsequently handed over to the Steering Group on Population for further consideration. In a surprise move, a shift from a $5^{1}/_{2}$-day working week to a 5-day week in the civil service was presented as one of the new pronatalist incentive in August 2004 to arrest the declining low fertility. This break from an ancient practice was reported in the press as the slaughter of a sacred cow.[48] Clearly, the government has come to the inescapable conclusion that a shorter working week is badly needed to give parents a longer weekend to spend more time with their children.

Under the new 5-day working week system, the total number of hours clocked in by an employee during the shortened week has still remained at 42 hours. What it means is that the hours previously observed on Saturdays are now redistributed and collapsed into the 5-day week with longer hours from Monday to Friday. An important requirement of the system is the continued opening of public counters and essential services on Saturdays by certain departments or sections within a department. It is not necessary to adhere to a common pattern of working hours during the 5-day week, and government departments and statutory boards are presented with a choice of five patterns of working hours to select in accordance with their own needs, but benefiting most of their employees (see Table 10.8).[49]

Equal Medical Benefits

One of the archaic terms of employment in the public sector has been the unequal medical benefits for the two sexes. A female civil servant is not entitled to claim medical benefits for her husband and children,

TABLE 10.8
Pattern of Working Hours for 5-Day Week

1.	Monday to Thursday Friday	7.30 am to 5.00 pm 7.30 am to 4.30 pm
2.	Monday to Thursday Friday	8.00 am to 5.30 pm 8.00 am to 5.00 pm
3.	Monday to Thursday Friday	8.30 am to 6.00 pm 8.30 am to 5.30 pm
4.	Monday to Thursday Friday	9.00 am to 6.30 pm 9.00 am to 6.00 pm
5.	Monday to Thursday Friday	9.30 am to 7.00 pm 9.30 am to 6.30 pm

regardless of whether her husband is employed as a civil servant. There has been constant calls to abolish this unequal treatment, but the government has without fail refused to change this policy. More recently, this issue was revived in the Remaking Singapore Committee and its recommendation for providing equal medical benefits in the civil service was submitted to the Steering Group on Population for consideration.[50]

Recognising the importance of adopting a comprehensive approach to the problem of solving the current baby shortage, the government finally decided to slaughter another sacred cow by giving equal medical benefits to female civil servants as part of the total package of pronatalist incentives offered in August 2004. With this change, female employees are allowed to claim medical benefits for their husbands and unmarried children under the age of 18 with effect from 1 January 2005.[51] It is hoped that this change will facilitate greater sharing of care-giving responsibilities between married couples and keep pace with the increasing tendency for women to play a greater role in supporting their families. This is in line with the new policy of promoting a more pro-family work environment and a better work-life balance in the public sector.

Work-Life Works! Fund

We have observed in the early years that an increase in the female labour force participation rate has been a significant factor in influencing the rapid decline in fertility. The difficulty faced by married workers in trying to maintain a satisfactory balance between work and family life will continue to assert a strong influence on fertility even when it falls below the replacement level. A conducive work-life environment will also benefit businesses since workers in a better position to care for their families tend to be more committed and engaged at the work place, thus enhancing the performance of companies. A good work-life strategy will enable companies to attract and sustain talented staff. In order to assist companies develop an effective work-life strategy at the workplace, the Ministry of Manpower established a $10 million WOW! (Work-Life Works!) Fund in September 2004.[52]

All private sector organisations, including non-profit organisations, can apply for grants from the fund to defray the cost of introducing measures that can help employees to better achieve work-life harmony. The government will co-fund up to 70 per cent of the costs incurred for approved projects, subject to a cap of $30,000 per project per organisation. The subsidy will help to mitigate the upfront costs of introducing a work-life strategy at the workplace, and hence spread the long-run benefits to more organisations. Prior approval must be obtained by the organisations before starting the work-life project which must be completed within a year. The grant will be disbursed in two instalments, the first 30 per cent for approved items after the approval of the project and the remaining 70 per cent after the completion of the project.

The WOW! Fund can be utilised for the following purposes:

1. Training of human resource (HR) managers and line supervisors on work-life implementation, including training to develop good HR management systems.
2. On a case-by-case basis, one-time infrastructural costs in implementing flexible work arrangements and selected employee support schemes that contribute towards care of dependants.
3. Engaging a qualified work-life consultant.
4. Employing or deploying staff dedicated to drive work-life implementation within the organisations.

In evaluating proposals from organisations, greater priority will be given to projects aimed at introducing flexible work arrangements which are deemed to have long-term benefits in facilitating work-life harmony. This pro-family stance constitutes an integral part of the package of pronatalist measures meant to create a better environment for working women to produce and raise children.

Overview of 2004 Measures

The 2004 package of pronatalist measures is by far the most comprehensive, offering a wide range of financial as well as non-financial incentives. It seeks to address, among others, three key issues that were raised through public debates and tripartite feedback from workers and their employers. Firstly, the new measures have sought to meet the concerns of parents in having larger families. The measures will give parents an opportunity to spend more time with their children, pursue a range of childcare options, and strike a better balance between work and family life. Secondly, as compared with previous ones, the new measures contain fewer conditions with the removal of mother's age and education as qualifying criteria for any of the measures. Thirdly, the new measures have provided parents greater flexibility in supporting the variety of choices that they make because of their differing circumstances, i.e., a wider range of childcare arrangements. A rough estimate of the cost of the new package to the government stood at about $300 million per year, bringing the total annual expenditure on pro-family measures to about $800 million.[53]

The general public has shown keen interest in the new package, seeking clarification on many issues and voicing their views in letters and the media, the Steering Group on Population and the Prime Minister. There were also numerous calls to the Parenthood hotline and emails to the Parenthood website. Public feedback on the new package has been positive, with many Singaporeans expressing satisfaction and strong support.[54] Responding to concerns that some families may become worse off with the new package, the Steering Group pointed out that the government has put in place some transitional arrangements to ensure that no Singaporean will be worse off under the new package. On whether some parents, such as stay-at-home mothers and employers not covered by the Employment Act, might not benefit at all, the Steering Group gave an assurance that the package will benefit most families. Responding to calls that the 1 August 2004 implementation date of some schemes be pushed back to encompass more families, the Steering Group emphasised that even parents with children from before this date will receive some benefits from the new schemes, such as childcare leave, infant care subsidy, lower foreign maid levy, and revised tax breaks.

It was mentioned that the pronatalist measures implemented in 2004 would benefit a larger group of families with the removal of age of mother, education of mother and income of parents as criteria qualifying for the measures. However, there is still scope for more babies to be produced if we allow these measures to be made available to all children and not only those up to the fourth order as in the extra paid maternity leave, baby bonus, parenthood tax relief and working mother's child relief. In this respect, the recently-introduced incentives may still be regarded as a limited kind of pronatalist policies, unlike those adopted in many European countries confronted with the same problem of below-replacement fertility.

The distribution of births according to birth order is presented in Table 10.9.[55] The number of births pertaining to the fifth and subsequent order amounted to 676 (1.7 per cent) in 2002, 628 (1.7 per cent) in 2003,

TABLE 10.9

Distribution of Births by Birth Order, 2002–2006

Birth Order	Number					Percentage				
	2002	2003	2004	2005	2006	2002	2003	2004	2005	2006
1st	17,524	16,434	16,624	16,887	17,266	43.0	43.7	44.7	45.0	45.1
2nd	14,873	13,548	13,330	13,319	13,784	36.5	36.0	35.8	35.5	36.0
3rd	6,009	5,515	5,112	5,182	5,205	14.7	14.7	13.8	13.8	13.6
4th	1,674	1,505	1,481	1,545	1,483	4.1	4.0	4.0	4.1	3.9
5th	446	421	405	364	384	1.1	1.1	1.1	1.0	1.0
6th & above	230	207	222	195	195	0.6	0.6	0.6	0.5	0.5
Total	40,760	37,633	37,174	37,492	38,317	100.0	100.0	100.0	100.0	100.0

627 (1.7 per cent) in 2004, 599 (1.5 per cent) in 2005, and 579 (1.5 per cent in 2006). It would make more sense to widen the eligibility of the incentives to all children since the proportion belonging to births for the fifth and subsequent order is very small. There would be savings in money and manpower in the administration of the measures if they are made available to all children regardless of birth order. Moreover, children who pertain to the fifth and subsequent order would not feel discriminated against and unwanted. The important consideration is that they do contribute to the national population number.

In the late eighties the Inter-Ministerial Population Committee was disbanded once it had completed its task and submitted its recommendations to the government. After the implementation of the latest package of pro-family measures in 2004, both the Working Committee on Population and the Steering Committee on Population were disbanded, and replaced by a permanent National Population Committee under the chairmanship of Wong Kan Seng, Minister for Home Affairs and Deputy Prime Minister, also appointed to be in overall charge of population matters. He said that his role as minister-in-charge of population issues is to "review the government's population and demographic objectives, and chart new directions for a comprehensive approach to these population challenges".[56] This is an improvement over the position in the late nineties when no Minister or committee was designated to look after national population affairs. The government even went a step further by establishing the National Population Secretariat

(NPC) in the Prime Minister's Office in June 2006. A detailed discussion of the NPC is provided in Chapter 11.

Notes

1. Singapore, *Employment Act 1968* (Singapore: Government Printer, 1968).
2. Singapore, *Population Trends* (Singapore: Ministry of Health, 1977).
3. Singapore, *The Income Tax Act (Amendment Tax) 1973* (Singapore: Government Printer, 1973).
4. *Straits Times*, 28 July 1977.
5. Lee Kuan Yew, "Talent for the Future" (Address delivered at the National Day Rally on 14 August 1983).
6. A full account is given in Saw Swee-Hock, "Singapore: New Population Policies for More Balanced Procreation", *Contemporary Southeast Asia* 7, no. 2 (September 1985).
7. See statement by the late Dr Tay Eng Soon, then Minister of State for Education, in Parliament, and reported in the *Straits Times*, 30 June 1984.
8. Singapore, *1984 Budget Statement* (Singapore: Government Press Release, Ministry of Culture, 1984).
9. See, for example, the various issues of the *Straits Times*, 7 March 1985.
10. Statement issued by the Prime Minister's Office on 2 June 1984 and published in the *Straits Times*, 3 June 1984; and the *Straits Monitor*, 3 June 1984.
11. Saw Swee-Hock, "A Decade of Fertility Below Replacement Level in Singapore", *Journal of Biosocial Science* 18, no. 4 (October 1985).
12. See, for example. Saw Swee-Hock, "When Couples Have Fewer Than Two", *Sunday Times*, 15 June 1986; Saw Swee-Hock, "Who Is Having Too Few Babies", *Sunday Times*, 6 July 1986; and Goh Chok Tong, "The Second Long March" (Speech delivered at Nanyang Technological University on 4 August 1986).
13. Singapore, *1987 Budget Statement* (Government Press Release, Ministry of Communications and Information, 1987).
14. Singapore, *1989 Budget Speech* (Government Press Release, Ministry of Communications and Information, 1989).
15. *1989 Budget Statement*, Singapore: Government Press Release, Ministry of Communications and Information, 1989.
16. *1987 Budget Statement*, Government Press Release, Ministry of Communications and Information, 1987.
17. *Straits Times*, 4 April 1987.
18. Inland Revenue Authority of Singapore, < www.iras.gov.sg >, 27 April 2001.
19. *Straits Times*, 7 March 1987.
20. Statement issued by the Ministry of Community Development and published in the *Straits Times*, 19 April 1987.

21. The details are given in a Ministry of Finance circular and published in *The Straits Times*, 7 March 1987.
22. *Straits Times*, 7 March 1987.
23. *Straits Times*, 4 April 1987.
24. *Straits Times*, 21 August 2000.
25. *The Employment (Amendment) Act, 1973*, Singapore: Government Printer, 1973.
26. *Straits Times*, 20 August 2000.
27. See "Bonus for babies and Mothers", *Straits Times*, 1 April 2001. This insert giving details of the Third Child Maternity Scheme was provided by the Ministry of Community Development and Sports.
28. Ministry of Community Development and Sports, < www.babybonus.gov.sg >, 17 March 2001.
29. *Baby Bonus*, Ministry of Community Development and Sports, n.d.
30. *Straits Times*, 17 January 2004.
31. *Business Times*, 29 August 2000.
32. *Business Times*, 29 August 2000.
33. Lee Hsien Loong, *Budget Statement 2004*. Singapore Government Press Release, Ministry of Finance, 2004.
34. *Straits Times*, 18 March 2004.
35. Ibid.
36. Ministry of Health. < www.moh.gov.sg > 5 October 2004.
37. Ministry of Manpower. < www.mom.gov.sg > 5 October 2004.
38. *Streats*, 1 September 2004.
39. Ministry of Community Development, Youth and Sports. < www.babybonus.gov.sg > 5 October 2004.
40. Ministry of Community Development, Youth and Sports. < www.childcarelink.gov.sg > 6 October 2004.
41. Inland Revenue Authority of Singapore. < www.iras.gov.sg > 10 October 2004.
42. Ibid.
43. *Straits Times*, 22 September 2004.
44. Ministry of Manpower. < www.mom.gov.sg > 5 October 2004.
45. Ibid.
46. Inland Revenue Authority of Singapore. < www.iras.gov.sg > 25 August 2004.
47. *Straits Times*, 23 August 2004.
48. *New Paper*, 24 August 2004.
49. Public Service Division, Prime Minister's Office, PMO (PSD) Circular No. 15/2004, 25 August 2004.
50. *Straits Times*, 23 August 2004.
51. Public Service Division, Prime Minister's Office, Press Release on "Civil

Service Moves Ahead and Changes to Promote a Pro-Family Environment and Better Work-Life Balance for Civil Servants", 25 August 2004.

52. Ministry of Manpower, "When You Need to Balance Work and Family", *The Sunday Times*, 5 September 2004.
53. *Business Times*, 26 August 2004.
54. Press Release on "Strong Support for Baby Package". < http://fed.citizen. gov.sg >, 7 September 2004.
55. Yearbook of Statistics Singapore 2004, Singapore: Department of Statistics, June 2004.
56. *Business Times*, 4–5 September 2004.

11

Immigration Policies and Programmes

The national population policies in Singapore have been dominated by fertility policies in the form of antinatalist measures commencing from the mid-1960s and postnatalist measures from the 1980s. The recent recognition that, despite the introduction of a comprehensive postnatalist programme, fertility will never return to replacement level to sustain the population size in the future, has resulted in a big shift in the national population programme towards immigration as the key answer to replenish the population in the years ahead. Not surprisingly, immigration rules have been relaxed to attract professionals and businessmen to re-locate to Singapore and accept permanent residence. Citizenship laws have also been liberalised to make it easier for those who have became permanent residents to take up Singapore citizenship by naturalisation.

NATIONAL POPULATION SECRETARIAT

We have observed the establishment of the Singapore Family Planning and Population Board (SFPPB) in 1966, vested with the task of providing birth control services during the period of high fertility. Having achieved its objective, the Board was eventually dissolved in May 1986 when fertility had already went down to below replacement level for almost a decade. But the closure of the Board was not replaced by another permanent organisation when the shift from antinatalist to postnatalist policies was put in place to prevent a further fertility downtrend, or better still to stimulate an uptrend. A permanent organisation responsible for studying the national population issues, proposing effective postnatalist measures, overseeing the implementation of any changes, and monitoring the effectiveness of the new policies would be essential for solving the population problems.

In an attempt to resolve some of the national population problems, the government had instead established various ad hoc committees. As noted in the previous chapter, the Inter-Ministerial Population Committee in 1984, the Working Committee on Population in 2004, and the Steering Group on Population in also 2004. These committees were immediately disbanded once they had submitted their recommendations to the government. As a member of the 1984 Committee, the author had recommended the formation of a Population Planning Unit in the Prime Minister's Office, but the Unit was established in the Ministry of Health, being reduced to a small organisation dealing with routine matters within the ministry. In 2004, the author made another attempt by forwarding a proposal to the Prime Minister, laying down the rationale for establishing a permanent population institution in his office.

A small step in the right direction was taken during the launching of the 2004 population programme changes when Wong Kan Seng, Minister for Home Affairs and Deputy Prime Minister, was designated as the Minister-in-Charge of national population issues. He was also appointed as Chairman of a permanent National Population Committee, set up in August 2004, with Lim Hng Kiang, Khaw Boon Wan, Tharman Shanmugaratnam, Ng Eng Hen, Vivian Balakrishnan, Lim Hwee Hua and Amy Khor as members. While the 2004 package of postnatalist measures were being formulated and implemented, it has became increasingly evident that these measures can at best raise fertility slightly but never back to replacement level. That being so, there is no alternative but to focus future efforts and resources on the promotion of immigration to compensate for the low volume of natural increase.

The shift in emphasis resulted in the formation of a permanent National Population Secretariat (NPS) in June 2006 in the Prime Minister's Office.[1] The NPC, with full-time staff, is entrusted with the two-fold task of providing support services to the National Population Committee and, more importantly, setting policy objectives and coordinating the work of Ministries in increasing more births and promoting immigration. The significance of the work of the NPC can be viewed in terms of its full compliment of professional staff, adequate funding, and the authority invested to deal, where applicable, with ministries, and statutory boards on national population issues.

The principal activity of the NPC has been directed towards the promotion of marriage and parenthood, engaging overseas Singaporeans, and encouraging immigration of suitable foreigners. A Citizenship and Population Unit (CPU) was established within the NPC to coordinate and drive the efforts of the relevant government agencies in enlarging the inflow of permanent residents and facilitating their acceptance of Singapore citizenship. Another unit refers to the Overseas Singaporean Unit (OSU), meant to assist Singaporeans working and studying overseas to stay connected with one another and with Singapore. The third unit, with a much wider portfolio, is the Strategies and Projects Unit (SPU). A more detailed account of the NPC will be presented towards the end of the chapter.

IMMIGRATION LAWS

It may be recalled that up to December 1942 Singapore and Peninsular Malaysia were considered as a single unit in matters concerning migration under the British colonial rule and various legislations were in force to control different classes of immigrants from China, the Indian sub-continent, and other countries. During the Japanese Occupation, which lasted until September 1945, the flow of immigrants into the two territories was completely halted, although there was some internal movement of people between them. The end of the Japanese Occupation brought migration under the jurisdiction of the British colonial rule once again, but the changing social and economic environment in the early post-war years necessitated a complete reappraisal of the whole issue of migration.

In the early post-year years, there was no attempt to revive any of the previous systems of encouraging immigration into the country. The only legislation available was the Aliens Ordinance 1893 which could still be employed by the Immigration Department to regulate the entry of aliens, particularly those from China. Prospective immigrants from the Indian sub-continent were not subject to the provision of this Ordinance because they were British subjects and not aliens. In addition to the lack of suitable legislation to oversee all aspects of migration, there were other new developments which emerged to force the colonial government to take a fresh look at the whole question of migration.

The overall demand for workers was not increasing at such a rapid pace as in the pre-war days, and there was now an adequate supply of labour from the earlier immigrants and their children. It was necessary to exercise a tight control on immigrants from all countries and to allow permanent entry only to those who could contribute to the social and economic development of the country. To this end, the Aliens Ordinance was replaced by the more comprehensive Immigration Ordinance 1953 which came into force on 1 August 1953.[2] This Ordinance, together with its many subsequent amendments, was employed to control not only Chinese immigrants but also Indian, Malay and other immigrants into the country.

The Ordinance restricted permanent entry to the following categories of people:

1. persons who could contribute to the expansion of commerce and industry;
2. persons who could provide specialised services not available locally;
3. families of local residents;
4. others on compassionate grounds.

In 1959, the Ordinance was amended to tighten entry under category 3 by prohibiting the entry of wives and children of local residents who had been living separately from their husbands for five continuous years after December 1954, and children of citizens who were 6 years of age and others.[3] In addition, children aged 6 and above of those persons admitted as specialists under category 2, or on grounds of economic benefit under category 1, were also prohibited from entering. The main objectives of the new legislation were to safeguard the employment and livelihood of residents and "to bring about a more balanced and assimilated Malayan population whose ties and loyalty are to this country alone without which the foundation of a true Malayan nation cannot be laid".[4] The amended ordinance provided a very strict and effective control over the number and quality of immigrants of all races entering Peninsular Malaysia and Singapore.

The entry of foreigners into Singapore nowadays is governed by the provisions of the Immigration Act (Chap. 133) and the Immigration Regulations.[5] Under these regulations, the following classes of passes may be issued to persons for the purpose of entitling them to enter and remain in Singapore:

(a) an employment pass;
(b) a dependant's pass;

(c) a visit pass;
(d) a transit pass;
(e) a student's pass;
(f) a special pass;
(g) a landing pass;
(h) a work permit pass.

Subject to the provisions of the Regulations, the issue of any pass shall be at the discretion of the Controller of Immigration. Furthermore, any pass may be issued subject to such special conditions as the Controller may think fit to improve.

Viewed from the immigration point of view, we are interested in the employment pass and dependant's pass since foreigners holding these passes are entitled to apply for permanent residence and even Singapore citizenship in due course. An employment pass may be issued to a foreigner for the purpose of engaging in any business or profession, or taking up employment with an approved company. The employment pass, valid up to a maximum of five years, is issued on condition that the holder should not change his employer. A dependant's pass may be issued to the wife or a dependant child of the employment pass holder to enable the wife and children to accompany or join the holder and to remain with him in Singapore. In general, the employment pass holder and his family members are eligible to apply for permanent residence, and after two years citizenship.

PERMANENT RESIDENCE RULES

Singapore, unlike some countries such as Australia and Canada, has never operated an immigration system to admit an annual quota of foreigners based on certain desirable qualities based on family affiliation, educational, attainment, and country of origin. What happens is that foreigners with already a job offer are issued with employment passes or work permit passes. The latter passes, normally valid for two years, are issued to unskilled workers drawing a monthly salary of less than $1,800. Most of them are construction workers and domestic maids, and are not eligible for permanent residence. The rules governing the granting of work permit passes are in fact directly associated with the import of foreign workers to supplement the local labour force, which will be discussed in the chapter on labour force.

Employment passes are issued to skilled foreign workers drawing a monthly salary amounting to $1,800 upwards. These foreign workers are eligible to apply for permanent residence after working for at least two years in Singapore, or at the time of submitting their employment pass application under some permanent residence programmes. Not all employment pass holders would be interested to acquire permanent residence, intending to stay in Singapore for only a few years and to move on to another country and back home. Such foreigners cannot be considered as immigrants, remaining as part of the non-resident population. For those who agreed to take up permanent residence, their spouses and children holding dependant's passes can also become permanent residents, thus contributing to the permanent resident component of the resident population. The number of permanent residents, as noted earlier, was enumerated in the 2000 Census as 290,118 or 8.9 per cent of the total resident population. The non-resident population amounted to 754,524 in the same year. By mid-2006 the permanent resident population had reached 480,000.[6]

The rules governing the granting of employment passes have undergone numerous changes over the years. A major revamp was made on 1 September 1999 when the Ministry of Manpower took over the administration of the employment pass system from the Ministry of Home Affairs. The system is intertwined with the import of foreign workers and the promotion of immigration. The prime objective of the system in offering the most attractive terms to foreigners is two-fold, one is to contribute to the continuous expansion of the economy as skilled workers or foreign talents and the other is to augment the resident population as new immigrants.

Employment passes have been divided into different categories according to monthly income and educational attainment. P1 employment passes are issued to the highest-skilled foreigners earning a basic salary more than $7,000 per month, and P2 passes to those earning a monthly salary between $3,500 to $7,000. Each employment pass is initially valid for two years, and can be renewed up to a maximum of three more years. The employment pass holders can obtain dependant's passes for their spouse and children, and also long-term social visit passes for their parents and parents-in-law to reside in Singapore. After staying for at least two years, the pass holders can apply for PR for himself and his family members. In this case, they would be considered as new immigrants and included in the resident population.

At the second tier, are the Q1 work passes issued to foreign workers earning a monthly salary between $2,000 and $3,500 and possessing five "O" Levels or a Level Two National Technical Certificate. From September 1999, these passes are also offered to foreign technopreneurs wishing to start a high-tech company in Singapore.[7] In addition, there were the Q2 passes which were replaced in 2004 by the S passes issued to workers earning a minimum of $1,800 and possessing an acceptable trade qualification.[8] The most important feature of Q1 and S passes is that the holders are allowed to bring their spouse and children to stay in Singapore on a long-term basis, and to apply for PR in due course.

Recognising the need to foster more immigration in the face of a slowdown in the growth of the local population, the government introduced from 1 January 2007 a completely new category of employment pass. This is known as the Personalised Employment Pass (PEP) tied to the holder rather than to a company.[9] The PEP, valid for five years, is issued to foreign professionals already working here or newcomers intending to relocate to Singapore. For those existing pass holders who have successfully converted their employment pass into a PEP, they can leave their existing employer and remain in Singapore for a maximum of six months to hunt for a job in another company. The newcomers possessing a PEP are permitted to enter Singapore and stay for also a maximum of six months to look for their first job.

In either of the above cases, the PEP is not renewable after the expiry of the five-year limit. If the PEP holders still wishes to remain and work in Singapore, they can do so by applying for the usual employment pass which will of course bind them to the new company. Alternatively, they can remain behind by acquiring permanent residence. The PEP category of employment pass system constitutes a fundamental shift in the immigration policy by allowing, for the first time, foreigners to enter the country to reside without having a prior job with a company in Singapore. It is obvious that the aim of the new scheme is meant to compete in the world for the highly-skilled foreigners, or foreign talents, to settle in the country.

On 8 May 2007, the government announced the introduction of a Work Holiday Programme (WHP) with effect from 1 December 2007 to allow undergraduates and young graduates from overseas to experience living and working in Singapore.[10] The programme has been designed to take advantage of the increasing tendency for well-qualified young people travelling abroad to gain experience and be exposed to foreign cultures in a globalising world. It is hoped that the initial experience of living and working in Singapore under the programme will encourage some of them to remain to work after the trial period or to return to work at a later stage of their careers. The Minister for Manpower, Ng Eng Heng, said, "The students and graduates are a rich source of talent whom we should try to tap on when they eventually join the workforce."[11]

The WHP programme is scheduled to commence with 2,000 passes for students and graduates between the age of 17 and 30 years. Applicants must be full-time students about to graduate or recent graduates from an official list of universities in any one of the following countries:

1. Australia
2. New Zealand
3. Hong Kong
4. Japan
5. United Kingdom
6. France
7. Germany
8. United States

Citizens of other countries, but studying or graduated from the approved list of universities in any one of the countries, are also eligible to apply for the WHP pass.

Successful applicants of the programmes are issued with a WHP pass, valid for a period of six months. During this period, they may seek employment to do any type of work, and there is no minimum salary requirement as in the case of other type of passes. However, they must be able to support themselves during their stay in Singapore and show proof of exit after six months. The pass will enable them to stay until its expiry after six months, even though they did not work and were on holiday all the time. But the WHP pass cannot be extended beyond the six-month period, regardless of whether they had been working or on holiday. If they wish to continue to reside in Singapore, they must apply for the other type of employment passes, and, hopefully, many of them will elect to do so, and become permanent residents.

If the work holiday programme proved to be successful in due course, the initial number of 2,000 passes could be increased and the number of approved countries could also be enlarged. The work holiday scheme, with some modifications, has been in operation in countries such as Australia, the United States and Hong Kong. But the aim is essentially the same, to attract young foreign talents to expand the pool of talent in the workforce and, in the case of Singapore, to augment the slow growing resident population.

PERMANENT RESIDENCE PROGRAMMES

The introduction of more liberal employment passes was supplemented by some special programmes designed to attract certain groups of foreigners by offering them permanent residence at the very outset. In 1988 an Immigration Affairs Committee was formed to woo professionals and other skilled foreigners to migrate to Singapore with the generous offer of permanent residence. The first batch invited to take up permanent residence consisted of selected Hong Kong people on the premise that, with political control of the colony due to be handed over to communist China many would be prepared to consider making Singapore their future home.

Some 31,000 were the offers in 1991 and 33,000 in 1992, but the scheme did not prove to be successful since only about 4,700 have actually taken up residence in Singapore.[12] Moreover, some of them returned to Hong Kong when the political environment improved or moved on to other countries. Some discernible concern was expressed by the minority races in Singapore to the effect that the inflows of new Chinese immigrants would dilute their relative share of the total population.[13] It was quite obvious that the underlying objective of the programme was to encourage the immigration of highly qualified or rich entrepreneurs from the Chinese community in Hong Kong.

Another special scheme is the global investor programme, which is managed by the Economic Development Board (EDB) to attract foreign businessman. Under this programme, foreigners from any country can be considered for permanent residence if they agree to invest in Singapore a minimum of $2 million. The investment can be channelled to a new business or in funds devoted solely to the economic development of the country. The range of investment was widened in 2005 by allowing them to invest up to $1 million in a private apartment in any residential development regardless of the number of storeys. Other foreigners are still restricted to the purchase of apartments in buildings with at least six storeys. The liberalisation of the programme was meant to further encourage "foreigners to bring their assets and families to Singapore".[14]

The latest programme was introduced by the Monetary Authority of Singapore (MAS) in December 2004 to woo rich foreigners with at least

$20 million by dangling the carrot of instant permanent residence. Such foreigners must invest at least $5 million with financial institutions registered with the MAS for a continuous period of at least five years in bank deposits, capital market products, collective investment schemes, and life insurance policy premiums. The two-fold objective of the programme is to boost the total assets under management in Singapore and to induce high net-worth foreigners and their families to take up residence in Singapore.

The above scheme will enhance the appeal of Singapore among rich foreigners because, according to a private banker, "wealthy investors don't just look at potential returns, but also other benefits such as residential status and tax structure".[15] The tax rates in Singapore are now lower than most Asian countries, except Hong Kong, and are certainly helpful in attracting new foreigners and even existing ones to continue to reside in the country.[16] Other well-known attributes that Singapore possesses are competitive business environment, good education for the children, and security for the whole family.

Apart from the above programmes targeted at specific types of foreigners, there are other programmes aimed at wooing foreign talents, viz. those with at least excellent tertiary education. In 1998 the government had established the Singapore Talent Recruitment Committee (STRC) under the chairmanship of George Yeo.[17] Another scheme employed to secure foreign talents is linked to the educational subsidy in the form tuition grants accorded to foreign students in tertiary institutions, permitted to enrol up to a maximum of 20 per cent foreign students. The foreign students pay, only slightly higher fees than Singaporeans instead of full fees, thus receiving tuition grants of about $12,800 per year. In return, these students from mainly ASEAN countries, China and India must serve a three-year bond in Singapore after graduation. It was reported that about 60 per cent of these foreign students go on to become permanent residents, adding to the talent pool in Singapore.[18] As for those who return home or proceed to other countries, they would probably have fond memories of Singapore and remain as part of the overall network.

RELAXING CITIZENSHIP LAWS

After successfully persuading foreigners to take up permanent residence, the final step in the urgent need to promote immigration is to put in place a set of conditions attractive enough for them to acquire citizenship. The citizenship laws, enacted soon after Singapore achieved independence in 1966, allow a person to become a citizen by descent or naturalisation. To be eligible to become a citizen by descent, a person must be born in Singapore to parents, one of whom is a citizen, or born abroad to parents with a citizen father. Unlike the position in other countries, a person born in Singapore to parents with foreign citizenship cannot claim to be a Singapore citizen. Citizenship by naturalisation is available to permanent residents who have stayed in Singapore for least two years. Most of the recent liberalisation of citizenship laws has been introduced with regard to persons acquiring citizenship by naturalisation.

Until very recently, the citizenship law has no provision for a Singaporean woman to sponsor her foreign husband for citizenship by naturalisation, though the foreign wife of a Singapore husband is eligible for citizenship. In order to promote gender equality and immigration, the laws were demanded in 1999 to allow the foreign husbands of Singapore women to apply for citizenship.[19] They must however satisfy two conditions, one they must have been permanent residents for at least two years, and the other their family must be able to support itself. These two requirements have been applicable all along for foreign wives of Singapore men. The new ruling will obviously be easier for the whole family to return or to continue to stay in Singapore, contributing to the greater inflow of immigration.

Another citizenship rule that is no longer consistent with the need to augment the population concerns children born overseas. Right from the beginning, children born overseas to Singapore men and foreign women can become Singapore citizens by descent. This is not so in the case of children born overseas to Singapore women but foreign men. There have been numerous appeals from different quarters to rectify the anomaly. The government finally amended the laws to permit, with effect from 15 May 2004, children born abroad to such mothers to be eligible for Singapore citizenship.[20] This policy change will eliminate the loss of babies born abroad to Singapore women, an important consideration viewed in terms of the current baby shortage. There is an increasing tendency for Singapore women marrying foreigners and starting a family abroad, and according to the Deputy Minister in charge of population, Wong Kan Seng, "we want them and their children to remain connected to Singapore".[21]

In relaxing the above citizen laws, the opportunity was taken to introduce a further liberalisation of the rule concerning the passing of citizenship to further generations. The ruling at that time did not permit Singapore citizens by descent pertaining to the group of children born abroad to Singaporean parents to pass on citizenship to their children also born overseas. This ruling was not quite consonant with the present state of affairs where more Singaporeans are travelling overseas to work, study or pursue their personal goals. From 15 May 2004, Singapore citizens by descent can pass citizenship on to another generation born overseas, provided certain conditions are fulfilled.[22] The Singapore citizen must have stayed in Singapore for a stretch of at least two years within the five-year period prior to the birth of the child. Alternatively, the child can qualify for citizenship by descent if the Singapore parent has stayed in the country for a cumulative period of at least five years up to the birth of the child. In a way, these requirements will avoid having a generation of "absentee" Singaporeans and provide some additions to the local population.

The liberalisation of laws in regard to the acquisition of citizenship by descent and naturalisation, coupled with persuading permanent residents to take up citizenship, appears to have some impact. The number of citizenship granted amounted to 6,500 in 2001, 7,600 in 2002, 6,800 in 2003, 7,600 in 2004, and, more importantly, 12,900 in 2005. The upsurge in 2005 will surely continue in the years to come, as evidenced by the 13,209 already granted in 2006.

In March 2007, the Immigration and Checkpoints Authority set up the online naturalisation eligibility tool, www.ica.gov.sg, to provide free self-assessment for foreigners interested in gauging their chances of gaining permanent residence or citizenship.[23] This internet system will enable foreigners working and staying in Singapore, or those in other countries, to make a quick check of their eligibility based on personal particulars such as type of work pass, occupation, annual income, educational qualification, nationality, marital status, and number of children. After completing the online forms, the internet visitors will at the click of a button ascertain how they fared.

The result will appear according the traffic light approach as follows:

1. Green: minimum qualifying requirements have been fulfilled, and application forms can be downloaded.
2. Amber: Not eligible now, but may qualify in one or two years' time.
3. Red: Does not qualify, but encouraged to try again when personal particulars change.

The online forms will take about five minutes to complete, and the result is given instantaneously. Previously, applicants for permanent residence have to wait at least three months for an answer from the Immigration and Checkpoints Authority regarding the success, or otherwise, of their application. The situation was even less satisfactory in the case of those applying for citizenship. They had to submit their completed forms in person and sit for an interview before they were given an indication regarding their chances of success. The online self-assessment system has been designed to encourage suitable foreigners, whether residing in Singapore or other countries, to obtain permanent residence or citizenship.

INFLOW OF ADOPTED FOREIGN CHILDREN

Rules governing the inward flow of foreign children adopted by Singapore parents have also been streamlined in recent years. With the drastic reduction in family size, the rising number of childless couples, and the shortage of local babies for adoption, Singapore couples tend to go out of Singapore to adopt foreign children. In 1999 the total number of adopted children was 655, and moved up to 672 in 2003 and 731 in 2004, with about 70 per cent foreign-born children. Some common basic rules are applicable to the adoption of both local and foreign children.

Most of the adopted foreign-born babies originate from China, and it is not surprising that a bilateral agreement was signed recently between the two countries. The agreement, taking effect from 1 April 2004, spells out the conditions under which Singaporeans can legally adopt children from China.[24] Among the major requirements for the Singapore couples are:

1. Singapore citizens;
2. Between 30 and 35 years old;
3. Annual household income of at least $32,000;
4. Be physically and mentally healthy;
5. Have no more than five children;
6. Have no criminal record relating to child abuse, drug abuse or sexual offence.

Couples satisfying the conditions must utilise only two adoption agencies, Tenah Community Services and Fei Yue Community Services. No middlemen, whether relatives or friends in China or private adoption agencies can be used. The two agencies, both accredited by the Ministry of Community Development, Youth and Sports (MCYS), are authorised to submit adoption applications and the Home Study Report to the China Centre of Adoption Affairs (CCAA). The CCAA will assess the couple's readiness and suitability to care for the adopted child according to the information contained in the Home Study Report, and, if satisfied, will then match a child to the prospective adopters. Once in Singapore, the child is brought to MCYS to be issued with a dependant's pass and visa, and the adopter is required to sign a security bond, about $1,000 to $2,000, undertaking to maintain the child. The adopter's lawyer files the adoption papers in the Family Court for hearing and the adoption order to be granted.

In the case of adopting children from other countries, the rules are less stringent. The prospective adopters can approach any MCYS accredited agencies, foreign agencies, friends and relatives to assist.[25] Once the child has been identified, the adopter submits the Home Study Report to MCYS, and, with approval granted, engages a lawyer to file the adoption papers in the Family Court. Once the Court grants the adoption order, whether for children born in China or other countries, the Singapore birth certificate can be obtained, showing the couple as adopted parents. The couple can then proceed to apply for permanent residence for the adopted child, and, in due course, Singapore citizenship.

INFLOW OF FOREIGN SPOUSES

Another source of immigration leading to an addition to the local population is the inflow of foreigners marrying Singaporeans. There have always been cases of local men and women marrying foreigners residing in Singapore or in other countries. It was reported that some 6,520 male Singaporeans and permanent residents married foreign brides in 2005, up from 5,210 in 2004 and 4,425 in 2003.[26] Detailed breakdowns of these figures by nationality are not available since the marriage statistics published so far do not give the bivariate distribution of grooms and brides according to nationality. When the foreign spouses take up permanent residence, and even citizenship in due course, they would constitute additional numbers to the resident population.

It would be safe to assume that some of the Singaporeans would remain single had they not married foreigners, and would not have produced offspring to contribute to the growth of the resident population. An idea of the extent of inter-nationality marriages and the number of offsprings originating from such unions can be surmised from the bivariate distribution of father and mother according to nationality.[27] Out of 38,232 births registered in 2006, as many as 9,025 or 23.6 per cent were borne to Singapore fathers and mothers with foreign citizenship. More interestingly, a much bigger figure of 12,644 or 33.1 per cent of these births were borne to Singapore mothers and foreign fathers, a reflection of the more common practice among women than men to marry foreigners already working and staying in Singapore.

Another emerging trend is the increasing tendency for male Singaporeans, faced with the difficulty of getting a local partner, resorting to arranged marriage to secure foreign spouses from neighbouring countries. This can be accomplished by the men proceeding to a foreign country to seek a bride, or alternatively approaching matchmaking agencies in Singapore. In the past, these agencies have catered to men with lower educational background, but they are now seeing more men with tertiary qualifications. The men are generally older in their late thirties and forties, seeking less-educated foreign brides in their twenties. The foreign brides handled by the matchmaking agencies usually come from Malaysia and Indonesia, but brides from Vietnam and China are becoming popular.

The matchmaking agencies, unlike the child adoption agencies, have created some problems due to the lack of strict government regulations. It is not uncommon for agencies to accept male clients without a thorough check of their marital status, financial position, physical health and criminal records.[28] Cases of sham marriages where the men marry foreign women just for financial gains have been uncovered and prosecuted in court.[29] The motive for foreign brides entering into such false marriages is to secure a longer social visit pass, and even permanent residence, to work and stay in Singapore. Since greater emphasis is now placed on immigration to compensate for the low level of births, it is time to put in place a set of more stringent rules to minimise abuses and problems emanating from matchmaking agencies.

ENGAGING OVERSEAS SINGAPOREANS

It was mentioned earlier that an Overseas Singaporean Unit (OSU) was established within the National Population Secretariat (NPC) in the Prime Minister's Office to help Singaporeans working and studying overseas to stay connected with one another and with Singapore. Clearly, the objective underlying this programme is to enhance the chances of these Singaporeans retaining their citizenship and, better still, returning home to augment the population and to contribute to the development of the country. It is hoped that the programme can develop an international Singaporean diaspora with Singapore the global city at the heart of this vibrant and diverse network. The Singaporean diaspora, numbering some 150,000, will undoubtedly expand in the years to come as globalisation creates more opportunities for Singaporeans to take up more challenging overseas jobs or to capitalise on the better business opportunities emerging in many parts of the world.

To enable it to function more effectively, the OSU has launched a website (www.overseassingapore.sg) to provide one-stop information to enable overseas Singaporeans to receive updates on developments in Singapore and to link up different overseas Singaporean communities in the world. For Singaporeans wishing to return home, they can have access to useful information such as availability of internships, job opportunities, and school admission policies for their children. Apart from the website, the OSU has introduced some face-to-face programmes to enable overseas Singaporean students and professionals to stay engaged and connected to Singapore. The overseas Singaporeans are our ambassadors and valuable assets, and no effort should be spared to facilitate their relocation home when they decide to return.

The OSU has formed a partnership with a number of top companies and the Public Service Division in the public sector to keep the overseas Singapore students informed about the availability of internships, and even job opportunities. The companies, local and foreign, have offered internships in various key sectors of the economy. The public sector has included overseas Singapore students in the Civil Service Student Internship Programme, applicable to all government ministries. The Distinguished Business Leaders Series was launched by the OSU in conjunction with Contact Singapore. Under this scheme, prominent business leaders from Singapore meet with overseas Singaporeans in major cities to talk about their personal and corporate experiences with the view of emphasising the business and job opportunities in Singapore.

Another networking activity organised by the OSU is the Singapore Day roadshow, which includes mini-job fairs, exhibitions and performances. The overall aim of this event is to remind overseas Singaporeans of their home and connect them with job opportunities in

Singapore. The OSU will be organising more activities in the future for students and professionals in cities, where a high concentration of them exists. The main aim of the OSU is to ensure that overseas Singaporeans stay connected, and, better still, to return home to work and stay permanently, contributing to the inflow of immigration.

CONCLUSION

The various measures embarked on recently by the government to encourage the inflow of foreigners to work and settle in Singapore have evoked some anxiety and concern among certain segments of the Singaporean community. Firstly, there are those, especially the recently unemployed, who feel that foreigners are here to take away their jobs. Secondly, some Singaporean men, who have served national service, expressed unhappiness about the older foreigners, on becoming citizens, did not serve in the defence force because they have passed the age of mandatory call-up. Thirdly, some Singaporeans would like to be treated much better than foreigners who refuse to take up permanent residence as well as those permanent residents declining to become citizens. Fourthly, there is some concern among citizens that many foreigners consider Singapore as a stepping stone, enjoying all the benefits while they are here.

To soften the grumblings from the ground, the government has come out to reiterate that while it welcomes foreigners, it will always look after the interests of Singaporeans. Towards the end of 2006, the government announced that the medical fees will be adjusted upwards in such a manner that permanent residents (about 480,000) and foreigners (about 876,000) will have to pay higher fees than citizens with effect from October 2007.[30] Notice was also given that foreign students (about 70,000), now paying slightly higher fees than citizens, will have their fees raised further from 2008.[31] Foreigners at universities and polytechnics, for example, now paying 10 per cent more than what Singaporeans are charged will have to pay more in two years' time. It was also announced in May 2007 that childcare subsidies for permanent residents will be phased out over the next two years. From 1 January 2008 permanent residents aged between 2 months and below 7 years will be eligible for only half the current amount of subsidy, and the subsidy will be eliminated entirely from 1 January 2009.[32] The adjustments to medical, school fees and childcare subsidy are meant to make a sharper differentiation between citizens and permanent residents and also between permanent residents and the others who are holding foreign citizens. This is, for sure, part of the government's attempt to win over the support of Singaporeans in its concerted effort to promote more immigration in the years ahead to counteract the slackening growth of the local population due to prevailing low fertility level.

Notes

1. "Addendum to the President's Address", National Population Secretariat, Prime Minister's Office, 4 November 2006.
2. Malaya, Immigration Ordinance, 1953 (Kuala Lumpur: Government Printer, 1953).
3. Malaya, Immigration Ordinance, 1959, No. 12 of 1959 (Kuala Lumpur: Government Printer, 1959).
4. *Straits Times*, 3 November 1959. Statement issued to the press by the Malayan Ministry of External Affairs and the Singapore Ministry of Home Affairs.
5. Singapore, The Immigration Act (Chap. 133), Subsidiary Legislation (Singapore: Singapore National Printers, 1990).
6. Li Xueying, "More Targeted Efforts to Get PRs to Become Citizens", *Straits Times*, 28 August 2006.
7. Jennifer Lien, "Work Pass for Eligible Foreign Talents", *Business Times*, 8 July 1999.
8. "MOM to Add New 'S' Category of Work Pass", *Today*, 28–29 February 2004 and Sue-Ann Chia, "More Flexible Work Pass System", *Straits Times*, 15 January 2005.
9. Chia Sue-Ann, "Personalised Employment Pass by 2007", *Straits Times*, 25 August 2006 and Daniel Bruenas, "Government Plans New Employment Pass to Draw Foreign Workers", *Business Times*, 24 August 2006.
10. http://www.mom.gov.sg.
11. Chen Hui Fen, "Come Over For A Working Holiday", *Business Times*, 20 May 2007.
12. *Straits Times*, 13 October 1992.
13. Zakir Hussain, "Immigration Will Not Affect Malay Numbers", *Straits Times*, 24 August 2006 and Mafoot Simon, "When Statistics Give the Lie to Perception", *Straits Times*, 9 October 2006.
14. "PR-Seekers Must Do More Than Bring Property", *Today*, 17 May 2005 and "Property Rules Based: Rules for Foreigners Relaxed", *Straits Times*, 20 July 2005.
15. Audrey Tan and Grace Ng, "Singapore Woos Rich Investors with New PR Scheme", *Straits Times*, 1 December 2004.

16. Genevieve Cua, "Personal Tax Cuts Will Attract and Retain Talent: Consultants", *Straits Times*, 28 February 2003.
17. "Star Search", *Straits Times*, 5 March 2000.
18. Lee U-Wen, "Tuition Grants Attract Overseas Talent: MOE", *Today*, 20 April 2005.
19. "Conditions Also Apply to Foreign Wives", *Straits Times*, 22 April 1999.
20. "Bill Introduces Auto-Citizenship Law", *Straits Times*, 18 March 2004 and "Citizenship Rules Ended", *Streats*, 20 April 2004.
21. Sue-Ann Chia, "New Citizenship Rule Recognises Marriage Trends", *Straits Times*, 13 March 2004.
22. "Citizenship Law Change Comes Into Effect", *Straits Times*, 15 May 2004.
23. Sheralyn Tay, "Want to Be a Singapore Citizen or PR? Click Here", *Today*, 13 February 2007.
24. Theresa Tan and Vivizainal, "Adoption Rules Get the Thumbs Up", *Straits Times*, 6 March 2004.
25. Arlina Arshad, "The Baby Trade — The Inside Story", *Straits Times*, 22 January 2006.
26. Goh Chin Lian, "Why Foreign Brides are Hot ...", *Sunday Times*, 1 October 2006.
27. Singapore, *Singapore Demographic Bulletin*, December 2006 (Singapore: Registry of Births and Deaths).
28. Ben Nadarajan and The Joo Lin, "Too Few Checks on Would-be Husbands of Foreign Brides", *Straits Times*, 25 December 2006.
29. Elena Chong, "Sharp Rise in Numbers Probed for Sham Marriages", *Straits Times*, 23 November 2006.
30. Lee Hui Chieh and Lynn Lee, "Foreigners' Medical Subsidies to be Cut", *Straits Times*, 11 December 2006.
31. Krist Boo, "Foreign Students' School Fees Up From Next Year", *Straits Times*, 2 December 2006.
32. Sumathi V. Selvaretnam, "Childcare Subsidies for PRs Being Phased Out Over 2 Years", *Straits Times*, 9 May 2007.

12

Labour Force

The amount of labour available for the production of goods and services in a country is determined by a variety of demographic, social and economic factors. The size of the total population and its composition with respect to sex and age determine the maximum limit of the number of persons who can participate in economic activities. Other factors such as race composition, the degree of urbanisation and the proportion of married women play an important part in influencing the proportion of the population in certain age groups in the working population.

Among the more important economic and social factors are the industrial structure of the economy, the mode and organisation of production, the per capita income, and the traditional attitudes towards working women and child labour. By and large, demographic factors are the principal determinants of the size of the male working population since by tradition nearly all men are engaged in some form of gainful work from the time they reach adulthood until they approach the retirement age. On the other hand, socio-economic factors seem to exert a greater influence on the size of the female working population.

The labour force of the country is that section of the population which is engaged in the production of goods and services during a particular period. By far the most complete and comprehensive statistics on the labour force are those made available in the regular series of population censuses. By means of these census data, an attempt will be made to examine the growth of the labour force and the participation rates in terms of various socio-demographic factors. Part of the chapter will also be devoted to an appraisal of the industrial and occupational patterns of the labour force which would in a way reflect the manner in which the people of Singapore earn their living.

CONCEPTS AND DEFINITIONS

Labour force statistics can be collected by means of the gainful worker approach or the labour force approach.[1] The older gainful worker concept was widely used before World War II and even during the early post-war years in some countries. In Singapore, it was last used in September 1947 when the first post-war census of population was conducted. According to this concept, the respondents were requested to state their usual occupation or gainful work from which they earned their money without reference to any time period. Those who were performing gainful work were considered to be in the labour force, while those without any such work were considered to be out of the labour force. Apart from the absence of a specific time reference for the figures, this method of collecting statistics cannot provide figures for the employed and the unemployed separately.

For the labour force approach, all respondents above a certain age were asked to state whether they were working during the reference period, and if not, whether they were actively looking for work. Working is defined as being engaged in the production of goods and services for pay or profit. All those who were identified as working or actively looking for work during the reference period were considered as economically active and included in the labour force. Those identified as not working and not actively looking for work were regarded as economically inactive and put outside the labour force. The labour force approach was used in Singapore in the five population censuses held in 1957, 1970, 1980, 1990, 2000, and in the General Household Survey held in 2005.[2]

Persons reported as working constituted the employed, while those identified as not working but looking for work and those planning to start their own business comprised the unemployed. The former group included persons who were actually working during the reference period as well as persons who had a job but were temporarily laid off on account of sickness, leave, strike, bad weather, and so forth, and would be returning to work in due course. The unemployed group consisted of persons who had worked previously and were looking for jobs during the reference period, as well as those who had never worked before and were looking for jobs for the first time. Actively looking for work was defined as registering at an employment exchange, inserting and answering job advertisements, applying directly to prospective employers, making enquiries from relatives and friends, or taking steps to start one's own business.

The economically inactive population included all persons who were not working and not actively looking for work during the reference period. Among the more important categories in the inactive population were those doing housework without pay, students, unpaid voluntary social workers, mentally or physically disabled persons, persons deriving their income from rent, dividends, interest, and so forth, and all others not engaged in economic activities. In Singapore, boys awaiting their call-up for national service are regarded as economically inactive. Among the economically inactive persons were those who had worked before and might re-enter the labour force in the future. A much larger number, mainly students, would not have worked before and would enter the labour force for the first time in subsequent years.

Persons who were identified as economically active during the reference period were always classified by industry, occupation and occupational status. Industry refers to the kind of economic activity or the nature of the business of the firm, establishment or department in which the person was employed. Occupation refers to the kind of work the person was performing. Occupational status refers to the status of the person with respect to his employment, that is, whether he is an employer, own account worker, employee, or unpaid family worker.

It is necessary to mention one important difference in the actual application of the labour force approach to the collection of statistics in the population censuses. In the 1990 and 2000 censuses and the 2005 General Household Survey, the minimum age of the population from which the labour force data were collected was fixed at 15, while in the previous three censuses the minimum age was 10. In Table 12.1 and other tables showing comparative data over time, the figures for the censuses prior to 1990 were adjusted to coincide with the minimum age of 15 adopted in recent years.

GROWTH OF LABOUR FORCE

Among the 2,770,290 resident population aged 15 years and over in 2005, 1,744,806 or 63.0 per cent, were returned as economically active persons according to the labour force approach. The remaining 1,025,484 persons or 37.0 per cent were economically inactive. The economically active population consisted of 1,647,294 or 94.4 per cent employed persons and 97,513 or 5.6 per cent unemployed persons. The relatively

TABLE 12.1
Population Aged 15 and Over by Activity Status and Sex, 1957–2005

Activity Status	Number ('000)						Intercensal Increase (%)				
	1957	1970	1980	1990	2000	2005	1957–70	1970–80	1980–90	1990–00	2000–05
Total											
Economically Active	471.6	717.2	1,112.1	1,562.8	2,192.3	2,367.3	52.1	55.0	40.5	40.3	8.0
Economically Inactive	355.3	552.4	648.7	806.2	1,005.0	1,142.6	55.5	17.4	24.3	24.7	13.7
Males											
Economically Active	388.5	533.8	728.6	934.3	1,324.3	1,376.5	37.4	36.5	28.2	41.8	3.9
Economically Inactive	54.3	114.9	165.7	247.8	308.8	382.8	111.6	44.2	49.5	24.6	24.0
Females											
Economically Active	83.1	183.5	383.5	628.5	868.0	990.7	120.8	109.0	63.9	38.1	14.1
Economically Inactive	301.0	437.6	483.1	558.4	696.2	759.9	45.4	10.4	9.6	24.7	9.1

low unemployment was a reflection of the fairly high economic growth rate and the persistent shortage of labour current at that time.

Table 12.1 shows that the economically active population stood at 471,600 in 1957, and thirteen years later it had increased by 52.1 per cent to reach 717,200 in 1970. By 1980, it had exceeded the one-million mark to touch 1,112,100, giving an increase of 55.0 per cent during the ten-year period. It continued to increase, but at a slower rate of 40.5 per cent during the next ten years to reach 1,562,800 in 1990. It continued to grow at almost the same rate, 40.3 per cent, during the latest intercensal period 1990–2000. In the next five years, the labour force grew by only 8.0 per cent, with the total standing at 2,367,300 in 2005. The much faster growth of the labour force during the 1970s is related to the high economic growth chalked up at that time, while the subsequent slower growth was due to the worsening shortage of labour resulting from the rapid fertility decline to replacement level in 1975.

The continuation of fertility well below replacement level until today cannot possibly lead to an increase in the supply of local labour in the future. At the same time, there are severe constraints to increasing further the already large pool of foreign workers on account of economic, social and political considerations. This has led the government to push towards the new economic strategy of moving away from labour-intensive industries to industries with a higher degree of automation, computerisation, or capital investment to produce higher value-added products and services.

A feature to note is that during the last four decades, the female labour force has grown significantly faster than the male labour force. The former increased by a much larger rate of 120.8 per cent during 1957–70, 109.0 per cent during 1970–80, and 63.9 per cent during 1980–90. In contrast, the male labour force increased by only 37.4 per cent, 36.5 per cent, and 28.2 per cent respectively. During the latest intercensal period 1990–2000, the female workforce grew just a shade slower, 38.1 per cent, than their male counterparts, 41.8 per cent, but resumed their much faster growth during 2000–2005. In terms of numbers, the female labour force grew rapidly from 83,100 in 1957 to 183,500 in 1970, 383,500 in 1980, 628,500 in 1990, and finally to 990,700 in 2005. On the other hand, the male labour force managed to increase by less than threefold, rising from 388,500 in 1957 to 1,376,500 in 2005. Viewed from another angle, some 41.8 per cent of the total labour force in 2005 were females, compared with

17.6 per cent in 1957. The more rapid growth of the female labour force may be attributed to the improvement in educational attainment of women, the more favourable attitudes towards female employment, and the better job opportunities for women in the rapidly expanding economy of Singapore. Women were able to find ample jobs in the labour-intensive industries, such as electronic products assembly and textile manufacturing and, more recently, in the financial and hotel services sectors.

We will now proceed to look at the economically inactive population. Table 12.1 shows that the economically inactive persons aged 15 and over numbered 1,005,000 in 2000, an increase of 198,800, or 24.7 per cent, since the census held in 1990. This was larger than the 24.5 per cent recorded during 1980–90 and the 17.4 per cent during 1970–80, but smaller than the 55.5 per cent during 1957–70. The higher growth of the economically active population must necessarily be accompanied by a sluggish expansion of the inactive population as all adults capable of working would have been induced to enter or remain in the work-force. However, we should not forget that foreign workers of all kinds of professions have also contributed to the comparatively higher growth rate of the labour force.

A contrasting pattern of growth between the active and inactive groups is exhibited by the two sexes. Since 1957, the men have experienced a slower rate of increase among the active groups than among the inactive group. But the reverse position has always been recorded by the women, which was caused by the increasing participation of women in the economic activities of the country. Another interesting feature is that the difference in the growth rate between the two groups is more pronounced among the women. For instance, in 1990 the women recorded an increase of 63.9 per cent among the active group, compared with 9.6 per cent among the inactive group. In the case of the men, the two corresponding figures were 28.2 per cent and 49.5 per cent.

LABOUR FORCE PARTICIPATION

In the preceding section we discussed the substantial increase in the labour force during the post-war period. To ascertain whether this increase was caused solely by population growth or also by a rise in the extent of participation of the people in economic activity, we need to examine the labour force participation rate, which is defined as the

percentage of economically active persons to the total population aged
15 years and over. This rate serves to give an idea of the proportion of the
population aged 15 and over who supply the labour on which the
economic life of the country depends. The participation rate will be
examined in terms of sex, race, age, and marital status.

The figures given in Table 12.2 reveal that the labour force
participation rate in Singapore remained almost stationary between 1957
and 1970 at about 57 per cent. Thereafter, it rose to 63.2 per cent in 1980
and to 66.0 per cent in 1990. The rapid upturn during 1970–80 coincided
with the exceptionally high economic growth chalked up at that time,
while the gentle rise during the following intercensal period was due to
the worsening shortage of labour mentioned earlier. The clear uptrend in
the participation rate was experienced by the Chinese only, with their
participation rate rising consistently from 55.2 per cent in 1957 to 65.1
per cent in 1990. In the case of the Malays, their participation rate did

TABLE 12.2

Labour Force Participation Rate by Race and Sex, 1957–2005

Race	1957	1970	1980	1990	2000*	2005*
Total						
All Races	57.0	56.5	63.2	66.0	61.7	67.4
Chinese	55.2	56.5	62.6	65.1	62.8	63.6
Malays	52.5	51.9	64.7	62.9	57.5	58.0
Indians	75.4	64.4	67.6	70.4	58.6	63.8
Others	61.0	57.0	61.2	81.7	54.7	67.1
Males						
All Races	87.7	82.3	81.5	79.0	74.5	78.2
Chinese	85.7	81.3	80.8	78.3	74.8	73.8
Malays	90.8	84.2	83.2	78.3	74.5	73.6
Indians	94.4	87.5	84.0	81.3	71.8	79.3
Others	90.0	84.4	85.8	91.1	71.3	82.7
Females						
All Races	21.5	29.5	44.3	53.0	49.1	56.6
Chinese	24.5	32.1	44.5	52.0	51.1	53.9
Malays	7.1	17.9	44.6	47.3	41.8	43.3
Indians	8.2	20.2	44.1	56.7	44.1	47.1
Others	30.0	27.3	34.7	74.9	40.3	53.1

* Resident Labour Force

not follow any clear uptrend, moving down from 52.5 per cent in 1957 to 51.9 per cent in 1970, up to 64.7 per cent in 1980, and then down again to 62.9 per cent in 1990. The Indians displayed a less irregular movement with their rate moving down from 75.4 per cent in 1957 to 64.4 per cent in 1970 and then straight up to 70.4 in 1990. The exceptionally high rate of 75.4 per cent in 1957 for the Indians and its decline thereafter was due to the steadily decreasing proportion of pre-war immigrant labourers, with a fair number of their families left behind in the Indian sub-continent.

For a better understanding of the labour force, we will examine the variations in participation rates recorded between the two sexes. The data set out in Table 12.2 reveal that, without a single exception, women in Singapore, like those in other countries, experience a considerably lower participation rate than men at all times. This world-wide sex differential is primarily conditioned by two deep-rooted traditional norms, namely, women are generally not expected to earn an income as a matter of course to support themselves and their families, and child-rearing and housekeeping tend to prevent them from engaging in gainful work outside their homes. In 1957, women participated in the labour force to the extent of 21.6 per cent as against the high of 87.7 per cent registered by men. Since then, there has been a steady narrowing of the gap as female participation improved faster on account of greater job opportunities and changing attitudes towards working women. By 1990, the female rate had advanced to 53.0 per cent and the male rate had fallen to 79.0 per cent, the former being about two-thirds of the latter, compared with the one-fourth that prevailed in 1957.

The labour force statistics are presented only according to the resident population in the 2000 Population Census and the 2005 General Household Survey. The figures for these two years shown in Table 12.2 are not quite comparable with those for the earlier years, which included the non-residents or foreigners. Bearing in mind that almost all these foreigners have been admitted into Singapore to work, we should expect the labour force participation rates to be higher for the total population than the resident population. Without any exception, this is reflected in the participation rates by race and sex remaining clearly higher in 1990 than in 2000 or 2005 in the table.

It is known that the extent of participation in economic activity varies considerably among different age groups. To study this pattern of variation, we will use the age-specific labour force participation rate, which may be defined as the percentage of economically active persons among the total population of a given age group. It is customary to calculate these rates for each sex separately in view of the traditional differences in the various age groups. In Table 12.3 are presented the rate for quinary age groups from 15–19 years to 65 years and over.[3]

A casual glance at the figures is sufficient to confirm the completely different pattern of age-specific rates displayed by each sex. Looking at the 1957 figures, we see that the male rate rises steeply at the young ages to a shade above the 90 per cent level at the early twenties and remain around the neighourhood of 98 up to the ages of 25 to 49. Thereafter, it

TABLE 12.3

Age-Specific Labour Force Participation Rate by Sex, 1957–2005

Race	1957	1970	1980	1990	2000*	2005*
Males						
15–19	59.4	55.7	47.5	30.0	18.0	10.7
20–24	92.3	92.9	93.4	82.8	75.9	59.3
25–29	98.0	98.0	97.2	94.8	96.5	89.2
30–34	98.6	98.3	97.9	95.4	98.3	91.5
35–39	98.5	98.4	98.0	96.4	98.2	93.7
40–44	98.0	98.1	97.6	96.7	97.5	93.6
45–49	96.9	96.2	95.6	94.7	96.3	90.0
50–54	93.5	88.1	89.6	88.2	91.2	88.6
55–59	85.1	73.9	70.7	69.0	74.4	75.3
60–64	66.9	55.6	52.5	49.5	49.6	52.4
65 and over		31.9	28.6	24.2	18.5	24.1
Females						
15–19	23.4	43.0	50.7	31.8	20.1	9.0
20–24	22.9	53.6	78.4	82.2	78.7	57.8
25–29	16.4	30.8	58.7	77.9	84.9	80.6
30–34	17.3	22.7	44.2	65.5	73.6	74.2
35–39	20.8	19.3	37.1	57.9	63.0	68.6
40–44	26.2	17.8	33.2	54.2	60.7	63.0
45–49	30.1	17.5	26.5	45.9	57.4	60.3
50–54	28.8	17.5	20.4	35.6	46.7	53.8
55–59	24.7	16.2	14.5	22.4	29.6	39.5
60–64	17.1	13.4	11.3	13.8	15.3	21.0
65 and over		6.5	6.4	6.1	4.1	5.2

* Resident Labour Force

falls consistently to touch the low of 66.9 per cent in the last age group of 60 and over when compulsory retirement and disabilities gradually remove men from the work-force. This general pattern, which continued to prevail in the next three censuses, merely reflects the traditional attitude that unless a man is sick or permanently disabled he should work even though he may be a person of some wealth.

The figures for females differ in two major respects: they are appreciably lower at all ages and their progression over the age range follows quite a different path. The pattern prevailing in 1957 was one where the rate moved downwards from slightly above 23 per cent in the first age group 15–19 to about 16 per cent in the late twenties; it then rose until the peak of 30 per cent was attained in the late forties, after which it fell continuously again. The withdrawal of women from the work-force on account of marriage, bearing and rearing children, and partly housekeeping was responsible for the dip, while their subsequent re-entry after these responsibilities had been resolved caused the second rise in the participation rate. By 1970 the pattern had given way to another type where the rate quickly peaked in the early twenties and then fell without any interruption with the advance of age as some women withdrew from the work-force primarily on account of family responsibilities. As can also be seen in Figure 12.1, this early single-peak pattern has remained until today.

It is clear that men have been subjected to less radical changes in their participation rates than women. In fact, the changes in male rates have been very minor for the major part of the working age range, with more conspicuous changes at the very young and old ages. The rate for the youngest age group 15–19 fell steadily from 59.4 per cent in 1957 to 47.5 per cent in 1980. This downward trend was due to the lower drop-out rate of school children at the Primary School Leaving Examination (PSLE), especially after the introduction of streaming after this examination into Normal and Express Streams. The more pronounced drop in the 20–24 age group recorded after 1980 was caused by more boys entering the university after serving their compulsory military service. A clear downward trend in the last three old-age groups also occurred over the years up to 1990 as mandatory or involuntary retirement at these ages became more common. An upward trend was recorded in the 55–59 age group in the nineties when these old workers were encouraged to remain in the work-force so as to alleviate the acute shortage of labour. The retirement age was in fact raised to 60 in 1993. The compression of

FIGURE 10.1

Age-Specific Labour Force Participation Rates by Sex, 1957 and 2005

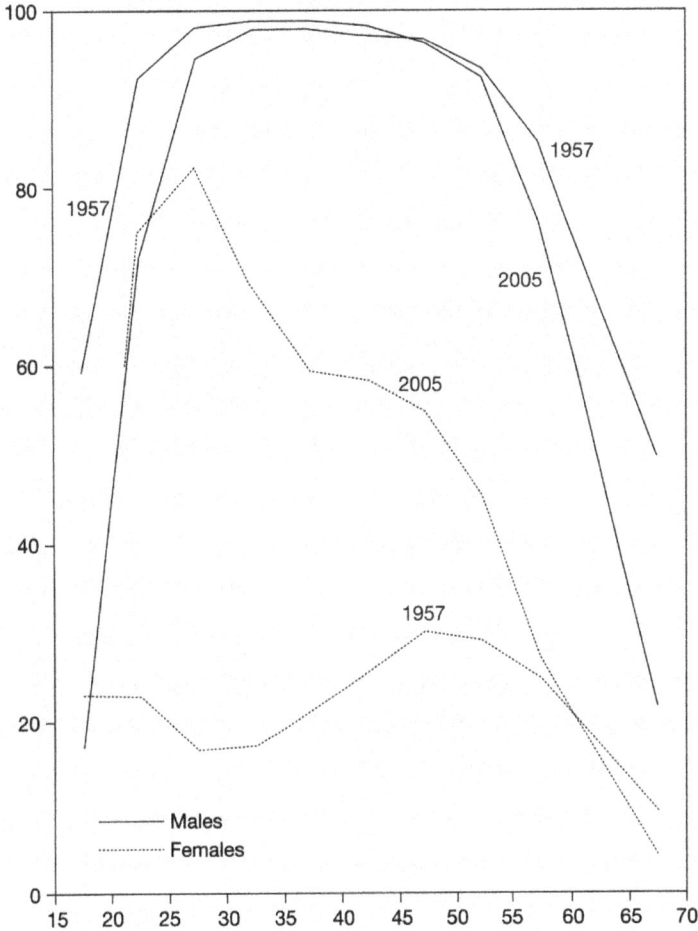

the working life span of men has been observed in most countries which have witnessed the growth of demand for secondary and tertiary education, the development of public and private pension schemes, and rising incomes, making it possible for more education of the young and earlier retirement of the old.[4]

Unlike men, women experienced more significant and interesting changes in their participation rates at all ages during the same period under consideration. Their youngest age group saw the rate increase from 23.4 per cent in 1957 to 50.7 per cent in 1980, and then decrease to 31.8 per cent in 1990. The decline gathered momentum thereafter, as reflected in the rate for the resident labour force falling to 20.1 in 2000 and 9.0 in 2005. Expanding job opportunities for girls caused the early rise, while the greater school retention and expanding tertiary education were responsible for the sharp drop in recent years.[5] In the age groups between 20 to 54 there was a marked rise in the participation rate in the last three decades. The decline between ages 35 and 54 during 1957–70 was quite exceptional, resulting from the disappearance of the twin-peak pattern.

Since housework and family duties tend to prevent women from engaging in gainful work outside their homes, it would be instructive to examine their participation rates according to marital status. As expected, the participation rate for married women in 1970 was the lowest, 14.7 per cent, among the four categories of marital status. However, it managed to shoot up twofold to reach 29.8 in 1980, and then more slowly to 45.6 per cent in 1990. By 1980, it had even exceeded the participation rate of 16.1 per cent among widows. The tremendous stride made by married women was in no small measure due to their improved educational attainment, the more favourable attitudes towards married women working, the provision of creches at minimal fees, the availabilty of foreign domestic maids, the higher tax reliefs for dependent children of working women, and, more importantly, the excellent job opportunities generated by high economic growth in the context of a tight labour market.

Better education, more favourable attitudes, and ample job opportunities have also resulted in a substantial rise in the participation rate of single women from 35.6 per cent in 1970 to 53.1 per cent in 1980, and thereafter a more moderate rise to 71.2 per cent in 1990. Divorced women also experienced a faster rise during the first rather than the second intercensal period, moving up from 47.6 per cent in 1957 to 61.7 per cent in 1980, and to 71.3 per cent in 1990. By far the least improvement was recorded by widows whose participation rate edged up from 15.5 per cent in 1970 to 16.1 per cent in 1980, and 18.9 per cent in 1990. In 1990, the highest participation rate was experienced by divorced women, followed by single women, married women, and widows. Divorcees are usually not past the prime of their working life and are often forced by financial circumstances to engage in gainful work to support themselves and their children. Widows are usually elderly women who do not need to work or face difficulties securing suitable jobs.

By comparison, changes in the male participation rate according to marital status seem to be less dramatic. Both married and divorced men experienced very minor reductions in their participation rate, moving down respectively from 89.2 per cent to 86.1 per cent, and from 85.0 per cent to 83.5 per cent during the period 1970–90. The widowers recorded a more conspicuous reduction, from 45.7 per cent to 37.0 per cent in 1980, and to 36.1 per cent in 1990. This was probably due to the lessening pressure on their part to work as family income increased. Single men were the only group that registered an upward movement in their participation rate, rising from 51.0 per cent to 72.2 per cent in 1990.

The figures given in Table 12.4 also reveal some interesting differences in the participation rate of men and women according to marital status. In 1990, married men experienced not only the highest participation rate of 86.1 per cent among all categories of marital status, but also a much higher rate than the 45.6 per cent recorded by married women. This is to be expected as married men, generally regarded as the head of the family, must necessarily engage in gainful work in order to shoulder the main share of the family financial burden. In contrast, the lower participation of married women is a reflection of the much reduced

TABLE 12.4
Labour Force Participation Rate by
Marital Status and Sex, 1957–2005

Marital Status	1970	1980	1990	2000*	2005*
Males					
Single	51.0	59.0	72.2	63.2	59.8
Married	89.2	87.8	86.1	84.7	83.2
Widowed	45.7	37.0	36.1	35.8	28.2
Divorced	85.0	83.8	83.5	84.3	82.0
Females					
Single	35.6	53.1	71.2	60.9	58.1
Married	14.7	29.8	45.6	49.2	53.0
Widowed	15.5	16.1	18.9	14.9	15.0
Divorced	47.6	61.7	71.3	71.8	71.9

* Resident Labour Force

necessity on their part to work. Of course, the greatest obstacle facing them appears to be the inherent difficulty of being involved in two conflicting activities, working outside the home and taking care of the family at home. The almost equal participation rate of single men and single women in 1990, 72.1 per cent and 71.2 per cent respectively, is explained by their freedom from household duties. The participation rates for both the widowed and the divorced were perceptibly higher for men than for women, which may be due to heavier responsibilities shouldered by men once they set up families.

INDUSTRIAL STRUCTURE

The labour force of a country, identified by means of the labour force approach is always classified according to industry and occupation. Industry refers to the economic activity or the nature of business of the firm, establishment or department in which the person was employed during the reference week. Occupation, on the other hand, refers to the trade or profession followed or the type of work performed during the reference week. The tabulation of the labour force by occupation serves to indicate the degree and nature in which division of labour is arranged, while the classification by industry serves to underline the integration of occupation and the type of units into which work is organised.

An investigation into the industrial structure and occupational pattern of the labour force will show how the people in Singapore are organised to earn their livelihood in the production of goods and services. The data on the industry and occupation of persons in the work-force, classified in varying degrees of detail and cross-tabulated by demographic and other characteristics, constitute a major source of information on the current stock of manpower. Such information provides the prerequisite basis for studying the labour market and employment growth potential of the economy and for estimates of key elements of the national income and product.

The collection of data on industry is possibly the most difficult and complex aspect of the census operation. Special care and effort have to be taken at all levels of the census operation to ensure the reliable and accurate collection of the data. The data were processed and tabulated according to the *Singapore Standard Industrial Classification (SSIC)*, which was updated regularly for use particularly in the decennial census.[6] This classification is based on the *International Standard Classification of All*

Economic Activities, with some modifications to suit local situations.[7] It is necessary to point out that in the 1980, 1990 and 2000 censuses the information on industry was collected from only employed persons, while in the two earlier censuses it was collected from the employed as well as unemployed persons with a previous industry. The figures for the latest three censuses therefore refer to the current industry of the working persons, while the earlier figures would also include those unemployed persons with a previous industry.

In studying the long-term changes in the industrial structure of the labour force, we will look at the data in terms of three broad traditional groups, namely, primary, secondary and tertiary. The primary sector is defined to include agricultural, forestry, fishing, mining and quarrying; the secondary sector to include manufacturing and construction; and the tertiary to include utilities, commerce, transport, communications, financial and business services, and other services. Broadly speaking, the trends in the percentage distribution of the labour force in the above three sectors would provide an idea of the past changes that took place in the economy. However, we will look at these trends for the period 1957–1990 when the data given in Table 12.5 refer to the labour force of the total population, while those for 2000 and 2005 refer to that of the resident population. The figures for these two periods are not comparable.

TABLE 12.5

Percentage Distribution of the Labour Force by Three Broad Sectors of Economic Activity, 1957–2005

Sector	1957	1970	1980	1990	2000*	2005*
	Number ('000)					
Primary	43.8	24.6	18.1	5.9	11.1	17.8
Secondary	91.4	186.2	396.5	569.6	380.6	356.8
Tertiary	336.7	440.1	662.5	961.5	1,090.9	1,272.7
Total	471.9	650.9	1,077.1	1,537.0	1,482.6	1,647.3
	Percentage					
Primary	9.3	3.8	1.7	0.4	0.7	1.1
Secondary	19.4	28.6	36.8	37.1	25.7	21.6
Tertiary	71.3	67.6	61.5	62.5	73.6	77.3
Total	100.0	100.0	100.0	100.0	100.0	100.0

* Resident Labour Force

The figures for the 1957 census reflect the influence of British colonial rule on the Singapore economy, which was entrepot in nature, serving the Malayan hinterland and the Southeast Asian region. In those early days, the people earned their living from trade and commerce and allied servicing industries in the tertiary sector, which accounted for 71.3 per cent of the work-force in 1957. At that time, agricultural activities in the rural areas were not insignificant since some 9.3 per cent were engaged in the primary sector. The proportion working in the secondary sector was relatively low, with only 19.4 per cent.

When Singapore attained the status of self-government in 1959, the government embarked on an industralisation programme to solve the serious unemployment problem and to raise the standard of living of the people. The success of this programme was reflected in the shift in industrial structure of the labour force. By 1970, the number employed in the secondary sector had reached 186,200, slightly more than double the figure of 91,400 recorded in 1957. As industralisation of the economy continued, the number of workers in the sector more than doubled again to reach 396,500 in 1980. Not surprisingly, the secondary sector share of the total work-force rose from 19.4 per cent in 1957 to 28.6 per cent in 1970, and then to the high of 36.8 per cent in 1980. The subsequent shift away from labour-intensive industries resulted in a smaller rise in the proportion employed in the secondary sector to 37.1 per cent in 1990.

The fate of those employed in the primary sector took a completely different direction. The number employed in this sector fell continuously from 43,800 in 1957 to 24,600 in 1970, 18,100 in 1980, and 5,900 in 1990. As a result, the already low importance of this sector was further diminished from 9.3 per cent in 1957 to only 0.4 per cent in 1990. In an extremely land-scarce country like Singapore, farm land has to give way to other more desirable developments like new towns, industrial estates, and reservoir reserve land. Other traditional labour-intensive farms have also given away to modernised capital-intensive farms producing orchids, tropical fish, poultry, fish, and prawns.

The tertiary sector underwent a somewhat different pattern of change, registering moderate increases over the years. The number employed in the sector was enlarged by 30.7 per cent during 1957–70, 50.5 per cent during 1970–80, and 45.1 per cent during 1980–90. However, the relatively faster growth experienced by the secondary sector inevitably led to a fall in the proportion engaged in the tertiary sector. From 71.3 per cent in 1957, it dropped to 67.6 per cent in 1970, and to 61.5 per cent in 1980. The decline in entrepot trade and related services was compensated by the growth of new service industries such as tourism, banking and finance. In fact, the recent de-emphasis on labour-intensive manufacturing activities and the development of Singapore as a financial and tourist centre saw a minor improvement in the relative importance of the tertiary sector, which absorbed some 62.5 per cent of the labour force in 1990.

The percentage distribution of the workforce by the three broad industrial groups for each of the three principal races for the last four censuses is presented in Table 12.6. All the three races were subjected to the same broad pattern of change whereby the secondary sector increased its share of the workers at the expense of the primary and tertiary sectors up to 1980. However, there was some variation in the magnitude of change in these proportions. By far the greatest change was recorded by the Malays who saw their proportion engaged in the secondary sector quadrupled dramatically from 10.1 per cent in 1957 to 44.3 per cent in

TABLE 12.6
Percentage Distribution of the Labour Force by
Industrial Sector and Race, 1957–1990

Industrial Sectors	1957	1970	1980	1990
Chinese				
Primary	11.2	4.4	2.1	0.5
Secondary	22.3	30.8	36.0	38.1
Tertiary	66.5	64.8	61.9	61.4
Total	100.0	100.0	100.0	100.0
Malays				
Primary	5.0	1.6	0.5	0.2
Secondary	10.1	22.4	44.3	35.9
Tertiary	84.9	76.0	55.2	63.9
Total	100.0	100.0	100.0	100.0
Indians				
Primary	1.7	0.7	0.4	0.1
Secondary	14.4	18.0	30.4	34.1
Tertiary	83.9	81.3	69.2	65.8
Total	100.0	100.0	100.0	100.0

1980. The corresponding proportion among the Indians only managed to double from 14.4 per cent to 30.4 per cent during the same period. A much smaller magnitude of change was registered by the Chinese whose proportion in the secondary sector was raised by less than two-thirds from 22.3 per cent to 36.0 per cent.

In the intercensal period 1980–90, the shift in the proportional distribution of the labour force was not similar for the three races. Only the Indians experienced a continuation of the previous trends, with a marked rise in the proportion in the secondary sector and a fall in the other two sectors. The Chinese witnessed a minor rise in the secondary and a decline in the other two sectors. A more radical change was recorded by the Malays; their proportion engaged in the secondary sector dropped sharply from 44.3 per cent to 35.9 per cent, and the proportion in the tertiary sector rose steeply from 55.2 per cent to 63.9 per cent.

It is interesting to note that the above diverse movements in fact resulted in a more similar pattern of industrial structure among the three main races. The 1957 census, taken towards the end of British colonial rule, shows that at that time the Chinese had a sizeable proportion of the workforce in the primary sector (11.2 per cent) and in the case of the Malays it was 5.0 per cent. In sharp contrast, the Indians have always had a negligible proportion employed in the primary sector, with only 1.7 per cent in 1957. Nowadays, the pattern of industrial structure is extremely similar among these races, with about one-third of the workforce in the secondary sector, two-thirds in the tertiary sector, and less than one per cent in the primary sector.

We will proceed to examine in greater detail the type of industrial structure that eventually prevailed among the three races as revealed by the results of the 2005 General Household Survey. For this purpose, the percentage distribution of the resident workforce by major industry sectors and sex for the three main races in 2005 is presented in Table 12.7. The Chinese had the largest concentration of workers in wholesale and retail trade, a manifestation of the traditional role played by this community in the trading and commercial activities of Singapore. In contrast, the Malays had an extremely low proportion of 10.9 per cent of their workers involved in this sector, and so did the Indians with slightly more, 14.2 per cent. In the case of these two minority races, the top position was occupied by community, social and personal services, which accounted for 23.6 per cent of the Malay workers and 24.5 per

TABLE 12.7
Percentage Distribution of the Resident Labour Force by Industry, Race and Sex, 2005

Industry	Chinese			Malays			Indians		
	T	M	F	T	M	F	T	M	F
Manufacturing	17.0	18.2	15.4	15.9	16.0	15.8	15.2	16.9	11.8
Construction	5.5	7.9	2.3	2.6	3.6	0.9	2.9	3.8	1.1
Wholesale & retail trade	20.0	19.3	20.9	10.9	10.1	12.2	14.2	15.4	11.8
Hotels & restaurants	6.3	5.3	7.7	6.8	4.8	10.0	5.3	5.1	5.7
Transport & storage	9.1	12.3	4.9	15.9	20.3	8.5	10.0	12.3	5.4
Information & Communications	3.8	3.7	3.9	2.8	2.3	3.6	6.3	6.6	5.7
Financial services	6.6	4.8	9.0	3.4	2.4	5.2	5.4	5.3	5.7
Business services	11.7	10.5	13.3	15.8	17.1	13.5	14.8	15.2	14.1
Community, social & personal services	19.0	16.8	22.0	23.6	20.1	29.6	24.5	17.8	37.7
Others	0.9	1.1	0.6	2.3	3.2	0.7	1.4	1.6	1.0
Total	100.0	100.0	100.0	100.0	100.0	100.0	100.0	100.0	100.0

cent of the Indian workers. The Malays had a much higher proportion, 15.9 per cent, engaged in transport and storage as against the 9.1 per cent for the Chinese and 10.0 per cent for the Indians. On the other hand, the proportion employed in financing services amounted to only 3.4 per cent for the Malays as compared with 6.6 per cent for the Chinese and 5.2 per cent for the Indians.

The figures for each sex separately reveal some interesting differences in the distribution of male and female resident workers according to industry among the three main races. Among the Chinese, the largest concentration of male workers was in wholesale and retail trade with 19.8 per cent, followed very closely by manufacturing with 18.2 per cent. The Malays had a predominant proportion of their male workers in transport and storage (20.3 per cent), but in their case a close second position was taken up by community, social, and personal services (20.1 per cent). A somewhat different situation was exhibited by Indian males in that the top sector was community, social and personal services (24.5 per cent), but the second spot was taken up by manufacturing (15.2 per cent) which was close to business services (14.8 per cent).

In the case of female resident workers, the Chinese had the largest concentration in community, social, and personal services (22.0 per cent), followed by wholesale and retail trade (20.9 per cent) in the second position. On the other hand, the Malays had a higher proportion of 29.6 per cent in community, social, and personal services, and the second position was taken up by another sector, namely, manufacturing with 15.8 per cent. A still higher proportion of the Indian women was to be found in the community, social, and personal services (37.7 per cent), with the second highest concentration in a completely different sector, business services with 14.1 per cent, as compared with that of the other two races. The Chinese women had a much higher proportion engaged in wholesale and retail trade than the women in the other two races. Another difference worth noting is that the Chinese seemed to have the widest dispersion of their female workers among the various industrial sectors than the other two races.

The data given in Table 12.7 can also examined in terms of the variation in industrial structure between the sexes for each of the three main races. It is quite apparent that male workers were dispersed more widely among the nine major industries than female workers. This followed essentially the same pattern as that of the total workforce of Singapore observed earlier. The narrower dispersion among female workers was most conspicuous among the Indians, with 42.5 per cent clustered in other services; the proportion of their male workers was 18.9 per cent in this sector. Some 74 per cent of female workers were concentrated in the top two sectors (other services and manufacturing) compared to 43 per cent of their male workers in the same top two sectors. Similar but less pronounced tendencies were exhibited by the Malays and the Chinese.

OCCUPATIONAL PATTERN

Having examined in some detail the industrial structure of the labour force, we will proceed to study the equally important aspect of the labour force in terms of occupational classification. The occupation of a person refers to the trade or profession followed or the type of work performed during the reference week. A tabulation of the labour force by occupation presents both an inventory of skills possessed by a country at any point in time and useful information on the rate of development of a country. Changes in the occupational pattern provide some indication of the social mobility of the people consequent on enhanced educational attainment and increased economic opportunities. In some respects, the occupation of a person gives an indication of his earning capacity and serves as a fair measure of his social status in society.

Data on the occupation of a person have always been collected in the population censuses conducted in Singapore. The data were processed and tabulated according to the *Singapore Standard Occupational Classification*, which was revised regularly to take into account particularly the emergence of new occupations.[8] This classification is based essentially on the *International Standard Occupational Classification* of 1968, prepared by the International Labour Organization.[9] The classification has been designed to present information on occupation in descending order of detail according to the one-digit, two-digit, or three-digit levels. However, in the 1980, 1990 and 2000 censuses the information on occupation was collected only from employed persons, while in the two earlier censuses it was collected from the employed as well as the unemployed with a previous occupation. The figures for the latest three consensus therefore referred to the current occupation of working persons, while the earlier figures would also include the unemployed persons with a previous occupation.

The distribution of the workforce according to occupation at the one-digit level for the last four population censuses is laid out in Table

12.8. During the intercensal period 1957–70, all the major occupation groups registered an increase in the number of workers, with the exception of agricultural and related workers, which registered a reduction of about 27 per cent. The other six groups, which showed increases in their

TABLE 12.8
Percentage Distribution of the Labour Force
by Occupation, 1957–2005

Sector	1957	1970	1980	1990	2000*	2005*
	Number ('000)					
Professional & technical	24.5	56.1	95.1	240.6	433.6	522.3
Administrative & managerial	8.6	15.5	52.2	132.1	211.8	216.3
Clerical	53.6	82.9	167.5	201.9	213.6	232.5
Sales	86.3	102.6	132.0	105.2	183.0	239.4
Services	71.1	88.7	112.2	228.0	183.0	239.4
Agricultural & related workers	37.1	26.9	21.0	8.9	1.2	1.2
Production & related workers	181.5	254.9	435.0	558.8	285.5	284.2
Cleaners, labourers & related workers	—	—	—	—	101.1	96.7
Not classifiable	9.1	23.1	62.2	61.4	52.8	54.7
Total	471.9	650.9	1,077.1	1,537.0	1,482.6	1,647.3
	Percentage					
Professional & technical	5.2	8.6	8.8	15.6	29.2	31.7
Administrative & managerial	1.8	2.4	4.8	8.6	14.3	13.1
Clerical	11.4	12.7	15.6	13.1	14.4	14.1
Sales	18.3	15.8	12.3	6.8	12.3	14.5
Services	15.1	13.6	10.4	14.8	12.3	14.5
Agricultural & related workers	7.9	4.1	1.9	0.6	0.1	0.1
Production & related workers	38.5	39.2	40.4	36.4	19.3	17.3
Cleaners, labourers & related workers	—	—	—	—	6.8	5.9
Not classifiable	1.9	3.6	5.8	4.0	3.6	3.3
Total	100.0	100.0	100.0	100.0	100.0	100.0

* Resident Labour Force

number of workers, grew at rates ranging from 19 per cent in the case of sales workers to 12.9 per cent in the case of professional and technical workers. The high growth rate in the latter group of workers was caused mainly by the great demand for this type of highly-skilled workers in both the public and private sectors during the early post-colonial years. The same reason applies to the second highest growth rate of 8.0 per cent recorded by administrative and managerial workers.

The difference in the rate of growth among the seven major occupational groups continued to persist, and more conspicuously during the next intercensal period 1970–80. The only group to witness a decline was again the one covering the agricultural and related workers, with a reduction of 22 per cent. This trend is not surprising in view of the need for farm lands to give way to industrial estates and suburban new towns. The most spectacular achievement was chalked up by the administrative and managerial group, which recorded a hefty jump of 237 per cent, with the number of workers raised from 15,500 to 52,200. Next were clerical workers which increased by 102 per cent from 82,900 in 1970 to 167,500 in 1980. The success of the industrialisation programme was reflected in the fairly rapid growth of production and related workers by about 71 per cent, taking the number from 254,900 to 435,000 by the end of the decade. A somewhat similar rate of increase (70 per cent) was registered by the professional and technical workers.

The slower growth of the overall labour force during the eighties, noted earlier, was manifested in the less rapid increase recorded by the major occupational groups. By far the greatest expansion was experienced by the professional and technical workers, which saw their members rise by 153 per cent, from 95,100 to 240,600 during the latest intercensal decade 1980–90. A close second was taken up by the administrative and managerial workers with an increase of 151 per cent. The relatively greater growth in these two groups of workers was reflective of the shift in the economy towards higher value-added industries employing a larger proportion of these workers. The increasing importance of the service sector resulted in a pronounced growth of the service workers by some 103 per cent. In sharp contrast, the number of agricultural and related workers shrank further to only 8,900 in 1990. Much lower growth rates were recorded by production and related workers (28 per cent) and by clerical workers (21 per cent). The extremely short supply of clerical workers led to the greater computerisation of many routine jobs performed by such workers.

The considerable differences in the rate of growth among the major occupational groups in the first three decades or so have obviously resulted in a shift in the proportion of workers engaged in these sectors. In 1957, production and related workers accounted for 38.5 per cent of the total work-force, way ahead of the second position of 18.3 per cent occupied by sales workers. The third spot was held by service workers with 15.1 per cent. Some 33 years later, the production and related workers continued to maintain their top position, with a slightly higher proportion of 36.4 per cent. The second spot was taken up by a completely different occupational group, the professional and technical workers, with 15.6 per cent. The greatest advance in its relative importance was made by the administrative and managerial group, improving about fivefold from 1.8 per cent in 1957 to 8.6 per cent in 1990. Another notable improvement was experienced by the professional and technical group which saw its proportion move up threefold from 5.2 per cent to 15.6 per cent during the same period.

It should be noted that the time-series data for 1957–1990 are not comparable with those for 2000 and 2005 since the former refers to the total labour force while the latter to the resident labour force only. Similar data for the non-residents or foreign workers are not available for 2000 and 2005. One clear example of the incomparable nature of the two sets of data is reflected in the drop in the production and related workers from 558,800 or 36.4 per cent in 1990 to 285,500 or 19.3 per cent in 2000. Most of the foreign workers were engaged in this occupational group.

In a multiracial society like Singapore it would be necessary to study the differences in the occupational pattern of the three principal races since there has always been some specialisation in their occupational pattern according to ethnicity. In Table 12.9 are given the data for the distribution of the workforce by major occupational group for each of these three races. The data for the period 1957–1990 refer to the total labour force, while those for 2000 and 2005 are for the resident labour force, excluding the non-resident workers.

The single most important occupational group among the Chinese in 1990 was still production and related workers who accounted for 39.7 per cent of their work-force. In fact, this proportion remained essentially unchanged over the years, 38.8 per cent in 1980, 40.1 per cent in 1970 and 38.9 per cent in 1957. Professional and technical workers occupied second position with 17.3 per cent, having moved up from the fourth

TABLE 12.9

Percentage Distribution of the Labour force by Occupation and Race, 1957–2005

Industrial Sector	1957	1970	1980	1990	2000*	2005*
	Chinese					
Professional & technical	4.7	8.5	9.1	17.3	21.9	32.7
Administrative & managerial	1.6	2.3	5.2	10.0	15.9	14.6
Clerical	9.9	12.5	16.0	13.8	13.5	13.6
Services & sales	35.9	28.8	22.7	14.5	11.7	13.8
Agricultural & related workers	8.7	4.3	2.0	0.3	0.1	0.1
Production & related workers	38.9	40.1	38.8	39.7	18.6	16.7
Cleaners, labourers & related workers	—	—	—	—	6.2	5.2
Not classifiable	0.3	3.5	6.2	4.4	3.7	3.3
Total	100.0	100.0	100.0	100.0	100.0	100.0
	Malays					
Professional & technical	3.4	5.7	4.9	9.7	20.4	18.8
Administrative & managerial	0.5	0.4	0.6	1.1	2.9	2.4
Clerical	14.0	13.1	14.5	15.4	20.0	18.6
Services & sales	20.1	27.9	20.9	14.0	16.2	20.3
Agricultural & related workers	9.9	5.3	2.3	0.3	0.1	0.0
Production & related workers	39.8	43.4	54.2	57.0	27.5	26.1
Cleaners, labourers & related workers	—	—	—	—	10.7	10.8
Not classifiable	12.3	4.2	2.6	2.5	2.2	3.0
Total	100.0	100.0	100.0	100.0	100.0	100.0
	Indians					
Professional & technical	3.8	7.9	8.9	12.5	30.7	35.4
Administrative & managerial	1.8	1.9	3.7	5.8	12.5	11.4
Clerical	13.0	13.0	13.9	11.7	15.4	14.0
Services & sales	35.4	40.9	28.8	14.8	13.7	14.7
Agricultural & related workers	2.9	2.2	1.4	0.9	0.0	0.0
Production & related workers	41.7	31.6	36.0	50.4	15.4	13.7
Cleaners, labourers & related workers	—	—	—	—	8.0	6.8
Not classifiable	1.4	2.5	7.5	4.7	4.2	4.0
Total	100.0	100.0	100.0	100.0	100.0	100.0

* Resident Labour Force

position with only 4.7 per cent in 1957. Another group of workers who recorded a pronounced improvement in their share of the total workforce were the administrative and managerial workers; their proportion moved up sharply from 1.6 per cent in 1957 to 10.0 per cent in 1990. Occupational groups experiencing a diminished share of the total work-force were the services and sales workers and the agricultural and related workers. However, a completely different picture is being portrayed by the resident labour force, with the 2005 top position taken up by professional and technical (32.7 per cent), followed by production and related workers in second position (16.7 per cent).

While a clear upgrading of the Chinese workforce has occurred over the years, as evidenced by a shift towards the higher skilled jobs, the same cannot be said about the Malay workforce. The proportion of administrative and managerial workers among the Malays has remained extremely small, not more than 1.1 per cent all the time. The relative importance of the professional and technical workers increased from 3.4 per cent in 1957 to 9.7 per cent in 1990, but this improvement was still less pronounced than that experienced by the Chinese.

Furthermore, the proportion of low-skilled jobs represented by production and related workers, in fact, rose from 39.8 per cent in 1957 to 57.0 in 1990. The key to the future shift in the Malay workforce towards higher skilled jobs lie in better educational qualifications. The occupational pattern of their resident workforce showed some improvement by 2005 when the proportion in professional and technical managed to reach 18.8 per cent. The dependence on production and related occupation was greatly reduced to 26.1 per cent.

The Indians experienced a moderate shift in the proportion of the seven major occupational groups. At the upper end, the proportion of professional and technical workers rose from 3.8 per cent in 1957 to 12.5 per cent in 1990, while that for the administrative and managerial workers also recorded a perceptible upward trend, from 1.8 per cent to 5.8 per cent during the same period. Apart from the clerical workers whose proportion remained almost unaltered, that of services and sales workers was lowered especially during the last decade. Production and related workers saw their share of the total workforce rise from 41.7 per cent in 1957 to 50.4 per cent in 1990, not as pronounced as in the case of the Malays. As in the case of the Malays, the Indian resident workforce displayed a wider dispersion of occupations by 2005, with the high of 35.4 per cent engaged in professional and technical occupations.

We will now examine the equally interesting differences in the occupational pattern between the two sexes, depicted in Table 12.10. The largest concentration of Chinese men was in senior officials and managers, which absorbed 18.4 per cent of the male workforce, and the second largest concentration of 17.3 per cent in associated professionals and technicians.

The third place was taken up by plant and machine operators and assemblers with 13.6 per cent. The Malay men had the biggest concentration of 21.6 per cent in clerical jobs, with the second largest taken up by plant and machine operators, and assemblers with 20.0 per cent. The third spot among the Malay men was occupied by production craftsman and related workers with 14.2 per cent. The ranking of the top three occupational groups of Indian men was completely different. The top position was taken up by professionals (19.6 per cent), the second by services and sales workers (16.2 per cent), and third by associated professionals and technicians (15.5 per cent).

TABLE 12.10
Percentage Distribution of the Labour Force
by Occupation, Race and Sex, 2005

Occupation	Chinese		Malays		Indians	
	Male	Female	Male	Female	Male	Female
Senior officials & managers	18.4	9.7	2.8	1.7	14.4	5.3
Professionals	12.6	12.6	3.2	6.9	19.6	15.5
Associate professionals & technicians	17.3	23.7	12.7	16.7	15.5	20.3
Clerical workers	5.1	24.8	9.9	33.3	7.2	27.7
Services & sales workers	12.2	15.9	21.6	18.1	16.2	11.6
Production craftsman & related workers	10.6	1.4	14.2	1.0	7.2	0.5
Plant & machine operators & assemblers	13.6	5.2	20.0	11.4	9.5	7.3
Cleaers, labourers & related workers	4.4	6.3	10.8	10.8	4.6	11.2
Other occupations	5.8	0.3	4.7	0.1	5.7	0.6
Total	100.0	100.0	100.0	100.0	100.0	100.0

Somewhat different occupational patterns were exhibited by the resident women of the three main races. Chinese women were concentrated in two occupational groups, namely, clerical workers with 24.8 per cent and associated professionals and technicians with 23.7 per cent. The Malay women were heavily concentrated in clerical workers with a high proportion of 33.3 per cent. The second position, with a much lower proportion of 18.1 per cent, was taken up by services and sales workers. The pattern for Indian women was slightly different in that the top occupational group was also clerical workers (27.7 per cent), but the second was occupied by associated professionals and technicians (20.3 per cent). What is perhaps more worthy of note was the relatively lower proportion of Indian women engaged as services and sales workers, and also the much lower proportion of Malay women working as senior officials and managers.

Notes

1. For a detailed discussion of these two concepts, see United Nations, *Handbook of Population Census Methods, Volume II: Economic Characteristics of Population*, Series F, No. 5, Rev. 1, Series in Methods (New York, 1958).
2. Singapore, 2005 General Household Survey (Singapore: Department of Statistics, 2005).
3. It is not possible to compute the age-specific participation rates for the census years prior to 1957 because the labour force tabulated by age was not provided.
4. John D. Durand, *The Labour Force in Economic Development* (Princeton: Princeton University Press, 1975); and United Nations ECAFE, *Interrelation Between Population and Manpower Problems*, Asia Population Studies No. 7 (Bangkok: ECAFE, e.d.).
5. The girls are not required to serve the two-and-a-half-year military service and can proceed to the universities at a younger age after obtaining their A-level certificate.
6. *Singapore Standard Industrial Classification, 1990* (Singapore: Department of Statistics, 1990).
7. United Nations, *International Standard Classification of all Economic Activities* (New York: United Nations Statistical Office, 1956).
8. *Singapore Standard Industrial Classification, 1990* (Singapore: Department of Statistics, 1990).
9. *International Standard Occupational Classification, 1968* (Geneva: International Labour Office, 1968).

13

Future Population Trends

INTRODUCTION

An examination of the most plausible course of population trends in the future and the social and economic consequences of such trends will be presented in this chapter. To do this, we need to prepare population projections on the basis of certain assumptions concerning the future course of migration, mortality and fertility, the three factors determining the rate of increase or decline in any population. In Singapore the future path of mortality movement is not difficult to decide, while the movement of fertility in the future is somewhat more problematic to resolve. It is of course quite impossible to reckon the flow of migration in the future, which depends primarily on the need for foreigners in the various sectors of the economy that is greatly dependent on external factors outside the control of Singapore.

Three sets of population projections based on three different assumptions in regard to the future course of fertility have been computed to provide us with a better insight into the possibilities of the growth and structure of the population in the years ahead. In addition, we have constructed another population projection on the assumption that the total fertility rate will move up to the replacement level of 2.11 and remain at this level indefinitely. The results of this projection based on a somewhat unrealistic fertility assumption are only meant to illustrate the previously-mentioned concepts such as zero population growth, population replacement, and stationary population.

METHODOLOGY

The population projections were prepared by the component method which involves the separate projection of the number of males and females in each age group of the population.[1] Since the base resident population in 2005 has been divided into quinary age groups, the projections are computed for five-year intervals of time so that at the end of the five-year period all the survivors of one age group would have moved into the next older age group. Each cohort of the sex-age group is diminished to account for the impact of mortality over time. This step requires a set of five-year survival ratios (P_x) which are deemed to represent mortality in each cohort during specific-periods of time subsequent to 2005. A multiplication of the original number in each sex-age group by the relevant survival ratio will give us the estimated number of persons five years older at a date five years later. A repetition of this procedure will yield the estimated population aged ten years older than those at the base date and at a date ten years later.

The second step involves the essential task of estimating the future number of children born in each five-year time interval subsequent to the base date in 2005 in order to fill in the vacuum in the first age group 0–4 at periods of time five years later. To begin with, it is necessary to fix the most plausible assumption concerning the future course of fertility in terms of the total fertility rate with its equivalent age-specific fertility rates from age 15 to 49. These rates are then employed in conjunction with the female population in the reproductive age groups to derive the estimated number of births to the various five-year periods. The total births are split into male births and female births by applying the sex ratio at birth with 0.516163 for male births and 0.483837 for female births. The number of births for each sex surviving at the end of a given five-year period is estimated by multiplying the number of births during the period with the survival ratio (P_b).

The three population projections were prepared on the assumption that the resident population is a closed one not subject to immigration and emigration. Mortality as measured by the life expectancy at birth is assumed to improve from 77.2 in 2005 to 79.6 in 2010 and to remain constant thereafter for the males, with the corresponding figure for the females improving from 81.2 in 2005 to 83.7 in 2010 and remaining constant thereafter for the females. In the case of fertility, three different assumptions are adopted to prepare the following projections.

Low Projection: Fertility is assumed to decline from 1.31 in 2003 to 1.21 in 2010, 1.11 in 2015, and to remain constant thereafter.

Medium Projection: Fertility is assumed to remain constant at 1.31
                     from 2005 onwards.
High Projection: Fertility is assumed to increase from 1.31 in
                     2005 to 1.41 in 2010 and 1.51 in 2015 and to
                     remain constant thereafter.

The results of the above population projections will provide a fairly
good idea of the possibilities of the growth and structure of the resident
population in the years ahead. As mentioned earlier, a fourth projection
was prepared on the assumption that fertility will move up from 1.31 in
2005 to 1.71 in 2010 and 2.11 in 2015, and remain at this replacement
fertility level thereafter. The results of this Replacement Projection will
allow us to illustrate the various aspects of a stationary population.

The 2005 base resident population classified by sex and quinary age
group from age 0 to 80 and over are obtained from the 2005 General
Household Survey conducted by the Department of Statistics.[2]

STATIONARY POPULATION

If a population is closed against migration and is subject to a net
reproduction rate of $R_0 = 1$ and a constant mortality indefinitely, the
population will eventually reach a stage where it will experience a rate
of population growth of r equivalent to zero.[3] At this point of time and
thereafter, the population is said to be a stationary population possessing
certain inherent properties. The size of the population will remain
constant, the annual number of births and deaths will remain not only
constant but equal, the age composition will be invariable, and the crude
death rate equal to the inverse of the expectation of life at birth. A less
restrictive population model is the stable population where the population
need not be stationary. It may be constructed from independent schedules
of mortality and fertility, permitting some annual increase or decrease in
r as determined by the level of the net reproduction rate R_0 above or
below unity. In a stable population the total size of the population varies
by a constant rate r, the crude birth rate and the crude death rate are
constant but the annual numbers of births and deaths vary at a constant
rate r, and the age composition of the population is fixed. It should be
noted that a stationary population is in fact a special case of the more
general family of the stable populations in which $r = 0$. The rate of
population growth in a stable state is known as the intrinsic rate of

natural increase or the Lotka rate. Lotka established the approximate functional relationship as $(1 + r)^x = R_0$, where $r = 0$ if $R_0 = 1$.

In life table terminology the annual number of persons reaching each year of age in a stationary population is indicated by the l_x column. The annual number of deaths at each age is given in the d_x column. The mid-year population at age x is shown by the L_x column, and the sum of the numbers in this column provides the total size of the stationary population which is equivalent to the value of T_0 shown as the first entry of the T_x column. The crude death rate is naturally the total annual number of deaths divided by this total population. The number of births occurring each year is equivalent to the value of l_0, ordinarily fixed at a constant number 10,000. The crude birth rate is therefore $\dfrac{l_0}{T_0} \times k$. Since the number of births and the number of deaths each year must be equal, the crude death rate is also equal to $\dfrac{l_0}{T_0} \times k$. Since the expectations of life at birth is $\dfrac{l_0}{T_0}$, the crude death rate and the crude birth rate are both equal to the inverse of the expectation of life at birth, that is, $\dfrac{l}{e_0} \times k$.

The results of the Replacement Projection based on constant mortality from 2015 onwards and also constant fertility at the replacement level of TFR = 2.11 from 2015 onwards are presented in Table 13.1. It is worth repeating that the possibility of fertility returning to this level in Singapore is completely out of the question. The figures given in the table are of very little practical use and can only serve to illustrate the kind of resident population that would emerge if we could in theory achieve the demographic goal, propounded in the seventies, of attaining a stationary population with zero growth in the future.

The data laid out in Table 13.1 demonstrate that the resident population is expected to grow from the initial size of 3,553,498 in 2005 to the peak of 3,901,193 in 2030. After that it will fluctuate somewhat, decrease to 3,867,583 in 2035, increase to 3,874,203 in 2040, down to 3,851,839 in 2045, and up again to 3,867,146 in 2050. Thereafter the resident population of Singapore is expected to remain stationary at about 3.9 million forever. The implied annual growth rate will be lowered from 0.5 per cent during 2005–10 to 0.1 per cent in 2025–2030, and after that it will oscillate slightly around zero growth. The small fluctuations in the annual growth rate after 2030 may be attributed to

TABLE 13.1

Future Resident Population According to
Replacement Fertility Projection, 2005–2050

Year	Resident Population	Increase	
		Number	Annual Growth Rate (%)
2005	3,553,498	—	—
2010	3,636,149	82,651	0.5
2015	3,733,489	92,340	0.6
2020	3,824,382	90,893	0.5
2025	3,886,744	62,362	0.3
2030	3,901,193	14,449	0.1
2035	3,867,583	-33,610	-0.2
2040	3,874,203	6,620	0.0
2045	3,851,839	-22,364	-0.1
2050	3,867,146	15,307	0.1

the initial disturbances in the age structure of the resident population which has engendered the unstable number of annual births in the first place. The base resident population in 2005 has an abnormal age pyramid with a bulge at the working ages contributed by permanent residents, most of whom were of working ages. If the initial age structure had the normal shape of a pyramid, the annual growth rate would remain about constant at zero after 2030 when the resident population would be in a stationary state.

FUTURE POPULATION GROWTH

The availability of two separate figures for the population of Singapore in recent years requires some explanation before we proceed to examine the results of the population projections. Resident population, the focus of our attention in this chapter, has been defined to include Singapore citizens and permanent residents. Total population, however, refers to the overall population which includes these two groups of persons as well as the transient group of foreigners collectively known as non-resident population. The latter comprised primarily of foreign workers on employment pass or work permit, foreign students on student visa, and foreigners on short-term social visit pass. According to the 2005 General Household Survey, the total population of 4,351,400 composed of 3,553,500 resident population and 797,900 non-resident population. Among the resident population, there were 3,113,000 (87.6 per cent) Singapore citizens and 440,500 (12.4 per cent) permanent residents. In 2006 the total population was estimated to number 4,485,900, split into 3,608,500 resident population and 875,500 non-resident population; separate figures for citizens and permanent residents are not available in postcensal estimates. As mentioned earlier, the resident population employed in the base year 2005 as the starting point of our projection was estimated to number 3,553,500. It is customary nowadays to use the figure for the resident population, without the temporary and volatile foreign component, to represent the population of Singapore.

The results of the three projections based on three different assumptions concerning the possible course of fertility in the future are summarised in Table 13.2 and Figure 13.1, while the detailed figures by sex and age group are presented in Tables 13.4–13.12 for the benefit of prospective users. If fertility remains constant indefinitely at the level of TFR = 1.31 as assumed in the Medium Projection, the resident population is expected to grow from the original size of 3,553,498 in 2005 to the peak of 3,635,225 in 2015, an increase of 81,727 or 2.3 per cent. After that, it will commence to skrink steadily to reach 3,398,337 in 2035, smaller than the size prevailing at the beginning in 2005. This contraction will continue to proceed up to the end of the projection period in 2050 when it will number 2,859,568. The implied annual growth rate will fall from 0.3 per cent during 2005–2010 to 0 per cent during 2015–2020, after which it will experience an accelerated negative growth rate to reach −1.3 during 2045–2050. This scenario will probably be the nearest the resident population will resemble in the future, and the detailed figures by sex and age group according to the Medium Projection are presented in Tables 13.9 and 13.11.

The above results of the population projections are based on the fairly reasonable view that fertility will continue to remain at the 2005 level in the future. However, there is a possibility that the 2004 comprehensive package of pronatalist incentives might be somewhat more effective as to move fertility up to the higher level of 1.51. As can be observed from the results of the High Projection, the resident population can now be expected to grow more rapidly from 3,553,498 in 2005 to the higher peak of 3,679,815 fifteen years later in 2020. Thereafter,

TABLE 13.2

Future Resident Population According to Three Different Projections, 2005–2050

Year	Resident Population	Increase	
		Number	Annual Growth Rate (%)
Low Projection (TFR = 1.11)			
2005	3,553,498	—	—
2010	3,604,305	50,807	0.2
2015	3,610,574	6,269	0.0
2020	3,582,934	−27,640	−0.2
2025	3,527,308	−55,616	−0.3
2030	3,427,986	−99,322	−0.5
2035	3,271,160	−156,826	−0.9
2040	3,094,054	−177,106	−1.1
2045	2,884,232	−209,822	−1.4
2050	2,670,729	−213,502	−1.6
Medium Projection (TFR = 1.31)			
2005	3,553,498	—	—
2010	3,610,810	57,312	0.3
2015	3,635,225	24,415	0.1
2020	3,631,634	−3,591	0.0
2025	3,600,366	−31,268	−0.3
2030	3,523,550	−76,816	−0.4
2035	3,398,337	−125,213	−0.7
2040	3,233,532	−164,805	−1.0
2045	3,047,917	−185,615	−1.2
2050	2,860,168	−187,749	−1.3
High Projection (TFR = 1.51)			
2005	3,553,498	—	—
2010	3,617,039	63,541	0.3
2015	3,659,721	42,682	0.2
2020	3,679,815	20,094	0.1
2025	3,671,950	−7,865	0.0
2030	3,617,732	−54,218	−0.3
2035	3,514,500	−103,232	−0.6
2040	3,373,130	−141,370	−0.8
2045	3,214,225	−158,905	−0.9
2050	3,055,913	−158,912	−1.0

FIGURE 13.1

Actual and Projected Resident Population, 1990–2050

Million

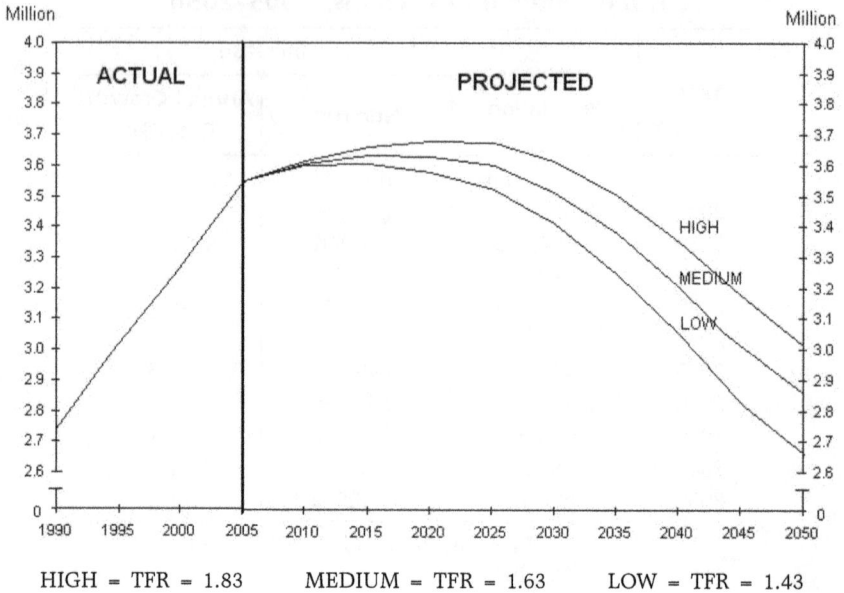

HIGH = TFR = 1.83   MEDIUM = TFR = 1.63   LOW = TFR = 1.43

the negative growth will trigger the shrinking of the resident population, but at a slower pace to reach the higher figure of 3,055,313 in 2050. During the uptrend, the amount of increase for every five-year period will become progressively smaller, being reduced from 63,541 during 2005–2010 to 20,094 during 2015–2020. The implied annual growth rate will slacken from 0.3 per cent to 0.1 per cent. A completely different picture will emerge during the downturn when the amount of decrease will worsen from 7,865 during 2020–2025 to 158,912 during 2045–2050. The negative annual growth rate will accelerate somewhat, moving up from 0.0 per cent during 2020–2025 to 1.0 per cent during 2045–2050.

If fertility happens to fall in the future as reflected in the Low Projection with TFR = 1.11, the resident population is expected to expand slower to reach a lower peak and thereafter shrink faster until the end of the projection period (see Figure 13.1). As the figures in Table 13.2 show, the resident population will grow slowly for ten years from 3,553,498 in 2005 to the high of 3,610,574 in 2010, after which it will reverse course to dwindle more rapidly to reach the smaller size of 2,590,129 in 2050. Under this pessimistic scenario, the annual growth rate will last for the first ten years only, being lowered from 0.2 per cent to 0 per cent during 2010–2015. Thereafter, the negative growth rate will gather speed to reach 1.6 per cent during 2045–2050. In all likelihood, this outcome of the future resident population will not take place considering the existing comprehensive pronatalist programmes, and the government introduce more generous measures should the need arise.

A common feature displayed by the results of the three projections is the inevitable shrinkage of the resident population after 2015, or the latest 2020, some forty or forty-five years after replacement fertility was attained in 1975. Though we do not have the projected figures to show, the resident population will continue to shrink beyond 2050. It may be recalled that the stationary population theory tells us that a population will not be able to replace itself in the future as long as fertility continues to remain below the replacement level. In other words, the excess of births over deaths will occur up to a point only, and beyond this point there will be a deficit of births over deaths as the former will be reduced progressively in the future. The decline in the annual number of births in all the three projections is depicted in Figure 13.2.

6.5 OR 5.5 MILLION PEOPLE IN 2050

The magic number of 6.5 million, which surfaced recently as a population planning parameter for the Singapore Government for the next 40 to 50 years, has intrigued many and sparked considerable public discussion.[4] For any discussion to be fruitful, however, it is imperative for all concerned to appreciate the basic population dynamics underlying this pronouncement.

In 2005, the total population of Singapore was 4.35 million, with 3.55 million residents (citizens and Permanent Residents) and 0.8 million non-residents. In Table 13.2, the Medium projection, based on total fertility rate (TFR) remaining constant at the current level of 1.31, reveals that the resident population will increase from the current number to the peak of 3.64 million in 2015. Thereafter, it will start to decline continuously to touch the low of 2.86 million in 2050.

The fact that TFR has consistently stayed below the replacement level of 2.1 since 1975 has made it impossible for the resident population to replenish itself through natural increase alone (births minus deaths) after 2015. Thereafter, the resident population can only grow with the addition of net migrational inflow (immigrants minus emigrants). To be precise, we need about 0.78 million — the difference of the resident population high of 3.64 and the low of 2.86 in 2050 — newcomers to enter Singapore after 2015 just to ensure that the resident population stays stationary at 3.64 million until 2050.

Assuming that the non-resident population rises from 0.80 million in 2005 to 1.01 million in 2015, the total population will amount to 4.65 million in 2015. However, if we want this total population to expand to 6.5 million in 2050, we will require an additional influx of 1.85 million newcomers after 2015. These newcomers may become PRs or even citizens, while others may remain as non-residents.

Taken together, the total number of newcomers needed to swell the total population to 6.5 million in 2050 will be as large as 2.63 million (0.78 + 1.85). This will have a major impact on the future composition of the population, with the proportion of newcomers arriving after 2015 constituting some 40.5 per cent of the total population in 2050 — the highest Singapore would have seen.

If we target a smaller figure of 5.5 million in 2050, the total number of newcomers needed after 2015 will be less, at 1.63 million. In this case, their share of the total population in 2050 will also be lower, at 29.6 per cent.[5] The 5.5 million target is not only more achievable viewed in terms of the type of newcomers we want, but also more conducive to the maintenance of a harmonious multiracial society.

These calculations are, of course, mere projections. In reality, how many newcomers will pick Singapore as their home — whether for a year or for good — will be dependent on economic conditions prevailing in the country and the world at large, which will determine the future demand for foreign labour. As such, it is almost impossible to ascertain the inflow of newcomers for the next 40 to 50 years.

FUTURE AGE STRUCTURE

Another aspect of the future resident population that we can examine is the changing character of the age structure presented in Table 13.3. In this table we have chosen to include only the figures derived from the Medium Projection, the most likely outcome of the future resident population. For a more convenient and meaningful analysis, the figures have been summarised in terms of four functional age groups. A well-defined shift in the age composition will be experienced in the first half of the present millennium when the first three age groups will record a contraction and the older age group an expansion. The number of young children aged 0–4, will fall consistently from 195,035 in 2005 to reach

TABLE 13.3

Future Resident Population by Four Broad Age Groups According to Medium Projection, 2005–2050

Year	0–4	5–14	15–64	65 & over	Total
			Number		
2005	195,035	502,953	2,558,606	296,904	3,553,498
2010	177,052	434,963	2,671,085	327,710	3,610,810
2015	161,010	372,540	2,683,489	418,186	3,635,225
2020	155,028	337,540	2,602,547	536,519	3,631,634
2025	153,329	315,550	2,457,793	673,694	3,600,366
2030	144,948	307,884	2,286,974	783,744	3,523,550
2035	129,684	297,819	2,133,038	837,796	3,398,337
2040	115,072	274,208	1,986,864	857,388	3,233,532
2045	105,069	244,376	1,880,904	817,568	3,047,917
2050	99,110	219,798	1,784,665	756,595	2,860,168
			Percentage		
2005	5.5	14.1	72.0	8.4	100.0
2010	4.9	12.0	74.0	9.1	100.0
2015	4.4	10.3	73.8	11.5	100.0
2020	4.3	9.2	71.7	14.8	100.0
2025	4.2	8.8	68.3	18.7	100.0
2030	4.1	8.7	64.9	22.3	100.0
2035	3.8	8.7	62.8	24.7	100.0
2040	3.6	8.5	61.4	26.5	100.0
2045	3.5	8.0	61.7	26.8	100.0
2050	3.5	7.7	62.4	26.4	100.0

the low of 99,110 in 2050. The corresponding proportion to the total resident population will decline from 5.5 per cent to 3.5 per cent during the same period.

A more clear-cut pattern is revealed by the figures for the schooling age group 5–15. The whole projection period will witness a continuous decrease in this age group from 502,953 in 2005 to 219,798 in 2050. This is accompanied by a downtrend in the proportion in this age group during the same period, falling consistently from 14.1 per cent to 7.7 per cent. Clearly, this tendency may not augur well for the supply of local labour in the future, but may offer excellent opportunities for improving the educational system. The lessening pressure for school places will provide a good chance for achieving enhanced quality education by

FIGURE 13.2

Age Pyramids of Resident Population
According to Medium Projection, 2005–2050

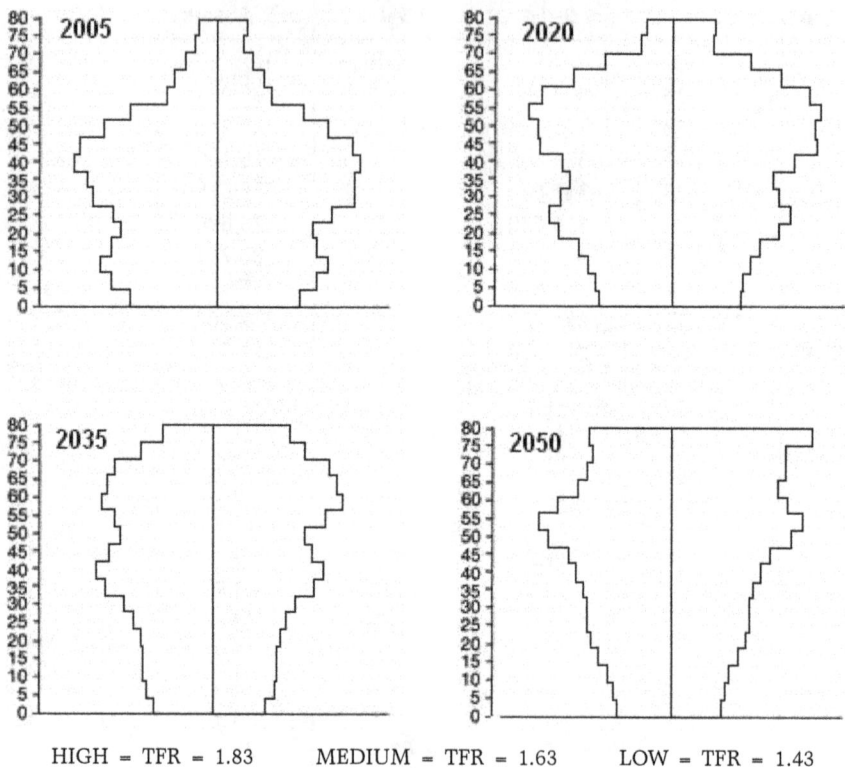

HIGH = TFR = 1.83   MEDIUM = TFR = 1.63   LOW = TFR = 1.43

eliminating double sessions, reducing class size, having better facilities, and maximising the utilisation of financial resources.

Except for a minor rise in the first decade, the working age group 15–64 will encounter a noticeable contraction from 2,683,489 in 2015 to the low of 1,784,665 in 2050. The proportion in this age group is expected to record a small rise from 72.0 to 74.0 per cent in 2010, and thereafter a steady diminution to 61.4 per cent in 2040. The deterioration in the supply of working age persons, already obvious since the late eighties, will offer no respite in the future and will surely perpetuate the current dependency on foreign labour. The other challenge concerns the nature of the dependency burden that will have to be borne by the working persons. The shrinking proportion of working persons will be obliged not only to shoulder a heavier dependency burden, but also to divert much of their personal effort and resources towards the care of the elderly rather than the young.

Another transformation of no less significance may be seen to occur in the last age group 65 and over. Since the statutory retirement age has been raised to 62 and some workers have had their retirement extended to 65, we have decided to adopt the cut-off period for the old age group as 65 rather than 60. The number of persons in this old age group can be expected to balloon from the initial size of 296,904 to the peak of 857,388 in 2040, an enormous expansion of some 560,484 or 189 per cent. Thereafter, it will fall to 756,595 in 2050. Their share of the total population will rise steeply from only 8.4 per cent in 2005 to 26.4 per cent in 2050. It is important to bear in mind that this continuation of the present rapid ageing process was mainly engendered by the sharp decline in fertility prior to 1975 and the subsequent below-replacement fertility rather than by a rise in life expectancy.

FUTURE LABOUR FORCE

The extent to which Singapore will continue to depend on foreign workers will of course be determined by the supply of local labour from the resident population. This aspect of the labour force dynamics can be examined in terms of the projection of the resident labour force, which entails two separate exercises. The first involves the construction of the resident population projections and the second the computation of the resident labour force by the application of the labour force participation rates to the population projection. The results of the work concerning the first stage have been presented earlier.

What we need to do is to proceed to the second stage by applying the age-specific labour force participation rates to the medium resident population projection by sex and quinary age-group to give us the resident labour force projection. The marked differences between the two sexes in regard to their population age structure and the age-specific participation rates necessitated the calculation to the executed for each sex separately.

The assumptions adopted in the first stage with regard to migration, mortality and fertility are the same as those employed in the medium population projection. In the second stage, we assume that the age-specific resident labour force participation rates from age 15 to 65 and over for each sex separately derived from the 2005 General Household Survey, already presented in the previous chapter, would remain constant during the whole period of the projection from 2005 to 2050. The detailed results of the resident labour force projections are presented in Tables 13.15 to 13.17, while a summary of the results is shown in Table 13.4.

TABLE 13.4

Future Resident Labour Force According to Medium Projection, 2005–2050

Year	Resident Labour Force	Increase	
		Number	Percentage
2005	1,744,806	—	—
2010	1,764,527	19,721	1.1
2015	1,761,533	-2,994	-1.7
2020	1,725,997	-35,536	-2.0
2025	1,649,443	-76,554	-4.4
2030	1,548,390	-101,053	-6.1
2035	1,438,690	-109,700	-7.1
2040	1,333,594	-105,096	-7.3
2045	1,239,907	-105,096	-7.9
2050	1,148,032	-91,875	-7.4

The resident labour force is expected to grow from 1,744,800 in 2005 to 1,764,500 in 2010, and to decline immediately in the next forty years to touch the low of 1,148,000 in 2050. Clearly, this continuous shrinkage of the resident labour force in the future must be compensated by the inflow of foreign workers if the economy of Singapore is to grow further. Just to maintain the resident labour force at the level prevailing in 2005, we would need some 600,000 new foreign workers. This is in addition to the existing pool of about one million foreign workers, which might have to be increased further if the economy is to expand in the future. The dependency on foreign labour, as noted earlier, is closely intertwined with the dire need to encourage suitable newcomers to take up permanent residence and more importantly, citizenship, to enable the total population to grow beyond 4.2 million.

The expected ageing of the resident population in the future will of course be accompanied by a similar ageing of the resident labour force.

FIGURE 3.3

**Projected Resident Labour Force
According to Medium Projection, 2005–2050**

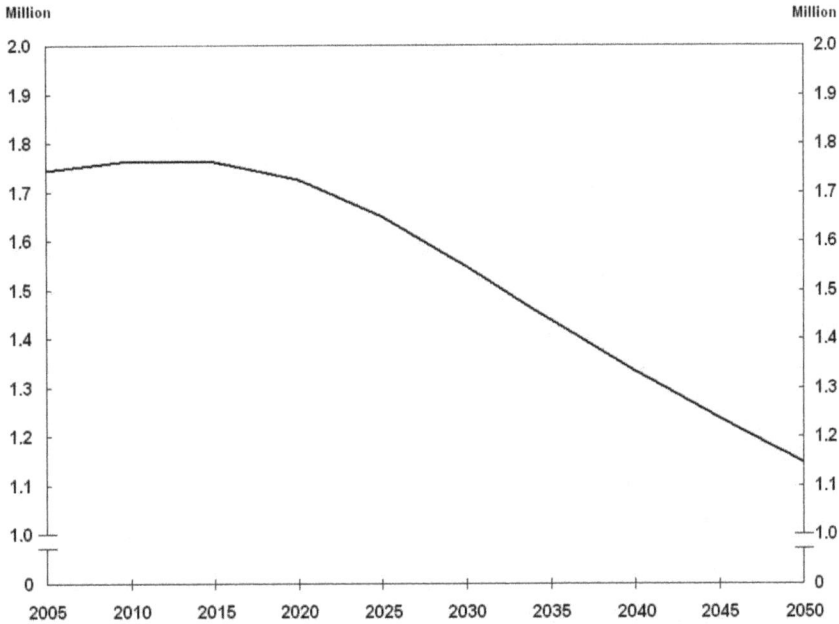

In Table 13.5, we have presented the distribution of the future resident labour force in terms of five broad age groups to highlight the nature of the ageing process that is expected to take place up to the middle of the present century. Most strikingly, the old resident workforce aged 60 and over is expected to swell from 76,382 in 2005 to the peak of 186,685 in 2035, up by 144 per cent. This number will fall slightly to 156,028 in 2050. As a share of the total resident labour force, the proportion of this old resident workforce is expected to rise steeply from only 4.4 per cent in 2005 to 13.0 per cent in 2035, after which it will fall very slightly to 12.7 per cent in 2045, and then jump to the higher level of 13.6 per cent in 2050.

An entirely different trend is underlined by the figures for the workforce in the youngest age group 15–29. Starting with 368,521 in this age group in 2005, the resident workforce is expected to move down and up during the initial period, reaching the high of 381,305 in 2020. From thenceforth, the resident workforce is expected to shrink relentlessly

TABLE 13.5

Future Resident Labour Force by Age Group, 2005–2050

Year	15–29	30–39	40–49	50–59	60 & over	Total
			Number			
2005	368,521	501,307	496,458	302,137	76,382	1,744,806
2010	353,264	452,063	486,986	365,994	106,220	1,764,527
2015	379,822	385,420	461,505	402,286	133,809	1,761,533
2020	381,305	374,019	415,455	392,010	163,208	1,725,997
2025	332,715	407,338	355,414	371,701	182,275	1,649,443
2030	277,912	407,645	346,026	331,640	183,196	1,548,390
2035	238,805	352,362	376,064	284,774	186,685	1,438,690
2040	209,027	295,877	376,840	280,717	171,133	1,333,594
2045	197,755	252,628	325,511	306,596	157,417	1,239,907
2050	190,635	221,751	276,094	303,524	156,028	1,148,032
			Percentage			
2005	21.1	28.7	28.5	17.3	4.4	100.0
2010	20.0	25.6	27.6	20.7	6.0	100.0
2015	21.6	21.9	26.2	22.8	7.6	100.0
2020	22.1	21.7	24.1	22.7	9.5	100.0
2025	20.2	24.7	21.5	22.5	11.1	100.0
2030	17.9	26.3	22.4	21.4	12.0	100.0
2035	16.6	24.5	26.1	19.8	13.0	100.0
2040	15.7	22.2	28.2	21.0	12.8	100.0
2045	16.0	20.4	26.2	24.7	12.7	100.0
2050	16.6	19.3	24.1	26.4	13.6	100.0

until it approaches the low of 190,635 in 2050, a drop of some 48 per cent from the initial level in 2005. A somewhat similar down-up movement will be experienced by the resident workforce in the 30–39 age group, but the overall reduction for the whole period was greater, 56 per cent.

One can expect a clearer downtrend to be displayed by the resident workforce in the 40–49 age group, falling during the whole period from 496,458 to 276,094. This is equivalent to a drop of 44 per cent. The second oldest age group 50–59 is expected to experience a more clear-cut trend, with the workforce rising quickly from 302,137 to 402,286 during the first ten years. Thereafter, the resident workforce in this age group will decline slowly to reach 303,524 in 2050, almost the same as the level prevailing at the beginning.

IMPLICATIONS OF FUTURE TRENDS

One of the vital issues confronting the people of Singapore pertains to the sluggish growth of the resident population up to 2015 and the inevitable shrinking of the population thereafter. The extremely low fertility in the past and the future has resulted in the inability of the resident population to produce enough babies to replace itself. Since 1987 the government has attempted to address this population problem by taking various pronatalist initiatives to encourage married couples to produce more babies. This intervention on the part of the government has culminated in the most recent package of pronatalist measures introduced in 2004, but this package is by no means exhaustive and final. It is still possible to strengthen this pronatalist package by fine-tuning some of the existing policies and adding new ones.

Listed below are some of the improvements that can be considered in the future:

1. The eligibility of pronatalist incentives currently restricted to births up to the fourth order can be extended to the fifth and subsequent births, amounting to less than 2 per cent of the annual births. Apart from the small additional cost involved, this will remove the discrimination, and stigma, against fifth and subsequent children and simplify the administration of these incentives, where applicable.
2. The quantum of money provided under certain existing measures linked to financial rewards can be increased to make them more attractive and effective. The government can afford to allocate more financial resources to the present population problem involving the very survival of the nation state.
3. The different incentive measures contained in the present package are certainly not all that can be adopted by a country to induce its people to produce more babies. The possibility of introducing other measures such as paid paternity leave can be carefully considered.
4. The Voluntary Sterilisation Act, legislated in the early seventies to control population growth, can be reviewed and amended to render it more difficult for men and women to undergo sterilisation, having served its original purpose.
5. The Abortion Act, also legislated in the early seventies for the same purpose, can certainly be re-examined and amended to make it less easy for women to seek abortion. Instead, pregnant married women

can see through their pregnancy, especially when the pronatalist package will provide financial and other assistance. For unmarried women, they can keep their babies or give away to deserving couples for adoption.

The anticipated shortage of births will require the relentless promotion of immigration to augment the resident population in Singapore. In this respect, we must bear in mind that the process of permanent residents taking up citizenship does not constitute an addition to the resident population. It merely represents a shift from the permanent resident component to the citizen component within the resident population. Addition to the resident population through immigration can only take place through the granting of permanent residence to foreigners already in the non-resident population as well as new foreigners entering Singapore. The possibility of enlarging the pool of permanent residents from the non-resident population is rather limited. Most of the non-residents, such as domestic maids and construction workers on work permit, are not eligible for permanent resident status. Those on employment pass are reluctant to become permanent residents as their primary purpose in coming to Singapore is to work for a few years rather than to settle down permanently. As discussed in Chapter 11, the rules governing the granting of permanent residence have been made as simple and generous as possible. The importance of attracting more immigrants has now been recognised by the government as mentioned by Mr Wong Kan Seng, Deputy Prime Minister in charge of national population affairs.[6]

The slackening rate of population growth, followed by a reduction in the proportion of persons in the working ages, will tend to reinforce the current dependency on foreign workers in certain sectors of the economy. What it implies is that the policy of allowing selected foreigners to work in Singapore on employment pass or work permit basis has to be preserved. Needless to say, the inflow of foreign workers would depend on the demand for such workers as determined by the health of the economy, and have to be supervised closely to minimise the number of over-stayers and illegal immigrants. As explained earlier, the admission of foreigners to work in Singapore is intertwined with the question of promoting immigration. Special consideration, or even incentives, can be offered to such foreigners to take up permanent resident status, thus enlarging the resident population.

TABLE 13.6
Total Resident Population by Age Group According to High Projection, 2005–2050

Age Group	2005	2010	2015	2020	2025	2030	2035	2040	2045	2050
0–4	196,035	170,547	142,804	131,355	129,843	122,317	107,894	92,525	80,532	72,922
5–9	239,320	195,799	170,394	142,676	131,238	129,727	122,208	107,798	92,443	80,460
10–14	263,633	239,164	195,671	169,837	142,210	131,153	129,642	122,129	107,728	92,383
15–19	238,053	263,314	238,874	195,434	169,040	142,037	130,994	129,485	121,981	107,597
20–24	222,422	237,463	262,661	238,281	194,949	168,619	141,684	130,668	129,163	121,678
25–29	253,710	221,696	236,681	261,796	237,495	194,306	168,061	141,215	130,237	128,737
30–34	303,587	252,830	220,906	235,831	260,856	236,641	193,608	167,455	140,706	129,769
35–39	310,093	302,322	251,781	219,964	234,818	259,735	235,623	192,775	166,732	140,099
40–44	331,244	308,196	300,485	250,255	218,610	233,365	258,128	234,164	191,581	165,698
45–49	314,470	327,991	305,195	297,579	247,842	216,466	231,064	255,583	231,854	189,691
50–54	260,456	309,638	322,965	300,571	293,116	244,138	213,155	227,505	251,645	228,277
55–59	202,772	253,375	301,237	314,220	292,510	285,319	237,665	207,394	221,319	244,801
60–64	120,799	194,260	242,734	288,616	301,087	280,419	273,638	227,970	198,743	212,022
65–69	104,281	112,218	180,444	225,461	268,129	279,772	260,800	254,688	212,244	184,702
70–74	79,660	90,854	97,809	157,261	196,486	233,714	243,910	227,565	222,395	185,385
75–79	56,244	64,029	73,017	78,656	126,449	157,978	187,964	196,224	183,316	179,352
80 & above	56,719	60,609	66,916	75,141	82,630	112,280	145,122	178,911	201,613	207,156
Total	3,553,498	3,604,305	3,610,574	3,582,934	3,527,308	3,427,986	3,281,160	3,094,054	2,884,232	2,670,729

TABLE 13.7

Male Resident Population by Age Group According to High Projection, 2005–2050

Age Group	2005	2010	2015	2020	2025	2030	2035	2040	2045	2050
0–4	100,914	88,004	73,688	67,781	67,001	63,117	55,675	47,744	41,555	37,628
5–9	123,389	100,783	87,942	73,636	67,734	66,954	63,073	55,636	47,711	41,526
10–14	135,575	123,303	100,712	87,880	73,584	67,687	66,907	63,029	55,597	47,678
15–19	122,317	135,358	123,106	100,551	87,739	73,466	67,579	66,800	62,928	55,508
20–24	112,243	121,889	134,884	122,675	100,199	87,432	73,209	67,342	66,566	62,708
25–29	120,844	111,693	121,292	134,223	122,074	99,708	87,004	72,850	67,012	66,240
30–34	145,707	120,216	111,112	120,661	133,525	121,439	99,190	86,552	72,471	66,664
35–39	152,150	144,789	119,459	110,412	119,901	132,684	120,674	98,565	86,007	72,014
40–44	166,766	150,948	143,645	118,515	109,540	118,954	131,636	119,721	97,786	85,328
45–49	158,829	164,631	149,016	141,806	116,998	108,138	117,431	129,951	118,189	96,534
50–54	131,464	155,382	161,059	145,782	138,729	114,459	105,791	114,883	127,131	115,624
55–59	101,243	126,666	149,711	155,180	140,461	133,665	110,281	101,930	110,690	122,491
60–64	59,084	95,290	119,218	140,908	146,055	132,202	125,806	103,796	95,937	104,181
65–69	49,977	53,052	85,561	107,046	126,521	131,143	118,704	112,961	93,198	86,142
70–74	36,815	42,111	44,702	72,094	90,197	106,607	110,501	100,020	95,181	78,529
75–79	24,838	28,035	32,068	34,041	54,900	68,685	81,181	84,147	76,165	72,480
80 & above	22,587	23,632	25,746	28,809	31,318	42,962	55,634	68,175	75,902	75,775
Total	1,764,742	1,785,782	1,782,921	1,762,000	1,726,476	1,669,302	1,590,276	1,494,102	1,390,026	1,287,050

TABLE 13.8

Female Resident Population by Age Group According to High Projection, 2005–2050

Age Group	2005	2010	2015	2020	2025	2030	2035	2040	2045	2050
0–4	95,121	82,543	69,116	63,574	62,842	59,200	52,219	44,781	38,977	35,294
5–9	115,931	95,016	82,452	69,040	63,504	62,773	59,135	52,162	44,732	38,934
10–14	128,058	115,861	94,959	81,957	68,626	63,466	62,735	59,100	52,131	44,705
15–19	115,736	127,956	115,768	94,883	81,301	68,571	63,415	62,685	59,053	52,089
20–24	110,179	115,574	127,777	115,606	94,750	81,187	68,475	63,326	62,597	58,970
25–29	132,866	110,003	115,389	127,573	115,421	94,598	81,057	68,365	63,225	62,497
30–34	157,880	132,614	109,794	115,170	127,331	115,202	94,418	80,903	68,235	63,105
35–39	157,943	157,533	132,322	109,552	114,917	127,051	114,949	94,210	80,725	68,085
40–44	164,478	157,248	156,840	131,740	109,070	114,411	126,492	114,443	93,795	80,370
45–49	155,641	163,360	156,179	155,773	130,844	108,328	113,633	125,632	113,665	93,157
50–54	128,992	154,256	161,906	154,789	154,387	129,679	107,364	112,622	124,514	112,653
55–59	101,529	126,709	151,526	159,040	152,049	151,654	127,384	105,464	110,629	122,310
60–64	61,715	98,970	123,516	147,708	155,032	148,217	147,832	124,174	102,806	107,841
65–69	54,304	59,166	94,883	118,415	141,608	148,629	142,096	141,727	119,046	98,560
70–74	42,845	48,743	53,107	85,167	106,289	127,107	133,409	127,545	127,214	106,856
75–79	31,406	35,994	40,949	44,615	71,549	89,293	106,783	112,077	107,151	106,872
80 & above	34,132	36,977	41,170	46,332	51,312	69,318	89,488	110,736	125,711	131,381
Total	1,788,756	1,818,523	1,827,653	1,820,934	1,800,832	1,758,684	1,690,884	1,599,952	1,494,206	1,383,679

TABLE 13.9
Total Resident Population by Age Group According to Medium Projection, 2005–2050

Age Group	2005	2010	2015	2020	2025	2030	2035	2040	2045	2050
0–4	195,035	177,052	161,010	155,028	153,329	144,948	129,684	115,072	105,069	99,110
5–9	239,320	195,799	176,839	160,816	154,841	153,144	144,774	129,528	114,933	104,943
10–14	263,633	239,164	195,671	176,724	160,709	154,740	153,045	144,680	129,443	114,858
15–19	238,053	263,314	238,874	195,434	176,510	160,514	154,552	152,860	144,505	129,286
20–24	222,422	237,463	262,661	238,281	194,949	176,071	160,115	154,168	152,480	144,146
25–29	253,710	221,696	236,681	261,796	237,495	194,306	175,490	159,587	153,659	151,977
30–34	303,587	252,830	220,906	235,831	260,856	236,641	193,608	174,858	159,013	153,106
35–39	310,093	302,322	251,781	219,964	247,818	259,735	235,623	192,775	174,105	158,329
40–44	331,244	308,196	300,485	250,255	218,610	233,365	258,128	234,164	191,581	173,027
45–49	314,470	327,991	305,195	297,579	247,842	216,466	231,064	255,583	231,854	189,691
50–54	260,456	309,638	322,965	300,571	293,116	244,138	213,155	227,505	251,645	228,227
55–59	202,772	253,375	301,237	314,220	292,510	285,319	237,665	207,394	221,319	244,801
60–64	120,799	194,260	242,734	288,616	301,087	280,419	273,638	227,970	198,743	212,022
65–69	104,281	112,218	180,444	225,461	268,129	279,772	260,800	254,688	212,244	184,702
70–74	79,660	90,854	97,809	157,261	196,486	233,714	243,910	227,565	222,395	185,385
75–79	56,244	64,029	73,017	78,656	126,449	157,978	187,964	196,224	183,316	179,352
80 & above	56,719	60,609	66,916	75,141	82,630	112,280	145,122	178,911	201,613	207,156
Total	3,553,498	3,610,810	3,635,225	3,631,634	3,600,366	3,523,550	3,398,337	3,233,532	3,047,917	2,860,168

TABLE 13.10

Male Resident Population by Age Group According to Medium Projection, 2005–2050

Age Group	2005	2010	2015	2020	2025	2030	2035	2040	2045	2050
0–4	100,914	91,428	83,083	79,996	79,120	74,795	66,918	59,365	54,218	51,142
5–9	123,389	100,783	91,309	82,975	79,892	79,017	74,698	66,831	59,288	54,148
10–14	135,575	123,303	100,712	91,245	82,917	79,836	78,962	74,646	66,784	59,246
15–19	122,317	135,358	123,106	100,551	91,099	82,784	79,708	78,836	74,527	66,677
20–24	112,243	121,889	134,884	122,675	100,199	90,780	82,494	79,429	78,560	74,266
25–29	120,844	111,693	121,292	134,223	122,074	99,708	90,335	82,090	79,040	78,175
30–34	145,707	120,216	111,112	120,661	133,525	121,439	99,190	89,865	81,663	78,629
35–39	152,150	144,789	119,459	110,412	119,901	132,684	120,674	98,565	89,299	81,149
40–44	166,766	150,948	143,645	118,515	109,540	118,954	131,636	119,721	97,786	88,594
45–49	158,829	164,631	149,016	141,806	116,998	108,138	117,431	129,951	118,189	96,534
50–54	131,464	155,382	161,059	145,782	138,729	114,459	105,791	114,883	127,131	115,624
55–59	101,243	126,666	149,711	155,180	140,461	133,665	110,281	101,930	110,690	122,491
60–64	59,084	95,290	119,218	140,908	146,055	132,202	125,806	103,796	95,937	104,181
65–69	49,977	53,052	85,561	107,046	126,521	131,143	118,704	112,961	93,198	86,142
70–74	36,815	42,111	44,702	72,094	90,197	106,607	110,501	100,020	95,181	78,529
75–79	24,838	28,035	32,068	34,041	54,900	68,685	81,181	84,147	76,165	72,480
80 & above	22,587	23,632	25,746	28,809	31,318	42,962	55,634	68,175	75,902	75,775
Total	1,764,742	1,789,206	1,795,683	1,786,919	1,763,446	1,717,858	1,649,944	1,565,211	1,473,558	1,383,782

TABLE 13.11

Female Resident Population by Age Group According to Medium Projection, 2005–2050

Age Group	2005	2010	2015	2020	2025	2030	2035	2040	2045	2050
0–4	95,121	85,624	77,927	75,032	74,209	70,153	62,766	55,707	50,851	47,968
5–9	115,931	95,016	85,530	77,841	74,949	74,127	70,076	62,697	55,645	50,795
10–14	128,058	115,861	94,959	85,479	77,792	74,904	74,083	70,034	62,659	55,612
15–19	115,736	127,956	115,768	94,883	85,411	77,730	74,844	74,024	69,978	62,609
20–24	110,179	115,574	127,777	115,606	94,750	85,291	77,621	74,739	73,920	69,880
25–29	132,866	110,003	115,389	127,573	115,421	94,598	85,155	77,497	74,619	73,802
30–34	157,880	132,614	109,794	115,170	127,331	115,202	94,418	84,993	77,350	74,477
35–39	157,943	157,533	132,322	109,552	114,917	127,051	114,949	94,210	84,806	77,180
40–44	164,478	157,248	156,840	131,740	109,070	114,411	126,492	114,443	93,795	84,433
45–49	155,641	163,360	156,179	155,773	130,844	108,328	113,633	125,632	113,665	93,157
50–54	128,992	154,256	161,906	154,789	154,387	129,679	107,364	112,622	124,514	112,653
55–59	101,529	126,709	151,526	159,040	152,049	151,654	127,384	105,464	110,629	122,310
60–64	61,715	98,970	123,516	147,708	155,032	148,217	147,832	124,174	102,806	107,841
65–69	54,304	59,166	94,883	118,415	141,608	148,629	142,096	141,727	119,046	98,560
70–74	42,845	48,743	53,107	85,167	106,289	127,107	133,409	127,545	127,214	106,856
75–79	31,406	35,994	40,949	44,615	71,549	89,293	106,783	112,077	107,151	106,872
80 & above	34,132	36,977	41,170	46,332	51,312	69,318	89,488	110,736	125,711	131,381
Total	1,788,756	1,821,604	1,839,542	1,844,715	1,836,920	1,805,692	1,748,393	1,668,321	1,574,359	1,476,386

TABLE 13.12
Total Resident Population by Age Group According to Low Projection, 2005–2050

Age Group	2005	2010	2015	2020	2025	2030	2035	2040	2045	2050
0-4	196,035	183,281	179,289	178,738	176,778	167,626	151,801	138,719	132,076	128,808
5-9	239,320	195,799	183,056	179,074	178,523	176,565	167,425	151,618	138,552	131,917
10-14	263,633	239,164	195,671	182,937	178,957	178,407	176,450	167,316	151,519	138,462
15-19	238,053	263,314	238,874	195,434	182,715	178,740	178,191	176,236	167,113	151,335
20-24	222,422	237,463	262,661	238,281	194,949	182,261	178,296	177,748	175,799	166,698
25-29	253,710	221,696	236,681	261,796	237,495	194,306	181,660	177,708	177,161	175,219
30-34	303,587	252,830	220,906	235,831	260,856	236,641	193,608	181,006	177,069	176,524
35-39	310,093	302,322	251,781	219,964	234,818	259,735	235,623	192,775	180,226	176,307
40-44	331,244	308,196	300,485	250,255	218,610	233,365	258,128	234,164	191,581	179,257
45-49	314,470	327,991	305,195	297,579	247,842	216,466	231,064	255,583	231,854	189,691
50-54	260,456	309,638	322,965	300,571	293,116	244,138	213,155	227,505	251,645	228,277
55-59	202,772	253,375	301,237	314,220	292,510	285,319	237,665	207,394	221,319	244,801
60-64	120,799	194,260	242,734	288,616	301,087	280,419	273,638	227,970	198,743	212,022
65-69	104,281	112,218	180,444	225,461	268,129	279,772	260,800	254,688	212,244	184,702
70-74	79,660	90,854	97,809	157,261	196,486	233,714	243,910	227,565	222,395	185,385
75-79	56,244	64,029	73,017	78,656	126,449	157,978	187,964	196,224	183,316	179,352
80 & above	56,719	60,609	66,916	75,141	82,630	112,280	145,122	178,911	201,613	207,156
Total	3,553,498	3,617,039	3,659,721	3,679,815	3,671,950	3,617,732	3,514,500	3,373,130	3,214,225	3,055,913

TABLE 13.13

Male Resident Population by Age Group According to Low Projection, 2005–2050

Age Group	2005	2010	2015	2020	2025	2030	2035	2040	2045	2050
0–4	100,914	94,575	92,515	92,231	91,220	86,497	78,332	71,581	68,153	66,380
5–9	123,389	100,783	94,452	92,395	92,111	91,101	86,385	78,230	71,488	68,064
10–14	135,575	123,303	100,712	94,386	92,330	92,047	91,037	86,325	78,175	71,438
15–19	122,317	135,358	123,106	100,551	94,235	92,182	91,900	90,891	86,187	78,050
20–24	112,243	121,889	134,884	122,675	100,199	93,905	91,859	91,578	90,573	85,885
25–29	120,844	111,693	121,292	134,223	122,074	99,708	93,445	91,409	91,129	90,129
30–34	145,707	120,216	111,112	120,661	133,525	121,439	99,190	92,959	90,934	90,655
35–39	152,150	144,789	119,459	110,412	119,901	132,684	120,674	98,565	92,373	90,361
40–44	166,766	150,948	143,645	118,515	109,540	118,954	131,636	119,721	97,786	91,791
45–49	158,829	164,631	149,016	141,806	116,998	108,138	117,431	129,951	118,189	96,534
50–54	131,464	155,382	161,059	145,782	138,729	114,459	106,791	114,883	127,131	115,624
55–59	101,243	126,666	149,711	155,180	140,461	133,665	110,281	101,930	110,690	122,491
60–64	59,084	95,290	119,218	140,908	146,055	132,202	125,806	103,796	95,937	104,181
65–69	49,977	53,052	85,561	107,046	126,521	131,143	118,704	112,961	93,198	86,142
70–74	36,815	42,111	44,702	72,094	90,197	106,607	110,501	100,020	95,181	78,529
75–79	24,838	28,035	32,068	34,041	54,900	68,685	81,181	84,147	76,165	72,480
80 & above	22,587	23,632	25,746	28,809	31,318	42,962	55,634	68,175	75,902	75,775
Total	1,764,742	1,792,353	1,808,258	1,811,745	1,800,314	1,766,378	1,709,787	1,637,122	1,559,191	1,484,509

TABLE 13.14

Female Resident Population by Age Group According to Low Projection, 2005–2050

Age Group	2005	2010	2015	2020	2025	2030	2035	2040	2045	2050
0–4	95,121	88,706	86,774	86,507	85,558	81,129	73,469	67,138	63,923	62,428
5–9	115,931	95,016	88,604	86,679	86,412	85,464	81,040	73,388	67,064	63,853
10–14	128,058	115,861	94,959	88,551	86,627	86,360	85,413	80,991	73,344	67,024
15–19	115,736	127,956	115,768	94,883	88,480	86,558	86,291	85,345	80,926	73,285
20–24	110,179	115,574	127,777	115,606	94,750	88,356	86,437	86,170	85,226	80,813
25–29	132,866	110,003	115,389	127,573	115,421	94,598	88,215	86,299	86,032	85,090
30–34	157,880	132,614	109,794	115,170	127,331	115,202	94,418	88,047	86,135	85,869
35–39	157,943	157,533	132,322	109,552	114,917	127,051	114,949	94,210	87,853	85,946
40–44	164,478	157,248	156,840	131,740	109,070	114,411	126,492	114,443	93,795	87,466
45–49	155,641	163,360	156,179	155,773	130,844	108,328	113,633	125,632	113,665	93,157
50–54	128,992	154,256	161,906	154,789	154,387	129,679	107,364	112,622	124,514	112,653
55–59	101,529	126,709	151,526	159,040	152,049	151,654	127,384	105,464	110,629	122,310
60–64	61,715	98,970	123,516	147,708	155,032	148,217	147,832	124,174	102,806	107,841
65–69	54,304	59,166	94,883	118,415	141,608	148,629	142,096	141,727	119,046	98,560
70–74	42,845	48,743	53,107	85,167	106,289	127,107	133,409	127,545	127,214	106,856
75–79	31,406	35,994	40,949	44,615	71,549	89,293	106,783	112,077	107,151	106,872
80 & above	34,132	36,977	41,170	46,332	51,312	69,318	89,488	110,736	125,711	131,381
Total	1,788,756	1,824,686	1,851,463	1,868,100	1,871,636	1,851,354	1,804,713	1,736,008	1,655,034	1,571,404

TABLE 13.15

Total Resident Labour Force According to Medium Projection, 2005–2050

Age Group	2005	2010	2015	2020	2025	2030	2035	2040	2045	2050
15–19	23,492	25,985	24,888	19,288	16,696	14,025	12,933	12,460	11,418	9,957
20–24	130,177	139,012	153,764	139,496	114,126	98,723	82,950	76,498	75,617	71,234
25–29	214,852	188,267	201,170	222,521	201,893	165,164	142,922	120,069	110,720	109,444
30–34	250,456	208,387	182,762	195,456	216,207	196,189	160,485	138,935	116,698	107,598
35–39	250,851	243,676	202,658	178,563	191,131	211,456	191,877	156,942	135,930	114,153
40–44	259,580	240,228	233,138	193,824	171,155	183,325	201,797	184,063	150,541	132,991
45–49	236,878	246,758	228,367	221,631	184,259	162,701	174,267	192,777	174,970	143,103
50–54	185,818	220,591	229,733	212,372	205,908	171,123	151,446	162,327	179,571	163,001
55–59	116,319	145,403	172,553	179,638	165,793	160,517	133,328	118,390	127,025	140,523
60–64	43,969	70,611	88,278	104,701	108,932	100,259	96,837	80,360	71,757	77,123
65 & above	32,413	35,609	45,531	58,507	73,343	84,937	89,848	90,773	85,660	78,905
Total	1,744,806	1,764,527	1,761,533	1,725,997	1,649,443	1,548,390	1,438,690	1,333,594	1,239,907	1,148,032

TABLE 13.16
Male Resident Labour Force According to Medium Projection, 2005–2050

Age Group	2005	2010	2015	2020	2025	2030	2035	2040	2045	2050
15–19	13,070	14,463	13,154	10,744	9,375	7,850	7,222	7,138	6,724	5,931
20–24	66,520	72,237	79,938	72,702	59,382	51,816	43,387	39,910	39,450	37,163
25–29	107,797	99,634	108,197	119,731	108,894	88,943	77,611	64,985	59,777	59,088
30–34	133,280	109,963	101,275	109,979	121,704	110,688	90,409	78,890	66,055	60,762
35–39	142,489	135,595	111,874	103,401	112,288	124,259	113,012	92,306	80,546	67,441
40–44	156,039	141,238	134,405	110,892	102,494	111,302	123,169	112,020	91,496	79,839
45–49	143,005	148,229	134,170	127,678	105,342	97,364	105,731	117,004	106,414	86,916
50–54	116,462	137,651	142,680	129,146	122,898	101,398	93,719	101,773	112,623	102,430
55–59	76,263	95,413	112,772	116,892	105,805	100,685	83,071	76,781	83,379	92,268
60–64	30,982	49,783	62,284	73,616	76,305	69,067	65,726	54,227	50,121	54,428
65 & above	23,985	26,239	33,610	43,244	54,136	62,436	65,408	65,281	60,839	55,921
Total	1,009,891	1,030,445	1,034,359	1,018,025	978,623	925,808	868,465	810,315	757,424	702,187

TABLE 13.17
Female Resident Labour Force According to Medium Projection, 2005–2050

Age Group	2005	2010	2015	2020	2025	2030	2035	2040	2045	2050
15–19	10,422	11,522	10,425	8,544	7,321	6,175	5,711	5,322	4,694	4,026
20–24	63,658	66,775	73,826	66,794	54,744	46,907	39,563	36,588	36,167	34,071
25–29	107,055	88,633	92,973	102,790	92,999	76,221	65,311	55,084	50,943	50,356
30–34	117,176	98,424	81,487	85,477	94,503	85,501	70,076	60,045	50,643	46,836
35–39	108,862	108,081	90,784	75,162	78,843	87,168	78,865	64,636	55,384	46,712
40–44	103,541	98,990	98,733	82,932	68,661	72,023	78,628	72,043	59,045	53,152
45–49	93,873	98,529	94,197	93,953	78,917	65,337	68,536	75,773	68,556	56,187
50–54	69,356	82,940	87,053	83,226	83,010	69,725	57,727	60,554	66,948	60,571
55–59	40,056	49,990	59,781	62,746	59,988	59,832	50,257	41,609	43,646	48,255
60–64	12,988	20,828	25,994	31,085	32,627	31,192	31,111	26,133	21,636	22,695
65 & above	8,428	9,370	11,921	15,263	19,207	22,501	24,440	25,492	24,821	22,984
Total	734,915	734,082	727,174	707,972	670,820	622,582	570,225	523,279	482,483	445,845

The ageing of the resident population is expected to gather momentum in the future as evidenced by the enormous expansion of old persons aged 65 and over. This rapid ageing process was triggered by the sharp decline in fertility since the early-sixties and the continued below-replacement level since the mid-seventies.[7] Among the more serious consequences of population ageing is the unavailability of social support system for the fast rising number of elderly persons. The family will have to continue to be the primary source of support for the elderly, viewed in terms of shelter and care, not forgetting the greater role to be played by institutional homes. In the course of time, senior citizen villages or condominiums run on a private basis might be able to provide additional shelter for the elderly.

Another implication of the ageing population is related to the modification of the health care system to meet the medical needs of the elderly population. Obviously, a higher proportion of the nation's resources, such as medical personnel, physical facilities and finance, will have to be devoted to the needs of the elderly sick. The expected rise in the number of chronic sick and disabled among the old population will require more old age nursing homes. The other issue that is of greater concern to the old people directly is in the area of personal finance. For most of them, the perennial anxiety is related to the adequacy of their CPF savings to enable them to maintain a reasonable standard of living during their old age. Extending the mandatory age for employees to retire, and even allowing some to work beyond this age under mutually-agreed terms, will help to ease the financial burden of the elderly and mitigate the tight labour market accompanying the sluggish growth of the resident population.

Notes

1. United Nations, *Manual III: Methods of Population Projections by Sex and Age*, Population Studies No. 25, New York: Department of Economics and Social Affairs, 1956.
2. Singapore, *2005 General Household Survey, Socio-Demographic and Social Characteristics*, Release No. 1 (Singapore: Department of Statistics, 2006).
3. For a discussion of the theory of stationary and stable populations, see Louis Dublin and Alfred J. Lotka 'On the True Rate of Natural Increase', *Journal of the American Statistical Association*, Vol. 20, No. 150, September 1925 and Alvaro Lopez, Problems in *Stable Population Theory*, Princeton: Office of Population Research, 1961.

4. Lydia Lim, "Singapore Gearing Up for 6.5m Population", *Straits Times*, 10 February 2007 and Lee U-Wen, "6.5m Is Planning Figure, Not a Target", *Today*, 28 February 2007.
5. Saw Swee-Hock, "What It Means to Have 6.5m Population", *Today*, 23 March 2007.
6. *Straits Times*, 4 September 2004.
7. Saw Swee-Hock, "Dynamics of Ageing in Singapore's Population", *Annals of Academy of Medicine* 14, no. 4 (October 1985).

Appendix

Sources of Demographic Statistics

INTRODUCTION

Since the establishment of Singapore in 1819, there has accumulated over the years a mass of population statistics collected in censuses held from time to time. A brief survey of the sources, methods of collection and reliability of these statistics is presented here. The census records can be conveniently divided into three periods, namely, 1824–70, 1871–1947 and 1957–90. The first pertains to the period when some form of census was undertaken, usually by the police at very short irregular intervals, and the second and third to the time when proper and systematic censuses by trained enumerators were taken at regular and longer intervals. The third period is differentiated from the second by the censuses conducted separately for Singapore and not as part of the pan-Malayan region. By and large, the census records for the second and third periods are by far more comprehensive and reliable than those for the first period. Apart from this, the original published results of the censuses taken in the last two periods are still available but those of the censuses taken prior to 1871 are apparently lost; what is left are the figures quoted by various writers in their published works.

THE 1824–70 PERIOD

The taking of a census of the population in Singapore dates as far back as January 1824 when the first census of the whole island was carried out. Besides the figures quoted by various writers subsequently, nothing is known about this first population count. Following this, many other counts were taken, at first every year and then at longer intervals. T. J. Newbold, writing about the population of Singapore in 1839, was able to collect the figures of eleven censuses taken annually between 1824 and 1836, except in 1835 when no census was taken.[1] The figures are classified by sex and race only, and they are rather defective. H. Marriott was of the opinion that the "figures for these early censuses cannot, however, be regarded as very accurate. In 1833... they were collected by the two constables who were attached to the Settlement and who had many other duties to perform. No fixed principle was adopted with regard to the headings 'Europeans', 'Native Christians' and 'Tndo-Britons'. Some enumerating officers appeared to have included as 'Europeans' all who wore European clothes".[2]

During the two-and-a-half decades between the eleventh census of 1836 and the end of this period, only three censuses were held. The figures of these three censuses of 1840, 1849 and 1860 were collected by T. Braddell in his valuable work on *Statistics of the British Possession in the Straits of Malacca*, giving the breakdown of sex and race only.[3] These figures were later quoted by Marriott in his study of the peoples of Singapore published in 1921. Very little is known of these three censuses except that, according to Marriott, the 1860 census was conducted by the police and, in his opinion, the figures of this particular census were absolutely unreliable.[4] Again, the 1871 Census Committee has this to say about the 1860 census: "We are inclined to agree with the statement made by Sir Harry Ord in his despatch to the Secretary of State on the 27 August, 1869, that no great reliance can be placed upon the returns of population stated to have taken in that year (1860), so that for any purpose of comparison now, they are of little or no value. There is a remarkable increase in the number of Malays, for which no adequate reason can be offered: the influx to the Settlement of 8,362 since 1860, is scarcely probable, while the Chinese race would appear to have increased by only 4,529 in the eleven years, which is still more improbable when the large increase in Excise forms since 1860 is taken into consideration. These discrepancies would tend greatly to show that the returns of 1860 are altogether unreliable".[5]

Apart from being somewhat inaccurate, the population statistics collected in these early censuses only included the bare characteristics of sex and race. Information on other characteristics normally collected in a population census of today is unobtainable. These early population counts, though of considerable historical interest, poses very limited value in terms of demographic analysis.

THE 1871–1947 PERIOD

Following the transfer of the settlement of Singapore from the India Office to the Colonial Office on 15 April 1867, the first proper census of Singapore as understood in the modern form was conducted in 1871. The year coincided with the decennial censuses taken in England and its other colonial territories. This first properly organized census of Singapore was taken by a committee of three census officers as part of the wider census of the Straits Settlements. The census report, comprising a brief three-page text and fourteen pages of tables, was submitted by the committee to the Colonial Secretary, Straits Settlements, and appeared in the 1871 Blue Book.[6] Besides sex and race, the tables contain information on age, occupation, town-country divisions, and houses. The age groupings are in terms of Under 10, 10–14, 15–19, and ten-year groups up to 89. As for occupation, the attempt to produce an exhaustive tabulation yields a long list of hundreds of occupations, with doubtful accuracy and utility.

The first island-wide census appeared to have been greeted with considerable apprehension among the local inhabitants who were under the wrong impression that the census was a preliminary to capitation tax. At one stage, the fear was so strong among the people that placards were put up by them in the town, urging all residents to resist the enumerators, who were mainly government employees. Under these circumstances, the reliability of the statistics collected was undoubtedly questionable. Even the census officers confessed that they "would not claim for them complete accuracy", but ventured to say that "they approximate very nearly to the truth".[7]

The next decennial census of Singapore in 1881 was carried out exactly along the same lines as the previous census, and the report by the six-man committee was published in the 1881 Blue Book. In addition to the usual account of the census administration and procedure, there was for the first time a write-up of the results of the census in this report. No new tables were added to those of 1871 but the age groupings were broken down further; single years for ages below six and quinary age groups for other ages up to 59. In planning the census, considerable publicity was given prior to the actual enumeration to try to eliminate the impression, prevalent in 1871, that the census had anything to do with the imposition of a tax. The co-operation of the inhabitants was consequently more forthcoming. The members of the census committee claimed that they "have every reason to believe that a really good Census has been taken, and that the numbers given fairly represent the population of the Settlement".[8]

In 1891 the population of Singapore was again enumerated as part of the census of the Straits Settlement, but this time the entire census operation was entrusted to a superintendent who was also responsible for producing the report. In this report, the first part presents the population and the census administration in the Straits Settlements as a whole, followed by three other parts in similar format dealing with each of the Settlements of Singapore, Penang and Malacca, respectively. The data on occupation were dispensed with because the government felt "that the value of such returns is not great, owing to the constant changes of occupation that occur among the Native Populations, especially among the Chinese".[9] Furthermore, the age classification was drastically compressed, with single years for the ages below 5, and quinary age groups between 5 and 20, and 20 and over as the last group. It appears that the emphasis in the census was on quality rather than quantity.

The 1901 census of Singapore was taken along the same lines as the previous decennial census, and the written text and tables of the report followed the general pattern of the previous report. One additional table on married men was included, but the superintendent opined that it was of little value in view of the great confusion regarding the term "married" among the different races. There was no uniformity in the age groupings adopted in the various censuses taken thus far; in this census the age classification was widened, with quinary age groups for ages below 20, and other ages up to 40 in ten-year groupings. For the same reason as in 1891, no information on occupation was collected. In 1911, the population of Singapore was enumerated on the same basis as the previous two decennial censuses, but with some enlargement of the scope of the whole census. New items on the place of birth, religion and industry were included, and occupation was reintroduced. The data on birthplace proved to be fairly reliable and of some value in the study of immigration, while the information on religion was confusing and of little value. The data on industry and occupation appeared to provide a more detailed analysis of the labour force, but the distinction between the two classifications is not sufficiently clear. The 1911 Census seems to be a more ambitious undertaking, and the form and content of its report differ significantly from those of previous reports.

A major change was introduced in 1921 when the population of Singapore was first enumerated as part of the census of the whole of Malaya, consisting of the Straits Settlements, the Federated Malay States, and the Unfederated Malay States. The innovation of putting the whole census of Malaya in the charge of a single superintendent ensured uniformity of definition and items to be included for the pan-Malayan region. In the census report, comments and tables relating to Singapore were included. In addition to the items covered in the 1911 census, information on literacy (ability to read and write) and language (ability to speak) was introduced for the first time. The next decennial census of Singapore in 1931 was conducted along the same lines and the items covered were exactly identical. However, this census report had an extra section on certain problems of vital statistics.

A population census of the Municipality of Singapore was conducted in 1936, but the records and report of this particular census are difficult to trace. A census was originally planned for April 1941, but with increasing difficulties arising from the commencement of World War II in Europe the project was abandoned. The long series of decennial censuses since 1871 was thus broken. During the Japanese Occupation in 1942–45, a registration system of the entire population was enforced by the Japanese authorities, but these records, not available now, were for food rationing, military conscription, and security reasons.

After the war, the population of Singapore was enumerated in 1947 as part of the whole census of Malaya under a superintendent responsible for the census operation and the report. In this first post-war census, information on religion and language was omitted because of practical difficulties and doubtful utility of the results. But then three new items on household, the number of children ever born, and the year of first arrival of foreign-born persons were included for the first time. The information on the year of first arrival of foreign-born persons was meant to supplement that on birthplace for the purpose of studying migration, while the information on the number of children ever born is extremely useful in the study of fertility. In contrast to the manual method of processing the results in the earlier censuses, a mechanical method using punched cards was employed to process the results of this census.

THE 1957–2000 PERIOD

The beginning of a series of censuses conducted independently in Singapore, not as part of Malaya or the Straits Settlements as in the early days, was instituted in 1957. However, the censuses of Singapore and the Federation of Malaya were held on the same day and some form of cooperation was maintained between the two census authorities. Another new feature of the Singapore census was the formation of a Standing Technical Committee on Census Matters, responsible for planning and offering advice on all matters connected with the population census.

In this census, some new developments in census methodology were introduced. By far the most important innovation was the use of the labour force approach to identify and separate the population ten years of age and over into economically active and economically inactive persons, with the former group further broken down into those employed and those unemployed. The statistics are of much better quality and value compared with those gathered under the older gainful worker approach used in previous censuses, though some practical difficulties were encountered in the application of the newer concept. The method of collecting age statistics was also improved with the introduction of the animal-year method of collecting the age statistics of the Chinese population. Briefly, the new method involves the gathering of extra information on the Chinese date of birth and converting the age calculated from the Chinese traditional system of reckoning age to the Western system of reckoning age. The results of the new method surpassed everyone's expectations, in that not only errors arising out of the Chinese system of counting age but also errors emanating from digital preference and overstatement or understatement of ages were substantially eliminated.[10] Another innovation was the timely publication of seventeen Preliminary Releases which gave detailed results in advance of the publication of the full census report.

In comparison with the 1947 Census, some changes in the items were introduced. The item on the number of children borne by women was omitted; the information would have been useful for studying fertility and testing the under-registration of births.[11] The item on language (ability to speak) was re-introduced. One completely new item on the place of usual residence was included for the first time, but appeared to be of little value because almost all persons enumerated had their residence at the place of enumeration. Information on age by very fine groupings — by single months below the age of one, and single years from 1 to 99 — was made available for the first time, thus, apart from other uses, allowing the analysis of digital preference and other errors in age statistics. On the whole, the tables incorporated in the census report were much more exhaustive than those of other censuses hitherto attempted in Singapore. However, the final census report was published many years later in 1964.

The 1970 Census witnessed further advancement in the history of census taking in Singapore in terms of the wider coverage of subject matter, use of sampling, and application of computer to generate the statistics. With the exception of the item on secondary occupation, all other items which were collected in the previous censuses was included in this census. In addition, new items on the type of age statement, citizenship, residential status, and country of origin (for foreign-born) were introduced. Information on the name and address of employer was also collected for the first time, and served to cross-check the accuracy of the items on occupation and industry. Information on the type of census house was also included. Items on the number of children born and still living, first asked in the 1947 Census but discarded in the 1957 Census, were re-introduced but on a sample basis. In the sample enumeration, further details on the year of first marriage (or age at first marriage), educational characteristics, characteristics of unemployed persons, and housing conditions were collected.

The results of the census were processed by computer and an interim release providing very basic information on the population by census division/district, race and quinary age group was published in late 1970. But the complete results were only made available more than three years later in two volumes published towards the end of 1973. Volume I contains the administrative report and the general review of the census results, while Volume II contains the detailed statistical tables from the main and sample enumerations. The long delay in releasing the tables created some difficulties for census users who were not given access to these data soon after the completion of the fieldwork.

The 1980 Census continued to adopt the previous procedure whereby the more important items were included in the main enumeration on a 100 per cent basis, and other items in a 20 per cent sample enumeration. Not surprisingly, this census was subjected to certain changes in the items included in the enumeration schedule. Three items used in the previous census were excluded, namely, place of usual residence, animal year of birth (according to the Chinese horoscope signs), and country of origin. The many new items in this census included income from work, address of work-place or school, usual mode of transport to work or school, languages and dialects spoken at home, and religion. The first three items were introduced for the first time in a population census in Singapore.

A user-friendly publication programme of releasing the statistics and findings was adopted to satisfy the varied needs of the different types of users. To enable users to gain earlier access to the census data, the statistical tables pertaining to different topics were published as and when they became available. A total of nine such statistical releases were published within a ten-month period, beginning from December 1980. Another innovation was the commissioning of specialists to prepare eight monographs to present the major findings of the census, the first of which, on *Demographic Trends in Singapore*, was published in February 1982. The third component of the publication programme was the release of the *Administrative Report* in late 1983, providing a detailed account of the census organization and operation, a brief analysis of the census results, and some important statistical tables.

The census conducted in June 1990 incorporated some valuable changes with regard to field-work and coverage. Prior to the commencement of the 1990 Census field-work, certain information already captured in the various government databases was utilized to pre-print some relevant particulars onto the personal and household schedules for the respondents to update or verify. This technique saves considerable time and effort during the field-work stage. Another important departure from previous censuses was the enumeration of Singapore citizens and permanent residents living abroad during the time of the census. The inclusion of these persons required the addition of a new item on country currently present in. Other new items included in the census were the number of leisure hours, participation in sports/ leisure activities, participation in arts activities, watching arts events, participation in voluntary social activities, and leisure activities. However, particulars pertaining to these non-traditional census items were collected from a small 2 per cent sample of the population.

A publication programme somewhat similar to that adopted in the previous decennial census was employed to make available to users the results and findings of the 1990 Census. The first publication, entitled *Advance Data Release* provided a few very basic results of the census and was released about a year later in 1991. The detailed results covering various topics were made available in six statistical releases published over a period of some three years from 1992 to 1994. The findings of the census were embodied in six census monographs, the first published in 1994 and the last in 1996. An obvious shortcoming of the 1990 census was the much longer time taken to release the results and findings to interested users. Another problem was the presentation of most statistical tables in terms of resident population rather than total population. This implies that it is difficult, if not possible, to examine the many important characteristics of the total population in 1990 and to compare these characteristics on a time-series basis in conjunction with the results of previous censuses.

More important changes were introduced in the latest census conducted on 30 June 2000. With regard to the method of collecting the information, a few data items were compiled from administrative records and the other data items were collected by means of a sample. Data on six basic items pertaining to sex, date of birth, age, ethnic group, marital status, and citizenship were compiled from the Household Registration Data (HRD) base. The HRD is a central population register of citizens and permanent residents maintained by the Department of Statistics, with the information being updated quarterly from various administrative records. The other data items were collected from a 20 per cent sample of households by a combination of internet, telephone and face-to-face interview.

Out of the list of 54 data items included in the census in the 2000 census, 15 were new items meant to gather information on educational upgrading, job mobility, home upgrading, overseas travel, and financial support for the elderly. Two items concerning age of mother when first child was born and income from all sources were dropped. The census results were made available in seven census reports, with the first entitled *Advance Data Release* published some nine months after the census. The *Statistical Release* Nos. 1 to 5 were published within a year, and the final one on the administrative report appearing another year later. On the whole, the census results were made available to users sooner than in the previous census. It is important to bear in mind that all the published statistics in the reports refer to the resident population (2,735,368), and similar figures for the non-resident population (754,524) were not published. This necessarily implies that one can only study the resident population and not the total population of Singapore.

Notes

1. T. J. Newbold, *Political and Statistical Account of the British Settlement in the Straits of Malacca*, Vol. 1 (London: John Murray, 1939).
2. H. Hayes Marriott, "The Peoples of Singapore", in *One Hundred Years of Singapore*, edited by Makepeace, Brooke and Braddell (London: John Murray, 1921).
3. T. Braddell, *Statistics of the British Possessions in the Straits of Malacca* (Pinang: Pinang Gazette Printing Office, 1861).
4. Marriott, op. cit.
5. J.F.A. McNair, C. B. Waller, and A. Knight, *Report of the Census Officers for the Settlement of Singapore*, 1871 Blue Book (Singapore: Straits Settlement Government Press, 1872).
6. McNair, Waller and Knight, op. cit.
7. Ibid.
8. S. Dunlop, W.A. Pickering, V. Cousins, H. Hewetson, A. Knight and A.P. Talbot, Report on the Census of Singapore, 1881, 1881 Blue Book (Singapore: Straits Settlement Government Press, 1882).
9. E.M. Merewether, *Report on the Census of the Straits Settlements Taken on the 5th April 1891* (Singapore: Government Printing Press, 1892).
10. Saw Swee-Hock, "Errors in Chinese Age Statistics", *Demography* 4, no. 2 (1967).
11. Saw Swee-Hock, "A Note on the Under-Registration of Birth in Malaya During the Intercensal Period 1947–1957", *Population Studies* 18, no. 1 (July 1964).

Bibliography

CENSUS AND VITAL STATISTICS REPORTS

McNair, J.F.A., C.B. Waller and A. Knight. *Report of the Census Officers for the Straits Settlement of Singapore, 1871*. Singapore: Straits Settlements Government Press, 1872.

Dunlop, S., W.A. Pickering, V. Cousins, H. Hewetson, A. Knight and A.P. Talbot. *Report on the Census of Singapore, 1881*. Singapore: Straits Settlements Government Press, 1882.

Merewether, E.M. *Report on the Census of the Straits Settlements taken on the 5th April 1891*. Singapore: Government Printing Press, 1892.

Innes, J.R. *Report on the Census of the Straits Settlements taken on the 1st March 1901*. Singapore: Government Printing Press, 1901.

Marriott, H. *Census Report of the Straits Settlements, 1911*. Singapore: Government Printing Press, 1911.

Nathan, J.E. *The Census of British Malaya, 1921*. London: Waterlow & Sons, Ltd., 1922.

Vlieland, C.A. *British Malaya: A Report on the 1931 Census and Certain Problems of Vital Statistics*. London: Crown Agents for the Colonies, 1932.

Del Tufo, M.V. *Malaya: A Report of the 1947 Census of Population*. London: Crown Agents for the Colonies, 1949.

Chua, S.C. *State of Singapore: Report on the Census of Population, 1957*. Singapore: Government Press, 1964.

Singapore. 1957 *Census of Population Preliminary Releases*, Nos. 1–17. Singapore: Government Printing Office.

Arumainathan, P. *Singapore: Report on the Census of Population*, 1970, Volumes 1 and 2. Singapore: Department of Statistics, 1973.

Khoo, Chian Kim. *Singapore: Census of Population 1980*. Singapore: Department of Statistics.

   Release No. 1. Advance Release of Basic Demographic and Geographic Data, 1980.

Release No. 2. Demographic Characteristics, 1981.

Release No. 3. Literacy and Education, 1981.

Release No. 4. Economic Characteristics, 1981.

Release No. 5. Geographic Distribution, 1981.

Release No. 6. Households and Houses, 1981.

Release No. 7. Income and Transport, 1981.

Release No. 8. Language Spoken at Home, 1981.

Release No. 9. Religion and Fertility, Administrative Report, 1983.

Lau, Kak En. *Singapore: Census of Population 1990*. Singapore: Department of
Statistics. Advance Data Release, 1991.

Statistical Release No. 1. Demographic Characteristics, 1992.

Statistical Release No. 2. Households and Houses, 1992.

Statistical Release No. 3. Literacy, Language Spoken and Education, 1993.

Statistical Release No. 4. Economic Characteristics, 1993.

Statistical Release No. 5. Transport and Geographic Distribution, 1994.

Statistical Release No. 6. Religion, Childcare and Leisure Activities, 1994.

Leow, Bee Geok. *Singapore: Census of Population 2000*. Singapore: Department of
Statistics.

Advance Data Release, 2001.

Statistical Release No. 1. Demographic Characteristics, 2001.

Statistical Release No. 2. Education, Language and Religion, 2001.

Statistical Release No. 3. Economic Characteristics, 2001.

Statistical Release No. 4. Geographical Distribution and Travel, 2001.

Statistical Release No. 5. Household and Housing, 2001.

Administrative Report, 2002.

Singapore. *1995 General Household Survey*. Singapore: Department of Statistics.

Release No. 1. Socio-Demographic and Economic Characteristics.

Release No. 2. Transport Mode, Households and Housing Characteristics.

————, *2000 General Household Survey*. Singapore: Department of Statistics.

Release No. 1. Socio-Demographic and Economic Characteristics.

Release No. 2. Transport, Overseas Travel, Household and Housing
Characteristics.

————. *Annual Report on the Registration of Births and Deaths*. Singapore:
Government Printing Office, 1940–1954.

————. *Annual Report on the Registration of Births and Deaths, Marriages and
Persons*. Singapore: Government Printing Office, 1955–1965.

————. *Annual Report on the Registration of Births and Deaths and Marriages*.
Singapore: Government Printing Office, 1966–1979.

————. *Annual Report on the Registration of Births and Deaths*. Singapore:
Government Printing Office, 1980–2005.

————. *Statistics on Marriage*. Singapore: Department of Statistics, 1980–1983.

————. *Statistics on Marriages and Divorces*. Singapore: Department of Statistics,
1984–2005.

Straits Settlements. *Annual Report on the Registration of Births and Deaths*. Singapore: Government Printer, 1886–1939.

OTHER OFFICIAL PUBLICATIONS

Malaya. *Immigration Ordinance, 1959*, No. 12 of 1959. Kuala Lumpur: Government Printer, 1959.

SFPPB. *Annual Report of the Singapore Family Planning and Population Board*. Singapore, 1966–1984.

Singapore. *Administration of Muslim Law Act 1966*. Singapore: Government Printer, 1966.

––––––––. *Annual Report of the Medical Department*, 1946–1996. Singapore: Government Printer, 1946–96.

––––––––. *1984 Budget Statement*. Singapore: Government Press Release, Ministry of Culture, 1984.

––––––––. *1987 Budget Statement*. Singapore: Government Press Release, Ministry of Communications and Information, 1987.

––––––––. *1989 Budget Speech*. Singapore: Government Press Release, Ministry of Communications and Information, 1989.

––––––––. *Christian Marriages Ordinance 1940*, No. 10 of 1940. Singapore: Government Printer, 1966.

––––––––. *Civil Marriages Ordinance 1940*, No. 9 of 1940. Singapore: Government Printer, 1940.

––––––––. *Employment Act 1968*. Singapore: Government Printer, 1968.

––––––––. *Immigration Ordinance 1959*, No. 18 of 1961. Singapore: Government Printer, 1957.

––––––––. *Muslim Ordinance 1957*, No. 25 of 1957. Singapore: Government Printer, 1957.

––––––––. *Population Trends*. Singapore: Ministry of Health, 1977.

––––––––. *Report on the Labour Force of Singapore*. Singapore: Ministry of Labour, 1973–1997.

––––––––. *Singapore Family Planning and Population Board Act 1965*, No. 32 of 1965. Singapore: Government Printer, 1965.

––––––––. *Singapore Standard Industrial Classification*. Singapore: Department of Statistics, 1990.

––––––––. *The Abortion Act 1969*. Singapore: Government Printer, 1969.

––––––––. *The Abortion Act 1974*. Singapore: Government Printer, 1974.

––––––––. *The Abortion (Amendment) Act 1980*. Singapore: Government Printer, 1980.

––––––––. *The Abortion (Amendment) Regulations 1981*. Singapore: Government Printer, 1981.

––––––––. *The Abortion (Amendment) Regulations 1982*. Singapore: Government Printer, 1982.

————. *The Income Tax Act (Amendment Tax) 1973*. Singapore: Government Printer, 1973.

————. *The Voluntary Sterilization Act 1969*. Singapore: Government Printer, 1969.

————. *The Voluntary Sterilization (Amendment) Act 1972*. Singapore: Government Printer, 1972.

Singapore. *The Voluntary Sterilization Act 1974*. Singapore: Government Printer, 1974.

————. *White Paper on Family Planning*, Command 22 of 1965.

————. *Women's Charter 1961*, No. 18 of 1961. Singapore: Government Printer, 1961.

————. *Women's Charter (Amendment) Act 1967*. Singapore: Government Printer, 1967. Straits Settlements. *Annual Report on the Administration of the Straits Settlements*. 1860–1861.

————. *Report on the Chinese Protectorate*. 1888–1932.

————. *Report on the Immigration Department*, 1933–1938. Singapore: Government Press.

————. *Report on Indian Immigration*, 1881–1911. Singapore: Government Press.

————. *Report of the Labour Department*, 1921–1938. Singapore: Government Press.

BOOKS

Braddell, T. *Statistics of the British Possessions in the Straits of Malacca*. Pinang: Pinang Gazette Printing Office, 1861.

Buckley C.B. *An Anecdotal History of Old Times in Singapore*. Singapore: Fraser and Neave Ltd., 1902.

Cheng, Lim Keak. *Geographic Analysis of the Singapore Population*. Singapore: Department of Statistics, 1995. Djamour, Judith. *The Muslim Matrimonial Court in Singapore*. London: Athlone Press, 1966.

————. *Malay Kinship and Marriages in Singapore*. London: Athlone Press, 1966.

Durand, John D. *The Labour Force in Economic Development*. Princeton: Princeton University Press, 1975.

Frejka, Tomas. *The Future of Population Growth: Alternative Paths to Equilibrium*. New York: John Wiley, 1973. Geoghegan, J. *Note on Emigration from India*. Calcutta: Government Press, 1873.

Hall, D.G.E. *A History of Southeast Asia*. London: Macmillan, 1958.

Hooker, M.B. *Islamic Law in Southeast Asia*. Kuala Lumpur: Oxford University Press, 1984.

Jackson, R.N. *Immigration Labour and Development of Malaya*. Kuala Lumpur: Government Printer, 1961.

Kuo, Eddie C.Y. and Jon S.T., Quah. *Religion in Singapore: Report of a National Survey*, Singapore: Ministry of Community Development, 1988.

Kuo, Eddie C.Y. and Tong Chee Kiong. *Religion in Singapore*. Singapore: Department of Statistics, 1995.

Marjoribanks, N.E. and A.K.G. Ahmad Tambi Marakkaya. *Report on Indian Labour Emigration to Ceylon and Malaya*. Madras: Government Press, 1917.

Newbold, T.J. *Political and Statistical Account of the British Settlements in the Straits of Malacca*. London: John Murray, 1839.

Parmer, Norman. *Colonial Labour Policy and Administration*. New York: Association for Asian Studies, 1960.

Purcell, Victor. *The Chinese in Southeast Asia*. London: Oxford University Press, 1951.

Raffles, Lady Sophia. *Memoir of the Life and Public Services of Sir Thomas Stamford Raffles*. London: John Murray, 1980.

Saw, Swee-Hock. *Singapore Population in Transition*. Philadelphia: University of Pennsylvania Press, 1970.

————. *Population Control for Zero Growth in Singapore*. New York: Oxford University Press, 1980.

————. *Demographic Trends in Singapore*. Singapore: Department of Statistics, 1981.

————. *The Labour Force of Singapore*. Singapore: Department of Statistics, 1984.

————. *New Population and Labour Force Projections and Policy Implications for Singapore*. Singapore: Institute of Southeast Asian Studies, 1987.

————. *The Population of Peninsular Malaysia*. Singapore: Singapore University Press, 1988.

————. *Changes in the Fertility Policy of Singapore*. Singapore: Institute of Policy Studies, 1990.

————. *Bibliography of Singapore Demography*. Singapore: Institute of Southeast Asian Studies, 2005.

————. *Population Policies and Programmes in Singapore*. Institute of Southeast Asian Studies, 2005.

Saw, Swee-Hock and Cheng, Siok-Hwa. *A Bibliography of the Demography of Singapore*. Singapore: University Education Press, 1975.

Song, Ong Siang. *One Hundred Years' History of the Chinese in Singapore*. London: John Murray, 1923.

Smith, T.E. *Population Growth in Malaya*. London: Oxford University Press, 1952.

Tietze, C. and S.K. Henshaw. *Induced Abortion: A World Review 1986*, 6th edition. New York: Alan Guttmacher, n.d.

United Nations. *International Standard Classification of all Economic Activities*. New York: United Nations Statistical Office, 1956.

United Nations. *Methods for Population Projections by Sex and Age*. New York: Department of Economic and Social Affairs, 1956.

————. *Handbook of Population Census Methods, Volume II: Economic Characteristics of Population*, Series F, No. 5, Rev. 1, Series in Methods. New York, 1958.

————. *Recent Trends in Fertility in Industrialized Countries*, ST/SOA/Series A. Population Studies No. 29. New York: Department of Economic and Social Affairs, 1958.

————."Population Trends and Related Problems of Economic Development in ECAFE Region". *Economic Bulletin for Asia and the Far East* 1, no. 1 (June 1959).

————. *Population Bulletin*, No. 6. New York: Department of Economics and Social Affairs, 1963.

————. *Assessment of Acceptance and Effectiveness of Family Planning Methods*, Asian Population Studies No. 4. Bangkok: Economic and Social Commission for Asia and the Pacific, 1968.

————. *The Concept of a Stable Population*. New York: Department of Economic and Social Affairs, 1968.

————. *Determinants and Consequences of Population Trends*. New York: Department of Economic and Social Affairs, 1973.

————. *Conditions and Trends in Fertility in Industrialized Countries*. Population Bulletin No. 7, ST/SOA/Series N/T. New York: Department of Economic and Social Affairs, 1976.

————. *Demographic Yearbook*. New York: United Nations, 1965–1996.

United Nations ECAFE. *Interrelation Between Population and Manpower Problems*, Asia Population Studies No. 7. Bangkok: ECAFE.

Wong, Aline K. and Eddie C.Y. Kuo, eds. *Divorce in Singapore*. Singapore: Graham Brash, 1983.

ARTICLES

Ahmad bin Mohamad Ibrahim. "Development in Marriage Laws in Malaysia and Singapore". *Malaya Law Review* 2, no. 2 (December 1970).

Biythe, W.L. "History Sketch of Chinese Labour in Malaya". *Journal of the Malayan Branch of the Royal Asiatic Society* 20, Part 1 (June 1947).

Chua, Sian Chin, "Speech by Mr Chua Sian Chin, Ministry for Health and Home Affairs, at the World Population Conference, Bucharest, Romania, 19–30 August 1974". *Singapore Public Health Bulletin* 15 (January 1975).

Da vies, T.A. Lloyd and R. Mills. "Young Mothers in Singapore". *The Medical Journal of Malaya* (1985).

Demeny, Paul. "Pronatalist Policies in Low-Fertility Countries: Patterns, Performance, and Prospects". *Population and Development Review* 12 (1986).

El-Badry, M.A. "Higher Female Than Male Mortality in Some Countries of South Asia: A Digest". *Journal of the American Statistical Association* 64, no. 328 (December 1969).

Freeman, Maurice. *Chinese Family and Marriage in Singapore*. London: Athlone Press, 1959.

Freeman, R. and A.L. Adiokha. "Recent Fertility Decline in Hong Kong". *Population Studies* 22 (July 1968).

Goh, Chok Tong. "The Second Long March". Speech delivered at Nanyang Technological University on 4 August 1986.

Lee, Kuan Yew. "Talent for the Future". Address delivered at the National Day Rally on 14 August 1983.

Lotka, Alfred J. "On the True Rate of National Increase". *Journal of the American Statistical Association* 20, no. 150 (September 1925).

Mohammed Din bin Ali. "Malay Customary Law and Family". *Intisari* 2, no. 2 (1965).

Saw, Swee-Hock. "Errors in Chinese Age Statistics". *Demography* 4, no. 2 (1967).

————. "The Development of Population Control in Singapore". *Contemporary Southeast Asia* 1, no. 4 (March 1980).

————. "Too Little Land, Too Many People". In *Singapore Towards the Year 2000*, edited by Saw Swee-Hock and R. S. Bhathal. Singapore: Singapore University Press, 1981.

————. "Increasing Life Expectancy in Singapore During 1969–1981". *Singapore Medical Journal* 25, no. 2 (April 1984).

————. "Singapore: New Population Policies for More Balanced Procreation". *Contemporary Southeast Asia* 7, no. 2 (September 1985).

————. "The Dynamics of Ageing in Singapore's Population". *Annuals of the Academy of Medicine* 14, no. 4 (October 1985).

————. "Who Is Having Too Few Babies". *Sunday Times*, 6 July 1986.

————. "When Couples Have Fewer Than Two". *Sunday Times*, 15 June 1986.

————. "Towards a Stationary Population in Singapore". *Asia-Pacific Journal of Public Health* 1, no. 2 (1987).

————. "Seventeen Years of Legalised Abortion in Singapore". *Biology and Society* 5, no. 2 (June 1988).

————. "Muslim Fertility Transition: The Case of the Singapore Malays". *Asia-Pacific Population Journal* 4, no. 3 (September 1989).

————. "Bringing Back the Baby Boom". *Current World Readers* 32, no. 8 (December 1989).

————. "Ethnic Fertility Differentials in Peninsular Malaysia and Singapore". *Journal of Biosocial Science* 22, no. 1 (January 1990).

————. "Muslim Divorce Trends and Patterns in Singapore". *Genus* 48, no. 2 (1992).

————. "What It means to Have 6.5 m Population". *Today*, 22 March 2007.

Skeat, W.W. and H.H. Ridley. "The Orang Laut of Singapore". *Journal of the Straits Branch of the Royal Asiatic Society* 33 (January 1900).

Tai, Ching Ling. "Divorce in Singapore". In *The Contemporary Family in Singapore*, edited by Eddie C.Y. Kuo and Aline K. Wong. Singapore: Singapore University Press, 1979.

Thomson, G.G. and T.E. Smith. "Singapore: Family Planning in an Urban Environment". In *The Politics of Family Planning in the Third World*, edited by T. E. Smith. London: Alien and Unwin, 1973.

Tungku Shamsul Bahrin. "Indonesian Labour in Malaysia". *Kajian Ekonomi Malaysia* 2, no. 1 (June 1965).

Yap, Mui Teng. "Changes in the Demographic Base". In *Management of Success: The Moulding of Modern Singapore*, edited by K.S. Sandhu and Paul Wheatley. Singapore: Institute of Southeast Asian Studies, 1989.

OTHER PUBLICATIONS

Annual Report of the Family Planning Association of Singapore
Singapore Monitor
Business Times
New Paper
Straits Times
Sunday Times
Today

Index

www.ingramcontent.com/pod-product-compliance
Lightning Source LLC
Chambersburg PA
CBHW021544260326
41914CB00001B/158